MW01716625

- TRUTH -

My Synchromystic Journey

3rd Edition

Niki Norlock

Astraea Nostos
Phoenix, Arizona

- TRUTH -

My Synchromystic Journey

Astraea Nostos, LLC
Phoenix, Arizona

3rd Edition
ISBN-13: 978-1-7336527-0-4

In Publication Data
Norlock, Niki
BISAC Categories:
OCC027000
Body, Mind, and Spirit / Spiritualism

Electronic versions of this text are available from fine e-book retailers.

Printed in the United States

{Table of Contents}

"In the Sacred Christian text Jesus Christ is quoted as saying 'I am the Way, the Truth and the Life'. But it never states what 'Way' he is, or what 'Truth' he is. In our typical humanness over the centuries we have boxed this 'Way' and 'Truth' into convenient understandable doctrine which has been taught as the reality of God. In short, the Christian church has often said, 'If you do not believe it as we teach it, you are going the wrong way and don't have the real truth'. This has often caused more harm than good, and has frequently set people looking in the wrong direction, which can regularly result in finding nothing, except despair of emptiness.

The reality of the Divine is far greater and far deeper than we can ever comprehend. The synchromystic world in which we live has a cosmically Divine orchestration and we must follow the path which lies before us, having given all of our inner self and preconceived ideas to the void and fullness of the Divine presence.

In *Truth—My Synchromystic Journey* Niki Norlock bravely unfolds before the world her deepest soul, showing us the journey which we all need to take. Not that we will all have the same experiences as she did, but that we will be fully open to whatever the Divine has for each of us, taking us beyond our understanding; right out of our comfort zone; and into a world which may seem like fantasy to those not taking the journey, but is the Ultimate Reality unfolding before us and within us for those of us who are.

It has been my pleasure to know Niki over the years. I know that, just as she has been a blessing to me and challenged me, through this book she will be a blessing and a challenge to all who hear her through the written word. *Truth—My Synchromystic Journey* has the potential to transform the way you live; to guide you into a better way of walking into your future; and reveal an unveiling of the Divine in ways you may have never dreamed possible, if only you let it.

David Cole author of *The Mystic Path of Meditation—Beginning a Christ Centred Journey* and *The Inner Journey—Prayers and Practices for Christ Centred Meditation.*

"Niki Norlock is a gifted writer and her awakening resonates with mine through a different twist of fate. My path was designed by the Divine, hers, through her awakening and discovering; a discovery of the true meaning of human existence by going to a different part of the world and learning a different way of life in a different culture. In her life travel, she discovered the power of forgiveness and gratitude to heal the human heart... the same discovery I had when I learned that forgiveness is a gift to myself; that is when all my brokenness was healed. Her book is powerful and one must read it to know her and understand her Sychromystic journey."

Julie Cox, author of *I Ordered My Future Yesterday.*

"Whether we realize it or not, we are all on a journey towards truth. Many will discover, just as *The Alchemist* did after a lengthy and complicated exploration, that it has been right here within us all along. However, many of us need to go on that journey, through its twists and turns, in order to appreciate the wisdom and its application to our lives. Many will never be brave enough to charter the murky waters of the heart and mind, but there are a handful of us who find strength and purpose in lending their voice, their eyes, their ears, and their pen to sharing the bold, shocking, earth-moving, daring, and yet strikingly simple and honest TRUTH that many are, for whatever reason, wearing blinders to. By George, it's not meant to be taken so seriously! Just admit it, own up to it, let go of the false perceptions and shame of it, and get on with it!

Niki Norlock has done just that. With her tongue-in-cheek humour, she very bravely and humbly places a looking glass over her own life journey as a demonstration of how all of us create elaborate schemes in order to avoid facing the simple truth. Only when we set fire to these illusory images of ourselves and the world around us, and stand out in the clear light of day, can we allow our TRUTH to arise from the ashes and no longer stand behind a guise of some fantastical tale that is perceived as acceptable. TRUTH is what it is regardless of how some of us may have tried, or continue to try, to explain it otherwise.
As Buddha has said, 'There are two mistakes one can make along the road to truth. Not going all the way and not starting'. Niki Norlock is going all the way!"

Nancy D. Gosse, fellow traveller on the path to TRUTH, Lightworker,
Author of *Obscurity in Your Face*
www.obscurityinyourface.com and www.inceptionalsoul.com

"The world needs more heroines. Or, better yet, the world needs to recognise that heroines don't have to fit into a box—quirky, vulnerable, over-the-top and even ridiculously emotional, heroines come in all shapes and sizes. But the stand-out thing about a true heroine is her capacity for bravery. In her deliciously transparent 'heart-on-sleeve' writing style (it's as though we're actually reading her thoughts), Niki Norlock maps one woman's courageous quest to discover her truth. And if Jean's first novel shows anything, it's that the world needs more heroines like Feenx."

Alexandra Wenman, Archangel Alchemist, editor, speaker, and author
www.alexandrawenman.com

{ Acknowledgements }

I would like to thank all the physical manifestations of George who were involved in the experience and sharing of this amazing adventure. You all know who you are, and I hope you ALL know how much I love and appreciate every single now moment we have shared.

{ Disclaimer }

No physical manifestations of George were harmed in the creation of this story…

{JVN's Fond Farewell...}

When this book was first published back in 2009 through Trafford Publishing, it was offered to the public as fiction, a wondrous imaginative tale birthed out of the imagination of Jean Victoria Norloch. I did it for several reasons, one of course being that my grandmother had warned me that if I ever tried to write my story as a 'truth', people would think I was nuts; in my family, when the lady of the house speaks, you listen. What my grandmother did *not* tell me to do was to change my name and hide myself away from the world. But… I let fear get the best of me, and in my desire to remain 'safe' I adopted a pen name, used pictures in my book and on my website that didn't show my face, and basically buried my head in the sands of time while *Truth* struggled to pull me out.

It wasn't long before I realized, through my work as a radio show host, that I am not alone, and that my story is not only 'not nuts', it is a perfect example of how Divine energy works in the world in which we now live. I suppose it was inevitable that I eventually would find myself stepping into the truth of who I was; you simply can't experience what I have experienced without learning enough about yourself to grow to love and accept yourself for who you are.

I have had a lot of help getting there, the birthing of this kind of story is certainly not a one-woman job; I have infinite gratitude to all those involved with helping me to see the truth about *Truth*. Each one of those people played an integral role in the publication of this book. In my heart, I know them all to be the gifts from our Creator that they are. There is one however that I have to expand on a little before we get into the rest of the story; my publisher Brian Kannard of Grave Distractions Publications. Back in 2010, I decided I wanted to get away from Trafford and find a publishing company more in alignment with my own heart, so I set out to find somebody who would 'get it'. Staying true to the theme of the story you are about to read, I googled 'Grail Seekers, Knights of the round table and publishers in one line and the first name at the top of the list was Grave Distractions. What's interesting about this is, at the time, they were a fledgling company, and as it turns out, I was in fact, the first book they ever published. Over the past few years I have had the privilege of watching Grave Distractions grow into a force to be reckoned with in the publishing industry, with their fierce determination to keep the company family/author oriented with a focus on environmentally sustainable print on demand publishing, Brian and his team have set an example for others on how to run a business based on basic human values and integrity. They have stolen the hearts of many an author, who, disillusioned with the old publishing mentality of 'money matters', decided that they wanted to work with a company who believed that the 'story' mattered more. In the process, Grave Distractions has earned the loyalty of many of us who recognize the value of this new business standard; long before transparency and honesty in business were 'cool', Brian was doing it simply because it's the right thing to do. Alongside Brian, stands his wife Laura, the mother of the company, who through her gentle encouragement and caring ways helped me to grow into my own skin and appreciate my own worth and value not only as an author, but as a human being. They have become like family to me… and without them, none of this would have ever been possible.

Of course, as I said, they are not alone on the list of people, who brought *Truth* to 'light' and so before you dive into the pages of this book, there are a few more things about it that you ought to know. First of all, it is Divinely inspired, and as terrified as I might once have been of making such a claim, there is no way, knowing what I know now, that I can deny that to be a *Truth*. It is in fact, at the insistence of Archangel Michael that this book is being presented as it is. It was he who demanded that I take ownership of both my story and my identity. Now when I say demanded I don't mean he stood over me with his sword and sternly told me it must be so, rather he gave the message to his channel, who kindly passed it along to me; it is however my experience, that when Michael makes a suggestion, it is often times in our best interest to heed it and so here we are.

Which brings us to the next thing you should know about this book; in its pages you will find a very casual approach to our relationship with the Divine. Messages from Angels, signs from God and experiences that some might describe as miraculous are presented as just ordinary everyday happenings because to be honest, they are. There is nothing miraculous about it if we consider our current understanding of the word 'miracle' – "*a surprising and welcome event that is not explicable by natural or scientific laws and is therefore considered to be the work of a divine agency.*" You see the problem with that definition is that it implies that the work of a '*divine agency*' is not '*explicable by natural laws*', when the truth is that divine intervention is the most natural thing in the world. The only thing 'special' or 'unique' about people who are able to communicate and work closely with the Divine is that they *asked* for help from the Divine and then allowed themselves to follow wherever it is the Divine led. Ask and ye shall receive; it's not just some over used expression that is based on some random quote in the Bible, it is step one on the 'how to' manual of life.

Finally, if you are looking for some great literary work of art in the traditional sense of the word, you will not find it here; I am not Hemingway. I ramble... I write the way I talk, and so, if you are not comfortable inviting me into your home for tea (I prefer red wine btw) and a chat then perhaps this is not the book for you. Still, as lax as my grammatical delivery may seem to some, it is the meat of the story that offers the sustenance, not the fancy julienned vegetables set on the side that are meant to dress the plate up. You will also find some very modern terms in this book, by way of emails, and text messages which may or may not include odd little additions like smiley faces and the occasional wink ;).

It's just who I am, and at this point in my life I have no desire to be anybody else. Which brings us back around to JVN's fond farewell; I realize there are those of you reading this who are rather fond of Jean, people who have closely followed her growth over the past few years. Be assured that she is grateful for the love and support you have shown her and though she may be gone, I doubt very much she will ever be forgotten as it is that she too is a very important element of this story.

Well now, I have taken up more than enough of your time, so let's get on with it then shall we...

but before I go, you should probably know...

I finished the last chapter of the new section of the book on my 3rd day of writing at 3:30 in the afternoon, and all of the new chapters were submitted to the publisher on St. George's Day which is celebrated by wearing a red rose boutonniere. St. George is the patron Saint of England his emblem is a red cross on a white background. He is often depicted riding a white horse and is, interestingly enough, one the rare Christian Saints who is also celebrated by Muslims. None of which I was aware of until I told my partner Richard that I was ready to submit my new chapters to the publisher, at which point he joyously informed me of what day it happened to be and all of which will make perfect sense to you once you get to the end of the book , and that's the truth.

Characters

Throughout this book there are several common themes; one of which is the significance of the meanings behind the names of the people involved in this trippy little tale. Each Character is this book is a representation of some incredible individuals who I have been blessed to share my life with. Their names have been changed (to protect their privacy) but the meaning behind the names were carefully researched and then those meanings used to find substitute names (much like my own original pen name) that would be an accurate description of the roles each individual plays in the tale. I was very careful to keep the meaning behind the names as true to the original names as possible so when you read what each name means keep an open mind and open heart to the possibility that coincidence is merely a sign post on the road of life.

Most of the meanings of the following names were found on the 'Behind the Name' website… I have searched extensively to find a website that provides a thorough and accurate representation of the etymology of names, and thus far www.behindthename.com is the best I have found. I would like to thank Mike Campbell for allowing us to use his carefully researched information, and both Mike and Tara Campbell for providing us all with an amazing resource. I highly recommend you checking them out once you begin your own Synchromystic journey.

Key Characters Not Mentioned or Explained in the Original Publication of this Book

Dan—Means "he judged" in Hebrew. Dan in the Old Testament is one of the twelve sons of Jacob and the founder of one of the twelve tribes of Israel. (Fitting given his role in the story of SOTH.)

Deo—Varient of *Dev*—Derived from Sanskrit देव (deva) meaning "god".

Dexter—From an occupational surname meaning "one who dyes" in Old English. It also coincides with the Latin word dexter meaning "*right-handed,* *skilled*". (I am not sure there is anything that Dexter couldn't do, when he put his heart and soul into it, he seemed to be good at *everything*)

Hannah—From the Hebrew name חַנָּה (Channah) meaning "favour" or "grace". (well duh…)

Jeffery—Medieval variant of *Geoffery*—From a Norman French form of a Germanic name. The second element is Germanic frid "peace", but the first element may be either gawia "territory", walah "stranger"

Nathan—Means "he gave" in Hebrew. In the Old Testament this is the name of both a prophet and a son of King David.

Randy—Diminutive of RANDALL, RANDOLF—From the Germanic elements rand meaning "rim (of a shield)" and wulf meaning "wolf"—hmmm… protective Wolf – now that's interesting.

In Native American Lore Totemic Wolf Meanings include: Loyalty, Cunning, Generosity, Intelligence, Friendliness, Compassionate, and Communication. Totem wolf symbols belong to those who truly understand the depth of passion that belong to this noble creature. The Wolf is a representative of deep faith, and profound understanding. In Norse mythology, the Wolf is a symbol for victory when ridden by Odin and the Valkyries upon the battlefield. As a Celtic symbol, the Wolf was a source of lunar power. Celtic lore states that the Wolf would hunt down the sun and devour it at each dusk so as to allow the power of the moon to come forth. In Asia, the wolf guards the doors that allow entrance to heavenly, celestial realms. The Wolf is also said to be among the ancestry of Genghis Khan.

Ruth—From a Hebrew name which was derived from the Hebrew word רְעוּת (re'ut) meaning "friend". This is the name of the central character in the Book of Ruth in the Old Testament, a Moabite woman who was the ancestor of King David.

Sister Flor—Diminutive of *Fluer*—Means "flower" in French. Also representative of the The fleur-de-lis or fleur-de-lys (plural: fleurs-de-lis)—a stylized lily (in French, fleur means flower, and lis means lily) or iris that is used as a decorative design or symbol. It may be "at one and the same time, religious, political, dynastic, artistic, emblematic, and symbolic", especially in French heraldry. It is used to represent the Divine Trinity and is reported to have been one of the symbols of the seal of The Knights Templar, the legendary keepers of the secret of the Holy Grail.

Richard Lee O'Shields (my business partner and treasured friend)

Richard—Means "brave power", derived from the Germanic elements ric "power, rule" and hard "brave, hardy". The Normans introduced this name to Britain, and it has been very common there since that time. It was borne by three kings of England including Richard I the Lionheart, leader of the 3rd Crusade in the 12th century.

Lee—From a surname which was derived from Old English leah meaning "clearing". (clearing = fresh start)

O'Shields—of the shield...

Bruce George Stevenson (my step father who played a significant role in both my upbringing and the keeping of secrets regarding the mysteries surrounding the death of my father 'Michael Joseph')

Bruce—From a Scottish surname, of Norman origin, which probably originally referred to the town of Brix in France. The surname was borne by Robert the Bruce, a Scottish hero of the 14th century who achieved independence from England and became the king of Scotland.

George—From the Greek name Γεωϱγιος (Georgios) which was derived from the Greek word γεωϱγος (georgos) meaning "farmer, earthworker", itself derived from the elements γη (ge) "earth" and εϱγον (ergon) "work". (and then of course there is that *other* George connection)

Stevenson—known most commonly as 'the sons of Steven'—From the Greek name Στεφανος (Stephanos) meaning "crown". However, after some digging with the assistance of Ayla, I found the meaning behind the family crest, the Stevenson family proudly bears the traditional motto of 'honor in secrecy' (apropos don't you think?)

Agnes Norlock (the grandmother referenced in this book as BABA – also the woman for whom my daughter's middle name was given)

Agnes—Latinized form of the Greek name 'Αγνη (Hagne), derived from Greek 'αγνος (hagnos) meaning "chaste". Saint Agnes was a virgin martyred during the persecutions of the Roman emperor Diocletian. The name became associated with Latin agnus "lamb", resulting in the saint's frequent depiction with a lamb by her side. Due to her renown, the name became common in Christian Europe, being especially popular in England in the Middle Ages.

Baba—(Persian, Urdu, Pashto; Sanskrit, Punjabi, Bengali, Hindi and Marathi: बाबा; father; grandfather; wise old man; sir) is a Persian honorific term used in several West and South Asian cultures. It is used as a mark of respect to refer to Sufi saints. The Bektashi Order, headquartered in Albania, use the term of baba for all its priesthood.

During the Muslim rule in South Asia it was also used for Hindu and Sikh ascetics (sannyasis) is also be used as a suffix or prefix to their names e.g.: Ramdev Baba, Baba Ramdevji, etc. Baba is also a title accorded to the head of certain order of Sufi saints: Baba Bulleh Shah and Rehman Baba. The Persian term was also adopted in Malaysia as an honorific of respect to address Chinese people born in British Straits Settlement. In Shona, a language spoken in Zimbabwe, and also in Yoruba, a language spoken by the Yoruba culture in the south western part of Nigeria, Baba is an honorific for father, wise man or, simply, elderly man.

What I find so interesting about this, is that as a small child the only reason I called my grandmother 'BABA' was because I could not properly pronounce the polish word for grandmother (babcia)—it was not until this year when doing some research for another project that I realized that all those years I had been calling her by a Sanskrit honorific reserved for spiritual leaders and saints. It appears that even as a small child I realized on some deep soul level exactly who and what this woman was, and what kind of influence she would have on my life. I remain to this day, in absolute awe of that fact that this amazing woman was gifted to me from the day of my birth.

Norlock—of the lake… (which means that she too was a lady of the lake)

And then of course there is me…

Niki—Diminutive of NICOLE—French female form of Nicholas—From the Greek name Νικολαος (Nikolaos) which meant "victory of the people" from Greek νικη (nike) "victory" and λαος (laos) "people". Saint Nicholas was a 4th century bishop from Anatolia who, according to legend, saved the daughters of a poor man from lives of prostitution. He is the patron saint of children.

Janine—English form of JEANNINE—Diminutive of JEANNE—Modern French form of Jehanne, an Old French feminine form of Iohannes Joan of Arc is known as Jeanne d'Arc in France. English form of Iohannes, the Latin form of the Greek name Ιωαννης (Ioannes), itself derived from the Hebrew name יוֹחָנָן (Yochanan) meaning "YAHWEH is great and/or gracious". The first is John the Baptist, a Jewish ascetic who was considered the forerunner of Jesus Christ. The second is the apostle John, who is traditionally regarded as the author of the fourth Gospel and Revelation.

Norlock—Means of the lake (which makes me the lady of the lake – more George humor)

The Original Characters of Truth

Alya—Means "sky, *heaven*, loftiness" in Aribic (given her role I would think I need not explain further)

Angel—Messenger of God (but of course she is)

Bob—From the Germanic name Hrodebert meaning "bright fame", derived from the Germanic elements hrod "fame" and beraht "bright". (given that my brothers alter-ego is the outgoing side of his personality this makes perfect sense)

Brigitte—Anglicized form of the Irish name Brighid which means "exalted one". In Irish mythology this was the name of the goddess of fire, poetry and wisdom, the daughter of the god Dagda.

Chelsea—An English name meaning messenger (pretty self explanatory)

Deacon—From the Latin *decanus* meaning 'chief of ten'

Derek—From a Germanic name meaning "ruler of the people", derived from the elements þeud "people" and ric "power, ruler". (who knows, if he is going to be rich enough to afford the car then maybe, just maybe...)

Jacob—Meaning 'may God Protect'.

Jean—Diminutive of JEANNE—Modern French form of Jehanne, an Old French feminine form of Iohannes. Joan of Arc is known as Jeanne d'Arc in France. English form of Iohannes, the Latin form of the Greek name Ιωαννης (Ioannes), itself derived from the Hebrew name יוֹחָנָן (Yochanan) meaning "YAHWEH is great and/or gracious".

Lina—Means either "palm tree" or "tender" in Arabic. Means "absorbed, united" in Sanskrit.

Again most of this makes perfect sense; palm tree, a remarkably strong and flexible tree that is able to withstand incredibly forceful winds. It's ability to bend with the wind allows it to survive powerful storms. Early Christians used the palm branch to symbolize the *victory* of the faithful over enemies of the soul, as in the Palm Sunday Festival celebrating the triumphant entry of Jesus into Jerusalem. Tender—she certainly is that when it's warranted and united we have stood for over 20 years.

Madison—Is English and means daughter of a powerful soldier; from the English surname meaning 'son of MAUD'. Maud—usual medieval form of MATILDA. Matilda—From the Germanic name *Mahthilds* meaning 'strength in battle', from the elements *math* 'might, strength' and *hild* 'battle'.

Natalie—From the Latin name *Natalia*, which meant 'Christmas Day' from Latin *natale domini.* Christmas represents the birth of hope… and to some it represents gifts… either way you have to admit it is fitting.

Norloch—Means of the Lake. (I think we pretty much covered that)

Revo—The first four letters in Revolution… Defined as:

> *1. an overthrow or repudiation and the thorough replacement of an established government or political system by the people governed.*
>
> *2. Sociology. a radical and pervasive change in society and the social structure, especially one made suddenly and often accompanied by violence. Compare social evolution.*
>
> *3. a sudden, complete or marked change in something: the present revolution in church architecture.*
>
> *4. a procedure or course, as if in a circuit, back to a starting point.*
>
> *5. a single turn of this kind.*

Feel free to choose any of the above, in the case of this particular story they all apply.

Reynard—From the Germanic name *Raginhard*, composed of the elements *ragin* 'advice' and *hard* 'brave or hardy'. It was brought to England by the Normans in the form of Reinard though it never became very common there. In medieval fables the names borne of a sly hero Reynard the Fox (with the result that *Renard* has become a French word meaning 'fox'.

The fox is often described as a crafty creature and is representative of Intelligence, diplomacy, Gentleness, wildness, persistence, adaption, and slyness. (all of which applies in this case, if you knew the man you would understand, he is ALL of the above)

Rose—Originally a Norman form of Germanic name, which was composed of the elements *hrod* 'fame' and *heid* 'kind, sort, type'. It was introduced in England by the Normans in the forms *Roese* and *Rohese*. From an early date it was associated with the word for the fragrant flower *rose* (derived from Latin *rosa*). When the name was revived in the 19th century, it was probably with the flower in mind.

In keeping with the theme of refusing to put only one name to the power that is our Creator, I remind you that a rose by any other name, would still smell as sweet.

The rose is believed by some to be a symbol used by the Templar Knights to represent Mary Magdalene.

Saul—From the Hebrew name שָׁאוּל (Sha'ul) which meant "asked for" or "prayed for". This was the name of the first king of Israel who ruled just before King David, as told in the Old Testament. Also, Saul was the original Hebrew name of Saint Paul.

Scott—The original meaning of the word Scot is debated, but it may mean 'tattoo', so given because Scotsmen often had tattoos. A little hint on this one, as it will not make immediate sense; pay very close attention to the final pages and the conclusion of the original version of *Truth*.

Sophia – Means 'wisdom' in Greek. Right like that doesn't make sense…

Theo—From the Greek name Θεοδωρος (Theodoros), which meant "gift of god" from Greek θεος (theos) "god" and δωρον (doron) "gift".

Victoria—Means 'Victory' in Latin or victory of/for the people. Victoria was the Roman goddess of victory.

There are several different versions of this name and its meaning yet all of them go back to the same word that can be found throughout this novel 'victory'.

Vincent—From the Roman name *Vincentius*, which was from Latin *vincere* 'to conquer'. This name was popular among early Christians, and it was borne by many saints.

This week I found the
Holy Grail and started
a revolution; now I'm
going to the Philippines
with Excalibur in hand
and the Black Madonna
shielding my heart-
to buy my wife a Louis
Vuitton Bag

My name is Feenx. I am
the Lady of the Lake,
and Genghis Khan has
risen from the ashes and
freed my soul.

Acknowledgments

Of course I have to start by first giving thanks to that wonderful Creative Energy that is the Universe in which we live, the Creator of all things and the inspiration behind all that I do. The Light that can be seen and felt in all of Nature. The Compassionate and Merciful Entity that brings to all mankind a message of love and hope. The Omnipotent Spirit that guides me and sends to me Angels to show me what I need to see and learn in order to move forward in my own personal quest for the Grail.

To my beautiful child who reminds me daily that the simple things in life like love and laughter are worth fighting for. To her father for giving me the most precious of gifts. To the family I have loved deeply and lost who taught me how to continue that fight before our Creator called them home. To my friends, all of whom I cherish and love for giving me the strength to keep fighting.

To my conqueror for leading me fearlessly to battle….

Finally to the people of the Philippines, for their lessons on compassion, family values and faith and for showing me that the most powerful weapon in that fight is love….

Preface
No, Seriously—I Made It All Up

He asked if I was a writer, while he was hovering over my table, fussing with the glass. "I always see you here, sitting, writing—you must be a writer."

He is a sweet kid, really; been serving me for two days. Yesterday he told me I have very kind eyes. Today he wants to know where I'm from. When I tell him I'm Canadian, from Toronto, his eyes light up. "What's it like there in Toronto? I've always wanted to go to Canada." Like I said, he's a sweet kid, and I would love to brag about my country, but at the moment the only lame answer I could come up with is that it's different there, very cold.

I know, it's strange that I can easily sit for hours and fill pages with colorful script, yet I can't answer a simple question. Perhaps it's the jet lag; perhaps it's the shock of being here at all. Right now, though, I am thinking it is more my own personal shame over the fact that the people in my world have so much more than the people here, yet they are constantly dissatisfied—always wanting or needing more. I simply can't look this gentle boy in the eye and tell him that the place I come from is a wonderful place. I can't agree with his misguided notion that my world is safer, more prosperous, and therefore a more comfortable place to be. I can't tell him that he should want to go there, that he would be happier, because I would be lying. I flat-out refuse to insult such a sweet-natured soul by telling him an untruth.

Oh I know, you are no doubt thinking I have lost my mind, and it was not too long ago that I myself was convinced I had. I can't argue with you and insist on my sanity when I am hanging on to it by a very thin thread. Honestly, what am I doing here? I've spent fifteen hours on a plane, flown halfway around the world, left my job, friends, family, and *my angel of a daughter*—God forgive me that—to join a man I love and admire deeply and embark on an adventure of spiritual growth. A quest I am hoping will lead to enlightenment and inner peace.

See, there you go—I am nuts, after all. Hmmm… You are probably right, and, if not for all the crazy and unexpected coincidences that led me here in the first place, I would take the advice you are no doubt telepathically sending my way, get back on a plane, and head back to reality. Unfortunately, it is much too late to save me from myself, and, though the logical thing to do would be to listen to you, I will remain and see this through to the end. Besides, I would disappoint a great many people—all those friends and family who, after seeing the previous two weeks of what some claim to be mini-miracles, are convinced that this journey is probably the most important thing I've ever done.

I did ask them, you see. I questioned them, sometimes relentlessly drilling them about their feelings and thoughts. The answer was always the same: "This you must do. This is what you were meant to do." Hell, we should probably all be committed together. It is extremely probable, in fact, that, being crazy myself, I have unknowingly surrounded myself with—unwillingly drawn to myself—others like me. I mean unstable, unbalanced, unreasonable people who are unable to see past their imaginatively invented illusions.

Somehow, though, I think if you knew them you too would put faith in their direction. You, too, would be reassured and sheltered by their faith in you. You would wrap that faith around you like armor and plunge headfirst into the battle we call life. You would not fear failure, nor would you fear the unknown, but rather thrive on uncertainties and unspoken possibilities. I swear you would. Their souls are pure, their spirits are strong, and their beliefs are grounded in the here and now while still having the uncanny ability to fly free on the wings of hope. They are, in short, the kind of friends that you yourself would wake up every day being thankful you had—the kind of friends that lift those they love to great heights, freeing them of doubt and enabling them to soar. Would you like to meet them? I know just where to start…

My most important living inspiration—my reason for being, my sole purpose in life—is eleven years old, with stringy blonde hair and beautiful hazel eyes. She has a sweet, not-so-innocent smile, which should be, but never has been, marred by the crooked teeth she had the misfortune to inherit from her loving English-bred father. Her name is Madison, a name picked out by one of my college roommates on the very same day she also picked out my wedding dress. I found out two years ago that Madison means "daughter of a great warrior." It remains to be seen whether that reference is to me or her father. I am not blind to the fact that it could be from the latter. He is a good man when you get to the heart of it, and he is a fantastic father. Human, yes, and prone to mistakes, but then you will see, if you choose to follow me through this adventure, that I, myself, am far from perfect. If I must be completely honest about the whole me/he situation, he has every right to be angry as hell at some of my past misdeeds. Yet he maintains the stance that our daughter comes first, and that, after all, is really all that ought to matter. I can honestly claim that if I *have* to have an ex-husband, I have probably managed to acquire the best ex-husband that a woman could be lucky enough to have.

Oops, I have gone off, haven't I? I apologize for that, but you will have to meet him eventually anyway, as he is one of the important influences that got me here in the first place.

We were, I believe, in the midst of an introduction to my daughter. I suppose her most remarkable and defining feature is her long legs. They are so long, in fact, that at present, with her being only a few weeks away from her twelfth birthday, her hips are a good inch higher than mine, though when she stands beside me she is a good two inches shorter.

I can't for the life of me figure out where her height comes from. I am only five feet, and her father is not much taller. I am pretty sure that his parents are not genealogically responsible, and my mother's side of the family could not have been much help in that area either. It could have been my father, Joseph, I guess, but as I don't remember much about him—other than the presence of a tall blonde lady named Christine and little brown bags of strawberry-marshmallow candies—I can neither confirm nor dispute the possibility.

Yes, physically, her legs are what stand out the most, but, if you can get past them and her quirky smile, you will eventually see the most magical part about her. I am blessed with a child who exudes a peaceful, gentle, loving nature. She is a kid, of course, and, being a kid, she has her less-than-perfect moments like all other children; yet, beneath the surface lies a strong sense of earthy connection. She abhors violence and pollution, is extremely uncomfortable with other people's suffering, and every once in awhile she comes out with a statement or observation about the world that would leave Socrates with his mouth hanging open. It is in these rare moments of profound wisdom that my daughter disappears, and I find myself searching her eyes for a clue as to who the ancient soul is hiding behind them.

Oh yes, I am the doting mother, aren't I—the one who spoils and coddles and is blinded by my love for my child. This time I will argue the point;

this time I will openly argue with you and tell you that your assumptions are wrong. If I were that kind of mother, I would be bragging to you about her accomplishments, would I not? I'd be telling you how high her grades are, how good she is in sports, how talented she is in the arts, and how popular she is. I won't, not because I can't (she does have some talent in the arts, but academically she is prone to laziness), but because I do not believe those things define who she is. They do not define her place in the world—not in the present nor in the future.

I would also like to point out that if I were so deluded as to think my child perfect, or gifted well beyond the norm—and had no grounds for that belief—then I would not willingly admit that, in those moments when it seems that someone else is watching me through her eyes, I find myself slightly afraid. Not of her, understand, but *for* her. I don't believe that, at her age, having a more advanced perception of the world and the energies in it can do anything but ostracize her from her peers. I doubt that she can find much of a comfort zone when surrounded by other youth whose main focus is how many people they can win over with their charm and wit. Okay, maybe that is stretching it a bit. I suppose charm and wit probably fall second to stylish clothes, expensive toys, and financial status of family. Though you may disagree with me, I think we sell our children short. I am sure they see much more with regard to social interaction than we give them credit for. It is not a big stretch to believe that at the age of eleven or twelve they could be capable of using that understanding to convince, sometimes deceptively, both adults and peers alike to give them what they want.

If you haven't noticed it, take the time to observe the younger generation of today. Give over for the moment your belief that they cannot possibly understand the harsh realities of existence and venture into the unknown; try to converse with them on a higher, more direct, level. You may very well be surprised at what you find. Take, for example, a conversation I had with my daughter over a year ago when I was driving her home from school. She was not yet ten and she had obviously had a rotten day. When I asked her what was up, she went into a detailed account of an incident involving one of her friends. Apparently there had been a falling-out of sorts, but, though my daughter seemed concerned about damage being done to a friendship she cherished, she seemed to be more concerned about the possible damage being done to her friend.

It went something like this.

"My friend Kate and I had an argument today; I wanted to play with her, but she seemed to want to ignore me. I probably shouldn't have pushed it, but I was a little disappointed, and we ended up fighting about something that shouldn't matter."

I would like to point out here that, though I would have liked to question or comment, Madison never gave me the chance. By the end of her story, I remember my mouth was hanging open with no words coming out, something that happens far too frequently for my liking.

"You know how we've been friends for over a year, Mom? I mean, we play together all the time, and we have a lot of fun. We like to do the same things, play the same games, we even like the same kinds of pets, but lately she has been hanging out with girls that are more popular. You know I'm not popular, right? Really, I'm okay with that. I mean, I don't see things the way they do, and I'm not very good at being mean. I don't want to hurt people to make them look bad so I can look good. Kate wants to be popular though, and that's okay too. She is my friend, and I want her to be happy, but sometimes at school I miss her a lot. I know why she has to ignore me though, and when we are together, just the two of us, we have a really good time, so I try really hard not to get angry. But, Mom, I'm a little worried. I mean, doesn't she know we won't be in this school forever? I wish she could understand that when we graduate, when we go to high school, she will have to do it all over again. They don't really care about her, anyway. It's okay. I know she doesn't understand, but when she grows up it will matter more that she is a good person—but that's the thing. I know she's a good person, and I don't want her to worry so much about being popular that she forgets that she is a good person. Mom, what should I do?"

Once you close your own mouth and recover from the brief shock you are no doubt experiencing, you can picture in your mind my own stunned silence. I mean, what is a mother to say to that? What great piece of wisdom can I impart to ease the burden of her troubled thoughts? At the tender age of nine she has just explained in depth more about interpersonal relationships than the average young adult at the age of twenty understands. I had no choice really, and, again, I remember this all very clearly. I simply turned to her and asked, "What the hell? You're nine!" It was not exactly the encouraging reaction she was hoping for, but, knowing my daughter as I do, I doubt that she was put off by my lack of comforting words. I doubt that she even needed to be reassured, but I did, after recovering a bit, take the time to let her know she was very perceptive for one so young. I also remember telling her that those perceptions and understandings would probably cause her as much discomfort in dealing with her peers as it would ultimately help the discomfort it was causing. Now I realize that, given the fact that she was being so open with her thoughts, I probably shouldn't discourage her. I did feel the need, however, to point out that others her age might not catch onto or explore that kind of reasoning until much later in life. I am still her mother, and though I occasionally find myself in situations where I am forced to concede to the unexpected wisdom of an eleven-year-old, it is also still my job as a mother to protect her from adversity and condemnation at the hands of others.

When my daughter isn't delving into the deeper recesses of the human psyche, she is busy being a kid doing all the things kids do. She, like all of her generation (much to my personal disgust and as a result of the shortcomings of my generation), loves to play video games. She also has a small addiction to the computer, which is turning out to benefit me by allowing me to keep in contact with her while I am off traveling the world. She also loves music—not much of a surprise, as her father was in school studying radio when I met him. She has a good voice, as well, when she forgets to be self-conscious. She can nail pretty much any song she happens to be listening to. She also seems to have a natural rhythm and beat and is currently studying hip-hop and ballroom dance as well as being a member of her school's step team (like stomp, but a different name). I have been trying to encourage her pursuit in the arts and to get her past her insecurities regarding how others will perceive her. It is the result of that encouragement that sent me to the airport in pursuit of a career I had long ago pushed aside.

You see, when my opportunity to re-explore my writing career arose, it was a conditional opportunity. It was not self-imposed, but, rather, the conditions were set by the man I travelled to the other side of the world to be with.

His first request of me was to ensure that my daughter understood and approved of my plans, as they would over the next year take me away from her on several occasions and for extended periods of time. It was important to him that I have my daughter's support if I were to embark with him on this adventure. He is, I have to point out, a different kind of man, with strong family values. You will get the chance to meet him later as well, given the fact that this book is our story, and he plays an integral role in the whole crazy adventure. I conceded to his wishes, of course, because they were both reasonable and touching. I took the time to have a heart-to-heart with my little girl. Her response? Keep in mind, please, that she is not yet twelve.

"Mom, you're always telling me to believe in myself and follow my dreams, but how can you expect me to listen to your advice if you won't follow it yourself? If you want me to do these things, shouldn't you set an example and do them yourself?"

Yet again I am left staring at my child with an open mouth, but, as I am now more accustomed to these little mature outbursts, I recover more quickly. This time I had the grace to thank her and let her know just how lucky I am to have a daughter who encourages me in such a selfless manner.

After you hear my side of the story, I am thinking that you may again be of the opinion that my mental capacity became impaired at some point in the past. Allow me to attack that fear from two opposite angles. You may latch on to whichever belief makes you most comfortable. Then we will be able to continue this journey together without the dangerous prospect of insulting your integrity or your sensibilities.

First, let's assume that everything I say in the previous and following pages is true. Fairly appropriate, wouldn't you say, given the title of the book?. Given that assumption, you would have to be wondering how I could possibly remember a conversation I had with my daughter over a year ago and share it with you in a manner that seems to be quoting her word for word. Realistically speaking, a word-for-word quotation at such a late date would seem to be nearly impossible, unless I had at the time enlisted the assistance of some kind of recording device. It's not likely that I happened to be carrying one in the car with me that day, or that I knew in advance that she would have something important to say when I picked her up, and therefore I was prepared in advance. A far more probable explanation is that I have a photographic memory and can somehow tap into past events by tuning my mind rather like you use a DVD player to track back to a place in the movie that you missed while getting your snacks. I, however, feel that is dangerous ground, as it suggests that I am far more intellectually advanced than I would like to believe myself to be. I fear both the complexities and responsibilities that a feeling of superior intelligence breeds, preferring merely to be a student of this life. I am not willing yet to breach the boundary between pupil and teacher. This leads me to suggest to you a safer and more reasonable manner in which to perceive what I am sharing with you, the reader.

I propose to you that this story be absorbed in the spirit in which it is being written—as a story, a tale, if you will—a fabrication that is perhaps occasionally interspersed with some very real observations. If you were to delve into these pages with the understanding that most of the adventures contained within are merely the result of an overactive imagination or even the unrealistic mental wanderings of an overly adventurous mind, then we might in the end come to an understanding. I get to safely share with you an interesting tale, and you get to read it with an open heart and open mind. After all, if it is *not* as the title indicates, then the contents and experiences throughout these pages hold no threat to you or your own beliefs.

It is, of course, up to you. It is not my place to tell you what to perceive as real; reality, after all, is subjective. Take, for instance, the Christian who believes that Jesus was crucified, died, and was raised again by a God who loves all his children unconditionally. That, to them, is reality, and the contents of the Bible are viewed as fact. Now, explore for a moment the Wiccan belief that the power of the world comes from the very earth itself and connects every living thing. To them, it is the manipulation, or, rather, controlled usage of that interconnected energy that allows what others perceive as magic to become a very real and very useful tool to maintain a comfortable and peaceful existence. To each individual, each situation, though coming from different ends of the spiritual spectrum, is very real. As such, reality becomes subjective, depending solely on one's fundamental needs and personal experiences. Before you ask, I will not share with you which belief system I myself follow. You will in time get to know me and will figure it out yourself. I merely wanted a way to illustrate my point, and I'm hoping that in doing so I have sparked in you, the reader, a little curiosity.

Here I seem to have hit a wall, which I assume for the moment means we are finished. But I leave you with one question: Fact or fiction? I know which I prefer, but I am curious what exactly it is that you find yourself wanting to believe.

Chapter 1
Out of the Fire and Flames is Born a New Life and a Renewed Hope

It's a crazy world in which we live, when two weeks ago I could be happily living out an average ordinary life in the city of Toronto, and then suddenly I could find myself uprooted and halfway around the world. I guess I would be exaggerating slightly if I said *happily* living, since, though I had a job, was surrounded by friends, and was living with a boyfriend who very obviously adored me, I, like many others living in my city, was completely dissatisfied with my current place in the world. Thing is, the unhappiness was never based on my need to attain a higher material status. I don't really want a bigger house or higher-paying job to pay for the bigger house. I can't imagine two things in life more likely to bring stress into my world, so I have very pointedly, for years, been trying to avoid both. No, if I was unhappy, it was lack of balance more than anything that was causing my distress. I had momentarily lost sight of the part of me that makes me whole. In ignoring that side of my nature, I had quite effectively managed to make myself sick. A weakened soul breeds a weakened body, and, as I had neglected to feed my spirit for far too long, my body had decided it, too, had had enough.

It was in the midst of my futile attempt to find help for my physical ailments that the cure for my spiritual ills accidentally (at the time I thought it was accidental) stumbled into my life. It is funny, you know, because when we met, there was no indication that we would have any kind of connection, much less alter the direction of each others' lives. Revo was a young, soft-spoken Asian who was studying to be an actor. He had just moved back to Toronto from New York, where his girlfriend was eagerly awaiting his return. My co-workers and I took him under our wing when he came to work with us. Although he had no experience, he obviously had a desire to learn. He managed to win us over with his friendly, open personality.

Our talks centered at first mostly around work, as I am one of those people who believe that I get paid to do a specific job, so I might as well get on with it. After we had worked a few shifts together, idle chatter turned to hobbies, and, in a brief exchange of words, a path was laid out before us that we would not initially recognize, but would ultimately end up walking down together. He discovered that I like to draw, and, after inquiring if he could see my portfolio, quite innocently asked if I would be willing to sketch up a logo for his band. When he told me the name of his band, I admit I was slightly intrigued, but I had not yet made any connection between my own personal quest and this sweet young musician. I told him I would, of course, be willing to do so, but as often happens in cases like this, life got in the way, and the idea was unceremoniously shoved to the back of my mind.

It wasn't until two months later, when he returned from a trip to New York on a casting call, that I was reminded of my promise. When he came back, he told us he had decided that he was going to give his notice at work so he could concentrate on his acting and his music. He claimed it was partly because of the encouragement of a few choice staff members that he had decided it was time to follow his dreams and stop worrying about the immediate effect on his wallet. I was apparently one of those encouraging voices in his ear. Yet, for the life of me, I cannot possibly see how, being stuck in a rut myself, I found the time or energy to inspire somebody else. Upon his return, he asked again if I would do the drawing. As I was agreeing to get it done before he left, I looked into his eyes, and something became immediately apparent—something I had not noticed until the very moment his brief visit into my life was about to come to an end. I knew this man, not in the sense that we were friends who talked and spent time together, but in the sense that the soul behind the eyes was one I had had encountered before. It also occurred to me that I had already drawn the logo—three years earlier, when I had first moved to the city. It was strange that I had not recognized it sooner. While we perused my drawings, we had briefly discussed the meaning of the name behind his band. We had also discussed the meaning of the medallion I have worn around my neck every day since Baba's (my Polish grandmother's) death. Yet, even given our common interests in an obscure and clouded legend, it had never occurred to me to dig deeper.

The evening of his return to the city I went home and redrew the old sketch, adding to it several unique symbols that tied into the theme of the band. When I brought it to him the next day, he was surprised that I had managed to finish it so quickly. I explained that I had drawn it three years ago and had merely been waiting for him to come and collect it. He was silently staring at it while I was quietly explaining the meanings behind the symbols buried in the piece I had drawn. I looked down and noticed that his hands were shaking, and the hair on his arms was standing up. What I had drawn had obviously touched him, yet again it would not become apparent exactly how deeply until a few weeks later, when our stories began to merge. His response at the time was that it was exactly what he had wanted and needed without being able to picture in his mind what it should look like. He wanted to know how I had managed to represent his thoughts so precisely without him having verbalized them; I wanted at the time to tell him that I knew his mind and his heart, but as we were only passing acquaintances, I was sure he would think me a little unstable, so I merely shrugged and explained that I had been visited by a brief flash of inspiration. He was content with the piece, but he never made these decisions alone; he still had to present it to the band. We left it that he would show it to his boys and let me know if they liked it. We parted ways thinking that we would see each other the next day, but he never did come back to work. Though his name once or twice crossed my mind, I did not much miss his presence nor did it concern me greatly that I might not see him again.

A few weeks passed, and life was pretty normal. I went to work, came home, took care of my house, tried to take care of myself, and basically maintained a safe, comfortable, mediocre existence. Then the phone rang, and a voice singing in my ear brought me out of my sleepy state. It was Rev, phoning to ensure that I would be attending the staff party at work. He claimed he had something for me, and the band was very interested in meeting the artist behind the graphic that he claimed encompassed all the meanings behind the band's very existence. I assured him I would be there and hung up the phone thinking to myself for the first time in weeks that I had something to look forward to.

My boyfriend and I arrived later in the evening at the restaurant and settled into the typical staff-party routine, exchanging pleasantries and excitedly hugging and wishing well to the same damn people I saw every day. It was in the midst of this pathetic ritual of false niceties that my little Asian demigod again walked into my world—and this time irrevocably changed the course of my future. I remember that when I saw him that night I thought that he truly was a beautiful creature. As he was pulling me aside, I realized that somehow, in the course of his absence from my day-to-day routine, my perceptions of this boy, no, this *man*, had changed. He handed me a white gift bag after pulling me into a hidden corner of the restaurant so we could be alone. I admit his behavior had me confused, but he explained that he and his band were only stopping by briefly and he had not bought gifts for anyone else. We fell into an easy banter about the band and the art. When I finally opened the gift I, much to my dismay and embarrassment, jumped up and down excitedly like a little schoolgirl. You see, it was impossible to hide my delight, as he had wrapped up for me a copy of the band's CD now labeled with my graphic and signed by the band. The other part of the gift was a very nice set of art pencils. The whole thing to me seemed to be a very straightforward message to not give up on my art. The way he smiled at my reaction made everyone else in the building for one brief moment disappear and turned an otherwise unbearably dull evening into the beginning of a magical journey.

When I was done making an ass of myself over this small, yet powerfully meaningful gift, I came to myself long enough to remember to give him what I had thought at the time a carefully prepared farewell gift. The drawing I had given to him earlier had been a copy of the original. When I am working on graphics for businesses, or tattoos, I never give my original sketches away. This time, however, I had decided that the original belonged with him and had rolled it up so I could safely carry it to him without it getting damaged. I handed it to him like that, rolled up, placing it in the palm of his hand, coincidentally upside down. He would later point this out to me as a sign that we had a journey we were meant to make together. This particular evening, however, we were both completely blind to the signs pointing the way, and, as the evening progressed, it played out naturally to a slowly building, yet extremely satisfying, friendship. I met his band and he introduced me to them as the artist. After I mingled a bit more, my musician friend pulled me aside once again, so he could show me something I had missed.

I hadn't noticed that something I had drawn, the Celtic-style image of a mother holding an infant, when turned upside-down took on the appearance of the hilt of a sword. It had actually been the band's bass player, Craze, who had been the first to notice. Looking back on it now, I am flabbergasted that I didn't see it at the time as more than mere quirky coincidence. I can only guess that had we forced the issue or connected too soon, then perhaps we would not have gone in the direction we were ultimately meant to go. Yet it is strange, again, for me to think that I did not see past the surface weirdness of the situation. After all, I haven't believed in coincidence for a very long time. As I said, I was in a slump. I had hit a wall and needed to break it down before I could continue my spiritual growth. It seemed to me at the time that though the wall was one I had built myself, it would take a great deal of effort to find a way to destroy it; I was not sure I was up for it. Later in the evening, I felt I needed to sign the drawing I had given him. So I asked to borrow it briefly. I found a corner to hide in to commence writing.

To Rev

Thanks for reminding me why Grail seekers seek—never give up the quest.

My heart to yours always,

Feenx

I signed it "Feenx" the name I use when signing my art. It was a name chosen for me by life and circumstance and represented rebirth and new life rising from the ashes left behind by a destructive, yet cleansing, flame. I suppose I should also point out that until three years ago, when I moved to Toronto after my house burnt down, the only time I had put pen to paper was to write.

Up until the very day I, for some reason, sketched out a Celtic style graphic design of a mother and child, I would have laughed in the face of anyone who suggested I turn to art as a hobby. I am, always have been, and always will be a writer—not because my blinded-by-love friends and family encourage me to be a writer, not because some self-absorbed critic justifies my work by claiming that in his superior expert opinion my work is worthy, and certainly not because you are reading this book. Rather, I'm a writer because, when life takes an unexpected twist or throws at me a challenge of seemingly insurmountable odds, I feel compelled to make sense of it all by writing it down. Eighty percent of what I have written in the past has been solely for my benefit. Writing has always for me been a way to heal any damage that has been done to my spirit during life's little annoying struggles. I went to school to become a journalist, and, though I both found myself giving birth and getting married during my fourth semester of school, I somehow managed to graduate and do it only a couple points below honours. I was told all my life that I was born to write by people who claim I had started writing poetry at the age of five years. Yet, through no fault of any one thing, I had forgotten, not that I am a writer, but, rather, what me being a writer meant.

So you see, when Rev gave me the gift that silently stated, "Don't give up on your art," it wasn't only in reference to the art of drawing. It awakened in me a realization that I had forgotten who and what I was. I had been drawn off-course by the day-to-day struggle of trying to maintain an existence on par with what society expected of me. Thus "Thanks for reminding me why Grail seekers seek." What I had really been saying was, "Thank you for reminding me to search out the truth of who I am, the truth of why I am here, and the truth of what I need in my life to keep me happy and balanced."

We met strangers and left friends, and though I was very careful this time to get his number, with a promise to myself not to lose it, I still felt a sense of sadness and loss at the prospect of this man no longer being in my life.

The evening was over, we were on our way home, and all I could think was that I was on the verge of losing something very special. I realized at the same time that I had been given a very precious gift.

I lay awake in bed that night, praying for guidance. It occurred to me that all I had dreamed was being overshadowed by my own personal guilt over past mistakes. My fear of losing the most precious thing in my life was holding me back from using my skills and my gifts to better myself—and maybe even better the lives of others. I continued my nightly meditation for over a week, before it occurred to me that, given what I was asking for, I was not offering a fair exchange. It was only several nights later that I opened myself up completely to the idea of change.

It is not natural or comfortable for me to think in terms of influencing others. Although I have always felt deep down that there was something more I was meant to do and was raised by my grandmother to believe in the talents I was born with; I found myself hesitant to delve into that part of me. Of course the thought of using those talents to make a difference in even one person's life was an extremely uplifting idea yet it was just that, an idea—a dream that upon my awakening dissolved into reality and, day after ordinary day, was never realized.

No more, I thought, lying there in the dark. If there is something I am meant to do, show me what it is; give me a sign in which I can put my faith. Guide me in the direction I am meant to go, and if it is necessary to sacrifice my life here with my friends and my family, if it is important that I be willing to let go of my reality, then so be it. I am ready. I will let go of my fear, accept my mistakes, forgive myself for all my misdeeds, and open myself to the idea of a way to atone for them. I will accept both the light and the dark within me and embrace my humanity and all that comes with it. The pain, the anger, the fear, and the joy—even the lustful hunger I have encountered more than once when in the arms of a man—all of it I will accept and know that it is these things that make me human. I will accept the hate and love, and all the emotions in between, that keep my spirit connected to this earthly plain. It is that earthly connection that I am here to experience, to learn from, and to revel in, allowing my spirit to grow. These things I will accept. I will put my faith in the belief that I am here to *do* more and to *be* more. When I accept these things, a path will be provided for me to walk safely down. There will be signs along that path, and there will be guides sent to keep me from veering off too far when it becomes necessary to steer around obstacles in that path. These things I accept; these things I believe; and, in believing these things, I will find the strength to walk that path. I will be given a clear vision with which to see those signs and granted the grace and humility to accept and be thankful for any help provided me along the way.

This was my final prayer late one night before I went to sleep. It was my plea to the powers that be—whatever you choose to call them—and my way of making peace with both myself and those powers. It was with hope that I could move on as a whole person; the torn spirit I had been would cease after that night to exist. I would learn to be grateful that, regardless of where the road led, for one moment in time I had given myself over to a higher power. I was completely secure in my faith in that power and my belief that this time I would get those answers I was so desperately seeking.

I am a writer and therefore prone to flights of colorful fancy. I revel in exaggeration, as it allows me to expand on my thoughts and ideas while remaining entertaining. Here today I put aside those exaggerations. They are no longer needed. What is reality now is more than fanciful enough and therefore more beautiful and attractive than anything my humbled spirit could create. As I was lying there, a comforting warmth was building in me and spreading over me. It seemed to emanate from, or perhaps enter, the area of my chest. My heart sped up, and my lungs seemed to breathe in a burning heat; yet, I clearly remember that for a moment I felt so detached from my physical self that I'm not sure I was even remembering to breathe. I fell asleep that way: wrapped in that warmth and secure in the knowledge that in the morning I would be embarking on a new adventure.

The next day I woke up, gave my wife a call, and offered to give her a ride to work. I walked into my boss's office and promptly quit my job.

Chapter 2
And Never the Twain Shall Meet... Not This Time

Yes, that's correct: I picked up my wife, took her to work, and quit my job.

I would like to point out that my wife, who happens to be a stunningly beautiful Black Irish woman with seductive Asian eyes, took the whole thing in stride. When I announced quite calmly that I was intending to quit my job in order to pursue my writing career, she merely cocked an eyebrow at me and passively stated, "This should be interesting…"

Now that I have your attention, allow me to clarify a few things for you. I can guess that my usage of the term *wife* has you a tad confused. I assume you have already ascertained that I am female. I have also mentioned that I live with my boyfriend, and though in this day and age a woman being wed to another woman is somewhat accepted in Western society, I doubt very much having both a wife and a boyfriend would be anything but frowned upon in any culture. Please allow me to explain. The term *wife* in this instance can be used both symbolically and figuratively. In the casual sense of the term, she is considered by those I work with as my at-work spouse, in that we communicate and relate to each other on a level of comfort very much on par with most long-time happily married couples. We don't need to say much to each other to accomplish any task at work that requires cooperation. It is well known, in fact, that we are able to read each other so well through the use of body language that there are times when we never say a word at all. It is also well known that we can fight as heatedly as any married couple. Yet we have a mutual respect and understanding of one another's views and refuse to let those arguments come between us on a deeper level.

If you would like to explore the term in a figurative sense, you will see our relationship is one of mutual support and commitment to each other's happiness, again much on par with most long-standing happily married couples. We stand beside each other, support each other, feel joy at the other's success, and suffer as the other suffers. We keep each other strong by refusing to judge either past or present foibles. We back each other, defending each other if necessary, against the criticism of others. We also have an intense respect for each other's private lives, which allows us to have multiple friendships that do not interfere with our own personal bond. We do not believe it is necessary to invade each other's personal space, clinging to each other in order to maintain our friendship. If you were to go to either me or her for support or advice, and chose to do so in confidence, you could feel very secure in the knowledge that it is not in our natures to run to one another telling tales and sharing gossip.

She is, when you get right down to it, the one woman in my life who, if I were inclined to go that route, I could quite comfortably share a home and future with. We would, however, have quite the difficulty explaining our future together to her very sweet, very loving husband Adam. He, by the way, also refers to me as *her* wife and finds the whole situation rather amusing. He is as white as she is black and as short and round as she is tall and statuesque. They will both kill me when they read this but, given time, will find the humour in it as well. When I say she is Black Irish, I mean she is a person of Guyanese/Jamaican descent who just happened to marry an Irishman.

I think combining his red hair and freckles with her own stunning features will make for uniquely beautiful babies. This is something they are supposed to start working on very soon; as I told Sophia, I look forward to meeting her son (yes, I predict a boy, but I very much doubt they will stop at one).

As to her complacent reaction to my abandoning her to the vultures at work (her words), it is not in her nature to question any decision I make that seems to be moving me toward a happier life. So, as with every other odd decision or idea I have come up with, she took it upon herself to support me in it, reserving judgment for a later date. Her comment on me quitting being "interesting" relates to the fact that she takes perverse delight in the discomfort of our restaurant management team. Being very much aware of how many hours I put in, and how many times during any given month I agree to cover shifts for others, she was of the opinion that my announcement would cause some squirming in the office. If it did, I never got the chance to relish in it. In fact, when I told my boss I wanted to work on my book, he encouraged me to take a leave, securing for me both my benefits during that leave and my position upon my return. It makes it much easier to stretch your wings and take that first leap into the unknown when you have the security of a safety net beneath you. I like to believe, though, that I would have done it regardless, as I was feeling compelled to move in that direction. I did notice that when my boss and I were finished talking he seemed to have a glazed look in his eyes, as if he were not sure he himself believed he was allowing it. The damage, as they say, by that time was already done, and I left work just a little more sure I was doing the right thing. Now for the shocking part: I still did not know for the life of me what I was supposed to be writing about. I had in my head an abstract idea, and I also had in my head a not-so-abstract title, but the actual content and the purpose behind that content had thus far eluded me. So here I was, a mere week away from three months off, with a laptop on order (something I had arranged the week before without knowing why) and nothing to go on but a title that in and of itself told me nothing.

I should explain here that it has always been my intention to write a book, and for the longest time I always thought I knew what it would be about. I had lived what on the surface appeared to be a fairly normal life. I was born, grew up, went to college, got married, had a baby, got divorced, and went to college again—nothing overly exciting to the casual observer; yet, to those who had shared some of that life with me, my stories and my experiences were both dramatic and entertaining. That, combined with the unrelenting belief and encouragement of my recently deceased Baba that I could someday be an inspiration to others, made it possible that my life story might just be worth putting on paper. There were, however, several drawbacks to the whole scenario as I saw it, and I was hesitant to explore that particular avenue. As I said before, I am uncomfortable with being responsible for other people's success. In order for me to inspire the general population, I had to embrace the idea that what I had to say might just be important; this was something I was not yet willing to do. Secondly, I would have to give up my somewhat-reclusive existence. I don't mean reclusive in the way that I was hiding myself away from society. I have a very outgoing personality with my friends and acquaintances. My reclusiveness was founded on the belief that the general public had no right to know anything about my personal life.

It is, as many have pointed out, practically unheard of for me to allow people into my life deeply enough that they can share my fear or my pain. Surface anguish does not count. Many people have seen me rant and rave; some have even seen me cry. Few, however, have been witness to the gut-wrenching emotional collapse that has occurred with each loss I have endured throughout my short life. As I have carefully built and surrounded myself with thick, protective walls, the very idea of breaking through them and sharing my inner self with the public was abhorrent. In saying that, I also knew that in order for anything I wrote to be inspirational those walls would have to come down. It was both a frightening and daunting prospect and, again, something I was unwilling to do. Lastly, I was not quite sure where to begin. I had tried over the years several times to start writing this particular story. Each and every time I would get a little way in and then get the feeling it was not yet time. Every previous attempt had begun at a different starting point and then been abruptly abandoned when the beginning ceased to flow toward a conclusion. It had been an exercise in humility and futility, and I was not eager to revisit such an emotionally draining experience.

I was mildly concerned about the effects such a story would have on the people in my life who are dear to me. In order to share my life story, I would have to expose as well pieces of others' private lives and essentially drag through the mud individuals I have over the years grown both to love and respect. My Baba, shortly before her death, had seemingly given me an answer to this dilemma. She reiterated a piece of advice she had given me several times throughout my life. She had told me over and over again that if I were ever to write my story that I should do it in the form of a fictitious tale, though she would never discuss with me exactly what she thought my story was. She would only say with certainty that someday I would write and publish a book. It was not until shortly before her death that she had given the advice with any sense of urgency. The last time she spoke of it, however, was the week before she died, when she made me promise—quite literally, on her deathbed—that I would never publish my story as fact. Having given that promise to the person in my life I revered above all others, I was now stuck on how to go about fulfilling her wishes. Nor did I realize at the time either the import or the implications of that demanded promise. I only knew I had to find a way to abide by it.

All these concerns combined to leave me pondering over exactly what I had left my job to write about. I was still somewhat secure in my belief that I would be given direction, but it would not be until several days later that I would experience the true meaning of the word *faith.*

Chapter 3
They Say You Do Not Find the Grail-It is the Grail That Finds You

While I was going my own way and doing my own thing, apparently, so was my musician friend.

Starting several weeks prior to my decision to randomly quit work, Revo and I were continuing to keep in touch via the computer. We had tossed a couple of emails back and forth, and he and his band had invited me to come to a show. The phone call began with *Hey Vicky you're* so... (This was a silly little song he had begun singing when we first met; it went to the tune of "Hey, Mickey.")

> *Okay, we gotta think of a new catchphrase. Hahaha*
>
> *Dearest Feenx,*
>
> *I've decided that I'm just gonna call you Feenx from now on... yes, the decision is made.*
>
> *The show is on the 25th of January at Raq Lounge and pool hall.*
>
> *I attached an invitation flyer and also the Raq Google map.*
>
> *Ummm, what else?... Oh, Craze told me he got your text msg. The guys think you're "really sweet." :)*
>
> *That's it; hope you had a good day at work today... how many guys hit on you? Lol*
>
> *Heart u, Revolution*

Throughout the days leading up to the show, Rev and I had tossed back and forth several emails, mostly pertaining to his band and my art and how the two seemed inexplicably connected. This leads me to the point in the story where it is necessary for a little background on both. I fear that without some explanation you may become lost in the imagery I will shortly be presenting. I will start with the connection between his band name and the medallion I wear around my neck. The name of his band is the Holy Grail, which is taken from the legend of King Arthur and the Knights of the Round Table. My own personal quest for the Grail had grown over the years from a different source. I wear around my neck a shield handed down to me by my grandmother. It depicts the Black Madonna and is representative of the shrine dedicated to her in Poland. The shrine itself is said to depict Mary, who the Polish people consider to be the rightful queen and protector of Poland as a free country. There are several legends and stories surrounding the shrine in Poland, as well as others dedicated to the Black Madonna, which are scattered throughout various countries on almost every continent.

Now, the story of King Arthur is pretty well known and really quite accepted in most cultures, regardless of their spiritual beliefs. The story of the Black Madonna, however, is much more controversial than a straightforward, albeit mystical, tale of a king and his courageous knights seeking the legendary Grail. For most people, the Black Madonna is simply a depiction of the Virgin Mary and child. Depending on what country you hail from, the reasons for her being black vary. Some believe that various paintings and shrines have darkened over the years as the result of age and exposure to smoke from candles burning nearby. Others believe her dark skin is the originally intended colour, though most of these paintings are exceptionally old and, in some cases, this can either be proven as fact or fiction. Some people believe the reason for the colour is to encourage acceptance of all races, creeds, and religions as children of God. They say the Black Madonna is an attempt to teach humans to embrace each other regardless of where they come from. I like the idea very much and support wholeheartedly the notion, though I myself am a member of a much more elite group of Grail seekers. After studying several of the paintings, as well as reading anything I could get my hands on, I have come to the conclusion that it is quite possible that the Black Madonna is not the Virgin Mary, but rather Mary Magdalene.

Oh yes, I know, you may think me a victim of Dan Brown's novel—though I support the idea myself, I am not sure I support the method with which he reached his conclusions. The truth is that it matters not, as I don't expect for one minute that you would alter your own belief systems to match mine. I am only clarifying a few issues of my own personal views, so that we can continue this tale in a manner that will not leave you lost and floundering.

Regardless of what you believe the Grail to be—either a magic golden chalice or the wife of Jesus and the mother of his child—the meaning behind the idea of the existence of the Grail remains the same. The Grail as a chalice was believed to contain God's light, his wisdom, and the truth of his existence. The Grail as the womb that bore and brought to life the direct descendants of Jesus was said to also represent the truth of his existence, thereby bringing light and wisdom to humanity. Either way, the Grail stands for truth. The Grail represents the truth of who we are, why we are here, and, ultimately, the truth of where we are headed.

My point to all of this is that both my musician friend and I had followed the Grail trail, down two separate paths, for most of our lives. As we discussed and explored each other's stories, we discovered a few things. I am a great believer in the meaning behind names. I think names come to us and that we are chosen by them, not the other way around. Out of curiosity, I looked up Rev's first name to see what it stood for. His middle name is pretty self-explanatory when you think about it, but that is a story for another time. His first name is Vincent, and I replied to his previous email with a reference to the meaning behind his name.

> *Dearest Revolution—(did you know Vincent means conqueror—what are you planning to conquer today?)*
>
> *Hey, sweetie: Thanks for the info, and, as usual, for making me smile. You are really good at that. I'll run with you calling me Feenx. If u r a good boy I might even let you see my Feenx tattoo someday. I will try very hard to be there on the 25th, but since I am going in for minor surgery on the 21st I may not be feeling the greatest. Don't worry; nothing major. They just found something that might be causing all my problems and they want to remove it and see if it helps get rid of my headaches. I do, however, really want to see you play as well as just get to see you before you take off again on another journey. Someday, I swear, I'll go with you on one of these trips of yours, just for the fun of it, but for now I guess I should let the doc try to get me healthy first. While I'm lying around in a drug-induced stupor, maybe I'll get the chance to do some writing or drawing. I get a week off work to recupe, but I don't think it will take that long. Well, hon, gotta run—still silly enough to be going to work every day, and I would hate to be late. Take care, luv, and play safe. Say hi to the boys—xo.*
>
> *Oh, I forgot—can I give your number to Sophia? She misses you…*

He wrote this back:

My dearest Feenx of the West,

You deserve every smile you receive from everyone,

I'll pray that the surgery goes well. The show on the 25th was cancelled; the owner came back from LA and some logistic stuff. I'm trying to set up another venue for Feb 1st, so hopefully you'll be fully recovered and back up to your lively self.

*It would be fun to go on a bunch of adventures with you. And you have a Feenx tattoo?! Mmmmm ... Okay, I'll try to be a good boy... *struggling* =)*

Someone once told me it means victorious, but I did not know Vincent meant CONQUEROR*! Lately I've been conquering myself. As soon as I'm done that, the world is next.*

And I swear... if I was ever a prince of the Grail in my previous life, you were surely my princess.

Greetings from the boys and yes, of course, Sophia can have my #. I miss her too. I've been pinching my own ass the past few weeks I'm missing her so much :)

Yours always, Revo

Shortly after my surgery, I sent a reply and took the opportunity to send him one more detail about my name that I had not yet bothered to mention. It was something another Grail-questing friend had pointed out several years ago as a joke and something I had forgotten about until recently. My last name, Norloch, means "of the lake." My rather large teddy-bearish friend had said a few years back that, given the fact that I am female, in a sense that meant I was also a lady (something I must point out here and now is a title I have categorically denied for years). He had finally gotten around to saying, in a convoluted and twisted way, that, in short, I was the Lady of the Lake—the very woman, in fact, who handed King Arthur his sword at the beginning of his quest for the Grail.

Dear, sweet Revolution,

I'm sorry your gig got cancelled; hopefully I will get to see you perform on the 1st instead.

The surgery seems to have gone well; my headaches are less intense, so that is a good sign. I would have written back sooner, but I have been on the couch sleeping for the last five day;, apparently my body decided I needed the rest. Overall, though, I feel good, so if you are playing on Sunday I will do my best to be there. (I work that night, but I can come up after work, so you will have to send me some info as to where and when and how the hell I can find it.

You know be good is one of those terms that can be relative to whatever current situation you find yourself in, so don't try too hard. Being a good boy does not always mean you should follow the rules—try to keep that in mind.

By the way, I know you said you were leaving again on another trip, but I can't remember when it is you said you are leaving, so drop me a line and let me know; that way, even if you don't have a show we can hook up for coffee and a chat before you leave. Very odd situation I find myself in; I already love and respect you, but I don't really know that much about you... strange to know so little about somebody I somehow feel so familiar with. I have no idea how often you check your email, but I am off work until Thurs lunch; if you get this and have time, give me a call. We can go out for lunch, and you can catch me up on all your plans to conquer the world.

Until then, my friend, play safe—and try not to give yourself too many bruises pinching yourself, because claims of self-mutilation will not save you next time you see Soph. She likes pain, lol. Say hello to the boys for me, and I will, of course, give Sophia a squeeze for you.

Oh yes, and here is your name info for today. One of my last names is Norloch, which means "of the lake," and, since I am a woman, it means I am the "lady of the lake" (coincidence is merely a sign on the road that helps us find our way).

My heart to yours ;) xo Feenx

Coincidences and colorful imagery aside, I am sure you can now see where I am going with this. Yet again, neither Rev nor I were putting any significance to these twists of phrase nor were we contemplating taking our passing acquaintance past a professional level. We both viewed the whole scenario as interesting, yes, as entertaining, certainly—but neither of us were allowing ourselves to read anything into it. I believed at the time, and so did he, that we were headed in two completely different directions. Yet the emails continued.

He sent me yet another invite to yet another new location for yet another new gig. I would have my daughter that night, and I had sent a message on Facebook asking if she could come with me. He answered immediately.

Hey, Viki,

I love reading your emails. You are an inspiration to my heart.

I'm glad the surgery went well. I was looking for turmeric the other day, which is a natural anti-inflammatory, but I couldn't find the right extract. Canada needs to step up on the natural remedies stage; in the US you can find it at any local drug store. I'll look again today; there's this good herbal store downtown.

I know; both shows got cancelled, but where 2 doors closed a window was shattered by a wave of wind that consisted of several TV producers, directors, and a record label. It's just in those times when we're down that God will give us a hand to get back on our feet, and—just like that video you sent—we have to on our feet again before we can start walking.

Thanks; now I know what you mean by "be good" =) hahahaha

I kinda felt the same way about you the first time I met you. In fact, people told me about you at the workplace, and it didn't seem like they were getting it entirely right. After a few conversations, there was this serendipitous feeling of knowing you.

Hmmm… Lady of the lake… like the lady of the lake in King Arthur's quest for the Grail. The sword got lost and the sweet protective lady gave it back to King Arthur. Funny how that works out—smile— my band's name Holy Grail … you made that beautiful sketch years ago… and when you turn the sketch upside around, it's the handle of a sword… and as soon as you gave me the picture, I left Tucker's to continue the journey.

Did you know that your name means "Victory of the People?"

I talked to the owner of the gig, and it's no problem. Just let them know you're with the Holy Grail, and they'll let her in. It's a friendly crowd, and the people are nice. If she's anything like her mother, I'm sure she'll fit right in, lol.

Some producers will be there, so if you need me to introduce her to some engineers and other artists, I will. If she has the voice you say she has, maybe we can nurture that, and who knows. =)

At a time when I was beginning to lose hope, a time I felt I lost my Excalibur… you gave it back to me in one flash: maraming salamat *(thank you very much in tagalog-Filipino language)*

With love, Revo

It was only days now until his performance, and I had just that day gone to work with my wife in tow and taken my boss up on his offer of a leave of absence in lieu of me quitting.

Hey, Revo,

I'm glad my emails make you happy, and as for me being an inspiration, it works both ways, 'cause, baby, have I got news for you (no, seriously, I do—it is BIG NEWS).

I harassed Craze and sent him a text, 'cause I wanna tell you in person, but you no call. I be thinking you r phone shy, yes? On a side note, I feel great—no headaches, and we will most assuredly be there Friday nite. My little girl seems to be looking forward to it, and me, well, I can't wait to c u play.

I've got a business proposition for you. I know you are not going to have a lot of time Friday night, 'cause you will be pulled in a million different directions, so call me when you get this—I know u r a busy boy—but I'll keep it short and relatively painless.

I'm so very glad you found your way to Tuckers. I am sure they had lots to say. I try very hard to keep people at bay and keep them guessing; if they belong inside my walls, they will find a way in. Unfortunately, it seems to give people a lot to talk about; luckily I don't much care, and the smart ones, the ones that matter, see through the stories anyway.

Teehee—what can I say? Next time round, don't make me wait this long. I've been in this city for 3 yrs waiting for you just taking your sweet time about coming round lol. I tease, but seriously, something tells me we have a connection from another time and place.

If I have helped set you on a positive path—if I can somehow set your heart free so you can soar—then I have done part of what I think I came to this city to do.

Maddi will be fine on Friday, I am sure; we'll meet whoever you want, but I also know you are there to work. Call when you can—write when you want—and play safe till I c u again.

Love, light, laughter, Viki

He never did call but I got a response.

Viki, what's your phone #?!

Lol

I saw Sophia yesterday... awww... I can't find your #. My phone is shitty and can only store 100 numbers, so once in awhile it deletes random numbers when I put new ones in there.

I have been busy preparing for my trip to the Philippines: all the contacts there and getting ready for the show tomorrow and some recording. I'm so glad you're better. =)

So, Maddi is coming. Yeah ... can't wait to see her in person; she's such a pretty little girl in her pic.

Um... yeah, sometimes I can be a little phone shy—I should get over it. Btw, got news too—will explain tomorrow at the show. xo

I wrote a very quick reply and then went on with my day.

Oh, u r such a bad boy, lol: 416-775-5575 (remind me to beat you later for losing my number) xo. I am home tonight and working from 11:30–4:00 pm Friday, but we will be at the show. She even made me take her shopping—having a girl is expensive. Love ya lots, Vik

I dropped by work the day of the show and took the opportunity to speak briefly to Sophia about a strange idea that had popped into my head—an idea I couldn't shake and the reason I wanted so badly to talk to Revo. I was having trouble bringing myself to write or create in my house. It was not a space that held much comfort for me. Rather, it seemed so steeped with negative energy that I felt it was draining me of my creative abilities. I told Sophia I had realized I had all this time off and I needed someplace magical to feed my spirit. As Rev was going to be taking a trip to spend a few weeks in the Philippines, I thought that maybe I could catch a plane and, using him as a guide, find some inspiration for my work. Crazy thought, eh?

I really felt bad asking Sophia what she thought, as I had been planning to take her and my daughter to Europe in the spring and could at the time only afford to take one trip or the other. I expected that maybe she would think me nuts, as I hadn't even spoken to Rev about the idea. Add to that the fact that I hardly knew him, then throw in an insecure and slightly jealous-of-his-prerogatives boyfriend—it was not, in general, the sanest of ideas. What did she say? Humph, I'll tell you what my grounded, down-to-earth, committed-to-reason friend said.

She said, "Okay, you can go, but only if you pick me up a Louis Vuitton bag while you are there."

I really do have the strangest friends…

The night of the show, I picked up a friend of mine and drove out with my daughter to the other side of the city. The friend in question is another person in my life who I have a very strong past-life connection with. We met through the same restaurant, which seems to me now to be a central meeting place for wayward spirits. When I first met him, I was slightly taken aback by this quirky little man. Honestly, he is shorter than me, and yet his self-assurance is so evident in the way he carries himself that at times he seems to me to be ten feet tall. He has a fantastically strange sense of humour, dresses to kill, and has a knack for getting out of trouble a split second after he gets into it—something that, thanks to his love of women, he manages to do frequently. When he isn't entertaining or challenging the world (depends on his mood), the quiet side of his personality emerges. He has a deeply buried and seldom-shared intellectual nature. Yet, when he does let it show, his confident advice and encouragement is often all that is needed to bring a friend back from the brink of despair. He always knows exactly what to say and when to say it—whether it be to lift up a friend or knock down an enemy; his words always hold a vast amount of wisdom, truth, and power.

He and his wife are both Jamaican, and when their youngest son was born they jokingly commented that he had my hair—near to impossible, given the fact that I am white and the new baby (my godson) is quite dark in both colour and origin. Yet, sure enough, when I finally saw him there it was: soft, wavy, medium brown hair.

I had recently asked my friend Conrad if he was interested in taking our baby (yes, my godson, my baby) home. I meant to Jamaica, to meet the family, something they have not yet had a chance to do. Conrad's answer was simply "My home is wherever you are, but, yes, I suppose some day we should take Deshaun to Jamaica." The answer was both touching and not that unexpected, as even his wife has commented that he and I have a connection that runs deeper than the here and now.

Again, I am only telling you these things so that later you can grasp each individual's part in this twisted tale—and if by the end of this you believe a single word, I will be absolutely amazed.

On arriving at the studio/lounge, we settled ourselves in, and I wandered behind the bar to teach the bartender how to properly make a Long Island Iced Tea. Rev saw me there and came up laughing, shaking his head and commenting that somehow I manage to make myself at home regardless of where I am.

Prior to the show, Rev and I had agreed to share our news after the band's set but instead spent the first hour together idly chatting. He played a visualization game or, rather, attempted to, but my answers were so twisted and far out of left field that he kept having to stop and backtrack. The most important part of the game turned out to be the part about a white stallion. I was to describe a horse, what colour it was, and use three words to represent the horse's personality. I chose majestic, powerful, and peaceful. He explained that the horse was supposed to represent my ideal mate, and the colour white, he said, laughing at me again, stood for purity. I found out later a deeper meaning behind the white steed, but we will in time get back to that. Eventually, the musicians had to go get organized, and I returned to my own table where Madison and Conrad were settled in ordering a late-night snack.

The first part of the show was a young drummer, a nine-year-old boy who could whale on a drum set better than several adult drummers I've seen. It was good encouragement for my daughter, who still held fast to the belief that, being young, it would be difficult to be taken seriously in the music industry. Yet here was a small boy who was being encouraged and applauded by a large group of adult musicians. Granted, he deserved it, but I could see the whole scene was having an extremely positive effect on my daughter's resolve to enter the world of music.

It is funny how the little things touch us in big ways. Here was this random guy I had met through work and who had no more than a passing interest in me—yet he was going out of his way to encourage my daughter to follow her dreams. It was touching, and it gave me a clearer inside view of who this man really was.

When the Holy Grail finally finished their set it was late, and Madison had her head buried in her arms, trying, but failing, to sleep through the noise. Rev and I still took the time to share our news, but, as the room was way too loud, we left Madison with Conrad and found a corner where we could talk. He told me to go first. So I told him I had decided to take some time off work and focus instead on my writing. He was very surprised, as he knew me as an artist, not a writer. Though he seemed pleased, he also had a slightly confused look about him. He asked me, "Really? You write?" Though I knew I should be getting Madison home, I stayed long enough to briefly explain my background and education in journalism as well as my ambition to write a book. He seemed a little more shocked than I had expected him to be. So I told him so. I also told him that, of all the people I knew, I would have thought *he* would be happy that I had decided to take a chance and follow a dream. He said, "No, no, that's not it," and he gave me a little grin. "It just seems quite coincidental that, given my news, you just recently decided to start writing."

Then he proceeded to tell me his tale. As he spoke, things began to fall into place. Apparently, his father had been a member of a revolutionary group before Rev was born. They had fought for the freedom of their people from oppression by a corrupt government. There was a legend taken from the time of the revolution that said someday a man would come to the Philippines and teach its people how to be free. The prophecy was made, during a large gathering of revolutionary soldiers, that the man's name would be Rebo, and he would be born of one of the men present. The only reason Rev knew about the tale was that his own father had been at that rally. He explained that his father had thought to Westernize the name, replacing the *B* with a *V*, and turning his name into the first four letters in *revolution*. Rev also pointed out that many children around that time had been named similar to him, and his own father had told him that it would likely be someone who had grown up to be a lawyer who would come forward to actively make change.

Rev's father was no longer involved, and, in fact, no longer even living in the country. Yet, for some reason, Rev said he felt himself being pulled back to his homeland. It was time to take a break from his music career and delve deeper into the meaning behind his given name. He also felt that somehow his people could be helped and inspired through the arts. Then he told me that the very same day that I had quit my job he had informed his band that he was going back to his home country and was not sure if he would ever come back. They had given up the lease on the studio, and he was preparing for an extended stay—when, up until only a few days ago, his intentions had merely been to have a short reunion with his family.

He had gotten it into his head to write a book exposing the corruption of the government, with the hopes that it would open the eyes of his countrymen. It was an idea he had been tossing around in his head for years, and then three days ago he had awakened with a strong desire to follow up on that idea. Now, here he was, on his way there, without any concrete plan for completing the challenge he was setting for himself.

He gave me another tiny smile. "You know, it is awfully strange that we both just happened to alter the direction we are going in on exactly the same day. I quit my band, and you quit your job. Now, I'm a musician, not a writer, and as I'm thinking to do some writing, I could probably use the advice of someone who is trained in that area. I think we need to talk more about this before I leave. Something tells me our time together is not yet meant to end."

It was my turn to look poleaxed, given my stop at the restaurant earlier to see my wife. I was also overcome with a panicked sense of urgency stemming from his decision to not return as intended. I happened just at that moment to glance over at Madison and realized that we had been talking a lot longer than I had originally intended. We made quick plans to meet before he left for the Philippines, and I gathered up my child. I left feeling both exhilarated and exceptionally confused. It seemed what I had suggested as a possibility earlier in the day was now turning out to be a very real and very scary probability.

It wasn't until Conrad made a comment to me in the car that I began to shake. Keep in mind, as I quote him, that while he was in the club with me, he was at the other end of the room and could not possibly have seen or heard a damn thing. I must also make it very clear that he and Sophia do not talk often. There is no way she would have breached confidence and shared our earlier discussion with him. Conrad was staring at me as I drove and, finally, after a few minutes of laughing to himself, he decided to share what he seemed to find a very amusing joke indeed. "I know you, Vik, and I know that look. You're going after this guy, aren't you? You are going halfway around the damn world to meet this guy." With my baby sleeping in the backseat, I tried to be reasonable about the whole thing. There was no way I could leave her for long. The whole idea was nuts. There Conrad sat, his smiling mouth split in an ear-to-ear grin, laughing his ass off at the fact that I was about to transverse the globe to follow a man I hardly knew. He was supposed to tell me not to do it. He is dedicated to his kids, and he knows how dedicated I am to mine. What he should have done while he had the chance was talk me out of it. Hell, until that night he had never met the guy. He had no foreknowledge concerning what type of person Revo was and no grounds to trust him. His love for me alone should have elicited from him the quite reasonable request that I at the very least think it through. Oh no, not him! When we finally got to his house, with him still giggling, his only comment on getting out of the car was: "Hey, have a good trip, eh?"

Chapter 4
Flying Cards, White Horses, and the Gospel Lady

It wasn't until I got home and had Madison safely tucked into her bed that I was willing to admit to myself that my story had found me. My instincts told me this was going to have an irrevocable effect on my life, and, though I hoped that in the long run it would be for the better, I was understandably afraid. Unfortunately, I have a bit of a wild side and—regardless of the impact to my safe, secure life at home—I found myself wanting to jump in: feet first, eyes closed, and hoping against hope the pond was going to be deep enough. I sent a quick text to Rev, then headed off to bed.

Hey, sweetie,

I forgot with everything else going on last night to tell you how much I love watching you play—you really are talented, and I hope you never give up that part of yourself. Listen, it occurred to me today that perhaps it is not my story I am meant to be writing, and though I know I will be seeing you on Tues, I wanted to give you something to think on until then. I am very serious when I say I want to come to the Philippines—and, yes, I know it's way out of left field, but I want to learn about your people, and I am wondering if you would teach me about them and tell me your story, the whole story—not just the stuff you briefly highlighted last night but all of it. I am willing to come there and learn if you would be willing to take the time and teach me. I figure if you have not by now run away screaming for fear that I have lost my mind, then maybe there is more to this. Perhaps if we collaborated our efforts: your knowledge and the gift that I was blessed with (the ability to pour my heart and soul onto paper), then maybe we can bring your people's story to the attention of the world. I feel so strongly about this and am willing to take the risk and invest the time, if you will help me by leading me to the information I need. If you are interested, you know how to reach me or you can wait until Tues and we can talk then—and, so you know, my full name means "Yahweh's great victory of the people." Perhaps the people who named me had a premonition—I hope you are open to the possibilities of us working together, because suddenly three yrs does not seem that long to have waited after al. Love, light, laughter. xo, Feenx

I didn't believe, of course, not at the time. I went to bed with all sorts of doubts in my head. Did the conversation we had really mean that this was a path I was supposed to follow? Did Rev really see it too, or would he take a look at my latest email and think *Man, crazy lady, got to get away.* What would happen if, by some off-chance, this was the road I was supposed to walk down? Where would it lead, and how many sacrifices would I have to make along the way? It was not a very restful night.

I still could not quite believe that I could write a book that would not only sell but would inspire the people who bought it. I'm not sure that even now I can reconcile the idea of me being anybody important enough to initiate change or affect the future of our world. My brother claims that it is the safe side of my personality keeping me grounded, so I can continue to do the work we are doing. I have discovered that as long as I am actively trying to help others, then the pieces just seem to fall into place, and answers are just sent to me as I need them. It is only when I begin to be concerned about my own security and make decisions based on those concerns that I find myself completely off-track and wondering how I got there. I can only guess that that is how it is supposed to work; I still haven't had the chance to sit down and ask God about it, so I will for the moment have to continue to draw conclusions based on what I've seen and been through. It makes sense, though, that if "the powers that be" want us to be selfless and compassionate, they would only actively help us when we are.

The next day Madison and I had an early morning hair appointment. When I attempted to wake her up, however, I discovered she was far too tired from the night before. So I left her sleeping and went on alone.

As per my now-usual routine, I quickly checked my email before I left and was pleasantly surprised to see a positive response to my email from the night before.

My Lady of the Lake,

Can we meet up at 12 instead of 1 on Tuesday? It's my last day and I have to be at the Airport 5 am Wed.

I'm home finally after 2 nights of late nights and music from Live Nights, lol.

I had dance this morning, then the gym, then the studio, then went to sell some equipment, then to my cousin's, then to Risa's and the guys, and I spent some bromance time together. I want to leave on good terms with them; it's another long story. Maybe your words of wisdom can solve the dilemmas we've faced.

Thanks! You know, I learn every time I go on stage, and the words never and give up have kind of been exhausted in my vocabulary by people who prefer instead to use the words believe and faith. So, the way I see it, winners never quit and quitters never win. The more battles I can find myself in in life, whether win or lose, the more I will ultimately learn the lessons I need to learn to win the greater war. Each step on stage or film is a battle, and I can only hope that with every step and every breath I breathe, I learn and improve—until one day the whole world is watching.

I think what the Philippines need is God's great victory of the people.

In high school, I was a pool shark and loved billiards. At this age, I hadn't read anything about the Arthurian Legends or the Holy Grail. I went out with my friend, and I bought a pool cue. When I went to the counter, the teller told me, "Nice pick, the Excalibur."

I said, "That's a cool name," and he told me I would never lose with it. I don't think I have to this day. It was only about 4 years ago when I discovered the tales of King Arthur and the Grail; soon afterward we formed the band.

Legend has it that the hilt had powers of its own. It was only when Craze turned your art upside down that we all saw what was clearly the hilt of a sword. And it was that night that you gave it to me, rolled up like a sword—and with it on my person, I felt all fear vanish. I'm thinking of that now, because I have it hanging on top of another picture in my room, and beside it is a card with the silhouette of Elvis that my mother got me for my trip to the Philippines. She wrote in it, "I hope one day you'll be like Elvis, only in popularity," as if to say: "but don't die so young."

Anyway...

I'm game with this entire scenario, with 3 conditions. And I guess we'll talk about them when I see you. That and . . . I'm just wondering: where did you come from? And where have you been all my life?

One of my acting coaches always told me, "Don't take care—take risks." =)

1. It's what you sincerely want to do and where you want to go.

2. It will make you happy and wake you up every morning with a greater purpose to stay focused and finish your book.

3. Your daughter supports it. I can see now—she was the window God opened when doors and walls had closed in on you.

As I drove, I realized I had to go. Yet the idea itself was so far out in left field and so unexpected that even if the prospect of a trip to the other side of the world was exciting, the reality was scary as hell. When I arrived at the salon, my stylist, Victoria, immediately noticed a difference in my demeanour. I believe she said something along the lines of "you're glowing." Now, taken out of context, that could mean my appearance was one of lighthearted happiness. Coming from Vic, however, it took on an entirely different meaning. Vicky is a spiritual child of the new age. Her journey to enlightenment has taken a different path than those who use structured religion as their guide. She is a believer in karma. She also believes that the energies that make up our world are what tie together and define our existence. She believes in the power of healing energy being shared and manipulated by others for the use of mending both body and soul. She also believes, like many others, that mankind is on the verge of a spiritual revolution. She can neither define nor describe, however, how that revolution will manifest. She can only say with certainty that it is inevitable. She feels that it is a necessary step in human evolution and that it will lead humanity toward a more enlightened state. She studies healing arts, spirit guides, chakras, and meditation. She relies on the powers of plants and herbs that nature has provided for us and looks to spirit guides to give her direction and confirmation. She is aware of the importance of recognizing signs, what some refer to as coincidence, and their place among us as a tool of encouragement and direction. She also believes in auras, the energies that come from within us and extend past our physical beings to connect with the rest of the world. Believing in auras as she does, she quite literally meant that to her I was glowing. My auras or energies at the time were exceptionally strong and vibrant, which (to her) visibly made my body seem to glow. She, of course, wanted to know why. I figured it couldn't hurt to bounce the idea off her. So, while she was working to mix up a new interesting hair colour, I began to explain what had happened. The more I talked about it, the more animated I became, and the more the whole crazy scenario seemed to make a great deal of sense. I explained how this man had a twisted past, having been born in a world where poverty and oppression are a part of daily life. I told her a bit about his name, how he got it, and what it meant to him. I also explained that, given the current state of economic and political instability in his country, what he was proposing could be extremely dangerous if we were not extremely careful.

I went into detail about how he himself had been gathering information for years in the hopes of using that information to inspire and awaken his people, and that through the use of his art, both theatrical and musical, he hoped to reach the younger generation and set them on a course for change. With all his ideals and beliefs, really, all he had was a dream, with no defined way to turn that dream into reality. I explained that what I was proposing to do was to go with him and collaborate with him to create a story that would both awaken and inspire. It had occurred to me that I had been, in fact, attempting to write the wrong book, and that is probably why I was never able to finish it. I asked her if she thought I was nuts. She said she didn't. Of course, I would expect a positive reaction from her, given her own spiritual quest. However, I had to make it plain to her that I could not honestly say how this journey would affect my relationship with my boyfriend. The catch there was that he is how Victoria and I met. He is her friend, not I. Here I was proposing to fly to the other side of the world with another man. She asked if I had told him, and I explained that I had not, as I was not yet sure that I was going, and I felt no need to upset his comfort zone. I also explained that if I were to do this it would have to be with or without his support—something I neither expected her to understand or encourage. She did both. In fact, she discussed with me the spiritual cost to myself if I decided not to take the trip. She inquired if years from now I would regret not going. She encouraged me to follow my instincts and base my decision not only on reason, but on awareness of the signs that seemed to be pointing me in that direction. She suggested that we go in the back to do a tarot reading. While we were back there and I was shuffling the cards, she was telling me that the cards would choose me by either poking out or sticking out or, very rarely, falling from the deck.

Just as she was finishing her sentence, one of the cards flew from the deck to land face-up on the other side of the room. I continued to shuffle as she went to pick it up, and I noticed that as her fingers touched the card they were trembling. I cocked an eyebrow at her, curious which card had set her so on edge. The card was an indicator card depicting a lady on a white horse and very pointedly saying that I was to embark on a journey.

The card also indicated that if I were to go on this journey, I would be provided with both direction and protection. What had left my good friend shaken was that she had never seen such a violent reaction from a deck of cards nor had she ever been witness to such an obviously straightforward message.

The next three cards also decided to fall out of the deck in rapid succession. The first card, the card that represented past issues, told us that I would need to let go of what was past; doubt, fear, and guilt were no longer welcome in my world, and I would not be able to embrace my future if I could not let go of the past. The card said the future was where I needed to be. The next card represented the present and also spoke of a journey, an adventure of spirit and awakening of self. The third card, representing the future, spoke of a peaceful end and a satisfactory completion of a spiritual quest.

Now, as I said before, it would do you, the reader, a great justice if you would take these words I write and believe they are a colourful, fanciful tale. I do hope you take my advice to heart, because, though the imagery contained within so far may seem to some rather mundane; to most it would seem quite fanciful. So I take this opportunity to once again implore you not to believe a word of it; it is a tale, a fabrication. It is an illustration of thought written only to intrigue and entertain you. I am certainly not sitting at this moment on the patio of a hotel restaurant in Pasay City, Manila. I am also not listening, as I write, to the animated banter from five Chinese businessmen sitting behind me. There are not several Asian children in the adjacent pool chattering away rapidly in their native tongue. I would also like to point out that yet another sweet young waiter here at the hotel did not just bring me another drink. I did explain to you before that it would be safer for you and for me if you would choose to embrace this story in that manner, and, as the tale is about to get that much more strange, I hope you are open to my suggestion. Now, I have to ask you: After all that Vicky and the cards had said, how could I deny that I was meant to take this trip? No, really. How could I doubt it? I did. It is in my nature now as I get older to second-guess every little thought and idea. I have in past years made too many mistakes that threatened to shatter the happiness of myself and others.

I was very excited, however, at the prospect of taking the chance that I just might be on to something. My apparent enthusiasm was enlivening my hairdressing friend. Our talk turned back away from the politics of the country in question and veered toward the prospect of a spiritual revolution. Vicky brought up the Mayan calendar and the fact that it ended in 2012. She asked if I thought that would be the end of the world, and I answered no. I have always believed, for my own reasons, that the end of the world would not be the catastrophic end of all things as predicted by many prophets. Rather, it is possible that it would be a shift in belief systems so monumental in magnitude that it would catapult humanity as a whole into a higher state of being. Books like *The Celestine Prophecy* and *The Secret* explore this shift from the point of view of each individual person. These books open people's minds to the energies that will eventually be required to attempt a shift that includes worldwide population. As to why the Mayan calendar stops in 2012, I have my own theory, which includes two reasons.

One: It is possible that in 2012 humanity will find itself at a crossroads and will either embark on a new enlightened path, and thereby reach a higher state of being (what some refer to now as *ascension*), or they will destroy themselves through greed and hunger for power. The Mayan priests had not been able to see past this fork in the world, as the choice had not been made. It would be impossible to tell what that choice would be. Humans are excruciatingly unpredictable in nature, allowing their thoughts and feelings to be their guides rather than relying on their inborn instinct. Knowing full well that it could end either way, it stands to reason that the priests could not be sure there would be a need for a calendar at all.

The second reason ties in directly with the first: If mankind went down the path to destruction, then they would cease to exist. Simple, yes? Okay, now following the reasoning I previously explored: if mankind actually found a way to attain that higher state of being, that ascension which New Agers tell us is possible, would they need a calendar? No one can say exactly what that higher state would be. Some predict a shedding of our physical shells and a return to our base state of energy. Some view it as *heaven on earth*, believing that we will maintain our physical form but will have accomplished spiritual oneness with ourselves, each other, and the nature that surrounds us. In doing so, we would shed our materialist needs and desires, living instead in our natural surroundings. If that were the case, would we need a calendar?

Please understand that I am not telling you these things are fact. They are theological ponderings that have been explored and discussed by minds much greater than mine for many centuries. These theories neither encompass all that I believe nor do they stem from a basis in proven fact. I do not expect you to alter your ideals and I do not wish to steer you away from your faith. I merely point out that these ideas exist and have existed from ancient times, all the way back to the pagans and their ritual worship of nature. I am not saying it is the right way, nor am I saying it is the only way. I do offer the chance, however, if you are curious, then, by all means, to explore the ideas yourself.

We do currently live in a world where information is readily available. God bless the Internet and its ability to put information at a person's fingertips. I caution you, of course, not to believe everything you read, but to read everything you can and take from that material only what you need to maintain a happy, balanced existence. I myself am still learning; as you will see, the beginning of this journey was merely an open door to a whole world of information. I am a curious being and, as such, am constantly asking questions—neither accepting nor denying what I learn. I continue to seek, to strive, and to grow from the knowledge I acquire, and I find that the more I learn the more questions I have. It is a continuous cycle, one I rather enjoy the experience of. If you, dear reader, can take anything from this book as fact, take this: knowledge is not power. It is not something to be used as a weapon against others, and it will not make you a whole person. The hunger and thirst for knowledge is where the power the lies. It is not a power that can be misused or misdirected; rather, it is a power that comes from within. It is the power to be able to open our minds, our hearts, and our eyes to new ideas, broadening our views and strengthening our resolve to be better people. It is in the *search* for knowledge, not the acquisition of it, that we achieve balance within ourselves and our surroundings.

This I know to be true. This I know to be real, and, if you learn nothing else from this story, learn this; the rest will fall into place, and you will believe what you personally need to believe and learn what you personally need to learn in order for you to be whole. As an aside, I do not know where you should start. The beginning of each person's spiritual quest is not something that should be guided from outside, it must come from within, and so I cannot be much help to you in that area. After saying that, I do advise that it doesn't hurt to ask questions and really listen to the answers. Again, you don't have to take each answer for fact; nor do you have to believe in everything you learn about, but it helps to be open to new ideas and to the views of others. They may have something to teach you, and, in turn, you may even have something to teach them. Think on it awhile as you read through the rest of my tale. Then, when you are finished, go out and explore the world. It is fun; really it is. When you get past the fear and the doubt you may even learn to enjoy it.

Back at the salon, we were wrapping things up when my phone rang. It was a number I didn't recognize, and, as I was in the middle of a conversation, I should not have answered. But I did.

The voice on the other end explained to me that her name was Sherry and she was inviting people to her church for gospel study. Um, no … you see, I have difficulty with believing in structured religion. It's not because the ideals behind it are unsound but because I find it very easy for people to abuse power they think they have secured directly from the hands of God. Consider the priest who tells you that in order to talk to God you must go through him. I am not sure about this, because I have not actually sat down with God and had a conversation over tea, but I can guess that he does not require the use of memos to hear and acknowledge our prayers. I am, as I said, not positive. I am no priest and so probably do not have the authority to make such a statement. Yet I can't for the life of me understand why a God who is all-powerful and all-seeing would not hear a prayer that was not first channeled through one of his chosen. I would like to know if I am right—and I intend some day to ask him—but it is my experience as a nondenominational spiritual pupil that my own prayers have been answered several times throughout my life *without* an intermediary or the use of idols.

I was very polite to this woman in my refusal and hung up the phone feeling only mildly guilty. I was on my way out the door when the phone rang again. It was the same number. Again, against my nature, but following my instincts, I chose to answer. I told this sweet little old lady, "Sweetie, you just called me, and I said I wasn't interested. Are you sure you have the right number?" She replied, sounding rather flustered, that she could not have just called me. She never calls anyone twice. Then it hit—maybe, just maybe, I am supposed to talk to this woman. So I tell her that I think for some reason I am supposed to talk to her, but, as I am in the middle of something, can she please call me back another day. She said she'd call me back the next day, and I hung up the phone. As I was now in a state of flux—should I stay or should I go?—I pushed the phone call to the back of my mind. I told Vicky I should probably call an old friend up and get my chakra centred before I embark on this bigger-than-little adventure. I left the store with phone in hand, now sure that I would like to go, but not yet knowing why. I got in the car, got on the phone, and, when my Pops answered, I told him simply: "Okay, I'm ready; it's time."

Chapter 5
Fairies, Horses, and Gifts from Heaven

He was, of course understandably confused, my poor Pops was, but, before I get into the why and the how, I should probably give you an explanation of how Pops came to be my Pops at all. Pops is not really my father. My real father, my biological father, passed away when I was three years old. There is still a great deal of mystery and many unanswered questions surrounding his death, but that, I think, is an entirely different book. Pops is also not my step dad. That title belonged to a loving, caring, and somewhat rambunctious man who passed away a day before my mother's own untimely demise six years ago. Lastly, he is also not the sweet, gentle, good-natured male half of the couple who upon my parents' unexpected deaths decided to take me under their wing and bring me into their family. It was an odd situation, to be sure, to be fostered at twenty-seven years of age. And yes, you guessed it; it is not yet time for that story either.

No, Pops is just another one of those random people who unexpectedly pop into your life, thus "Pops." Two years ago, I was working as a waitress in my united nations of restaurants, when I inexplicably felt a pull toward this little decrepit old man who was sitting in my section having lunch with his friends. I overheard bits and pieces of their conversation as I was serving them and the tables around them. Their animated discussion intrigued me, and I found myself repeatedly wandering past the table.

They were discussing the theory that coincidences are not just random occurrences, but rather signs that are meant to guide us down the road of life. What fascinated me so much was that this group of men, all well past the age of sixty, was having a very loud, very open discussion about this theory. I have seen this belief proven true several times in my own life, and I had often heard it discussed. The more spiritually advanced already know there is no such thing as coincidence and eventually get to the point where they don't feel the need to state the fact. The people who usually talk about such things were, in my experience, much younger, and they were also usually people who had just begun their journey to enlightenment. This was not a discussion, therefore, that I expected to hear from a group of men who were very obviously closer to the end of their personal quests. I also noticed that all three men were taking turns following me around the room with their eyes—none more so than Pops, who seemed somewhat drawn to the medallion around my neck (at least, I think it was the medallion he was staring at—it couldn't be my cleavage, as I don't have any). The lunch crowd eventually thinned, then vanished; yet, these three men stubbornly remained. They were well aware that the restaurant was well past closing time, and they had paid their bills what seemed to me eons ago. I approached the table one last time to offer more coffee before going off to cash out and wrap up my day. *Very strange little man*, I remember thinking.

I was rewarded with confirmation of that assumption by way of an offhand comment when I arrived at the table. "You know, you look like the daughter I never had… Yes, yes, I think you are. Would you like to be my daughter? I very much feel that you already are."

He stated this so placidly, yet with such conviction, I couldn't help but giggle—at which point he quipped, "Yes, my daughter would sound like that; hmmm… you must be her."

Normally a person's natural instinct would be to run, but I really wasn't feeling anything other than mildly amused. Realizing that he hadn't managed to scare me off, he asked yet again, "Are you my daughter"? His friends were rolling their eyes while attempting to crawl under the table. However, I couldn't let him win this battle of wits, so I merely arched an eyebrow at him and responded, "Sure, Pops, I am your long-lost daughter; you've been missing me, haven't you?" They were strange words coming from a little waitress girl, but it immediately put his friends at ease, and an odd, but educational, friendship was born.

It turned out Pops is an author himself and a healer. He has written and published books on metaphysics and, at the time I met him, was working out of his house as a spiritual healer focusing on the realignment of chakras. During a brief discussion that day, we discovered our birthdays happened to be one day apart, his being July 4, mine July 5. We agreed to meet for lunch on his birthday to celebrate them both and exchanged numbers with the intention of keeping in touch. As usual, time and circumstance got in the way, and in the next year we did not find many chances to meet. We did keep our birthday date, and when he had a hip replaced I dragged Sophia to the hospital to pay him a visit. We kept in touch by phone, and he kept trying to convince me to let him do a healing, something I continually told him it was not yet time for. My Baba, after being extremely sick for a year, finally succumbed to her illness, and in the spring of this year she had passed away. Pops began a vigil by phone, repeatedly calling to check on my well-being. Each time he called he offered healing, and each time he offered I told him, "No, not yet—it isn't time."

Well, now it was time. Though he didn't immediately recognize the significance of those words, I do recall him asking me where I was flying off to and explaining that he could feel the energy over the phone. He said an energy that strong indicated flight. We talked briefly, and I explained that I had this opportunity that I was contemplating taking a chance on, and, as I was going on this trip, I thought now might be the ideal time for a healing session. I also explained that I felt I would need as much strength and balance as I could get. Having him align my chakras would probably help with that. He emphatically agreed, and we set a date for a session the following Monday. I hung up the phone and headed home.

At this point I was figuring: *Okay, cool—game on.* I mean, as his earlier email had shown, Revo obviously understood my priorities and supported them. It suddenly felt like a very safe venture—not in a physical sense, but emotionally, which we all know can be the more damaging of the two. Still, I was not entirely positive I was going; Rev and I had still not met in person to go over details. Therefore, I didn't feel the need to broach the subject with my daughter just yet. Taking Rev's conditions to heart, however, I did decide to see if my cosmically connected little girl could find it in herself to approve without me having to voice aloud what it was that needed approval. One of my bosses, Alya (oops, that would be ex-boss), had given us a joint gift for Christmas, and I decided it was high time we tested it. In order for this to make sense to you, I must again present a bit of background on this new character. Our history centred around my job at the restaurant. It was Alya, in fact, who had hired me when I had chosen to wander in off the street, resume in hand. I would like to clarify a couple of things.

First: When I originally applied for the job, it was completely at random. I had just moved into the city and had been driving around aimlessly trying to decide where I wanted to work. I am not even sure how I ended up in the plaza where the restaurant is located, as it is both quite a distance from where I was living and well off the beaten path. I certainly did not know the restaurant was there, nor, for that matter, that it even existed. I had no foreknowledge as to what kind of restaurant it was, and I happened to luck out as far as getting in the door on that particular day. You see, unbeknownst to me, the restaurant closed between the hours of 2:00 PM and 5:00 PM, and it just so happened that I stumbled on the restaurant and slipped in the door exactly at 2:00 PM, as the hostess was coming to lock up. I asked her if they took resumes; she gave me an application and told me I should sit and wait. The hostess, a young lady by the name of Sarah, told me she had a feeling that Alya would want to meet me and went off to find her, as I sat down and flew through the process of filling out the application. I needn't have bothered. Alya didn't look at it until several minutes after she decided to hire me. When she sat down to interview me, she said she had the feeling I belonged there. We talked a bit about ourselves and shared a bit of our experiences. Then we eventually turned our attention to the matter at hand.

Before she looked at my resume, she said, "Since I've already decided to hire you, I suppose I should see what kind of experience you have."

We talked some more, going over minor details with regard to uniform, dress code, etc. Then I left some thirty minutes later with a promise to return that evening to start training. It was without a doubt the most unique interview I have ever had, and I remain thankful to this day that I was lucky enough to stumble blindly into her world.

The three years I have spent there have overall been happy ones. The friendships I have built with the people there have been both a comfort and a blessing.

Alya herself is a vibrant, independent woman who hails from a strong spiritual background steeped in both Christianity and mysticism. Over the past couple of years we have fed, energized, and encouraged one another. We have watched each other grow and taught one another various lessons along the road. We have also clashed numerous times, both being strong personalities secure in our places in the world. Though it has been proven repeatedly that we do not always agree, our bond has remained strong. It was shortly before Christmas of this year that Alya decided that her time at the restaurant was done. Her last act as manager had been to hire Revo—something I recalled later as being another one of those coincidental occurrences. She had come to me on her last night of work and confided that she had been asked to do one last interview. She felt that as she would not be there to train this individual, she should not be the deciding factor in his obtaining the job. She admitted, however, that she felt compelled to meet this character. I encouraged her to follow her instincts, as they were usually pretty accurate. She did the interview, and, oddly enough, she hired him. The reason I say *oddly* is because the man had absolutely no experience in the restaurant industry—unless, of course, you wish to count dining out. Now, given that Alya takes her job and responsibilities very seriously, it is not in her nature to hire someone who hasn't got a clue what he is doing. It is also not in her nature to cease taking that responsibility seriously until the job is in fact complete. So it is not likely that she hired the boy simply because she no longer gave a shit. That is simply not an attitude she is capable of.

Sometime around Christmas, Alya had held a dinner for close friends. The dinner was for adults, but, as I believe that where I go, my daughter also goes, Alya was nice enough to invite her as well. She welcomed Madison with open arms, even going so far as to get her a small Christmas gift.

There were actually three small gifts, both tiny in size and momentous in meaning. The first was a small crystal charm pendant of an owl, which Alya had lovingly wrapped up for Mad and to which she had attached a small note. The second gift was for me, and it was a framed picture of a statue of Mary Magdalene that currently resides in the Louvre in Paris. The picture was one Alya had taken herself, and attached to it was a note saying: "Some gifts come from very far away and need no explanation." She was, of course, well aware of my fascination with the Grail and had, in fact, given me a card when she left the restaurant that thanked me for many long talks and wished me well in my personal quest for the Grail. It is with the opening of the last gift that we can continue our tale.

Alya had managed to find a tarot deck that depicted fairies as the guiding spirits and had included a card that read: "To aid in the mother-daughter bond that is the belief in magic." It was an especially touching gift in two respects. My daughter has for years collected fairies, and it was very sweet of my friend to acknowledge that hobby and include it in the gift. It was also my daughter's first tarot deck—something that I cannot in retrospect see coming from any purer source.

It was this very deck that on the Saturday afternoon after my hair appointment I decided to open and test. My daughter was playing once again on the computer, so I decided to cleanse the deck, tune it to me, and then do my own reading before bringing her over to teach her how. I shuffled the deck with the intention of doing a simple three-card spread, and again the cards decided to jump out. They were, of course, different in appearance, as it was a completely different deck—yet their meanings matched exactly the meanings we had read earlier in the day. I really wasn't that surprised but was most curious to see what would happen if the deck was instead tuned to my daughter. I called her to come sit with me on the floor and proceeded to instruct her on what to do with the deck. After I was satisfied that she had completed the ritual cleansing, I again began to shuffle the cards. Yet again, three cards leapt out in rapid succession, and yet again their meanings were crystal clear. This time, however, they were three different cards, but the direction they gave was the same as both the three I had done myself and the three from the salon. The thing that stood out, however, above all others was the fact that in every single card there was somewhere buried in the card a picture of a white horse. It wasn't until later that I would understand.

I was anxious to respond to the email I had read that morning from Rev. Once we were done the reading, I asked Madison if I might use her computer to check on an email that I was expecting from a friend. She said, "Sure Mom, say hi to Rev for me," and a big, goofy grin split her face. You know, you would think it would be easier to raise the smart ones!

My Holy Grail,

12 is fine my sweet—you do mean 12 noon, right? No matter if you mean midnight, it won't matter; I'll be there either way. Just let me know, okay (T-bones)? I am glad you are getting a chance to say goodbye; it is something I will have to make time to do over the next couple weeks. I figure it will take that long to get the passport settled and make arrangements for the flight and the million other things I'm probably not remembering I need to do. As far as your friends go, I have learnt that they will be your friends (no matter where you are and how long you happen to be gone for) only if they are meant to be in your life; if, on the off-chance your time with them is done, then you have already learned all you need to from each other and the memories and lessons will stay with you always, even if they cannot…

There are a million things we will have to talk about on Tues so perhaps I can answer a few of your questions now. It is not only what I want; it is what I need. I have known all my life that there was more that I was meant to do. I have prayed countless times for the wisdom to recognize the signs I was sure I would eventually receive to lead me down the path I need to follow. I can say with complete conviction that I have never felt so secure in any decision I have ever made—I actually feel at peace and free for the first time in years, and, though I look forward to telling you this all again in person so you can see the truth of it in my eyes, I know also that you need to know it's real—so have faith, and run with it, and we will both end up where we need to be…

As for Maddi understanding, I think she will support me only if she feels that I am content, and if it is something I believe in she will be disappointed only if I don't do it. It was Mad that did one of the tarot readings that confirmed for me that this is where I need to go—and she used the cards that Alya bought her at Christmas to do the readings—the connection being that Alya is the one who, three years ago, hired me at Tucker's without looking at my resume. I walked in, we met, and she told me she thought I belonged there, and that was that…

I have never been more at peace or so focused on a goal. I have absolutely no fear of where this will lead; my heart and mind are more open to this than I could have ever dreamed they would be, and I am so grateful that I finally get to start what is sure to be one of the greatest adventures I will ever have.

I will tell you this again in person when I see you—so you can see and feel the truth of my words…

I came from your past and, as to where I have been, I've been here: living, and learning, and waiting for you to find me and set me free.

It will be an adventure, don't you think?

I will see you soon—xo

I now decided it was past the time of trying to decide if I should go and well into the time I should start trying to figure out how to tell my family and friends that I was going. The next day went by rather slowly. Maddi was back at her dad's for the night, and I did not really want to broach this subject of my leaving with my boyfriend. I feared a negative reaction to my decision and was not looking forward to the conflict I expected to come.

It was during this day of restless uncertainty that I decided to look up Genghis Kahn. Revo had told me that he had been informed a few years ago that his spirit guide was the Mongolian conqueror, and I thought it prudent at this point to find out exactly what I was getting myself into. I was entertained to discover that his wife, Borte, was often depicted in white and riding a white horse.

Chapter 6
Brooms and Broken Burdens-Honestly, I'm Working on It.

Looking back, I realize I should have been more open right from the beginning with my boyfriend regarding both my reasons for going and the feelings of dissatisfied restlessness that had built up over the previous months. It wouldn't be until after Rev left that I began to really be aware what kind of impact this trip was going to have on my current relationship.

My state of mind now, however, was one of clouded uncertainty, and I found myself looking to others for distraction. I had agreed to meet with Rev on his last day in Canada. We wanted the chance to say goodbye, and we still had not made any concrete plans as to what kind of work we were planning on doing. We had in our heads a very generalized idea, but nothing definitive. On the day of his departure, I had agreed to do some marketing work with my boss. I was willing to do anything that would keep my mind occupied, and, as a result, I was now spending the morning touring around the city with my manager, working to promote the restaurant. It was in the midst of this traveling around that Revo called and asked if I could find my way to his home rather than meet him at the restaurant we had agreed on. He was only hours away from leaving and still had not managed to pack for his trip. I agreed to go to him, thinking I would meet with him briefly and return to the restaurant later to continue my work with my general manager. I never did make it back to work, as we ended up spending almost the entire day together talking and discovering more about our history.

The whole thing started innocently enough, with me arriving to find him desperately trying to throw together things he would need to take. At first we only swapped idle chatter while he walked around his room tossing stuff into an open suitcase. He indicated at one point the drawing I had done, which was now hung on his wall, and he started explaining to me his girlfriend's reaction on seeing it. Now, you have to understand their relationship was pretty solid. They were used to being apart, and she had never shown any kind of insecurity or jealousy. In light of that fact, Revo had been extremely surprised when she had gotten angry over a simple drawing mounted on his wall. He had told her, "But, you met her, remember?—I introduced you at the restaurant," to which she had responded that she did indeed remember and that she very much did *not* want the drawing on his wall. We discussed the night in question, as I remember very clearly meeting this girl. He had been working late, and she had just flown in from New York and was sitting at the bar waiting for him. I was working that night as the bartender and thought that I would try to be friendly and make her feel welcome. I offered to get her something from the bar while she waited. She wasn't interested. Rev had come in a few minutes later and formally introduced us, at which point I again offered to get her something. Again she refused. He recalled that later in the evening she had admitted to feeling extremely threatened by me, though she could not understand why at the time. She had conceded that we did not seem to have any chemistry between us, and that, combined with the fact that I was quite obviously an older woman, led her to rationally consider that I was not a threat. Yet, for some reason, the whole idea of me talking to him had really pissed her off. The whole story reminded me of an incident that had occurred only days before Revo's girlfriend had flown in from New York, when my own boyfriend had been hanging out at the bar waiting for me.

Rev had walked by, and I'd thought I'd be nice and introduce the new guy. My boyfriend was well known by the staff, and, though he had on occasion shown jealous tendencies, it had never before been directed at the people I worked with. Rev made a comment to my boyfriend about how he must be doing something right for me to be so loyal. He said that I was always getting hit on by customers and that my first response had always been "Sorry, I have a boyfriend." Rev said that it must be nice to be in a relationship that was built so strongly on trust. Strangely enough, my boyfriend made some really condescending response (I can't remember what exactly), but I did remember that it had left Revo looking like he'd been slapped. I had questioned my boyfriend on it later, and he admitted that he couldn't explain why he had said it. He, too, had apparently felt really threatened, but could not understand why. Revo threw another shirt into his suitcase and joked that maybe they had seen something we had missed. Even with me sitting there alone with him in his room neither of us felt any kind of sexual tension, and it wasn't until much later in the day that we figured out why.

We sat there on the bed for awhile, continuing to talk, though our attention was now turned to the reason I was to join him in the Philippines. He explained that he had the desire to help his people, but he had no idea how to go about it. He told me about the research he'd done into the political history and that he had studied the historical whys and hows of the political corruption. The problem he was running into was how to present that knowledge to the people in a manner that would not only interest them but also inspire them to do something about it. Most importantly, he had to find a way to do it safely. He told me that is why he felt he needed to go back to his country to pursue his acting career.

He said actors there are sacrosanct, and they are in such a positive position in the public view that those in power are hesitant to openly move against them. He felt that if he could amass enough popularity then he could find a way to safely make a move against the corruption in his country. It was a bold plan and one I was not entirely sure would work. I did, however, see how his contacts there in the media industry could open the doors for both of us—but maybe not the way he thought. I did not immediately make any kind of proposal, and our talk eventually moved into the area of our childhoods. We had both been raised surrounded by oddities and strange occurrences and legends. We had also both been raised to believe we were meant to do something important. Neither of our families, however, had bothered to tell us what that was. We swapped strange stories about our younger years. He told me about his father's history and the revolution, and I told him about the high weirdness that occasionally went on around my family. The first story I told him was about a time when I was very young and my mother and I had been staying at her mother's house.

The grandmother in question was extremely entrenched in the Catholic faith, and though my own mother had left the Church shortly after my birth, she still tried to be respectful of my grandmother's views. I remember being asleep in bed with my mom (beds were not in abundance there) and waking up to my mother screaming. There my grandmother stood in the doorway, staring at me, saying nothing. My mother grabbed at me and was screaming at my grandmother that she would not allow it.

She kept repeating: "You can't have her. I won't let you use her."

It went on for a very long time, and, being young, I was absolutely terrified by the whole experience. Eventually, other members of the family awoke and made their way to the room. I was led away and tucked into bed with my godmother, but still my mother continued screaming.

I kept asking my godmom why, but all she said was, "Shush now; time to sleep."

I guess I eventually passed out, because I awoke in the morning and all was quiet. In fact, when I went down into the kitchen everyone was sitting around having coffee acting like it had never happened.

I tried to talk about it and ask what it was all about. I wondered, was my mommy sick?

My grandmother casually reached across the table and slapped my face hard enough to make my head snap back. She quietly whispered: "It did not happen, and you will not speak of this ever again. Do you understand?"

All I could do was sit there with tears streaming down my face and nod. I was only a six-year-old child and had no one to turn to for comfort or answers. It was never mentioned again, at least not within the confines of my family. I have told a few friends over the years and, other than agreeing the whole thing was supremely screwed up, they really didn't have any answers for me either.

The next story I told him was about a trip I had taken with my aunt (also my godmother). We had gone out of town overnight to pick up a new car that she had purchased. During the night I had woken with a sense of foreboding about the next day and our return trip. I was sixteen at the time and had learned already to follow my instincts. While talking to my dad the next morning on the phone, I had asked him to talk my aunt into staying an extra day. He agreed to try, as he had also grown used to relying on my instincts. Unfortunately, she didn't listen to him any more than she had listened to me. Shortly after I had hung up the phone, we were driving down the road, and, as it was winter, the roads weren't the greatest. I wasn't wearing my seatbelt—given my premonition and the driving conditions, that was, I admit, pretty stupid of me. About an hour into the trip, I got this very strong urge to put on my seatbelt. I heard a distant disembodied voice whispering in my head, "Do it now." I listened—wouldn't you? I mean, really, how often is it that voices in your head actually give you good advice? As my seatbelt clicked into place the car started to spin, and the next thing I know there was a rather large tire staring at me through the windshield. My parents later told me that she had lost control and broadsided a highway snow plough doing ninety kilometers an hour. I don't know if you have ever seen one, but they are very large pieces of equipment, and my aunt's car was only a little hatchback. It was completely written off. This is only hearsay, however, as at the time I saw none of it, and when I asked later, my parents refused to let me see the car. They said something about it being too much of a shock for me in my current fragile state. I do remember whispered conversations days later (they would exclaim, seemingly in awe of the fact that I had managed to survive) as we sat in the hospital by my aunt's bed waiting for her to give in to her injuries. She had been taken off life-support, after the doctors had declared her brain-dead and told the family there was nothing more they could do. Oddly enough, it was me to whom the family turned when they were confronted by the decision.

I was pulled into a hospital room three days after the accident by my grandmother (on my mother's side), and she sat me down and asked me what I wanted them to do. She explained to me that I was the closest thing to a daughter my godmother had had, and so the final decision was up to me. It was an easy decision to make. The first time I had seen my godmother after the accident had been in a long room with about ten beds lining the wall, separated by plastic. The whole scene was like something out of a futuristic horror movie—a long line of bodies, with wires sticking out of them, were connected to machines to keep them alive for whatever twisted purpose the mad scientists had cooked up in their warped little brains. I didn't think my aunt would like to live like that, and that is exactly what I told my grandmother. She agreed and thanked me for being able to make such an adult decision. She apologized for having had to ask me, and I remember that even though I was at the time going through hell, it was one of the only times I would ever in my life really connect with the woman. For that brief moment we understood each other completely, and for that brief moment of understanding I am eternally grateful.

My godmother left us peacefully a few days later, surrounded by her family, and everyone in the room that night agreed they had felt her leave. My cousins and I had discussed it later, and they had agreed that there had been a sense of contented peacefulness in the room the night she moved on, but what I never told them is that I heard her whisper thank you. Perhaps it was a necessary delusion created by my own fragile mind to help me come to terms with the decision that I had made, but I like to think that I had done the right thing and she took the time on her way out to let me know that she would be okay.

On the day of the accident I vaguely remember crawling out the window and yelling at the driver that he had killed my aunt. I remember also that police and ambulance were on the scene almost immediately, but they seemed for some reason to be ignoring me completely. It was instead a passerby who took me to her own vehicle, saying that it would be warmer there. It was in the van that things started to get a little weird. She told me she was a healer and she had been sent to make sure I was okay. She said it wasn't my time yet, so I had to let her help me. It was an odd situation to be in, to be sure. I had just crawled out the window of a completely wrecked automobile, and nobody from the medical team or the authorities seemed in the least concerned about my welfare or my whereabouts. I stayed with this woman, sitting in the front seat of her van. Honestly, I was too dazed to argue with the woman, so I leaned my head back against the seat and let her get on with it. She offered up a little prayer, then began to run her hands up and down the length of my body. She never actually touched me—her hands stayed hovering about an inch over my flesh—but even from that distance I could feel the heat off them. I had a similar experience much later in life when I sought a Reiki healer to find a way to manage the pain in my back, but at the time of the accident I had never heard of Reiki, so I had no way to connect what she was doing with any kind of reality-based healing method. All I knew was that there was amazingly comforting warmth spreading through me, and, as she continued to whisper prayers while moving her hands around me, I felt this warmth starting to heal me, both physically and emotionally.

I left her van a few minutes later, feeling much of my strength returned to me. I wandered over to where the fireman were trying to get my aunt extracted from the twisted metal that had been her car. They asked me to talk to her, to reassure her that I was okay, and so I stood there beside the car for a long time talking to her, telling her I loved her and that it would be okay. I don't think I could have done it if I hadn't spent the time in the van with my mystery angel; she restored to me both my strength and my faith, and it was with her in mind that I managed to get through the next few days without completely losing myself to feelings of anger and guilt. I at one point looked back to where the van had been, and I couldn't find either it or the lady who had come to my rescue. Although I never got her name or found out where she came from, I know that she is probably still out there somewhere bringing peace to others in need. Maybe someday she will even get a chance to read this and know what an amazingly positive impact she had on me that day.

If you are out there somewhere… thank you.

I did eventually make it to the hospital, and they did eventually check me out and tell me I could go. But where was I to go? At sixteen years of age I had no money and was in a strange city far away from home. What could I do? My parents couldn't come for me, as the storm had gotten worse, and the roads were closed. So there I sat by myself in the hall of this massive emergency unit until a nurse approached me. Well, she said she was a nurse, but she was in jeans and a T-shirt, so, who knows? She told me I was to go home with her until my parents could come for me in the morning. I didn't sense any danger in it, so I agreed to go along as long as I could call my mother. This lady reasoned that it would be better to call from her house where I would be able to sit comfortably and take the time to assure my mother I was okay. Again, I felt no threat from this woman, so I decided to go. Looking back on it, I do not remember her name, what she looked like, or where she lived. I cannot picture in my mind her house or the face of her husband. I do remember that her husband had gone out and gotten me a toothbrush, some pyjamas, a robe, and some slippers. The clothes he had bought had fit so well that I naturally assumed my mother had given them my size. Not so; when I finally called my parents they were extremely surprised to hear that I was in this house. There ensued a very long conversation between said nurse and my dad. I was not privy to the conversation, as the nurse's husband had chosen that moment to insist that I go take a bath to help ease some of the bruising. If I had to do it over again, I would have been questioning every step of the way, but I was young, and scared, and felt very much alone.

When my parents picked me up in the hospital the next day, where the nurse had dropped me off, my mom went to the nurses' station to ask for the girl's name so she could thank her in person. The hospital staff had absolutely no clue who she was talking about.

It was only several years later, as I began explaining to Revo, that the full impact of what had happened that day really hit me. I had gotten an MRI to try to find the cause of back pain I was having. When the doctor pulled me into the office to discuss my results, he asked if I had been in an accident. I told him not recently, and he asked how long ago it was and how bad it had been. I wanted to know what this was about and told him I would not answer any more questions until he gave me some kind of explanation. He explained that I had a recent fracture in my back that was more than likely causing my current problems, but it was the evidence of old injuries in my body that had him confused. Apparently, there had at one time been multiple fractures throughout my body that had long ago healed. There was nothing in my medical record to indicate such a massive amount of damage. He said my accident at sixteen was recorded as resulting in only superficial bruising, but the injuries described to him by the technician who had done the MRI were extensive and would more than likely have ended with loss of life. He could therefore not see how the picture could be accurate, because on the off-chance that I had survived such an injury, then I would certainly have remembered it. He wanted to do more tests to confirm the results. He was now sure there had been a mix-up between patients, so back I went for more tests. It turns out the pictures *had* been mine—my back was broken, and my doctor now turned his efforts to finding a way for me to manage the pain until it healed. The other injuries were never mentioned by either me or him again.

There I was, sitting in this man's room, telling him this, and he didn't even flinch. Not a "that's crazy," not a "no way," not even a "yeah, right"—nothing. He just listened and nodded and stroked my arm, trying to comfort me, knowing full well that just telling the tale was bringing up some pretty negative memories. That's right; that's what I said—stroking my arm, something he had apparently been doing the whole time I had been talking. I also realized only at the end of the tale that I had been lying there talking to this guy with my head on his chest for over an hour. It had been so natural, so comfortable, that I had not even noticed. After my story we decided to get up, go out, have lunch—and more conversation ensued.

We got into a detailed discussion about God and our views on both his existence and his impact on society.

It was Rev who started it all by calling me on something I not realized he had picked up on.

"You know, I don't get it. You obviously believe in God; we've talked about him several times, but, for some reason, when I make reference to the Bible I can sense you flinching inwardly. It's not anything that you're doing with your face or body language, but something in your eyes says you have issues with the scriptures."

It would take awhile to explain, but I figured, as we were still waiting for our food, time was something I had.

"Oh, it's not God I have a problem with; it's structured religion I find myself questioning. Too much blood has been shed over the debate about whose God is the right God. Thing is, I've spend the greater part of my life exploring different religions and have found that they all teach the same fundamental life lessons that humans need to grow spiritually. So it angers me that instead of following those lessons and learning from them, people waste their time and energy on arguing about which teacher is right, without realizing that all those teachers are working off the same lesson plan."

He gave me a quizzical look. "So, you don't believe that structured religion has a place in our world?"

"No, that's not what I mean at all," I answered hurriedly. "Humans need guidance in order to know which direction to take for answers to all of life's questions. They also need something greater than themselves to believe in: something to bring them strength, encouragement, and comfort in times of sorrow. People just need to stop fighting over what to call their God and get on with living the life he wants them to live."

"So, you think that if there were one central religion that the world could stand behind, the fighting would stop, and the world would find peace?" He was starting to sound slightly put off. "I'm surprised at you; it sounds like a Nazi mentality: one race, one religion, one belief system. You're Polish aren't you—how can you, of all people, agree with Hitler—have you forgotten the camps? How can you bring yourself to think that way?"

"Again you are making an assumption based on only part of the story. You should know better than that—hell, you should know *me* better than that," I said heatedly.

"Oh I do," he laughed, "even if we just met. All I want is for you to be able to explain it, so you don't find yourself getting into trouble down the road—so, go ahead, explain…"

"Oh, I see…" And I did; he was thinking to help me get it straight in my own head before making the attempt to present the idea to the world. I got the sense that in the past he had always played the role of teacher, with me the willing pupil. I was a little more independent, though, this time around, and we would have to see how that would play out in the end, but for the moment I decided to maintain the status quo and bow this one time to his will.

"Okay, so you think that I have Nazi head because I want people to stop fighting over religion, but I am not saying that they should all follow the same religion. The idea is ludicrous; each person, each culture has their own needs, their own views on how life should be lived. The world is a vast place with different climates and living conditions. Each of the religions that exist have grown from a combination of those climates, the history of each individual culture, and the needs that those cultures have to continue to survive, grow, and thrive. It is not for me or anyone else to judge their way of life or their belief system, when I have never lived as they do, or learned as they have learned. My views of the world are different than theirs, and, therefore, so are my own personal needs for a faith to follow. My point is that I respect each individual religion and culture, regardless of what that is, because, as long as it is a positive belief system that teaches patience and understanding, it is a good thing. I don't much care what you call your God, as long as that God shelters you, protects you, and guides you to a better way of life—with emphasis put on respect for life and the need for spiritual growth.

My big problem lies in the constant battle between the leaders of these religions, who seem to think that it is necessary to insure the continued loyalty of their followers by proving to each other and the world that they are right. Their God is the only God, and if you do not follow their God's teachings you will no doubt suffer terribly. Depending on the religion in question, you will either go to hell, or you will be punished here on earth by having all of the good things in your life taken away. These leaders use threats and promises of Utopia to maintain their followers' faith instead of merely teaching those same followers compassion and understanding. They forget that we all have a right to live here, that we all must learn to live together. Their need for domination and control blinds them to the reality of the world being a diverse, complex organism that can only maintain its existence if there is a continued balance between the organisms that live here—which are, by the way, merely an extension of that central core that is our planet. We seek power and control and destroy the very world in which we live, the very world we cannot exist without. How can we justify the need to be right if that need comes at such a high cost?"

He leaned back in his chair, and, glancing down at the table, then back at me, said, "You know the world isn't going to change yet, right?"

I also glanced at the food that had been delivered during my one-sided dialogue. "Sure, I know that, but wouldn't it be nice if it could..."

I popped a piece of bread in my mouth and waited; surely he had more to say than that.

"Okay, so your own belief system stems from humanity's need to accept their own diversity and embrace and encourage that diversity while still maintaining their individual belief systems and cultures. Do I have it right?" He sat there staring at me with a little grin on his face as if to say

'Ha !! After you said all those words, I summed it up in one sentence'. I sniffed, "Yup, that's about it, and I honestly believe that someday humans will get there; it is only a matter of time."

"Hmmm… yes, well, that is what we are supposed to be working toward then, isn't it, but not yet, my love, not this time …" He leaned forward. "Now, what about you—how do you see God, and how do you reconcile your belief for understanding with your obvious disdain for things like the Bible?"

"Okay, well, first of all, it isn't what is written in the Bible that I have a problem with," I looked him straight in the eyes, "It is a fantastic, wonderful, uplifting, and enlightening story that has brought hope to millions. However, it is a story, written by men, and—though those men were witnesses to some of the most incredible miracles that have ever occurred on this planet—they were still men, human men, and in being human they were fallible and imperfect."

"Ouch, you question the validity of the most popular and most widely published piece of literature ever created …;" cocking his head to the side, he looked at me and asked, "what gives you the right?"

"I don't question whether or not the content is valid," I said, laughing, "as I said, the very existence of and impact of that particular book is what makes it valid. What I question is the fanatical study of its teachings with a mind closed to any outside influence that may contradict those teachings. By all means, study it, learn from it, but, for God's sake, learn to take the lessons within and put them in context with the world in which we live. Open your eyes and see the people around you. Although they may not believe the same as you, they are still going out into our world and making a difference for the better by actively working to help others in need. Does the starving child on the street need to believe in God in order for a Christian to be willing to feed him? I do not think that is what Jesus taught do you. When a man is dangling from his fingertips off a cliff, do you think it appropriate to stop and ask him if he has faith before reaching down your hand to help him up? Come on, stop looking at me that way—you know exactly what I'm saying!"

"Oh, you are too cute when you're pissed—," he reached down for a bit of bread, "but you only answered half the question; how do you see God? What is God?"

"Well, you may not agree with this one, but if I were to define God as an entity then it would have to be the central core of a massive ball of energy that extends around and encompasses everything that exists. God is something akin to the brain that controls and manipulates this enormous mass of energy, and when a person feels like he is being guided or sent in a certain direction to do God's work or God's will, then it is very much like you stretching your arm out so you can pick up that piece of bread."

"So, every person, every living thing is like one of God's limbs that he moves around at will to help him accomplish any given task?" He smiled, "I couldn't have put it any better myself ... you have learned a lot this time around, haven't you?"

"Yes, well, I've been through a lot, then, haven't I? It's kind of hard not to learn something when God is constantly ramming lessons down your throat, isn't it?" I looked down at the table. "You know, we have hardly eaten anything—too much talk—but we have to get going; you have a lot yet to do today."

"Very true," he agreed, calling the waiter over and asking for the check. "Let's get out of here."

As we were leaving the restaurant we were holding hands, and he gave me a little kiss on the lips much like the kiss a husband would give his wife on his way out the door while rushing off to work. We stopped by work so he could say goodbye to Sophia and let her pinch his ass one last time. I took the chance to corner her while he was saying goodbye to our boss, and I asked her: "Did you see this coming? I mean, I didn't see this coming. It's right, it's natural, but it's way beyond unexpected."

She gave her answer with a wink and a smile: "Sure, hon, but would you have believed me if I told you?"

I concurred that I certainly would not, and we left it at that. Next I took him up to his studio for one last jam with his band, and I lay there on the couch on my stomach listening to him pound away on the drums. The whole thing seems ridiculous when I look back on it. We were not dating, had never even discussed or (at least on my part) considered the idea—yet, here we were acting like a couple who had been together for months. His bass player finally arrived and seemed not all surprised to see me there stretched out on the couch. I told them I'd leave them to it, gave Rev a quick kiss goodbye, and told him to call me when he needed a ride home. It was on my way home that it really hit me.

What the hell was I doing? I had a boyfriend at home who loved me, and, though I already knew we would not likely stay together as a couple, I did still love him. I most definitely did not want to hurt him, and he certainly deserved better than this. Strangely enough, as much as I wanted to save, at the very least, our friendship, I felt uncontrollably drawn to this other man on a level that I couldn't explain or at the moment even attempt to understand. When I finally got home that night, I wandered around the house, very restless. I went on the computer and went out of curiosity more than anything over some of the emails that had been flying back and forth. They were all very familiar in nature. We were like two old friends bantering about common interests. There was one in which he asked me to look up Jose Rizal. I had, and had discovered that he had been a great hero to the Filipino people: a writer, a politician, a philosopher, etc. (accomplishments too numerous to mention). He had later in his life worked very hard at pulling down the corrupt government in power. He had failed in the end, but not before managing to win the hearts and support of a nation. His battle ended when he was executed by the political power of the time. Sadly enough, it had happened only shortly after his marriage, and he left behind a woman who had stood beside him throughout his brief battles. She had chosen to fight with him and was left a grieving widow. It was that small detail that I had casually passed over the first time I read it and that small detail that stood out now as being exceptionally large. I did not like the idea a bit. It was not the fact that it seemed so sad, or the fact that it seemed so familiar. I most assuredly hated the fact that I felt it was destined to happen all over again.

The whole process of revisiting these emails did not take very long. I soon found myself pacing the house, bitterly confused about what to do, so I did the only thing I could think of. I reached out to a friend, but the direction of my reach was perhaps odd in nature. I called my boyfriend's sister. We had, during the last year, grown close over many heart-to-heart chats, and I knew I couldn't tell her about this minor (well, really, I thought it would go away—I mean, it *had* to go away, because it was threatening to really screw everything up) problem of confused emotion.

I could, however, let her know I was leaving and why, and I could confide in her my fear of the reaction I would get when I finally got the nerve up to tell my boyfriend I was leaving. She was way beyond supportive, and, out of respect for our mutual high level of trust, I will not break confidence here regarding our talk. However, I will say that I hung up the phone reassured that regardless of what came of this I would remain close to at least one member of the family. I also felt comforted by the fact that if on the off-chance that my boyfriend did not take well to the changes that seemed to be forthcoming, he would at the very least have the strong support of his family. It was only a few minutes after I had hung up the phone that my boyfriend wandered in the door. While waiting for Rev, I had called Sophia and offered to give her a ride home from work, so I couldn't stay and talk for long. I did feel I owed him something, though, so I told him we would make time and have a heart-to-heart about what was going on. We had been seeing each other only in passing over the last couple of days, and, even though he knew something was up, he had no idea how big a something it was.

I promised to make time and then practically ran out the door. The truth about what was going on scared the hell out of me, and I was not yet willing to face it. I picked up Sophia at work, and as I drove her home I told her everything that was going through my head. As usual, she didn't judge, but she had some good advice to give.

We were sitting in the car in her driveway, when she looked at me and smiled. "Are you happy?"

Oh, hell, I couldn't help it; I answered quite frankly, "Ecstatically."

She then said, "Well then, if you are happy, that is all that matters, because when you are happy you can soar to great heights, but you must remember to always be honest in your happiness: honest to yourself and honest with others, because when we are not honest happiness gets taken away."

It is a hard lesson to learn this thing called honesty. Perhaps of all the lessons it is the most painful. It is the most damaging, and it is the one lesson that finally frees us to live the rest of our lives comfortable in who we really are. I abhor the process of learning this lesson, and I repeatedly fail the various tests given to me on it. I rail against the powers that be like a stubborn child throwing a temper tantrum. If I could only get it right this time, then maybe I will be done and won't have to come back and do it again. Something tells me this won't happen; regardless of how well I do this time around I will have to do it all over again anyway. So I stubbornly persist on bending some of the rules, and, having a rebellious nature, I choose the one rule that seems to be of the utmost importance. Being antagonistic in nature, I openly question the rule and the lesson attached. Is there not a time and a place for dishonestly? Are we not required, for the benefit of others, to stretch the truth just a little to soften the blow when reality strikes? Hell, we all do it—except for Sophia, who boldly proclaims, "I might be a bitch, but at least I'm an honest bitch."

Oh, I see her point, I really do, and, as I said, I am working on it—but I am more concerned at the moment about being honest with myself: about my nature, my core, what makes me tick. As she said, we have to be honest to be happy. I am learning (slowly, I might add) that if I am honest with myself about what I want and need it is a hell of a lot easier to find a way to get it. I am also learning that by being honest with myself it prevents me from having to be dishonest with others. They may not like the truth—in fact they may very well detest the truth—but then I do not have to force myself to make them happy by telling an untruth. I am not responsible for their happiness, only my own. With that realization comes the freedom to walk away from the presence of those whose judgmental attitude makes me essentially unhappy.

It is a vicious cycle, this need to belong. The more we bend ourselves to fit the expectations of others, the closer we come to breaking. I don't particularly feel like breaking just yet. I have way too much left to do in this life to waste time with breaking. So I am attempting to straighten. A few people have placed some weight on my shoulders along the way, but then I willingly bent my back, allowing them to unload their own burdens. Some of those burdens will, no doubt, hit the floor as I slowly rise, but with each determined stroke of the pen I come that much closer to standing straight. When I'm done, there may be a mess of broken burdens at my feet, but I will find a broom and help to sweep up the mess I have made. Somebody is going to have to hold the dustpan, though. They weren't all my burdens to begin with, so I think maybe I deserve a little bit of help.

Chapter 7
Questions, Answers, and the Art of Arson

I'd like to say I did the right thing that night (what you might think would be the right thing), but Sophia did say to be honest.

Revo called; and I went. It was a simple decision that set us on twisted path of coincidental encounters and symbolism bordering on high weirdness. He hopped in the car when I picked him up, and, after a quick kiss hello, we sat and chatted for awhile. He told me more about what he was hoping to accomplish but admitted he had no idea how to go about it. I explained to him that the one promise my Baba had made sure to get out of me was that I would write my story as fiction. As every other piece of advice she had ever given me had been extremely beneficial, I figured maybe that's what we should do. He seemed to like the idea.

I had in my mind the idea that we could marry my idea of the upcoming spiritual revolution with his desire to see a more prosperous future for his people. I was proposing the story of two people on a spiritual journey, but if we based the story in the Philippines we could incorporate all the issues of the people there and in other Third World countries. I hoped to inspire people to work toward change. With slow, steady steps forward in a positive direction the worldwide population would slowly move toward a more positive future. Of course, I wasn't deluded enough to think one book or one story could change the world, but in my mind every little piece of individual inspiration was one more piece added to the big puzzle that is our undetermined future. I made the suggestion, he took it to heart, and we began hammering out a few more details.

We talked about the dangers of asking the wrong questions, and he seemed very much concerned about the possible threat to our safety. I pointed out that, as we were already acting like we had been together forever, it would be believable to the casual observer that I was just his Canadian girlfriend out for a visit. I also explained that it would be easier for him to access certain information than for me. He could easily steer conversations with friends or family toward politics in a noninvasive manner. I, on the other hand, would very likely end up shot if I even brought up the subject with the wrong person. We also agreed that any major information that we managed to find would not be put on paper until I returned to Canada. Again, he was concerned about safety and cited the execution of one of Philippines's greatest national heroes as an example of what happens to those in his country who question authority. At this point, I believe I mentioned not particularly wanting to lose him again when I had only now found him—which took our discussion in a new direction.

This time his concern was more passionate in nature, and he admitted to being very worried about the fact that it seemed too familiar. We had been down this road before, we both knew it, and we also both knew the outcome. The problem was he wasn't sure he could do it again. He was positive that he didn't want me to have to do it again. We could run with the idea that we had to follow the path we both saw as being chosen for us, but the price could be extremely high. We had paid it before, more than once, but although he was more than willing to suffer himself, he was not at all happy about the idea of me suffering at his side. It seemed I had a decision to make and not much time to make it.

He sat there looking at me with sad eyes, imploring me silently to walk away. He had to know; I doubt for one minute he believed I would, but what we want and what we are forced sometimes to accept are two entirely different things. To me, it didn't seem much of a choice, really: lose him now or lose him later. I went with later. There was no way in hell I was going to give up any of the precious time I could have with him. I had spent an entire lifetime feeling incomplete and hungering for that connection that would make me whole. In the space of a couple of hours I had found, recognized, and accepted that other half willingly into my life. I'll be damned if I was going to give it up. And that was exactly what I told him.

He was left feeling torn: knowing that keeping me away from him would keep me safe, but also knowing that we would both be completely miserable if I actually listened to him and let him go.

He gave up after several minutes of pained silence. He merely shrugged his shoulders, "So, you're coming home with me, and we are going to start a revolution."

I had to laugh; the whole situation was hysterical. Here we were, two reasonably responsible adults, sitting in a car, having a rational, open discussion about having shared our lives together several times in the past and our concerns over doing it all again. Seems completely crazy, doesn't it? I swear there were no drugs or alcohol involved, and neither of us would be considered by society as an unsound or potentially dangerous personality.

Of course, viewing someone as potentially dangerous is subjective. When you think of all the people you meet along the road of life and the effect they have on yours, you can see my point. Next time you are out in public, take a look around you, and, if any of the people you see are a threat to your safety, your happiness, or your way of life, try to figure out why. Where you are in your life at the time will drastically alter who you perceive as a danger.

If you are a young woman, then perhaps the well-built, muscular young thug standing on the corner is more a potential playmate than a potential threat. If you are a little old lady struggling home with a couple of bags of groceries, then that young man likely looks twice the size he really is and three times as dangerous. To the cop driving by in the cruiser, the young thug is probably more a potential nuisance than a potential threat. To the baby mamma staying at home awaiting his arrival, he is possibly her salvation. Think about it. To the baby mamma he represents the food and shelter he provides. The cop is wondering how the young man goes about providing that food and shelter, and the old woman is hoping that in his quest to provide food and shelter for his own family he does not take hers away. As for the young woman, she is not likely thinking much beyond the fact that he is a hottie, and if shelter crosses her mind it is only in relation to the bed that may found inside.

So, you see, it completely depends on you and what you perceive as the reality of the situation. Though I am willing to bet the average person might well find the conversation between me and Revo verging on insane, there are just as many others out there nodding their heads and thinking to themselves, "Sure, I can see it—I've been there myself." The conversation eventually died, and tension started to mount. We really could only stay there so long before we both got restless. It was either drive or jump each other, and, as having sex at the time was not going to accomplish anything, I chose to drive. We headed to a quiet place on the bluffs where we would be free for the moment from busy city life.

As we drove, I told him yet another story about my Baba, trying to explain to him why it was so important for me to heed her warning. In retrospect, the explanation really wasn't necessary; he trusted me completely and took me on my word. At the time, however, it was a much-needed distraction from the looming shadow of fear that had begun to worm its way into our minds. Our hearts would stay true, but rationality and reason have a way of taking over emotion when that emotion involves danger to one's heart.

So, I drove and talked, and he listened, quietly, intently and openly…

I told him about a conversation I had had with Baba shortly before she died. It had been hard in those last couple of weeks to get any straightforward answers out of her. I had still not asked her everything I wanted to know about my father's death or my mother's crazy behaviour, and I was still very curious about how my stepdad fit into the picture. Yet, as her time drew nearer, I felt less inclined to trouble Baba with things that might upset her in her last days. Of course, it didn't help matters much that she had begun for some reason to speak randomly and fluently in German. It was a language I did not understand, and I was therefore not able to communicate with her in it. I had never heard her speak German before, and until two weeks before her death I had not been aware that she was fluent in more than one tongue.

It was during the last week of her life, in one of her rare, seemingly lucid moments, that she had told me two short tales. One began after I asked if she had been there when I was born. I was curious, as it seemed to me that she had both always been around and that she was more of a mother to me than my own mother had been. Her answer was not one I was prepared for.

She closed her eyes a moment while she spoke, leaning her head back against the wheelchair. "Oh no, I wasn't allowed to be there, but I was waiting for you. Yes, I was. They brought you to me straight away, as soon as you were born. You were only a day old when I first held you in my arms. I remember it so well. They brought you to my home and handed you to me. I was so happy. You were so beautiful, and I was so grateful for this gift. They left right away, of course, but we were okay, you and me. We didn't need them, we had each other."

I was a little confused by some of it, so I asked her, "What do you mean, they left?"

"Well they brought you to me, handed you over, and went away. It isn't hard to understand." Her eyes popped open, and she stared right at me. "They went away; they had to go away."

Now, I don't know if any of you have kids of your own, but the very idea of bringing a one-day-old infant to stay with Grandma while the happy couple goes off on holiday is completely foreign to me. I did not really want to think of the reasons behind it. In fact, being a mother myself, I am still not able to reconcile the idea at all. I had to know, though—that accursed human curiosity did me in yet again!

So, timidly, I queried, "Where did they go; I mean, how long were they gone?"

She reached out and laid her wrinkled, gnarled hand on my arm. "I don't know, child. They brought you, placed you in my arms, and then went away. It was a long time, a very long time, and that, as they say, is that."

Then, with a little twinkle in her eye, she smiled a lopsided smile. "I wonder if we are having rice pudding for dessert. You know they feed us too damn much rice pudding; every day with the rice pudding…"

The conversation was in her mind over, and I was not one to attempt to change her mind. So we spent the next hour playing cribbage and discussing rice pudding vs. tapioca.

On the day I told Revo about my crazy adventures in Baba Land, I was no closer to wrapping my head around the answers to the puzzle of my birth than I had been on the day I found out Ma and Pa had left me at Baba's. These things we discussed as I drove. In truth, I talked and he listened. It wasn't until halfway through my next story that he had anything to offer other than a smile.

As I was pulling in to park the car, I started in on the tale of a shopping adventure my Baba had told me about. Apparently, sometime shortly after acquiring for herself this little infant girl, she had needed to go to the mall to get groceries. It was a really mild fall day, with the sun shining and not a cloud in the sky. Baba had just parked the car and was in the process of getting me out of the car seat in the back, when she looked up to see a black car at the stoplights out front of the mall parking lot. For whatever reason, something about the car scared her, and she stopped a moment to stare at it. Suddenly realizing what was wrong, she went about the hurried, panicked task of getting me to safety. By way of explanation, she told me a week before her passing, "The car was still on the road, but I thought to myself, 'Oh my God, you're right, it's going to hit us.'"

Now, at this, Rev looked at me and said, "'You're right?' Hold on, *who* was right?" and I explained that Baba told me that I had somehow warned her that the car was going to hit us. He was sitting there looking at me, and he asked, "Vick, how old were you?"

I answer quite frankly, "Three months."

Again you would think again at this point he would be getting the urge to run away from the crazy lady and her stories, but no…

He just smiled and said, "So, was the car totaled?"

That's right, not "What happened?"; not "How does a three-month-old baby tell anybody anything, let alone see the future?"; and certainly not "Okay, can we maybe go home now? I… um… have to get some sleep before my flight."

No, not him; he just wants to know how much damage was done. Completely content to believe the rest, he is only curious about the outcome.

I explained to Rev that, according to Baba, she had had lots of time to get me out and we were well out of the way and standing in the mall entrance when this black car finally came barreling through the parking lot ten minutes later. Baba told me the driver had later claimed to have lost control and that he had managed to get away with only a few bruises, but both the front end of his car and the back of my Baba's (where I would have been sitting) were completely obliterated. I also told Rev that it was minutes after hearing that story that I ceased to ask any questions of my grandmother pertaining to my past. The answers I was getting really only left me with more questions.

The evening was wearing on, but neither of us cared at this point if we got any rest. There was one more thing I had yet to tell him before I could let him go home—a secret part of my past that, in my eyes, threatened what was left of our time together. It was not a story I wanted to share with this man, but it was also not conceivable for me to keep any secrets from him either. He hadn't turned and run so far, but in light of what I had to say that didn't really mean anything. Unbelievable stories about strange occurrences and random coincidences were one thing. The truth about past decisions resulting in arrest and conviction were a different matter altogether.

It might, however, be our last night together for a long time, and I could not let him go without testing the waters of my newfound urge to be completely open and honest. So I told him that there was one possible problem with this whole scenario, one glaring oversight that I had neglected to mention. He was, of course, understandably curious, but he reassured me that whatever it was we could probably work around it.

So I blurted out rather abruptly "I have a record, a criminal record, and I'm not even sure yet that I'll be able to get a passport and, if I can, how it will affect the work we want to do."

He smiled and asked innocently, "Okay, what'd you do?"

I didn't want to tell him. Hell, I don't particularly want to tell you. I am not proud of my behaviour in the past, and though it is with time getting easier to face, the wounds are, as they say, still fresh. I could not, however, lie to this man, so I offered up a piece of my life I have worked very hard to hide.

Shortly after my parents passed away, I started dating this man who ultimately ended up moving in with me. At first I thought it a selfless act of love. He had left his home, family, and friends to move six hours away to a town he had not known existed. Things went well for the first few months. I went back to school for auto mechanics, and, as he was not working, he helped out by taking care of the house and picking my daughter up from school. Sometime during those first few months, however, my back had really started to hurt, and I was finding it more and more difficult to function. The less I was able to do, however, the more he helped out, and, in the beginning, I was very grateful. But time passed, and as my quest to find a diagnosis and cure for what was now crippling back pain progressed, so did his inability to find work. We were at the time living off my student loans and the small inheritance my parents had left me. As the savings dwindled, however, so did my ability to attend school. After being diagnosed as having a fractured spine and herniated disc, I was forced to drop out, cutting off my student loan funding.

Still he was not working, nor did he seem at all inclined toward the notion of finding a job. Several other factors came into play, of course. I had tried to financially help out a friend, who ended up screwing me over, thanks to her addiction to cocaine. Although my parents' house was now rented out, the money coming in was not even covering the expenses on the property. I soon found myself in a situation I had not seen coming. Something had to give. He was quite literally sucking me dry, and, on the verge of being broke, I made the attempt to kick him out. This is when the demon entered, and my sweet, supportive boyfriend turned into a manic-depressive suicidal maniac who refused to leave. Fights ensued, and I found myself standing at one point in my kitchen with a chair flying past my head. Thing is, I am only five feet tall and 110 pounds, but he was six foot four and all muscle. I figured I was screwed. So I called the police, and, though they did come, they ultimately ended up leaving him there. They did acquire from him his promise to leave, but only after I willingly signed over one of my cars in the presence of the officers into his possession. The idea was that if this man had a car he would have the means to drive away. The police told me I had not been hurt yet, so they couldn't do anything. So, all I could think of to do was give him the car so he would go away.

He did for awhile, driving out to Alberta to find work, but his hold on me was not easily relinquished. He started phoning daily and leaving ten-to-twenty-minute-long messages on my phone. Each message was a mixture of sobbing and begging me to reconsider, blended in with threats on my person. I called the police again, and they again said that he had not hurt me yet, so there was nothing they could do.

As all this was going on, I had been trying to find another source of income. With a broken back I was now technically disabled and unable to either work or finish school. I tried to apply for disability, but, as I owned property, I was refused. I tried to apply for welfare and was told I had to sell my parents' house. So I put my parents' house on the market, then went about the task of trying to be honest with my landlord: asking, hoping for a little understanding. He told me that I could grow or sell pot for him in lieu of rent. Big help he was.

Still the phone calls continued, and eventually my crazy ex began the habit of driving all the way back to Ontario on his days off. I would wake up at 3:00 AM to find him standing over my bed staring at me. Still the police said they could not intervene.

Desperation can, I have learned, cause temporary insanity, and it was not long before I became a victim of the human weakness of mental deterioration. Luckily this whole time my daughter had not been affected. She had neither witnessed any of the violence nor been exposed by me to the reality of our desperate situation. A phone call that threatened to change that finally prompted me to act.

It was yet another message on my machine, but this time it was a very calm, self-assured voice that spoke: "You honestly have no idea what it's like, do you, to have everything, then lose it—just like that it gets taken away. Well, you will know very soon what it is like. You will know what pain is. You think you've suffered before? No, only after I have taken away everything you have, only after I take away from you the one thing you cannot live without, only then will you know what it's like to have your life stolen from you."

"Hell no, you didn't—oh hell, you did!" That was the thought I had immediately after hearing that message. He was coming back, and he was coming back to take my baby. I had to do something, but, as the police had thus far refused to help, I took the road less traveled and went to the one person I trusted to make it right.

Now, all my life I have managed to fit in with almost every available social circle. It is well known by my friends that a large part of my youth was centered around criminal activity. I had grown up and gone clean the moment I felt that first tiny spark of life inside of me, but even after the birth of my daughter I maintained my contacts with those I had worked with in the past. Honestly, you never know when either someone in leather or someone connected to someone in leather will come in handy. The price for any assistance they give may at times be high, but they do have ways of accomplishing seemingly impossible tasks. So, instead of bringing the recorded message to the police, I travelled instead into the bushland hills of northern Ontario to meet my fate. After hours of discussing my options, we came up with a plan to torch the house, collect the insurance money, which I would then take to relocate, and lose myself in one of the bigger cities.

The offer was at one point made to help my ex-boyfriend disappear altogether. Something about it being very hard to locate a body in the northern parts of Ontario bush country. The offer was also made to do the drive out to Alberta, hunt the asshole down, and give him a warning beating that would leave him contemplating, while fighting for his life, whether harassing me all this time had been worth it. I could live with neither. I may have a criminal mind at times, but my heart far outweighs the power that mind has over me. I do not like to see others suffer, and, regardless of what he had done, I could not bring myself to go that far. I couldn't bring myself to ask a close friend to go that far.

As much as the world may think that what the man who torched my house did was wrong, it was done out of love for me. It was his way of trying to help when nobody else had, and it was an action taken with great risk to himself. I have not seen him since, but someday I hope to get the chance to say I am sorry for putting him in the middle of a situation he had no business being in the middle of. I hope also someday to face his family and tell them he is a good man, with a good heart, and though at times it may be a little misdirected, his loyalty to his friends and family is far beyond what the average person is capable of. My friend's name was Jacob, and he did, in the end, live up to his name. May God bless him for his sacrifice.

We settled on the fire. It was my way of sacrificing a little to gain my freedom and safety for my child. To the flames I would lose almost every material object I owned, including all of my parents' furniture, some of which held great sentimental value. It was a small price to pay, however, and as I now felt that I was very much on my own in this, I agreed to the requested price and we set about planning.

The time came, the house burned, and the insurance company paid up. We moved and settled into a life in the city, and though I felt deeply shamed by what I had done, I was, for the moment, free. Karma, though, has a way of catching up with you, and, as a result of my firebug friend pissing off another criminally minded individual, we got ratted out. Police picked me up while I was visiting friends in my old town, and there I stayed, trapped by my bail conditions, awaiting my day in court.

Strangely enough, in the end it all worked out. I explained to the detective why I had done it, and he admitted that in this case the cops had really screwed up. He might even, he added, have done the same in my place. So, between my lawyer, my confession, and a detective who sincerely believed I did not deserve to be in jail, I ended up serving an eighteen-month suspended sentence—much shorter than the twenty-five years to life that I could have gotten. I was instead released into the community with strict conditions and curfews and allowed to maintain a somewhat normal existence with my little girl. I was even encouraged by my parole officer (a very kind and gentle man) to pursue the art I had discovered on escaping to the city. Instead of serving my community service in the usual manner, I instead did a painting representing life and hope that was later sold at an art auction, with the proceeds going to the Hospital for Sick Children. All that I really had left to do was come up with the $120,000 to pay off my debt to the insurance company—a debt I do fully acknowledge and accept as mine and a debt I wholeheartedly intend to pay.

Throughout the entire story, Rev had once again sat silently listening, not uttering a sound—until at the very end he broke into laughter. I was not sure how anything I had just said could possibly be perceived as hysterically funny, but I let him laugh himself breathless and patiently waited until he was able to speak.

"Too funny" he said, still snickering. "Here I am thinking it is something horribly bad, and here you are thinking I will think it is something horribly bad, and it turns out we are more alike than I thought. I am an arsonist too." With that, he went back to losing himself in a fit in laughter, and if not for the fact that I was already sitting down, I probably would have fallen on the floor laughing myself.

Chapter 8
Linear Life Lessons and the Cost of Acceptance

Okay, so maybe we shouldn't have been laughing about it, and I just know you are thinking we are a couple of sick, twisted individuals. In our defense, we were only laughing at the discovery of yet another unexpected parallel in the lives of people from two entirely different worlds. We did eventually sober up, and he looked at me quite seriously and said, "But I never thought to do it for money."

Argh! "But—" I protested, with my face starting to flush, "I was not—"

He never let me finish. "No, that's not what I meant," he laughed, giving me a little grin. "You had your reasons, and I will not begrudge you those. You do what you have to do to protect your own. Children's safety always comes first. "No," he said, shaking his head, "What I meant was: I did it because I am really fascinated by fire… I like watching things burn."

I wish I could have seen my own face. I must have looked funny as hell, because I was totally shocked by his admission.

He laughed at me again. "It's okay, really; I have it under control now," and he started to quietly explain that while he was younger he had accidentally set two separate fires, destroying both the back room of his home and a school bathroom. He never went into much detail about the first, but he did tell me the story of his bathroom adventures at school.

Apparently his friend and he had been playing with lighters in the boys' bathroom, using them to burn toilet paper and a few other things they had found lying around. The bell had rung and they had had to hurry on to class, so Rev tossed the last piece of paper in the nearest garbage can and left. Of course, burning paper tossed into garbage containing more paper is going to eventually turn into a large quantity of burning paper. Fire spreads and takes on a life of its own when left unattended. It was that very principle my friend had been counting on when he torched my house. Of course, kids don't think of these things. They think along the lines of "Shit, gotta get to class, so we don't get in trouble."

Long story short: the bathroom got torched, and the school authorities went in search of the culprits. Rev and his friend ditched their lighters and agreed not to tell a soul, but as the day went by Rev overheard comments by other classmates, which led him to the conclusion that his friend had a big mouth. Too many smirks in his direction left him feeling extremely uneasy, and when he finally did get called into the office he knew in his heart he was most definitely busted. He was a stubborn one, though, and had no intention of 'fessing up. He knew if he did it would be guaranteed expulsion, so, when confronted by a very irate principal, he categorically denied his involvement. The head of the school produced the lighter belonging to Rev's friend and asked Rev to whom it belonged. Loyalty outweighed reason, and Rev answered that he didn't know. After what seemed to Rev to be hours of interrogation, the principal finally switched tactics and tried to cajole him into confessing. He explained to Rev that if it were an accident, and if he would own up to it, perhaps they could come to some kind of understanding. Eventually Rev conceded defeat and took the high road. He admitted his crime, and, instead of being expelled, he was rewarded for his honesty by the chance to remain in school and work at redeeming himself. He was put into counseling, but, as he wasn't really a firebug, they soon let him discontinue his sessions. The counselor concluded that he had learned his lesson and really had no need of further assistance.

I was dumbfounded by the similarities in our stories—not the cause so much, but the effect. In both cases we had been handled with gentle, compassionate understanding by those who had been in a position to irrevocably destroy all our future hopes and dreams. Both of us had begun by stubbornly denying our mistakes with the intention of protecting the other person involved, and, finally, in both instances, because of our willingness to live up to our mistakes and accept the consequences, we were given a second chance by some remarkably understanding individuals. The only major difference was in the timing, but then we had led essentially different lives and taken two entirely different roads to get where we now were. I thought at the time, *It will be very interesting to see how these two roads will end up merging.*

I honestly couldn't help thinking that the whole situation was funny as hell. I picked up the phone while we were still sitting in the car, and I gave Sophia a quick call. At first Rev was asking me what the hell I was doing; it was one of the rare times he seemed to be completely caught off-guard by anything I have done or said. When he heard her laughing hysterically on the other end of the phone, he understood. She is one of those rare people in my life who completely understands where I am coming from, and, as she has the same sick sense of humour as me, I figured I would take the time to share a giggle with her. After all, given all that she does on a daily basis for me and others in her life, the least I could do is put in as much effort as possible to make her smile. Before she hung up the phone, she told me to remind Rev to take me shopping for her Louis Vuitton bag, adding that she needed one for her niece as well. Letting her go, we turned back to our own conversation.

We talked a bit about our younger years, trying to discover any more similarities between them. We ended up on the topic of pool halls and found we had both put in a fair amount of time in these when we were teenagers. He never told me much about actually playing. I myself had partnered up with a boyfriend at the age of fourteen and embarked on a year-long, highly entertaining adventure in hustling.

Every time we would enter a new pool hall, the boy I was with would "teach me" how to play pool. He would lean over the table with me, directing the cue and openly giving me pointers. There is a sucker born every minute, and eventually another male of the species would wander over and offer to play a few friendly couples' games, enlisting the help of their usually less-than-enthusiastic acquaintances. It would only take a couple of games with both girls sucking and the boys cleaning up for the newcomers to get bold enough to wager a bet. My partner and I would lose one more, and then, suddenly, beginner's luck would kick in, and I would accidentally either hook my opponent or just have a short lucky run at sinking a few balls. It was more than enough to tip the scales and allowed us more than once to make a killing at the tables. It wasn't obvious enough, however, to get us in trouble, though I suppose it helped that I always played in low-rise jeans and a low-cut top. The point is, we never got busted (not for that, at least) and it turned out to teach me a thing or two about human nature and the power of female flesh over men. I am a lot older now, and my body is admittedly not what it once was, so I do not use those tactics in battle very much anymore. I do still, however, rely on men's natural instinct to underestimate the intellect of a cute girl. Though I am now usually fully clothed, it is still fairly easy to get what I want without giving anything up.

As I said, all Rev would tell me was that he had spent a fair amount of time playing pool, but he gave no gory details on how he had learned to play or why. He had already told me about his pool cue Excalibur. He thought it was pretty funny considering he had discovered King Arthur later in life.

He mentioned that he wanted to bring it with him, but he didn't have a lot of room left. He was bringing presents for his family, as is the tradition in the Philippines. I offered to pack the cue up with my stuff, if he would trust me with it, and he laughed again. "So, the Lady of the Lake is going to bring me my Excalibur. You know, it seems to fit, doesn't it?"

We again broke into peals of laughter, both agreeing during brief rest periods that the whole story was indeed turning out to be a strange one. We eventually came back to the topic of us and how comfortable it felt just being together. "You know, you realize that we have been sitting here talking for hours like two people who had known each other their entire lives," he said, smiling. "There is still so much about your life that I have to learn, but I already feel like I know exactly who you are."

The thought warmed my heart, if only because I knew he was right. It seemed that all the other surface day-to-day crap didn't really matter. There was a deeper connection, something warm and comforting about being together. There was no urgency or need to explore the future, because with him I was perfectly content to be in the *now*.

I agreed wholeheartedly, telling him, "We have time, I think, to explore all that other stuff; I'm just glad I finally found you." Jokingly, I added, "Just don't make me wait three years next time. I'm a very impatient person."

He smiled at that. "Sorry, I have always believed in being fashionably late."

Oh, stop it—we are not nuts, and, if you ever get the chance to meet someone you connect with on that level, you will more than likely find yourself having the same conversations. I have, in fact, had chats very similar to this with several different people I have met along the way. So, instead of sitting there grinning inwardly at our inability to accept reality, open your mind to the idea that you, too, have been here more than once. Then, next time you meet someone for the first time and it feels when you look in their eyes that you have met them before, open your mouth and say, "I know you." Maybe, just maybe, you'll discover a long-lost friend who will gladly and willingly come back into your life and make it richer and fuller with his or her presence.

It was getting late, and the time to let him go was coming close. As we drove back to his house that night, we continued talking. "You already know I wrote that song three years ago," he mumbled, half to himself. "I just never knew who I was writing it for. I thought maybe I was writing it for myself, you know, knowing that I wasn't really where I needed to be."

He looked at me then, and there was a hint of sadness in his eyes I couldn't understand. "Maybe I was writing it for both of us; maybe I knew there was someone out there I was meant to find…" His voice trailed off, and in the silence that followed there was a brief moment of pain. In a flash it was gone, as he continued his tale. "The guys insisted on recording it. You know, it was the first song we put on CD. I didn't think it was the one. I didn't think it was good enough, but the guys made me do it anyway." He was smiling again, "I am glad they did." So he had rescued us briefly from an uncomfortable moment, but the thought lingered in my mind: *Why is he so damn sad about all of this? What is he seeing that I am not?*

I couldn't bring myself to ask, and I didn't want to ruin our last few minutes together. I left it alone, preferring to steer the discussion back to safer ground. I asked when the flight was, and, as we pulled up to his house, we were safely back to talking about mundane topics like the weather and jet lag. I was grateful for the rest. It had been an emotionally draining day. The problem was that as surely as I felt the connection between us I also felt the inevitable severance of that connection. It seemed to hover there just out of reach like a shadow in the corner of a brightly lit room. It was a darkness that was at once out of place yet also had every right to exist. It didn't threaten for the moment to spread out and consume the light, but just by its presence the promise remained unspoken that it would eventually come forth.

I ignored it, as I am wont to do in situations that I do not approve of. I wasn't ready to accept it, so therefore it could not harm me. I never told him that I saw it too. I wasn't prepared to have that discussion. I still don't want to face it even now, but then I have discovered recently that I am not much in control of what happens. The only thing I seemed to have any power over was how I dealt with each new situation or challenge as it arose. So even though I maintained my state of denial, I was aware of the threat that shadow posed and I could acknowledge the price it will finally ask me to pay when it comes forth into the light.

Our night together was over. He had a plane to catch, and I had a life here I had to continue to live. After he ran quickly into the house to grab his cue, he placed it carefully into the trunk, saying, "Take good care of it please; keep it safe."

I assured him I would and then turned to him, burying my face in his chest. "Please be safe," I whispered to him. "I'm not ready yet to lose what I just found."

He held me for a moment, stroking my hair, trying to reassure me that he would and that he would see me soon.

Then he was gone, and I was left to drive home alone, trying very hard not to allow the shaking in my hands to spread. I knew I'd see him again; that wasn't my fear—it was the fact that I recognized how much damage our chance meeting would cause to some of the people in my life that I had grown to love. I knew I was being slowly pulled away from the life I now had and that, for good or bad, I would allow myself to be led. I didn't think it was all about him, however, and that bothered me as well. It would be nice to have the comfort of having somebody else's presence at the end of the road, but for the moment I did not see that as being possible. We had been brought together for a reason; we would use each other's love and strength to accomplish what we had to do, and then he would be gone.

He had foreseen it, and it saddened him. Even knowing the outcome I was willing to try, and as I lay in bed awake that night I prayed he would find a way to take the risk. I knew even if our time together was brief it would be beautiful—if, and only if, we could let go of tomorrow and find a way to live for today.

I had asked Rev to send me his info—where he would be staying and where I should be heading, so I could begin to make arrangements for my flight and hotel. As was my habit, though it was late and I was tired, I made the time to check my email.

After I had dropped him off he had apparently taken the time to leave me a message.

Pasig City Metro Manila

That is where my aunt is. Remember the writer I told you about that was on the 5-dollar pesos? Whose book inspired a revolution? His name is Jose Rizal—Pasig City was the Capital of Rizal province before Metro Manila was formed.

So, we're staying in the capital of the revolutionary writer who stirred shit up. Isn't that great? =)

I hope to see you and ex very soon.

My lady of the lake, a wave of inspiration has come upon us. I just pray we have the discipline, strength, and wisdom to hone in on this great power.

Yours always, R

I wrote back quickly just to let him know I was going to try to get there as quickly as possible. I never bothered to tell him I already knew about Jose, it was a topic for another time. For the moment, he was mine and that was all that mattered. I figured he would not get the chance to read it until he arrived, but I needed to let him know I was with him; it wasn't much, but I would learn later it had been enough...

Rev,

Thanks for the info—I will book my flight tomorrow. I will keep your sword safe, my heart, until you and Ex can be reunited. I think it will be an honour to stay in the same city—perhaps senior Rizal will pay us a visit some night and lend us his wisdom and his vision. If we keep the faith, my love, we will find the strength and the wisdom to see this through—play safe, xo

Always yours, Vik

Sleep was a long time in coming that night; I lay awake for hours trying to come to terms with the emotions raging through me. I was ecstatic that he had found me and terrified of him being taken away; yet, there was a certain peace to be found in the feeling of faith I had in what we wanted to achieve together.

I felt him fly away that night as I drifted off to sleep, and, though he was gone, I could still feel him with me. It was an odd sensation, this entity hovering near, but it was comforting, and I knew then that even when the time came to let him go he would still always be with me.

As a side note, because my first real acceptance of the possibilities that life was presenting had largely been due to that first tarot reading at my hair salon, I was now (more out of curiosity than anything else) checking out my daily tarot online. The cards continued to coincide with my daily activities, and checking my card at the end of each day was becoming an entertaining evening ritual.

Today's card was the *Ten of Wands*. It suggests that my power today lies in conscience. "He ain't heavy, he's my brother." I own responsibility for the baggage I have chosen to carry, but I am ready to lay the weight of a burden or secret I have been hiding behind, where it belongs, in order to reconcile my conscience. Do I want to be right or be alone? I am empowered by blind faith in fulfilling my purpose or greater good to "just do it," and I transform through passion or direction in principle.

Chapter 9

Fear, Faith, Flight, and Wisdom in a Child's Eyes

When I got up I headed straight for the computer and discovered a little secret about my newfound long-lost love: the man hardly sleeps…

He had left me yet another message.

Tomorrow you need to read up on Jose Rizal. Sometimes my relatives joke about how I look like him. He was taken from his sweetheart when the Spaniards persecuted him for his book. This isn't the first time we're doing this. I have a feeling we've done this before… many times over and over.

Now I understand what you mean by "I was taken away." I was… I wasn't careful enough last time. One of our last journeys might have been with Rizal, only this time, we'll be more careful.

Goodnight, so much to talk about... so much to say…

Xoxo

What does a woman say to that? What would you have said in my place? There it was in black and white (and by now you know I much prefer colour)—everything I felt, everything I feared, staring at me from my computer screen. It was an unreal reality looking me straight in the eye and challenging me to take it on. I never have been one to back down from a good battle, so I wrote back, knowing this time there was no way he'd get the message before he landed.

I know sweetie,

I feel the same way: we have done this before, and it feels like every time you have been taken from me it was for a greater good but the pain of it has lingered. I've always felt like I was born missing a part of me but at the same time knowing that you would find me again eventually. I had to learn patience and faith, but it will be worth it in the end; as I said, I will take whatever comes, as long as it comes from following the path we were meant to follow. I thanked the gods again today, and I will continue to do so every day, for finally bringing you to me. You are right—there is so much for us to talk about and explore, but I feel safe in the knowledge that we will be given the time we need and the strength to believe in this when obstacles are presented. I was thinking that since I had already offered to take Soph to Italy, perhaps it was because I knew that was one of the places I would have to go. I'm hoping you will think on it; I think it might be safer to do some of my research there after I learn about your people and live among them, and I would love it if you would come with me. I know it is one of the countries she feels pulled toward, and I would like to give her the chance to see it before she starts building her family—a way of saying thank you to her for keeping me grounded and sane. I'm not scared anymore—all my fear and doubt have disappeared, and this feeling of contentment and peace has taken over me. I will be leaving very soon to go make arrangements to join you, but for now I am going to do some research and read up on Jose Rizal. I already started writing this morning, and I think I will have to do a bit each day whenever I feel the need to put pen to paper. If you get the chance to write down some of your thoughts and feelings in the next few days, do it—the book will flow really well if it can come from both sides of the story as it unfolds. Please stay safe, and, like I said in the text, lie low—all will come in time, but we need to be very careful. I do not want to lose you yet... my heart to yours, xo

After sending it off, I gave myself a moment to gather my strength, then set about the task of finding out what I needed to travel to the other side of the world.

As much as I have always been a free spirit who suffers from wanderlust, I have not had the opportunity to travel. Both a commitment to my daughter and responsibilities to my ailing parents had kept me grounded. I had also been very aware in previous years that my time with my beloved grandmother was short. I was hesitant to stray far from her, as I felt I had yet much to learn from her strength and wisdom. I do not regret what some would view as restrictions on my freedoms. Through my commitment to my family and my desire to stay close to them, I have learned much about myself and my own limitations. I have also learned through my mistakes, and as those mistakes creep into and meld with this tale, I will be more than happy to share them with you as well as the lessons learned along the way. Let's face it—after the last few chapters there aren't very many secrets left for me to keep.

Besides, if you can accept where you have been and find a way to use the knowledge you've gained, it becomes easier to see where it is you are supposed to go. It's like a boxer training for a fight—every swing that life throws at us, every time we are either hit or manage to dodge the punch, our reflexes become faster. With each practice round our skills are honed, so that when the "big fight" finally arrives we are prepared for it. I am positive that the powers that be arrange these little challenges for us to train us for the real thing; we get knocked down, we get up, we wipe the blood from our eyes, and the next time we know when to duck and when to punch. I have learned to be thankful for all the woes that have befallen me and can say with all honesty that I am grateful for the times my soul has cried out in agony, "Please God, no more." It was by surviving those times that I learned compassion and understanding for others who suffer, and I built up the emotional strength to make it through my next personal battle.

I have a strong belief in looking for the good that always comes along with the bad. If you are aware that you need to look for it, it is only a matter of time before you see it. Unfortunately, one first has to be willing to accept the possibility that it is there to find. I, through my own experience, have learned how difficult it can sometimes be to see past the pain. I now feel quite blessed by all that I have been through, as it has shown me a clear view of the reality of life. Rather than hold me back, it has helped me build a strong foundation. From there, when the time was right, I could (as my friend Sophia says time and again) take flight.

I have a friend I grew up with who has told me several times over the years that each loss has been just another test. Her name is Chelsea, and she is a sweet-hearted girl, who, although she doesn't always agree with my way of doing things, has always understood the reasons behind my actions. I have decided when this is all done I will have to send her a copy and a note to say thank you. I need to let her know that she was right and that it is partly her faith in me that over the years has helped to keep me on my feet. Perhaps she saw that in time things would change, and eventually I would find my way.

Time did pass, and circumstances did change; I suddenly found myself able to explore the world and write about what I'd learned. The fact was, though, that I did not know how to go about it. I was flying blind, so to speak, and I had to rely on my more travelled friends for guidance. My first project was to get a passport, something I had never attempted to do. My criminal record could at this point completely destroy any hope of my pursuing this new endeavour. As much faith as I had that Rev and I were supposed to meet, I am still human and, as such, am prone to fear and uncertainty.

I discussed it with Sophia, and she told me that in her experience most countries were open to people like myself. She encouraged me to at least make the attempt, explaining that the only sure way to fail at something was never to try. Still it worried me, and it was with fear again in my heart that I made my way, application in hand, to the passport office. I got there late because I had made an impromptu phone call, and the lineup, of course, was absolutely horrendous.

I made another quick phone call while I was waiting in line. I called an old friend by the name of Natalie, thinking I would catch her up on what I was up to. Natalie and I had met six years ago, shortly after my parents had passed away. I had been staying in our family home after the funeral, trying to wrap up my parents' personal affairs. I was spending time with old friends, while I was working out the details of what I was going to do with a property that had suddenly been handed over me and at the time was over eight hours away from where I was living. I was trying to give myself time to heal surrounded by friends I had grown up with, friends who had known my parents and who could understand and share my pain with me.

My parents had been ill for a very long time, but their death was still a shock, in that they had passed away only a day apart. We were all having a hard time coming to terms with the reality of a married couple dying from two completely different, yet natural causes, in two different hospitals, in two distant cities. My dad had passed away on May 8 when his kidneys and liver had shut down, and my mother had passed on May 9 when her lungs and heart gave out. Coincidentally, May 9 that year happened to be Mother's Day—something I think my mother had purposely arranged, as I had managed for years to repeatedly forget her birthday. I can imagine she was determined for me not to forget this particular date. It was a very surreal experience for all of us, and the bonding between old friends had been absolutely essential to our survival. Natalie was a young woman to whom my friends had introduced me. I recognized immediately on meeting her that she had an absolutely beautiful soul. She was hardworking, intelligent, kind, and dedicated to her family—yet it seemed she was stuck in a world in which she didn't belong. She had dreams of getting away from the small town she was living in and finding her own way in the world. However, at the time she did not have the means.

I found myself touched by her plight and, surprisingly enough, in a position to help her achieve her goals. I offered to give her my parents' car. She was understandably shocked. We had, after all, just met, and the idea seemed to her to be a bit on the crazy side. She was concerned that she could not pay me, but I assured her that no payment was necessary. I explained that, as I already had a vehicle, and as my parents no longer needed their material possessions, that the car might as well go to someone who needed it. I asked only that she repay me by using the car to escape the life she was wanting to flee and drive to a better, happier place. My faith in this girl was much rewarded. She has since established herself in a small town in Southern Ontario; she bought a home and is currently engaged to a man who makes her exceptionally happy. He is, oddly enough, a Mexican Mennonite, who speaks five languages fluently, and who appears (though I have not met him) to be her perfect counterpart in that he himself is a well-rounded, earthy personality.

It was this young woman I now chose to call, and it was while I was speaking with her that I managed to regain a little of my strength. We were talking about her upcoming wedding and the honeymoon that was expected to follow soon after. She, however, also has a criminal background, and though she has never been officially convicted, she still has a few things left over from the past hanging over her head.

She was not so much concerned with the acquisition of a passport or her ability to leave the country. She was worried, however, about her return to Canada at the end of her trip. If she did, as she had been warned years ago by an officer of the law, still have unanswered charges in the system, then the authorities would no doubt pick her up on her way back into Canada. I asked her why she hadn't dealt with this sooner. I was quite confused as to why someone I viewed to be quite intelligent would be so blind to the fact that the problem would not simply go away on its own.

She assured me she was well aware of the fact, but as she had never had any desire to travel, it had not really been a problem—until now. I told her that if she wanted to get on with her life, she had better also get on with sorting out her shit. I spoke with her for a long time while I was waiting, and I told her repeatedly that she would not know if she didn't try. I was encouraging her to take the chance and find out what her issues with the authorities were and then take the responsibility and deal with those issues appropriately. The problems would not work themselves out. She would have to let go of her fear and face them head on. The more I tried to convince her, the more I managed to convince myself.

By the time my number was called, I was feeling fairly confident. I boldly approached the desk and declared to the girl behind the counter that I had a criminal record. I explained the ability to travel would be very important to my work and that I needed to know what, if any, restrictions would be placed on that ability. She very kindly did some digging and explained to me that for some reason or another she could find no record on file. She also explained that she was privy through her system to more information than customs agents would find available to them when looking at my passport. She concluded that if there was nothing for her to find then there would also be nothing for them to find. I got the information I needed so I could send my proof of flight to her later, thereby expediting the process. I also obtained the date my passport would be ready for pickup: February 11th. As I was leaving, this very sweet young lady used a strange choice of words when she said goodbye: "So now you know you are free to fly, you better go find your wings." Her name was Angie.

The rest of the day went smoothly enough. I made my way to the travel agency and attempted to book the flight and hotel. Thanks to Revo's timely message, I could move quickly on getting my travel arrangements made.

All seemed to be going fairly well, given that I had such short notice for the trip. My agent managed to find a flight that thankfully didn't stop over in the States. Restriction-free passport or not, there are still some places I doubt I can go and chances I'm not willing to take. My agent also put a reservation in a hotel at Passay City; she did not recognize the name of the city that Revo told me he was staying in. Thinking that I had maybe misspelled it, we both made the assumption that he had meant Passay.

The flight was booked for February 12th, with return flight twenty-three days later, and the ticket information faxed to the passport office. I was now well on my way to leaving. The hotel was on hold, and I would not find out about it till the next day, but I was far from worried. I figured things would work themselves out but decided to focus my energies instead on how to explain to my daughter that I was leaving the country. The only time I had ever been separated from her for longer than two weeks had been four years earlier when I had been arrested. I had been restricted in my travel, due to my bail conditions, and was not allowed to leave the small town in the Ottawa Valley that I was being detained in. As my daughter was in Toronto on the day of my arrest, I was not able to go to her, and, understandably, her father was hesitant to bring her to me. There ensued a three-week mini-adventure involving interfering family members, Children's Services, and outright miscommunication between everybody. The whole distressing process did work itself out in the end, and it was ultimately through the help of both Children's Services and my arresting officer that my ex-husband was finally convinced that he should bring my daughter to me.

It is strange to think that only after the system had failed me completely, and only after I had been forced to act out of desperation, that my faith in that same system would be renewed and made stronger. In this instance, it was either my ex-husband or a member of his family who had called Children's Services on me. It was also in this instances that Children's Services, after meeting me, apologized for intruding and then actively acted on my behalf to have my daughter returned. Combine their belief that I was no threat to my child, and the efforts of the detective who had arrested me in contacting my ex-husband and explaining that he was violating our custody agreement, and—voilá! My baby girl was once again safely in my arms.

I would like to point out that at the time I was disgusted and angered by the whole affair; yet, looking back on it now I harbour no ill will toward my ex-husband for trying to protect our child. It is, after all, his undeniable love for her that makes him such a wonderful father. I can be proud to say that my baby's daddy will always put his daughter's safety and happiness first. So, you see, we grow, we lose, we learn… It's a good thing, and for that gift we must learn to also say thank you.

This time, however, I would be leaving her by choice—not something I am comfortable doing. As I said, she is only eleven, and I thought it would be many years yet before I would be willing to leave her side. It was with much trepidation that I looked toward telling her I had to go. When I picked her up from school, we were intending to go directly to her dance class, but the instructor called asking if we could push the lesson back an hour. I agreed, thinking it would give me time to explain matters as best I could. As we were driving toward my daughter's favourite restaurant, the phone rang again. This time it was Sophia, wondering how plans were progressing.

We got into (with my daughter in the car beside me) an in-depth conversation about my upcoming trip. I at one point told Sophia that at least now I didn't have to find a way to broach the topic with my little girl, as she had inadvertently done it for me. My discussion on the phone was more than enough information for Maddi to base her yay or nay on. So when it was time for us to sit down and eat, I merely had to ask her if she had any questions. She had only one. How long?

I told her that it would likely be a three-week trip, but that I would be back in time for her birthday. She seemed heartened by the notion, but said quite pointedly that she would miss me. I agreed wholeheartedly and told her leaving her would be the hardest part. I did reassure her, however, that part of my reason for going was to secure a better quality of life for us both in the hopes that in the end we would be free to spend more time together. After dinner we went on to her dance class, and as she was partaking of her lesson I took the opportunity to call her dad. Again I found myself looking up at a rather large wall I myself had created. How would he take the whole idea? I needed his support in this. He would have to be willing to alter his schedule in order to accommodate three full weeks of child care. He would have to make arrangements to travel inconveniently to the other side of the city to accommodate her dance lessons. I was leery of asking this extremely large favour of him. He owed me nothing, really, and had every reason to be selfish and unaccommodating.

Prior to our divorce I had put him through hell, but I had been working very hard over the last few years to establish a safe, communicative relationship with him for the benefit of our child. I had repeatedly bent over backwards to make things easier for him in the hopes it would prevent confrontation. I had willingly signed off on child support so that he would have the money to go back to school. I had often altered plans with my daughter so that plans he had made at the same time could be realized. I had allowed my daughter (much to the disgust of my family) to call his girlfriend Mom; that had cut very deeply, but I felt it was for my daughter to decide who she would allow into her life. I put my faith in my belief that my daughter would know me in her heart as her mother and that that bond between us could not be threatened. Even though I didn't believe that the woman not yet married to my ex had any right to be called Mom, I did believe and have faith in my own child's intuitive abilities. She would know in her heart who did and did not love and care for her. In my mind, any extra love given my child was ultimately a good thing.

My friends and family did not agree with my methods. Being, however, the black sheep in the flock, I continued to go my own way and ignore their advice to stand up to this man. It seemed my perseverance would pay off in the end. When I finally got up the nerve to call Saul, he encouraged me to take the opportunity presented and set about assuring me that we could work out the details as we went. He also gave me some good advice with regards to phones and using them abroad. He did not question me on particulars, for which I was grateful, but instead he put faith in the fact that I was being honest with my intentions. I was yet again shocked and amazed and extremely grateful to him for his understanding. I hope someday to get the opportunity to apologize and admit to him that my treatment of him during the end of our marriage was disgraceful. I could have found better ways to deal with the issues we had, but I was young and had much to learn. Our divorce, however, has taught me much more than I believe our marriage could ever have, and I am extremely thankful for going through the experience of both. I doubt very much that he has the same view, but then, I have never bothered to ask him. I suppose someday I should, perhaps on the same day I say thank you for helping me get this far.

After Mad's lesson I had a brief discussion with the instructor about the upcoming trip. I was fortunate that the mother of Mad's dance partner was also present and agreed to change the day and time of dance classes during the period I would be away. I very much wanted to make things easier for Saul. I owe him so much more, I realize, but at least I could start with giving him that.

We were on our way home, and I wanted to confirm that my daughter was okay with the whole idea. I explained that I was very concerned about her nonchalant attitude toward my upcoming trip. I made it very clear that I value her opinion with regard to the decisions I make, as those decisions ultimately affect her as well. Yes, I used those words, all of them. As I have already told you, she understands, as all children do, much more than we give them credit for. Her answer gave me strength, courage, and reassurance. I told you at the beginning of this story what she said, but when you put it into context it is that much more enlightening. Given all that we have been through as a family, both together and apart, it is remarkable to know that it took being willing to leave it all behind and follow my heart to find out just exactly where my heart was. God bless the unselfish wisdom that can be found in the eyes of a child, as it is through those eyes that we are able to see the true beauty and love that surrounds us.

The *Six of Wands* suggests my power today lies in validation. I rise to the occasion and am motivated or confident to take it to the next level by the recognition, admiration, praise, or accolades put on my achievements or personal success. I am newly aware of and proud of my sense of empowerment, and I transform through acceptance.

Chapter 10
Black and White vs. Colour
Logic and Reason vs. Me

My day started out with an average routine of getting up, showering, hopping in the car, and dropping by Tim's on my way to the next appointment. (I skipped over checking my email, as I figured he was either still on his way or having just arrived, had not had time to send me anything.)

This time it was the doctor I was off to see, a follow-up on a CT scan done three months earlier. It had been a part of a series of doctors' visits and tests ordered in a futile attempt to find the cause of blinding headaches I had been suffering from for over a year. I don't even know why I bothered going. I had finally had surgery, and the headaches were now gone. It had been a dental surgeon, of all things, who had accidentally stumbled on the probable cause and taken a long-shot chance at operating to cure it. He didn't even think at the time that it would work, but I had agreed to it anyway. I was long past caring how they took the pain away. I only knew I wanted it gone. I was now fully recovered and was having trouble remembering what it had been like to have a blinding headache twenty-four hours a day. Honestly, it was one of those things I didn't mind forgetting. Still, I thought I had better follow through with getting my test results, figuring that it would be good to know if there was anything else wrong with my head.

While I was on my way, I got a call from an old friend. I had given him a shout the previous morning, before I had wandered off to the passport office. That call to him had been the reason I had been late getting there; it was the reason I had been forced to sit waiting there for over an hour. I wasn't even sure why I had called him, except maybe I was still looking for a little confirmation that I was on the right path. Deacon is the one person in my life I can absolutely count on to play the devil's advocate, keeping me reasonable and grounded with his steadfast belief in logic. The man's very presence in my life is a paradox and therefore should not be; yet, he remains a huge part of my world, and I am very grateful for his honesty and his guidance. We had started dating shortly after the fire, while I was still living in the Ottawa Valley.

I still remember the first time we met. It had been a blind date set up by his sister, and his reaction to my appearance was comical, at best.

I had hopped into his truck, and he had taken one look at me and said quite bluntly, "I don't usually date girls with tattoos and shit in their face."

His reference was to the piercings I have, but even though he was blunt as hell, he was at least still smiling when he said it.

I told him that I didn't usually date people without, so we were both taking a chance. Right then, I knew if nothing else came of this I had at least made friends with someone I could respect. Respect him I do, and date we did. He stuck by me through my arrest, with much risk of condemnation by his peers, and we continued to try to make it work even after I moved to a city four hours away. It couldn't last, though, not in that way, and it was on one of my biweekly overnight visits that the romantic part of our relationship came to an end. I remember that night very clearly. We were lying in his bed talking about me leaving in the morning, when he decided for his own reasons to cut me loose.

"You know, Vick, it can't continue." He tried to say it gently, but gentle doesn't come naturally to him, and as he talked I was relieved to hear the strength return to his voice. "I can't take care of you there. I can't watch over you and protect you when you are so far away. You shouldn't be alone all the time. It isn't right for someone like you to be alone. You are never going to find someone else if you are still here clinging to me, and I really need to know that you are safe. I need to let you go so you can find someone who can take care of you … someone who will love you."

I could have argued with him, tried to make him see reason, but it felt wrong to do so. I understood him then as I understand him now, and I know that in this one moment of agonizing openness he was making an extremely difficult and selfless decision.

"I don't think this is what God wants for you. You are not meant to be stuck here. There is so much you can do." He did at this point manage to lower his voice. "Do you understand? Can you let me let you go?"

I did understand, and I couldn't tell him because I couldn't trust my voice, so instead I snuggled up to him and, putting my head on his chest, I slowly nodded my head as the tears started to flow. I laid there like that, silently crying in his arms until he fell asleep. Then I offered up a little prayer in the hopes I could give him one more gift.

For years he had been suffering from stomach pain that had at times disabled and distracted him from his very active, very passionate role as an adoring father to his two little girls. I lay there with my hand on his stomach and I concentrated all my energy into healing him of this affliction.

I prayed to the powers that be that he be allowed to be cured of this ailment. He is a selfless man and deserves the strength of body to go along with his intensely powerful soul. I never spoke of it to him, but I have often asked him over the past couple years how his tummy is. Every time we speak his answer is the same: "No problems, Vick; don't know why, though, I haven't changed any of my bad habits, but it seems to have gone away."

He would not believe it if he ever read this story. He is too strongly chained to the here and now. Thankfully, though, he never *will* read this book, so I won't ever have to explain my reasons for bringing him into the tale. He would be pissed at me, I assure you, as he very much values his quiet, humble existence. He would not welcome the intrusion of the outside world. It would cause him to flee and find a shack in the bush, no doubt, in which he could hide. That is why I say he will never read this book. He does not believe in mixing business with personal. Though he fully acknowledges and accepts my artistic side, he rails against the idea that he may somehow be part of or an inspiration to that art. This is also why I say that his existence in my life is a paradox.

He sees the world in black and white. There are no grey areas. Life is either truth or lie, no in-between. You either live that life in the right or you do wrong. He will not acknowledge or accept any choice that is anything but one or the other. The road of life for him is well defined by his principles and integrity. Every step forward is thought through carefully and analytically. He weighs the pros and cons of his decisions, picks apart possible consequences, and then makes his decision based on the ethics of those decisions. Ethics and morals are his signposts on the road of life, and there is not much room on his chosen path for deviation or drastic change of direction. He is, in all honesty, my exact opposite—and I love and cherish him deeply for it.

What makes our relationship so undeniably strange is that he seems at once appalled and fascinated by my view of the world. He does not understand how I can so openly attack life with seemingly no regard for the future. He does not understand the colourful spectrum that I see when I look at life and all its possibilities. He does not understand my distaste for reality—and not understanding is not something I think he is used to. I doubt very much, in fact, that he has ever encountered anything or anyone in his life who he could relate to less. Being who and what he is, his natural instinct should be to remove himself from anything that threatens to endanger or destroy his solid belief in logic and reason. Yet he remains in my life a close friend who is always there if needed. He seems unable to remove himself completely, and, though he refuses to read my work or see things my way, he continues to be an inspiration to me in a strangely detached way. He sees in me a goodness that I had ignored for a long time myself, and, through his faith in that positive half of my soul, he has constantly encouraged me toward being a better person.

The very thing he tries so hard not to be—my teacher, my guide, my inspiration—he manages to accomplish by his insistence that it is not his role. As our friendship has grown and strengthened I have found myself exceptionally grateful to have him in my life. Even if we are not meant to be a couple, I love him dearly, and he is one of the few men in my life who I can see myself growing old with.

I have a vision of us sitting by a lake in our later years thinking back and laughing at all the previous stupidity that was us. I can picture us both, beers in hand, lounging against the backs of padded chairs, swapping tales of "you remember when…" and "did I ever tell you the story of…?" It is a comfortable prospect for the future. Though he insists that he will never marry again, I doubt very much we will need any kind of vow to hold us together. They say you are supposed to marry and grow old with the man in your life who is your best friend, and I can quite honestly say I am content with merely the *growing old with* part. As I said, the two of us are happy to just be, and that by itself is a beautiful thing.

I would like to address one more remarkable characteristic that Deacon possesses, but, as it is of a sensitive nature, I will try to approach it gently. I would like to point out that I am merely making observations here, not judgments or condemnations. The world is the way it is for a reason; I support and embrace religious and spiritual diversity. Yet the issue I am about to tackle has to be mentioned eventually, so I will take the risk and hope against hope that you receive it in the spirit in which it is given. Now, Deacon is so special because he is a follower of God's law, although he views the law as merely an exceptionally respectable guideline for his own personal moral code. The man quite literally lives by the Ten Commandments; this to me is a remarkable feat for anyone living in today's society. If you don't believe it would be difficult, then look them up…

I can think of a few, off the top of my head, that the average person has trouble with.

THREE: You shall not take the name of the Lord your God in vain

I am sure I do not have to explain this to you. Don't claim you don't hear it that often, because I hear it all the time. Don't claim you don't do it; I do it, and many others in my world do it; hell I've even heard priests and ministers do it (oh, shocking, isn't it?). Now, I don't have any clue what the consequences for disobeying are but that is not my concern. The point that I am trying to make is that Deacon somehow manages to live his life by these rules, and I have to marvel at the discipline needed.

FOUR: Remember the Sabbath Day, to keep it holy

Oops! Does that mean we are not to be at work on Sunday? Hmmm... it sounds pretty straightforward, but then, maybe it just means we need to make sure we put aside a few hours on Sunday to go to a church and worship; then again it does say *day*, so...

TEN: You shall not covet your neighbour's house; you shall not covet your neighbour's wife, or his male servant, or his female servant, or his ox, or his donkey, or anything else that is your neighbour's

Well, now, all we do is covet, isn't it? *He has a shiny new car, so I want a shiny new car. He has a big, beautiful house, so I should have a big, beautiful house.* We are constantly seeing those better off than we are, and, instead of saying, "Wow, good for them," or "They must have worked really hard for that," we instead ask ourselves "Why can't we have that too?"

TWO: You shall not make for yourself a carved image: any likeness of anything that is in heaven above, or that is in the earth beneath, or that is in the water under the earth

Now, I can only take this to mean that we are not to have false idols... and, you know, this is one of those times when I am going to keep my mouth shut and let you figure it out on your own...

You will, in time, ask your own questions on this one, and you will find your own answers.

All I know for fact is that these commandments were in Exodus, in the Bible's Old Testament, and, though they are commonly known to be God's law, given by God for his people to follow, I have so far only found one man who does follow them. What he was doing with someone like me, I will never understand.

It was with all of this in mind that I had called Deacon on my way to the passport office the previous day. I figured if anyone in my life would have a good reasonable argument for me not to go it would be him. I told him about my three month leave from work, my intentions to write a book, and my crazy plan to go to the Philippines. He knew, perhaps more than anyone, the risk I was taking. I would be using money I had put aside to secure my child's future, and there was no reasonable way to conclude that I would ever get that money back. That risk was against all the fundamental principals he himself used to dictate his own life: safety, security, and structured planning for the future. I should have, could have, and originally intended to set that money aside for my daughter's education, and it was a huge leap of illogical faith in what I viewed to be my possible destiny. He knew all of this, and I half expected him to ask me where the hell I had come up with such a harebrained idea. Much to my confusion and delight, he did not. Instead, he joined me in my leap of faith and temporarily spread his own wings and jumped with me off a cliff into the unknown.

"Okay," he quipped over the phone, "So you have to go to the other side of the world to write a book. It sounds like something you would think necessary. In fact, it is very probably something you should do. It might be very good for you."

I was speechless. Here he was telling me to go for it instead of lecturing me yet again about how twisted my view of reality was. Perfect, I thought. The one person I can rely on to bring me back to the real world, and he decides now to join me in the twilight zone. Great, now what do I do? Hmmm… I guess I better go. All this had run through my head that morning, as he spoke to me over the line, encouraging me to follow my dreams. He did also suggest that I keep my eyes and ears open for possible problems along the way. He also mentioned that I should be prepared to pay a price for the freedom of exploring the world and the opportunity that had been presented.

"There is always a cost. You know that nothing in this world is free."

I promised him that I would indeed be careful, and when I hung up the phone I was thinking that I would next talk to him upon returning to Canada. Not so. As he had apparently taken it upon himself to at least make sure I made it there in one piece, he called me again while I was on my way to my appointment.

"Hey, how long are you going for?" he questioned me over the line, not even bothering to say hello.

"Nice to talk to you too," I shot back. "Not that it matters much, I'm thinking, but I am going from the twelfth to the ninth. Why?"

"Yeah Vik, that's the thing—it does matter." He sounded slightly exasperated. "If you're there longer than twenty-one days, you need a visa."

"What the hell?" I asked, "My travel agent didn't say a damn thing about a visa."

"Figures, good thing I called then, eh? Look, I can't talk long; I'm at work," he explained quickly "I went online yesterday and checked out the information from the consulate, and any visit longer than twenty-one days needs a visa."

"Well, what the hell do I do?" I asked, feeling a bit panicked. "How do I get one? How long does it take?"

"Relax, it can be expedited," he explained again. "You can get one in twenty-four hours usually, if you are willing to pay extra."

"Great, no problem; I can do that." I was now thinking I was in the clear, until he threw another curve at me.

"Yes, but you need a passport to get a visa. When did you say you were getting your passport?" he asked, again sounding rushed.

"Um, I think I'm screwed," I mumbled "I get my passport on the eleventh and I'm on the plane on the twelfth. So…"

"Yep, you're screwed!" he agreed with me, and then he started chuckling to himself. "It's a good thing I decided to stick around, then, eh? Look, I do have to go, but I'll send you the consulate number in TO and a link through your email, so you can check the site out yourself. Good luck, eh?"

Soon after he hung up, the number for the consulate came through in a text message, and as soon as the car was parked I started dialing. I figured there was no need to panic yet. I still had a couple of days, so I should be okay. I kept trying to call while I was waiting in the doctor's office. It was one of the rare moments when you are grateful that the doctor is never on time. I tried calling again after the good doctor had seen me and had given me a clean bill of health. I called again while waiting in line upstairs to make an appointment at the travelers' clinic for my shots and twice again on my walk back to the car. I had to leave it alone while I drove, but as soon as I was parked where I was picking up my new computer I tried one more time. Still nothing. The line was busy yet again. For the moment it looked as if I was not going to get anywhere.

Eventually, I managed to complete the few errands I had been running and found my way back to the house. I immediately went online and into my email to get the link to the consulate. I went to the site in question, and, as I started reading, my heart started to sink. The requirements were fairly well explained, but there seemed to be way too many for my liking. By the time my boyfriend Reynard arrived home at 6:00 PM, I was pretty convinced my trip was about to be cancelled. One of the things I needed was proof that I had enough financial security to stay for an extended length of time. It was a reasonable request, no doubt, but, as I had neither a credit card nor a large amount of money in the bank, I really had no way to provide the consulate with that kind of information. Yep, I was most assuredly screwed. When Rey walked into the bedroom, I was sitting on my bed with my head in my hands, trying to figure out what to do. I explained briefly what my problem was, and as I was verbalizing my needs I came up with an answer.

So I got on the phone to the travel agency, thinking I'd just change the flight and shorten my stay. Easy solution, right? Oh no, not for me. Turns out the office is closed, and the only person left there answering the phone is an unlicensed trainee left behind at the end of the day to clean up. To make matters worse, my agent has the next few days off. On the upside, the sweet young lady volunteers to try to contact the airport and make them aware of my situation. She explains that if she leaves a note in the office one of the other agents might be able to assist me. The young woman puts me on hold, and, as I'm waiting, I am wondering to myself if this might be a sign I shouldn't go. After about ten minutes of silence, a friendly familiar voice came on the line.

"Julia!" I exclaimed, "I thought you had gone home."

She explained that she had indeed gone home and had been almost to her door when she had realized she had forgotten something and had been forced to return to the office. She apologized profusely about the mix-up with the visa and promised to fix it immediately if I didn't mind holding a bit longer. I certainly did not, and I leaned my head back against the pillows on my bed and closed my eyes in relief. I didn't have long to wait. She was back soon enough with news that she had changed the flight and would have new tickets for me in the office the next day.

"Oh yes, and by the way," she added, "Your hotel fell through, but another one of much better quality had a cancellation and is willing to give you a room for only twenty dollars per night more than the original hotel. So, really, you'll be staying in a five-star for the price of a three-star. I tried to call you earlier, but your phone was busy, and, since they need an answer by tomorrow morning, I'm glad I have you on the phone now. I can call them as soon as we are done here. That is, of course, if you want to take it."

Well, hell yes, I took it, and I was yet again reassured that I'd be making my way across the ocean. Of course, the entire time I was on the phone, my boyfriend (is it fair to continue calling him that?) had been standing by my bed listening. We had finally had a chance a few days prior to briefly discuss my trip, but I had not gone into an in-depth explanation about my reasons for going. He was still confused over my quick decision to leave, but he had decided for reasons of his own to support me. Just as he was turning to leave the room, he made a suggestion.

"You know, life would be a lot easier for you if you had a credit card. These things would not be such a hassle." He smiled a little. "I know you can't get one, but I can get you a copy of mine. I would feel better knowing you had an emergency backup plan."

I started to protest, but he was already on the phone to his credit card company. By the time I had followed him into the living room, it was too late. He was already hanging up, telling me, "It should be here in a couple of days." The idea made me extremely uncomfortable. I was torn between feelings of gratitude and guilt. He was trying so hard to help me do this thing, even though he really had no idea what the thing was that I was doing.

It was time for me to sit down and be as honest as I could be. He deserved to know that this new path I was starting to walk down just might lead me away. To be honest, it already had, but it was one of those times when a gentle half-truth would cause less damage. I was concerned about destroying him. Although he was in his mid-thirties, he had never shared his life with another woman. He had had plenty of girlfriends, but never one he had lived with. We had struggled with the change to both our lives when we got together, but, though the road had been rough, we had both assumed that it was going to last. I had made it clear several times that I would not remarry, but it remained an unspoken presumption that this was indeed a long-term commitment, just with no legal paper required.

I knew now the change that was coming. I could not continue living the way I had and still move toward my future in the arts. I needed to be free to wander and discover the world, and it worried me that accepting that freedom would mean leaving certain parts of my life behind. A much as I would like to think I could still be myself and continue to play a domestic role, I was becoming more aware every day of the impossibility of balancing both.

It also occurred to me that there was no way I could give up even a remote chance that Rev and I could be together. I had spent long, lonely nights hoping and praying for that other half of my soul to somehow find his way to me. Looking into the eyes of my past, present, and future had awakened in me a burning desire to stand by his side. I could not—would not—deny myself. In my mind I already belonged to this man; heart, body, and soul, I was his. I always had been. I had shared my life with others, given them as much of myself as I was able, but I had never been able to bring myself to give it all. There had always been a reason to hold back, the knowledge that someday I would be faced with a choice. Someday a person would come to take me away from my world and pull me into his. I had never cared if it would be a man or a woman; I knew that when the time came I would go.

It was a painful realization, if only because I was desperate to avoid hurting Reynard, a man I had grown to love. I resolved to explain as much as I could to him. I sat down in the living room with him and started to talk.

"I am not sure that the card was a good idea; I am not comfortable with using your money to make this trip. It makes me feel as if I am being unfair to you."

He was surprised at that. "But, why? You need a safety net. Hell, I need you to have a safety net. Besides," he grinned at me, "It's not like I won't be able to find you to get the money back. I know where you live, remember?"

It made me sad to think about what I was about to do, but it was necessary, so I continued.

"You don't understand: this trip, this journey, it is something I have to do to save myself and get back to who I am. I don't know where it will lead or what kind of impact it will have on my future. I do know that it will lead to change, and in order for that change to occur I must give myself over to it with everything I have got. I can't hold back or be afraid about what might come of this. Do you understand what I am trying to say?"

He still looked confused. "Of course I do, and I said I would help in any way I can. Why are we discussing this?"

Poor soul, he wanted to support me, and, in the blindness that his love for me was causing, he was unable to see the possible danger to himself.

"Look, hon, what I'm trying to say is that I have to commit all of my time and all of my energy to this book and to this trip."

He grinned again. "I know that—I've hardly seen you for days, and you're not even gone yet."

In my mind I was thinking, *Oh, but I am, a part of me is already on the other side of the world …* I wanted to make it clear to him if I could.

"Try to understand this," I said pleadingly, "I no longer have the energy or the time to dedicate to you, this house, or our relationship. I need to harbour that energy and use it for my work."

His eyes flashed for one brief second of realization and then glazed back over. It appeared he had chosen to return to a state of denial. "Once you're back, it will be fine. Go do what you have to do, and then we will go from there. Okay?"

Stubborn, obstinate creature.

"I don't know when I'll be back," I mumbled with my eyes downcast.

"What the hell are you talking about?" he groaned. "Your flight is back on the fifth."

I looked up, forcing myself to look him in the eye, "I am talking about the fact that I do not know when or even if I will be able to come back to this on an emotional level. I am not sure anymore this is the life I was meant to be living."

"Oh," he said quietly and moved his body back on the couch. "Well, can we not just wait and see?" he said hopefully. "I mean, you go, do what you have to do, come back, and we'll deal with it then. Okay? You said yourself you don't know what's going to happen, so don't assume this trip will change anything. Keep in touch while you are there, and let me know you are safe. I'll be waiting for you when you get back. It will work out." He added angrily, "And take the damn credit card with you, so I will at least believe you are safe."

I realized I would have to accept his offer…

All I could do was sit there and stare in wonderment at this intelligent, reasonable man suddenly being reduced to a creature suffering from unreasonable denial of fact. I gave up the argument. I wasn't going to win. Part of me didn't really want to, but eventually the truth of our situation would have to come out—whatever that turned out to be.

I went to Madison's room and logged in to send Rev a quick message.

> *Hey sweets,*
>
> *Hope all is going well over there and that u r getting settled in—I also hope u will be checking your email, since I don't wanna call you and wake you up if you are finally getting some rest. If you get the chance, give me a shout; I know the time zones are way off, but I don't care if you wake me up. I can always sleep later. Everything seems to be working out here; the flight is booked, the hotel that I*

had reserved at 100 a night which was a 3-star fell through, but then the 5-star hotel that we looked at yesterday that wanted 210 a night called my agent today and told her they had a cancellation and would give it to me for 120 a night, so all is well.

Thanks to my friend Deacons' quick thinking, and the random fact of the travel agent forgetting something at the office and having to go back, a possible problem with regards to me needing a visa was solved today—we changed my return date so I won't need a visa this trip—and now I have the option of getting a 58-day travel visa later if I need or want to go back (did you know they will only issue you one per person?) I am learning quickly.

I was just talking to Maddi online and she said to say hi to you so, "Hi"—she is being so totally supportive and selfless about this whole adventure—you are right, she was my open door. She has brought me back from many a dark dangerous place more times than I can count—I really am blessed. Well, hon, I will hopefully hear from you soon. I will be running around like crazy till I leave, but I'll check my mail at random times and my phone is with me always. See you soon, xo

I went to bed shortly thereafter to lie awake and ponder what would come of this. Before I went I checked out my daily tarot, and, as I read, I let out a little audible groan…

The *Nine of Swords* suggests that my power today lies in realizing that I am not my mistakes. I can't do this alone or pretend anymore. The illusion of comfort in denial or sacrifice is no longer mine. There is no shame in my suffering, no healing in silent torment. It is here at the surreal crossroads of the "soul search," where dawning truth meets the anguish of overwhelming resistance in mind over matter, that I can finally wake up, change my mind, let go of what no longer works, or my own losses or choices. I am empowered by intense acknowledgement or epiphany, and my virtue is gratitude or relief in recognition.

Chapter 11

Eyeliner, Angels, and Backseat Drivers

Shortly after waking, once I had a coffee in hand, I took the time to check my email. I was glad to see that Rev had made it safely, but a little concerned about some of what he had written. I was pretty sure I did not want this piece of art I intended to create to become political; I personally can't stand politics and avoid the subject whenever possible.

Unfortunately, my other half has always somehow managed to immerse himself in the politics of whatever age he happens to be in, and, as much as the peaceful priestess in me would prefer to initiate change through positive spiritually based inspiration and enlightenment, it seemed to me that the two were interconnected. One issue could not be addressed without the other, a fact that irritates me no end—but then, I suppose that is why there are two of us. I can't imagine trying to tackle both at the same time without help; I think exhaustion would put an end to the battle long before the government or the churches even bothered to try. However, at the time I read the email we had only begun our journey together; there were several realizations yet to come, and at the time I knew very little about where we were headed. I did know that we had something we were meant to do, I knew that we were meant to do it together, and I knew we had been down this road before. I also knew that my instincts were telling me that becoming ensnared in politics could pose a threat to both of us, a risk I myself was not yet willing to take.

Vik,

It costs 210 dollars a night at a hotel and I found out today it cost 250 dollars a month to OWN *a condo. Because of the recession, real estate prices dropped so much. Well, it's 9 pm here, and I've survived day one and made it to the evening, so my body adjusted extremely fast. My uncle told me it would take me a week, but I think you're right when you said your body will tell you where you belong. After only a day, I've almost fully adjusted.*

Such a weird thing happened today. We were driving, and the traffic was just horrendous. My cousin's fiancé was driving, and we started talking about the corrupt government. I guess I got a bit enthusiastic and began talking about ways to improve the infrastructure. Then, out of nowhere, as a joke, my cousin yelled, "Vote for Revo!" and her fiancé told me to consider running for congress. I feel, however, there will be a new medium of power that will circumvent the use of politics. The people do not need a voice; they need an ear to listen to them.

So far in the last 3 days I've only had a total of around 11 hours of sleep, but my energy levels are extremely high.

I've written a bit. When I type it seems as if something takes over my hands and types away. The weather is so great here. I'm so lucky to be staying where I am. I'm being treated really well, and I know not a moment of it can be taken for granted.

Your dearest always,

R

I figured maybe I would get lucky, and he would stay on safe ground if he focused on his belief that he could inspire people through the arts—but there was no point in trying to give him direction. He would more than likely go his own way regardless of what I said. Besides, I had chosen to leave my life for the man—the least I could do was offer my support, regardless of how uncomfortable the idea of politics made me. I dropped him a quick line, then got ready to go. I had a long day ahead of me yet and much to do…

R,

It seems so crazy that a condo can be so cheap, when it costs so much for just one room, but I guess it doesn't really surprise me—the economy between nations is so far out of balance because there are too many different factions struggling for power and control of the almighty dollar. It's 3 pm here, and I have been running full-tilt trying to get all the arrangements made. I'm glad your body has adjusted so nicely and that you are not completely exhausted. Your family sounds like they will stand behind you no matter what crazy decision you make—which is an incredible feeling. I would know, because I am getting the same support here. I will have my hotel info for you later today, but I have my flight info for you now, so you know well in advance when I am coming. My flight leaves here at 12:15 am on the 13th with a 2-hr stop in Hong Kong, then on to Manila. My flight should touchdown in Manila at 5 am on the 14th—so I guess u r right: I will be seeing you on Valentine's day. I was curious about the significance of the date, so I looked it up and found out that Valentine's day was originally a pagan celebration honouring life and fertility, but it was the Catholic Church that changed the meaning as well as the date—the original holiday was apparently on the 15th, so, hey, we have two days to celebrate life and love. Let me know when you can if you will be able to meet me at the airport—I'd feel safer with you there, but, like I said, I know you have a lot of things to do and people to see. Enjoy your visits and your adventures, but please stay safe—we still have so much left to do. Keep in touch

Yours then, now, and always.

A quick shower, then back in the car with Timmies in hand, and on the road to another new and strange encounter. The fact that I was driving toward this particular destination at all was really rather odd. For some strange reason, I had gotten it in my head a few weeks prior that I should get my eyeliner permanently tattooed on. This was an extremely strange decision, as I am generally a low-maintenance type of girl. Even working in an industry where appearance can translate to dollars (if you look good, people tend to tip more), I had never been one to spend a lot of time on hair and makeup. Not that I don't want to be attractive, but I really can't be bothered with all the effort involved.

I am still, however, a woman, and occasionally it is expected of me to put a little effort into my looks. This had recently started to pose a problem, as the vision in my right eye was deteriorating rapidly. It was, as a result, becoming increasingly difficult to put eyeliner on without completely making a mess of things. Still, I am not one to turn to extreme measures to improve my outer beauty. I am, however, rather partial to the way my eyes look when they are lined in black. They are a unique hazel that tends to change to reflect whatever I am wearing. When lined in black, though, they cease being merely interesting and become darkly intense eyes, eyes that I have been told by many give people the impression that I can see right through to their souls. I rather like the idea of being able to enter a person so deeply merely by looking at them. It's not with the intent to invade their inner being, you understand, but I am fascinated with humans and spend a great deal of time studying them. I rely on my eyes to in effect hypnotize others into being more open and honest with me. They have always been my most striking feature, but with a little help in the makeup department they become a useful tool in my exploration of the human psyche, a tool I was now in danger of losing.

I had spent days looking online and questioning friends, trying to find out if the procedure was even safe. If there was too much risk involved it would be a "no go," but I had discovered that it was in fact safe, and I decided to go for it. I had searched several sites online for clinics that specialized in that kind of work. For some reason, I had put the number for the first site I came to in my phone. I then went through about fifteen more sites before returning again to the first. Something in the name drew me in, and I bookmarked the site and decided that if I ever got the urge, she was the lady I would call.

I had gotten the urge. Sitting outside the bank in my car one morning while waiting for Sophia to do her banking, I had one of those random spur-of-the-moment ideas that end up leading to an enlightening encounter of the spiritual kind.

Today was the day. As I drove, I went over in my head all the things I had done in the last few days. I had a good hour of driving to lose myself in thought: conversations I had had with friends, along with all the little signs and symbols that seemed to be pointing the way, ran through my mind. Several of them had been extremely strange and seemingly coincidental. It was during my reflection on these signs that I had a momentary loss of faith. How could I be sure I was doing the right thing in going? Even though I felt a sense of direction for the novel I was aspiring to write, my faith in my ability to actually finish it was dwindling. All the support I was getting was amazing, but I reasoned that the support was coming from the people in my life who were only in my life because they always *had* supported me. I also reasoned that I could have misinterpreted all the little signs and portents. Perhaps they meant something else, or perhaps they meant nothing at all. I had prayed for a sign of some kind, and it seemed I had been given many, but, again, how could I be sure? What if I went ahead with this, investing a great deal of time and energy, and then nothing came of it? How would I be able to justify risking my daughter's future security on the chance that I would be a success? Doubt crept in and soon threatened to consume me. Really, it wasn't too late to change my mind. Was it? I was completely torn in two. *Do I stay or do I go?* I was starting again to doubt my sanity, so, in a last-ditch effort to hold onto it, I offered up another prayer to the powers that be. I drove the car and spoke to the air. I started by being thankful for the opportunity, but explained that I was still suffering from uncertainty. Was there any way, and I realize I was asking a lot, that I could get a more definitive sign?

When I think back on it now, I feel I was being selfish, but at the time I really needed to know. I mean, let's face it, signs and symbols aside, though many of us talk to God on a regular basis, it isn't as though he is likely to talk back. He doesn't often lean over your shoulder and whisper sweet nothings in your ear, and you are not about to get the chance and sit with him over tea and ask his opinion on world issues. It just doesn't work that way. Guidance comes through more indirect means, and, unless our hearts and eyes are open, that guidance is easy to miss. Even with an open heart, even when we are able to see the signs, they are sometimes difficult to accept. This was the problem I was having.

I had recently acknowledged that I was now no longer driving the car that was taking me down the road of life. I was, it seemed now, in the passenger seat but was still trying to clutch at the wheel. I was hesitant to relinquish my control over my direction and destination. The problem is that a car is not meant to have more than one driver. Too many hands on the wheel can have disastrous consequences. Thankfully, I was blessed, and God took his eyes off the road ahead long enough to look at me and shout, "Let go of the wheel before you make me crash the car!"

I had not yet had the benefit of this warning, however, when I pulled up in front of the house of pain. I call it that only because, man, it really hurts having a bunch of needles rapidly and repeatedly piercing tender flesh. I knocked on the door and was greeted by a strikingly pretty woman by the name of Brigitte.

"Welcome to Auriel's Touch," she smiled. "Come on in; I'll be right with you."

The house/clinic had an extremely warm and inviting atmosphere, and I immediately felt my fears regarding the upcoming procedure melting slowly away. My other fears would not be far behind. She was right; I didn't have long to wait, and she was soon sitting with me going over options. Before I knew it I was on the table, and she was getting set up to begin adding a little extra colour to my life.

"Do you mind if I talk while I work?" she asked me, while she was leaning over my eye with the needle. "It makes the time go faster."

I told her I didn't mind at all; in fact it would probably be good to have something to distract me. As she talked and began to tell me a little about herself and her business, I began to feel an affinity with this woman. She and I had been through similar situations with our husbands and our divorces. We both had one child who seemed destined to follow us in the arts, and we had both had to struggle with our exes on the topic of allowing our children to pursue a career that was a little off the beaten path. She, too, had just reached a new level of comfortable communication with her ex and was in the midst of changing the direction of her career. The only difference, really, was that she was already successful and well established. That was probably due to the fact that she was also ten years older. Still, our stories were shockingly similar, and I enjoyed listening to her ramble on about life and love. She was also a very spiritual creature with a strong faith in God and his presence in her life. She told me repeatedly how she had been both blessed and challenged by him over the last few years. Each time she had been given a test of strength and character she had also been taught a valuable life lesson. She, like me, believed that with every painful tragedy that befalls us there is always the presence of something good and positive. It is this balance that helps us grow and prepares us for our next challenge or lesson. She also believed, apparently, in acknowledging the gifts that God gives us and in being grateful for opportunities as they are presented.

"Oh, and by the way." She smiled an angelic smile. "I am supposed to tell you that when God opens a door for you, it is appropriate that you to take the steps forward to walk through the door—stop doubting, stop fearing, and start walking."

What? What? Now, wait a minute. I had not told this lady a thing past the fact that I was a writer and that I was leaving soon to go to the Philippines to visit a friend. No details about my life or my intentions had been discussed. In fact, I had not had much of an opportunity to talk at all, as I had been given strict instructions not to move. Here I was, lying on my back, staring through teary eyes at the face of this woman and feeling like I had been kicked in the head. I was for the moment completely numb, and my mind wasn't able to function. Well, I had asked for it, hadn't I? I had wanted some kind of definitive sign.

You know, at this point I am thinking that there is one very obvious lesson to be learned: when God kicks you in the head to send you flying through the door that he has opened, you would probably do well to smile and say thank you as you are flying by!

Brigitte didn't give me a chance to recover. She merely continued on with her work, as if she had not said anything particularly interesting. I couldn't say anything. I still wasn't able to move, but it was now more a paralysis caused by a giant shock to the system than one caused by fear of a misplaced needle.

She started in about an interesting tale on how she had acquired her business name. It was a story that stuck with me and one I would need to make use of in the near future. She told me that when she decided to move her career out of the area of artistic tattooing and into the field in which she now worked she had decided she needed a name that better suited the work she was doing. As she would be working to cosmetically improve the appearance of people like burn victims to help them be more confident and comfortable within themselves, she needed a name that had a nurturing connotation. She also believed that she was being given the chance to work with people like that so she could help restore their faith and give them back their trust that they would find their way out of the darkness they were currently experiencing. Her problem was that she had no idea what name to use. After weeks of pondering, she decided to simply go online and look on the business registry to get ideas. When she went to her computer, however, she could not get it to turn on.

Not having much spare time in those days, what with changing careers and all, she put the idea aside. She had intended to get someone to look at her computer, but she forgot to do that as well. Approximately a week later, she had been walking through her living room and noticed a piece of paper lying on the floor. She bent to pick it up and realized that it was a list of all the archangels' names. It was a list she had kept in her room by her bedside for years and had no business being on the floor in her living room. One of the names seemed to draw her eye. No matter how many times she glanced away and then back to the list, her eyes always seemed to fall on Uriel. On a whim, she decided to go to the computer she had abandoned a week earlier and see if it would work, so that she could look up the meaning of the name Uriel. Here's what the site she found read.

> *To build self esteem and confidence, inner peace and tranquility; untangling knots of anger and fear and effecting peaceful resolution of personal problems, both social and professional; inspiration for*

nurses, doctors, counselors, teachers, judges, public servants, and everyone in the service of others.

All these things tied into the work she would be doing, and she decided to use the name. She noticed that there was a variation available for the spelling, a variation which she chose to use for her business name. I am not sure at the time she realized what she had done by choosing to add the *A*, but I intend to go back some day and ask her.

As I realized later in the day, when I finally looked it up, there is also an archangel Ariel, and, when combined, the two names represent the very core of whom and what this woman is. One thing that did strike me immediately was the association with water. I am a water sign, Rev is also a water sign, and it was across oceans I would soon travel to a land surrounded by water in the hopes of finding out where it was I was meant to be.

Symbolism has a crazy way of creeping up on you, and, when it does, it is best to be wary. Sometimes the presence and the seeming insistence of the message the symbol represents can leave you feeling completely powerless and overwhelmed. Really, it was a bit much, and though I left soon after, feeling grateful for being given the chance to meet her, I was a bit shaken. It was very hard to accept the idea that somebody like me, with all the bad things I had done haunting my past, could be forgiven, accepted, and openly guided by God.

I was again humbled at the thought. I found myself crying as I drove home and praying that in the end he would find me worthy of his faith.

I arrived home in late afternoon and decided to look the angels up online. I found a site, as I mentioned earlier, and discovered both angels Ariel and Uriel. I looked to a site called *Angel Focus* and read the following:

Ariel means "lion of God," and is often associated with lions. When Ariel is near you, you may begin seeing references to or visions of lions around you. Ariel is also associated with the wind. Found in books of Judaic mysticism, and cabalistic, Ariel works closely with King Solomon in conducting manifestation, spirit releasement and divine magic. Ariel also oversees the sprites, the nature angels associated with water. Ariel is involved with healing and protecting nature, including animals, fish and birds. If you find an injured bird or other wild animal that needs healing, call upon Ariel for help. Ariel also works closely with Raphael to heal animals in need."

Uriel means "'God is Light," "God's Light," and "Fire of God." Uriel is considered to be one of the wisest archangels because of his intellectual information, practical solutions, and creative insight.

Uriel warned Noah of the impending flood, helped the prophet Ezra to interpret mystical predictions about the coming Messiah, and delivered the cabal to humankind. He also brought the knowledge and practice of alchemy, and the ability to manifest from thin air as well as illuminate situations and give prophetic information and warnings. All this, considered Uriel's area of expertise, is divine magic, problem-solving, spiritual understanding, studies, alchemy, weather, earth changes, and writing. Considered to be the archangel who helps with earthquakes, floods, fires, hurricanes, tornadoes, natural disaster, and earth changes, Uriel is called on to avert such events or to heal and recover from their aftermath.

In the eighth century, the Christian Church became alarmed at the rampant and excessive zeal with which many of the faithful were revering angels. For some unknown reason, in 145 AD, under Pope Zachary, a Roman counsel ordered seven angels removed from the ranks of the Church's recognized angels; one of them was Uriel.

On another site, called *Connecting with the Light*, I found the following:

Ariel—Name means "lion or lioness of God." Ariel is known as the Archangel of the Earth, because she works tirelessly on behalf of the planets. Ariel oversees the elemental kingdom and helps in the healing of animals, especially the non-domesticated kind. Call upon Ariel to become better acquainted with the fairies, to help with environmental concerns, or to heal an injured wild bird or animal.

Uriel—He is the wise angel who sheds light on all darkness. When you are feeling depressed, angry, victimized, or confused, call on Uriel. He will come and pour his golden light over you. He will help you release anger, unforgiveness, and any other negative emotions that may be clouding your vision and judgment. He will help you find peace and answers.

Well, perhaps, in my dazed state of pain with multiple needles penetrating my eyelids, I had misheard. Perhaps Brigitte knew exactly who both angels were. In fact, I am sure now she did, but I still intend some day to go back and ask her. For the moment though, try to picture me silently sitting in front of my computer, eyes flying across the screen, "Ask and ye shall receive" would not stop repeating in my head.

I couldn't help myself. I had to share this story with someone, and I was soon on the phone with Sophia. I told her the entire tale, as crazy as it seemed, and waited for her response.

"So, I guess you've been told." I could hear the grin in her voice. "Honestly, it takes you long enough sometimes."

"Really, Soph?" I moaned, "It's been a weird day, and I'm thinking you are being just a little harsh."

"No," she shot back, "I don't think I am. Jesus boots. What more do you want for proof? You are the one who has been saying for years that there is no such thing as coincidence. You've been getting signs and guidance for weeks. You've had the support of everyone you know since you started this crazy quest, yet you have the balls to continue to question it. You dare ask for yet another sign."

Her words were angry, but her tone was not, and I knew she was only trying to rekindle the fire that she feared might be starting to go out.

"But, for God's sake, Soph! I'm a sinner, not a saint." I was getting a little annoyed.

"You have the mind of a criminal, yes, but we both know that your heart is pure," she said gently.

The thing was, she was right. I shouldn't have doubted, and I made a silent apology to God for losing sight of what he was offering. "Okay, you're right. I deserve that. I really do."

Her voice was soft. "Everybody else has faith in you. Don't you think it's time you had a little in yourself?"

As usual, I couldn't say much in argument. She is almost always right in her interpretation of situations. I was being extremely ungrateful, and it was time to stop asking "Why me?" and start saying "Thank you." Still, I wasn't sure what I could possibly do to be a positive influence and initiate change. I told Sophia this, expecting to get another earful. I was surprised to hear her agree.

"I don't know either," she admitted. "But I do believe that God will let you know what you need to know when you need to know it. I don't think you are meant to plan ahead. Hell, I don't think at this point it would make a difference. He'll take you wherever he wants. It is your job to go along and watch and learn from what he has to show you." She started to laugh, "Do you think you can stop him if he decides to use you?"

"No," I frowned, "probably not."

"Okay, so just go with it, and stop asking who, what, where, and why. You're acting too much like the journalist, questioning and analyzing everything. Stop for awhile, and just let yourself live. Analyze later. It will all come together eventually. For now, just enjoy the moment."

"Okay." It was so true what she was saying. It all made a great deal of sense. I promised her I would heed her advice and stop trying to figure out where we were headed. After all, when God is driving it is a pretty safe bet that you will get there eventually.

I left a quick message for Rev and then went off to bed, content for once to let someone else do the driving.

> *Hey sweetie,*
>
> *Here is all my contact travel info. Hotel: Heritage Hotel, Roxas Blvd., PO Box 454, Passay City, Metro Manila, 1300, Philippines. I am thinking all the info you need is there, if I missed anything, let me know. Hope you had a good sleep and pleasant dreams (very pleasant)—hopefully I'll hear from you before you run off for your daily adventures. Your emails make me smile—just knowing you are having a good time puts me in a happy place. Here's hoping my emails still make you smile too. Have fun wandering, but don't do anything too crazy without me. Hate to miss all the fun—Muah (see, I learn, lol).*
>
> *xo to you, my baby, see you soon.*
>
> *P.S. remind me when I get there to tell you about the sweet angel from God I randomly met today—it is a story that so needs to be told in person but one I am sure you will enjoy.*

Oh, I almost forgot my daily tarot.

The *Knave of Wands* suggests that my power today lies in experimentation. I enthusiastically initiate new, extreme, or novel opportunities for adventures, fads, connections, or enterprises and am an active and image-conscious player in the game of life. I am empowered by signs of approval for my performance and transform through arousal and charisma.

Chapter 12
Shots, Shopping, and Sweet Sophia

A new day, a new coffee, and a new chance to discover new things…

Of course, a morning would not be complete without checking the email.

> *Lady,*
>
> *So far nobody is willing to talk. It might be too dangerous still, baby. I'm meeting up with a director, and my aunt asked me, "What will you say if they ask you where you got your name?" and I was silent, then said "I'll say it's from the revolution," and she cut me off and said, "Nooooo, just say that your dad picked it… don't say anything about a revolution or anything. Okay?" and I said, "Okay…" I have a strange feeling that my family knows* EXACTLY *why I'm back in the Philippines. Which is why I'm practically being treated like a king: fed, my clothes washed and ironed for me, driven around, I'm even given my cousin's room with its own private bathroom. It's so bizarre, baby… but none of them think I know the story… well, they at least know that I don't know the details of it. Maybe this is part of the plan, for me* NOT *to know all of it, so I can go about innocently without attracting too much attention.*
>
> *Maybe to take the pressure off me…*
>
> *It's quite unbelievable… I almost feel guilty sometimes at how good I'm being treated… maybe I shouldn't though, huh?*
>
> *I got a meeting with a director today. I have a good feeling about it. Wish me luck.*
>
> *I watched King Arthur yesterday, the movie. I think the latest one they made is the best version.*
>
> *Mmmmmuah, xo*
>
> *Anyway, off to my adventure for the day. Muah =)*

I wrote a quick note back.

Rev,

Baby, you are sooooo stubborn—listen to your Aunt PLEASE*!!!!!!*

No more questions, no more investigating until I get there. I have an idea on how to get this done in a safe way that will have a very positive impact—maybe not in just the Philippines but in other countries as well. Try to trust that things will fall into place as they are supposed to, but we have to be very careful as to what direction we take this in, so again I am asking you to concentrate on your art and your contacts through art and for art until we have a more concrete plan. Your purpose is pure—I already know that—but I agree that this story is not meant to play out in a political arena. We are there to write a story, yes, but we are not there to upset the people who run the country—if we do, this story will never get told and we will have to go through all this again next lifetime and start from scratch. Behave yourself, my love, and stay low, stay safe, and wait for me. As far as letting people treat you well—if that is their wish, then let them do what they want, but do not let them lead you down a stray path. Enjoy your time there: get to know your people, their culture and spiritual beliefs, their hopes and dreams—the rest will come…

Have sweet dreams—I will be with you soon, xo

I soon found myself sitting in my car again, waiting for Sophia to come up from her dungeon, so we could get on with our day. Two things you can count on with this woman: she will always tell you the truth, and she will always be late. She lives in an apartment in the basement in her mother-in-law's house, and I find myself envying the relationship the two of them have. I consider Sophia to be a very lucky girl to have for a mother-in-law a fiery, quick-tempered redhead who loves her unconditionally.

The old woman absolutely amazes me. She drives a little red sports car, spends more time out of the house than in, and when she is at home she can usually be found wearing a bathrobe and holding a beer either in hand or within reach—crazy bird, she is.

Sophia seems to take it in stride when mamma switches from sweet little old woman to dragon lady in the blink of an eye, something that happens daily. Though they are both opinionated and stubborn as hell, it hasn't seemed to negatively affect their relationship. I do have to feel sorry for Sophia's poor husband, because, when the two women decide to join forces to convince him to do something, it must be very similar to being trapped between a ship and an iceberg: crushed, cold, unable to breath, and with legs dangling in midair. I doubt he ever has much of a chance to outrun their powerful will.

It was certainly taking Sophia long enough to get out to the car. I was not willing to wait for long—we had way too much to accomplish in such a short time. She came stomping out of the house with a scowl marring that beautiful face of hers.

"Morning, I guess," she moaned as she dropped into the seat. "Why is it so damn early?"

"Oh, quit whining, and drink your coffee," I grunted, as I backed out of the driveway.

"Mmmm, caffeine, yes, that should help," she finally smiled at me. "So, what do we have left to do?"

I ran down the list. We had to be at the clinic for shots at 9:30 AM, had to hit the bank one more time, then head off to the mall to pick up the hotel voucher. I also wanted to tackle my growing list of essentials but was a little concerned about time. I still had to make it to my brother's for dinner, and, as he lived an hour away, I would be pushing it.

"So?" she asked as I drove. "You hear from Rev?"

"Sure!" It was my turn to frown. "He's running all over the damn place with his cousins, visiting people, and having discussions with everybody he meets about politics and the need for change. Hell, he even sent a message telling me that they were driving around the city when his cousin stuck his head out the window and called 'Rev for President.' Not exactly what you would call lying low."

She whistled through her teeth, then exclaimed, "Well, you did say he was pretty passionate about wanting to help his country."

"Yeah, yeah, I know, but I also recall saying he needs to be careful. He won't be able to accomplish anything if he gets killed." The thought made me really angry. "He has to find his place first, set down some kind of foundation, so these people can trust him. Besides, you know how much I hate politics. I just wish he'd focus more on his acting and his music, as he originally intended. His cousins are encouraging him to follow a more political path. I just don't feel it is the right way to go about it."

"Hmmm, sounds like you also have plans for him. Don't you think, though, that it would be better to let him find his own way?" She had a point…

"They are thinking politics, you are thinking spirituality and arts, and it is him who will have to make the choice. Let him go for now, see what he does, and if it starts getting dangerous then talk to him. Don't discourage him, though. You're the one who is so sure he needs to do this, so let him do it," she grinned at me. "Don't worry, hon, he'll be very much alive when you get there."

"I know, I know," I conceded. "I have to have a little more faith. It is hard, though, when he is so very far away. We had so very little time to make plans before he left. I honestly think we can create something special to put into print, but we have so much more to discuss about how to do it."

I know I was sounding pretty whiny and, given my experience the day before, I really ought to just let it go.

"I guess I have to work out some of my own issues, too. Besides, I have a lot to do before I can even get on the plane. I had better put my efforts into getting there. The rest will probably work itself out."

"There you go," she grinned, "You're learning. You know you saw it yesterday. You admitted it yourself. You've had your proof now. Put yourself in God's hands. Let him guide you. Rev will be fine, and you two will see each other soon. You'll lift each other up and soar to great heights together. Be confident, be patient, and let the book write itself." Laughing, she added, "In fact, after all you told me, I think it already is."

I had to agree with her there, but, even with all the interesting stories and symbolism I had already witnessed, I still had no clue as to what kind of conclusion I would make at the end of it all. I supposed she was right, though. For the moment, it was the journey that mattered, not the destination.

We arrived at the clinic and, after driving around for fifteen minutes, finally found a place to park. We kept up an easy banter about mundane things like weather, drama at work, and how much I had left to do. While we were waiting for the doctor, she asked me about Rev's reaction to my criminal activities.

"He took it pretty well," I answered, "but then he doesn't seem much surprised by anything I tell him."

As I finished speaking, I realized we were in a very busy, very public, waiting area, not the kind of place one should be discussing these issues. Oh well, I shrugged inwardly: I am who I am. It's about time I stopped trying to hide from it.

"So," she arched an eyebrow, "Did you tell him everything?"

Hmmm, I was thinking, *Did I?*

"Yup, I think I did. You know, I don't think I could lie to that man if I tried. He knows at least as much as you." I winked at her, "and he, like you, doesn't seem to give a damn where I've been. He seems much more concerned about where I'm going."

"I knew there was something I liked about that man—other than his delightfully pinchable ass, that is." She smirked at me, then added seriously, "I'm glad you guys got past that so quickly. It will make things easier for you."

"Me too," I agreed. "If it was anybody else, I'd be concerned, but nothing fazes the man. You know, I told him a few of my crazy family stories and he never even blinked."

She laughed, "Well then, I guess if he took those in stride you have nothing to fear. Which ones did you tell him? Not that they aren't all pretty much messed up, but I'd hate to see you scare him off."

So I went over the stories I had told him already, adding that our time had been short, so I hadn't been able to tell him all of them.

"Too bad you never got to tell him about the three days you spent camped out in the kitchen with your mother and her rifle." She laughed as the woman beside her shot her a surprised look. "That one would be a sure test of his ability to accept the weirdness that has been your upbringing."

"Oh sure, I'm positive he would love to hear all about my mother keeping me hostage in the kitchen. I mean, it's not every day one's mommy decides that someone is coming to take her daughter away. Certainly I can see his amusement as he pictures in his mind my mother lying by the patio doors, rifle in hand, waiting patiently for the bad men to come so she can pop a cap in their ass. I shook my head, "No, I'm not sure he's quite ready for that one yet."

Just then I was called in to get several needles stuck into both shoulders. After I was done, we hurried out and wandered toward a store across the street, where my wife proceeded to pick out a few cute little dresses for me to wear on "vacation."

Once we were back in the car, she queried, "You know, you never told me how that ended. I mean, why did your mom put down the gun?"

"Oh, that," I shrugged. "Dad came home from wherever he had been for the last week and told her it was okay—they had taken care of it." I shook my head, "And before you ask—no, I have no idea what the hell it was all about or what it was *they* had taken care of or who *they* were. I was only nine years old and I wish I couldn't remember any of it."

"No need to get stressed about it now, hon." She shook her finger at me. "You've had years to get used to your messed-up childhood. Use what you can from what you went through, and let the rest go." She grinned at me, "There had to be a reason for it. You know God never makes us go through anything we can't handle even if we suffer for it at the time. Over time, and with the help of people who love us, we find a way to survive." She added while once again laughing at me, "The good with the bad, remember—it's what you're always preaching to people. Balance: it makes the world bearable."

Too true. Once again she had found a way to throw my own ideals back in my face without insulting me in the process. She was right (I realize I say that a lot). It was my religion—the one belief I relied on beyond all others to keep me from giving up, the one thing beyond all others I wanted my daughter to learn. I felt it would give her strength to make it through all the challenges life would present to her. I had been trying to both show it to her and prove it to her since the day she was born. Even when she was an infant I would talk to her about the need for the universe to maintain a balance. Every time something had gone wrong in our lives I would find the good in it and point it out and explain it.

My daughter had proved to be an apt pupil, and, as she began to believe, I could see it helping her come to terms with some losses in her life. Only this past spring when my Baba had passed away, my baby girl had come to me and tried to comfort me by saying, "It's okay, Mom, Baba isn't suffering any more, and we still have each other. Baba taught us that, Mom—that family takes care of family, right? Besides, now we have one more guardian angel to look out for us and to protect us so we will be happier, safer, and stronger."

With that, she had given me a hug and one of her lopsided little smiles, then run off to get back to her computer.

I was reflecting on this as I pulled into the bank parking lot. "You know, Sophia, you're right. There is always a light that shines through the dark. Sometimes it just takes a little wisdom from our family and friends to help us to see it."

"Of course I'm right," she said as she climbed from the car. "Look up the meaning of my name sometime; it wasn't given to me by chance."

We spent the rest of the day rushing around trying to get everything done. We picked up the tickets and Soph paid the balance on my hotel. We rushed through Sears picking through luggage until we found a set that met Sophia's requirements. We must have gone through every set in the department store before she settled on one. She insisted that it be the lightest we could find, explaining that I would probably be bringing some gifts back and had to take that into consideration. She also pointed out that if it was a mundane, common colour it could easily be lost. Of course this is what I rely on my friends for, it seems every time I get a crazy idea in my head to go off on a new adventure they find a way to make it work. We grabbed a quick lunch, did a quick look around the mall for sandals (impossible to find in Toronto in winter), then gave up and headed home.

On the way home, I popped in the *Holy Grail* CD. "I want you to hear something, but, before you do, tell me what is the one thing I've been saying since we met?"

"You?" she wrinkled her brow. "You keep saying that you are tired, that life has already exhausted you, and that you are more than ready to go home." She looked at me quizzically. "Why, what does that have to do with—"

"Just listen," I said, cutting her off and pushing play.

The song played out while we drove, and when the chorus came on, her eyebrows made a very good attempt at climbing off her forehead.

"Damn, chica, Rev wrote that?" She mumbled, "Girlfriend, you in trouble."

"Don't I know it?" I agreed as the words "Come home, come home, I'm coming home" played in the background.

"It just occurred to me—did you ever tell Rev about that dream you had six months ago?" she asked as I pulled into the driveway.

"No," I said, confused, "Why would I… Oh, shit!"

"Yes, dear, I know…" she said, shaking her head. "And all this time you thought the faceless person in the dream was Deacon." She laughed at that. "Surprise! So, you gonna tell him?" she asked me seriously.

"I dunno; I mean, the whole point to the dream was that he came for me on his own. If I tell him, doesn't that kind of negate the purpose?" I looked at her sideways. "What do you think? Should I tell him?"

"Sure, I can see that going well—how do you tell your newfound soul mate that you had a dream six months ago that involved you sitting on your couch watching a discussion between your current boyfriend and a faceless man you couldn't identify. How do explain that this faceless man came in to get you and sat your boyfriend down to tell him that you really didn't belong to him, that you actually belonged to him, the faceless man?" She arched a brow, "What was it this ghost man said?"

"Um," I looked down a little sheepishly, "That I was his wife, had always been his wife, and had only been on loan, but that it was time for Rey to give me up, so I could go home where I belonged."

"Oh yes, "she purred, "Now I remember: his wife, on loan, go home… right."

"But it was just a dream," I argued

"Oh no you don't," she answered firmly, "You're not getting away with that crap, and you said yourself, at the time, you knew it would happen." She added, giggling, "You just had the wrong guy!"

"Hmmm…" I admitted, "I guess I did at that. I didn't see that one coming."

"Well, now you know," she smiled, "But to answer your original question: no, I don't think you should tell him yet; see what happens first. There may be a time he decides to come back and explain this all in terms Reynard can understand, and, if not, it doesn't change the fact that the faceless man has finally come to claim his bride." She added sadly, "Poor Rey."

"I know," I pouted, "It really isn't fair to him, is it?"

"Well, chica, like I told you, you have to be true to you, or you'll never be happy," she grinned at me wickedly. "Besides, the man is hot, girl—you lucked out…"

I didn't have much time to get back on the road and headed to my brother's, but we took a moment more sitting in her driveway to say goodbye.

"You know, I'm glad you and your brother are back in each other's lives," Sophia reflected. "I think you are going to need him around to support you on this journey."

"Oh, he'll be around," I assured her. "Even in the three years we weren't talking he was still a part of me. After all, he was pretty much the only parental figure I had growing up, other than Baba. He provided pretty much my entire early education in life. Most of my personality traits are his fault. He apologizes all the time for giving me such a jaded view on relationships, but I keep telling him a lot of my strength and survival instincts are wrapped up in those views, so it's okay."

"What do you mean?" she asked. "We have a great relationship!"

"No, woman!" I laughed, "I mean the way I deal with the opposite sex."

I gave her a long look up and down, "One of which you are most definitely not. No, he thinks I'll have a hard time finding a life mate who can both understand me and keep up with me. He taught me at a very young age to be free and independent. With Mom being a little off at times and Dad not being around, it fell to him to raise me during the winter months. He wanted me to grow up confident and able to take care of myself, so he drilled it into my head that the only person I could count on was me."

"Ouch, no wonder you are not good on crying on people's shoulders." She pointed out, "Yet, you have some really solid, safe friendships with both men and women. So, how does that work?"

"Oh, well, those people are in my life because they don't need to hear from me every day to know I love them. They let me go my own way secure in the knowledge I will always come back around." I reached over for a smoke, lit it, and blew a puff out the window, "But when you are in a committed relationship with one person, that changes. I mean, the average man isn't going to be comfortable with his girlfriend or wife constantly wanting to go their own way. I need to be with someone who knows I am with them in spirit even when I can't be in the flesh. Theo knows that and he very much fears I will never find that person."

"Do you think that it will happen?" she asked me quizzically. "I don't think such a man exists," she added, laughing.

"Who knows, but either I will find one who will set me free, or I will find one who I will finally willingly get in a cage for. Either way, if I end up happy, like you said, that's all that matters."

"True dat, sister, true dat." She gave me a quick hug. "Have fun, stay safe, and have a good flight okay? Oh yeah," she added, "Say hi to the Holy Grail for me, tell him to stay sexy, and pinch the rump!"

She got out of the car and then stuck her head back in the door. "You're going to experience a lot of things that many do not get to, so enjoy the people, culture, and, most precious of things, life. Your heart will be so full that you will soar above your wildest dreams past the clouds. Just save a little piece of it for me. You may be leaving the country, but know that you are always close within my heart."

With that she was gone, and I would not see her again until I returned weeks later a changed person. Her words, however, stuck with me—a lesson on life and love. As I traveled, she continued to send me inspirational words and encouragement. The emails she sent to me in the following days were full of light, laughter, and love, and they helped to keep me focused on the positive. I have been extremely blessed by her presence in my life. Most of what she tried to teach me to see, believe in, and have faith in, eventually did come to pass, though at the time I had no idea just how prophetic her words would be.

All I could think of that day as I watched her walk up her drive was, "Damn, I have the hottest, sweetest, most beautifully souled wife in the world."

I swung by my house to send a quick email to my boo, but he was one step ahead of me…

Hi, baby,

I had a good sleep. Actually had my first 8-hour sleep last night. Did you already pay for your hotel? That hotel is about 15 km from where I am, but that 15 km can turn into a 1-hour to an hour-and-a-half drive from where I am because of the traffic. I asked my cousin and he said there's Holiday Inn and Crowne Plaza that's closer. Crowne Plaza Galleria Manila, Quezon City or Holiday Inn Galleria Manila—these hotels are 30 minutes even with traffic.

We're going to the gym now. See you on Valentine's =)

I sent a quick note back.

Hey, babe,

Yup, hotel is paid for, but that's okay for this time around—it was such short notice and with no way to phone you to make arrangements I figured it wouldn't hurt just once to live it up a little. If we can find a place closer once I get there, I can see about getting a refund in a couple weeks—but I did get it for cheaper than the regular rate, and since it's a 5-star, it has a gym and Internet access as well as several other amenities that we probably don't need. But it will be fun, so no worries. I wonder if they have mopeds for rent—then 15 km won't be so bad—if you get time look into it.

I have been running full-tilt trying to get all the arrangements made—I got my shots today, just to be safe, and Sophia took me shopping; with everything else going on she still manages to bring me back to reality on a regular basis by making random mundane decisions like buying me a couple new summer dresses so I would have something to wear 4 you if we end up going out on a dinner date. She really is too sweet—wow, what else—um, I have my luggage and, though I still have a huge list of equipment to buy before I come out, I did manage today to get all the pads of paper and pens and all the non-techie writing tools I'll need while I'm there, so my to-do list is slowly getting cut down. I'm on my way to see my bro tonight and spend some much-needed downtime, but I'll check the comp again tonight or tomorrow and see what u r up to—miss ya, xo

I grabbed my stuff, jumped in the car and headed out.

Chapter 13
That's Appropriate

I completely lost myself in the music that was playing on the radio. Before I knew it, I was pulling up in front of my brother's house.

I let myself in and hollered down the stairs to his basement entertainment room.

"Hey, baby, I'm home..."

"Come on down, just playing with my toys," came his baritone reply.

I dropped my stuff in the hall and descended the stairs to find him sitting in this favourite chair toying with his remote. When I say *remote*, I am being a little flippant—my brother is a gadget junky and his idea of a remote control is a five-thousand-dollar computerized device that is wired into and programmed to control every electronic device in the house. He's a smart guy, my bro, and he has spent the last two years completely rewiring his home. He has speakers on the ceiling in every room that are connected to a master stereo that is controlled by his super remote. He also has an extra stereo upstairs that can be separated or linked into the system depending on whether or not he wants different things playing in different rooms. The crazy mini-computer he calls a remote also runs this extra sound system. His massive wall-to-wall screen and projector in his entertainment room, as well as his other, smaller TV (only 106") located in his workout room are also—yes, you guessed it—run by the same remote.

Now, don't get the wrong impression; he's not rich, just very handy when it comes to electronics. I remember the first time my mother brought home a computer—I was about six years old at the time, which would make him sixteen—anyway, he took it apart to see how it worked and then put it back together again while Mom was at work. She never found out until years later, and by then it was much too late to punish him for it. He also, at the age of fifteen, wired a headset into his bedroom phone so he could tinker and talk at the same time. His love of electronics led him into the field of robotics, and he now happily (except when his bosses are ticking him off) works as a troubleshooter for a company that makes both electronic and robotic equipment.

As I said, everything he has done to his house by way of improvement he did himself—including renovating and designing my favourite room in the house.

It is my room, he says—designed apparently with me in mind during our three-year separation. Aside from the giant screen and kick-ass sound system, it also has deep burgundy walls with black trim. A floor-length black velvet curtain covers the one and only window. The coffee table is a beautifully carved stone dragon with a glass top, and the wall sconces are little gargoyles hidden in each corner holding little balls of dimmable light. In short, it is the most comfortable room I have ever been in, and it is so me!

He glanced up from his electronic baby and, after giving me an up-and-down once-over, commented, "Good to see my sister finally came back to me."

A little confused, I commented "I came back to you months ago—so what are you talking about?"

"So you did," he said, standing up, "but judging by the clothes you're wearing, the real you, the part of you that makes you *you* has decided to come out to play."

I glanced down at my long, brightly coloured hippie-style shirt. "I suppose she has at that." Then, laughing, I added, "You know, I never noticed..."

"You never do," he added. "Every time you go off down some new adventurous road you revert back to your natural tree-hugging state. I have to keep track of these things, you know; helps me to know which of your personalities I am talking to."

"Oh, yes, well I'm rather hoping this one sticks around for a bit. I think I'm onto something, and she's a big influence in a positive way. I'd hate to lose her halfway through and end up not finishing what I've started." I spread my arms and shrugged. "Besides, she's much more low-maintenance than that other one. It helps that I don't have to spend a lot of time on my hair and makeup—have too much to do."

"Right, well let's get out of here; you can tell me all about it over dinner," he said as he reached down and turned off his system. As I followed him up the stairs, he added "But don't put that other girl too far to the back of your head, you'll need her yet before this is over."

We hopped in the car, and, as we drove off, I reflected on what he had said. I did have two very different personalities.

One is an extremely bad girl who enjoys challenging and confronting the world by doing the exact opposite of what everyone expects. She is a strong, determined spirit who goes her own way, regardless of who it hurts, as long as it gets for her whatever it is she wants at the time. She usually keeps company with other criminally minded individuals who find warring against society as entertaining as she does. She has been known to take over completely at times and wreak havoc on my otherwise quiet existence. She wears tight jeans, tight tops, shows off her cleavage (what little she has), and uses her sexuality to persuade men to do what she wants. She is an extremely dangerous girl; if you threaten her or those she loves she will gladly slit your throat and not waste a second of her day on feelings of guilt. She is manipulative and conniving. She has a vengeful nature and is willing and able to expend a great deal of energy on plotting the demise of anyone who hurts her or gets in her way. All these traits are what have allowed her to survive the various challenges life has thrown at her. She is a nasty, hardened individual and is usually present when life is exceptionally difficult.

However, she can, like he said, come in handy. She knows how to take care of herself, and the walls she has built over the years provide an extremely strong protective shield. The problem is that with her domineering nature it is difficult at times to convince her that she is not needed at the moment. Even after she successfully gets us through whatever rough spot we are in, she boldly clings to her control, and it can sometime take months to talk her into letting go. I do need her, and I have learned over the years to even love her, but, quite frankly, she can be a real pain in the ass.

My core personality, the one who my brother was saying welcome back to, is a creative, spiritual entity who delights in exploration and adventure. She is a gypsy, an explorer of the world and all that it contains. She adores people, animals, and nature. She is an inquisitive little thing who constantly pokes her head into new places and asks way too many questions. Anything new is something to embrace and learn from. She, unfortunately, does not take being tied down very well. She suffers from wanderlust and cannot thrive until she is set free to venture forth into the world without commitments or responsibilities. She usually wears long skirts and baggy clothes. Her hair is almost always tied back, but occasionally, when she is not actually writing or painting, she lets it down.

Her strength comes from an open, honest personality that she uses to draw those to her who will help or support her. She has a gentle warmth about her that people feel very comfortable to be around, and they are therefore more than willing to allow her into their lives. She is an artist, a writer, and a free spirit. It is very easy to love her, but when the bad people come into her world, she runs and hides behind her counterpart. "Her Evilness" takes over, and God help the people who tried to mess with the "Gypsy Princess."

Now, please understand—it has taken me years to come to terms with and learn to manage these two completely opposite entities, and, no, I neither need nor want your damn medication. I have it well under control. The two of us have come to an understanding, and, now that we are no longer battling each other for control, we are quite balanced and at peace with each other. Using our individual talents and personalities and blending them together, we have managed to create a strong, loving, soulful individual who recognizes the need to break free of societal expectations and has the strength and willpower to do it—with the underlying desire to hurt as few people as possible along the way.

Oh yes, I agree it is an absolutely crazy concept, but then I already told you perhaps we should all be committed, and there you were, thinking I was referring to my friends and family. Oh, okay, you got me—I was at the time referring to exactly that.

Speaking of those very people, I would like to take the opportunity to say thank you to all of them for having the good grace to never throw it in my face that I do indeed have a split personality. They have learned over the years to recognize and embrace whatever side of me happens to be facing the world on any given day. I am sure they (friends and family, not my two me's) have had to face their own inner battles concerning my emotional issues. Yet, for some reason, none of them has ever confronted or accused me (apart from Saul, but then, who can blame a man for getting completely confused and stressed out over being married to a crazy lady?). They have never tried to make me be anything other than who I/we am/are—for which I am exceptionally grateful.

Oh, and by the way, I am thinking that you should not fault them for not insisting I seek medical or psychiatric help. Apart from the fact that being left to find my own way has allowed me to make my way here, I am sure the whole journey has been entertaining as hell to witness. I myself would not want to stop watching such a comical show. Laughter does make the world go round, and thanks to my idiosyncrasies my friends have had a lifetime of it.

It is interesting to note that my brother also has an alter ego, whom he refers to as Bob, but that is something we will no doubt explore at a much later date.

When my bro and I sat down at the table, I promised him I would hold tight to my dark side, though I admitted I don't think many people like her.

"What the hell do you care what other people think?" he asked, reaching for the menu. "There are people in your life, you know, who love all of you; as for the rest of the world ... screw 'em."

"True," I agreed, "But it has posed enough problems over the years. Look at what it did to my marriage. Saul never could learn to accept what he often referred to as my double life. It's not easy for people to come to terms with."

"No, but that's not what wrecked your marriage, is it?" he asked, glancing over the menu. "What destroyed your marriage was that *you* never accepted it. The problem wasn't him, sis. It was you. Now that you have learned to acknowledge the existence of both of you, you aren't in danger of hurting anyone else through your denial."

Yes, I thought, as he ordered his steak. I suppose he's right. If I am aware of it I can manage and control it. I can also stop trying to run from it and hide it. If I am open with others, then no worries; either they accept me or not. If they do, that's perfect; there will be no surprises down the road and nobody will get hurt.

"Only one problem with that, hon," I said, pointing my order out to the waitress. "There's still going to be one more victim when all is said and done."

"True, true, but if you handle this right he won't get too damaged, and you can both get on with your lives." He glanced at a passing waitress and grinned, "Good view tonight! Listen, Rey's gonna get hurt, yes, but you can't help that now. Just be careful not to do it again—you keep trying to settle down like this, and it's just not what you were meant to do."

"I know." I glanced at another passing waitress. "You're right, the view is good tonight. I just hate the fact that he's going to get hurt at all, though, you know. He's a really good guy; he deserves better."

"Yeah, but you have to take care of you," he said, shaking his head. "I guess, though, that me trying to drill that into your head all these years is probably half the problem. Sorry about that, I really am, but you know, maybe there is a guy out there somewhere who's strong enough to handle being with you." Laughing, he added, "Being with all of you, as you, that is. No more denial, okay?"

"Okay," I agreed, "I will either marry Superman or die single—it's agreed."

He changed the subject. "So you gonna tell me what woke you up this time? Does he have a name? Or is it a she? No matter, really, fill me in on what's going on."

Over dinner I caught him up on everything that I'd been doing; it took the entire meal to do, then dessert, then coffee, and most of the car ride to Future Shop. I went over all the conversations I'd had with various people to give him a better sense of where I was headed. He already knew where I was coming from. I ended my tale with, "But so far the book seems to be writing itself."

As we pulled into the parking lot, he turned to me and smiled, "Well you certainly haven't made it easy for yourself this time, have you?"

"Do I ever?" I answered, grinning.

"Ain't that the truth. But we'll have to talk more later," he exclaimed, looking at his watch. "Shit, it's almost nine. Come on, they're closing soon. I hope your list isn't very long."

When we got into the store it was almost empty, but, given that it was two minutes before closing, that wasn't really a surprise. I had several things I needed, and I would need help finding them all. We finally found a salesperson and I briefly explained what I was looking for. It was very entertaining to watch the interaction between the young sales guy and my brother. The young man would look at my brother and ask a question with regard to the stuff I needed. My brother would shake his head, then gesture to me and say, "You're asking the wrong person—the lady is buying."

The kid would then ask me the question. I'd give an answer, and he'd go off and find what I needed. Yet, when he'd get back, he would direct his next question or comment to my brother, who would again chuckle and say, "You're asking the wrong person—the lady has the money."

This went on for a good twenty minutes before the youngster finally clued in and focused on me instead of my brother. I can understand the mistake; my brother is a rather robust gentleman at six foot two, with striking blue eyes and greying hair that gives his overall appearance an air of distinction. He certainly doesn't dress like he's out to make an impression (something he does purposely to keep materialistic personalities at bay). His quietly confident demeanour, combined with a handsome, distinguished face, has a way of giving the impression to strangers that he is somebody of importance, which of course he is to me—but I know him well enough to know that if he was ever viewed by the general populace that way he would probably fall down laughing.

I, on the other hand, am a very petite, hopefully young-looking female with (as Deacon says) shit in my face and tattoos. Not someone you would immediately recognize as having money, status, or possibly even an education. That's how I like it, though. Let them underestimate me. Let them underestimate me all they want; it just gives me more room to manoeuvre.

Once this young gentleman realized he had been focusing on the wrong person, we actually started to accomplish something. With a little talking, pretty soon I had four sales people running around the store finding me what I needed. My brother stood off to the side watching and giggling to himself, as teenager after teenager came running up with various pieces of equipment. He watched in wonder as one of the sales boys talked me out of buying a phone and instructed me instead to buy one in the Philippines, explaining that it would be cheaper.

I turned to Theo/Bob and laughed, "Did you see that?"

He sniffed, "Yeah, you realize what he just did, don't you?"

"Sure," I answered. "But to which part are you referring—him losing a sale or gaining a guaranteed return customer?"

The activity continued for a good half hour until I had everything I needed. Surprisingly enough, they even managed to find me a computer bag that looked like a hippy-style backpack. Good boys they were, but the biggest surprise was when we were cashing out.

"Listen," said the dimple-faced boy behind the counter. "You had to wait a bit, so I'm going to throw those flash drives you need in for nothing. Okay, we have three eight-gigabyte drives left, and you can have them—my way of saying sorry for the delay. Oh and there's a store wide sale on today so you get a discount, I guess you lucked out, the sale ends tomorrow."

Hey, who am I to argue? I ended up leaving the store with everything I needed, as well as having 20 percent from the bill and my free flash drives. Not a bad night of shopping.

As we were getting in the car, our young helper from inside came out, got into the car beside us, and off he went.

"You amaze me, you know that?" My brother put the car into gear. "You absolutely amaze me..."

"Me?" I asked innocently. "What did I do?"

"Hmmm, let me see," he said as we headed home. "You walk into a store at two minutes to closing, with a list of shit you need a mile long. You somehow manage to get the entire staff involved in helping you out. I mean, Jesus, Vik, they even went rummaging in the back room for twenty minutes to get your voice recorder. Then you get everything you need and go to cash out almost an hour past closing, and instead of the guy being annoyed that you just kept them all there way past closing, he for some reason feels guilty for making you wait, so he gives you free stuff." He was shaking his scruffy head yet again. "Do you not notice the effect you have on people? From where I was standing, it was pretty amazing to see. The funniest part about it is you're not even trying. You don't have to do a damn thing. People literally crawl up your little finger and wrap themselves around it."

"Oh," I admitted sheepishly. "No, I never noticed. I just thought they were being nice."

That sent him into peals of laughter, which he did not recover from until the car was in his garage and we were comfortably seated outside drinking coffee and smoking cigarettes.

"So, it would seem, as I said earlier, that you have set yourself a bit of a challenge," he said mildly. "If I get the gist of what you are telling me, you're proposing to travel alone to the other side of the world to meet a man you just met, but have a past with; not only have you chosen a Third World country, but you have chosen to broach the topic of political and spiritual independence in a country that is dominated by two very powerful factions. On one hand you have the Catholic Church, and on the other you have a politically corrupt government backed by an equally corrupt military. Now, if I get this right, you want to go in there, learn as much as you can from the inside, then come back here and write a book that will both expose the corruption and encourage the people to do something about it. But, wait for it; you want them to do it peacefully and without violence. Oh, yeah, and while you are at it, you want to toss in the idea that the world needs to learn a little religious tolerance and understanding if the human race is going to have a chance at moving toward its next step in its inevitable evolution." He put his smoke out. "Did I cover everything?"

"Yep, that's pretty much it," I said, grinning up at him. "You missed two very important facts, though."

"Oh yeah?" he asked. "What's that?"

"One, I intend to come back in one piece, and two, I have absolutely no idea yet how to pull it all off."

He laughed till he cried.

I gave him time to recover; then I added quite seriously: "I know exactly what I want to do, but I'm at a loss as to how to do it. My biggest challenge so far has been myself. Everyone else seems to have faith in me, but I am having trouble believing I can make any kind of impact. I am a complete unknown and without a good story to back me up I will fail. It's the story I need, the actual content and events that uplift and inspire." I shrugged. "If you have any ideas, don't hesitate to throw them out there."

"You said yourself that the book seems to be writing itself and, quite frankly, if all you have told me is true, then I agree that certainly seems to be the case." He lit another smoke. "So, maybe you should just go out there and see what happens. In this particular case, maybe no plan is the best plan."

"You know, I think Sophia's been trying to tell me the same thing," I realized. "I am thinking maybe I should listen to both of you and stop worrying about it. I have been trying just to concentrate on getting there and let the rest just fall into place, but it is hard not to over think everything that's happened so far."

"Keep busy. If you are too busy to think ..." he trailed off.

"I've been trying, but everything I do seems to be a reminder of where I'm going. I stopped at the bank, and the woman behind the counter, a lady I've never met, spent thirty minutes talking to me about the need for change and her hopes for the next generation. She wasn't Filipino, but her husband is, and they had lived there for ten years. Then I stopped at the drugstore to get a Medical Alert bracelet, and the guy behind the counter started talking about spiritual growth and his hope for the future generation. Hell, he was barely old enough to not himself be part of that future generation—and they didn't even have the bracelet I needed."

"I know. I get what you are saying, but maybe you were just meant to tuck all that information into the back of your mind," he grinned. "I mean, listen—really listen—to the tale that you told on how you got to this point. It is most definitely not your average story. I'm half expecting you to change water into wine at some point, and I'm fully expecting that you will finish, publish, and sell this book."

"You see, you all have faith in me that I can't justify." I looked down at my feet. "Even if what I have to say is important, who is going to listen?"

"They'll listen if they are meant to listen." It was his turn to shrug. "You know I don't go to church, and I don't go in for all that religious stuff, but it would seem you are being given a task, so I would think you should probably stop whining about it and get on with it."

"Okay, okay, enough. Can we maybe talk about something else? I'm getting tired already, and I haven't written a word," I said half jokingly. "How about the weather or maybe the economic crisis? No wait, I've got it. How's your love life?"

"Right, three topics that have been beaten to death verbally. No thanks." Scrunching his nose at me, he added, "How about we call it a night. Okay? You have a lot to do tomorrow, and I have some walls to rip open."

"Sure thing, but I want to check my email before bed, okay?" I said as I walked past him into the house.

Sitting downstairs in my favourite room, I read Rev's latest email.

Hi, baby,

Okay, if you're sure. I don't think you should ride a moped here. Once you get here, you'll know why, lol. The traffic is bad, a lot of people don't follow the traffic regulations, drivers are very aggressive, and the pollution is terrible 'cause half the cars use diesel. If you can talk to your travel agency and switch hotels, there might still be time. If you don't want to go through the hassle, then that's fine.

Sometimes the taxis here are shady, especially to tourists who don't know their way around town. If you want, you could get a car and a driver that my family knows and trusts. To rent a car + driver would cost around $400 Canadian for 3 weeks. What do you think? Just do it for 2 weeks or something. Saves you the hassle of getting a taxi every day. It's a fixed rate, and you can focus on other things while you're getting driven instead of the frustrations of driving around such insane traffic.

We can pretty much get anything we need here at its cheapest rate 'cause my family has been here forever and know the ins and outs. I was thinking of starting a business here that would just earn money immediately. Labour is cheap, and there could be an even stream of revenue.

Keeping my days busy. It's so great here. I drove by where my condo is being built.

So weird. I was hanging out with my cousin's girlfriend and her friend and my other cousin, and they got me talking again, and they told me I sound like I would be an honest president. They drove me to a few malls to get my pictures printed. I think I know where I can get the unlocked cell phone and SIM card, that shouldn't be a problem.

Yes, I'll see you at the airport; can you please give me all the details: flight #, local time of arrival, and airport. Also, can you buy products from online? Like amazon.com ... wasn't sure whether you used a credit card or not.

I'm falling in love with this country more and more the more time I spend here.

A lot of the young people have such a passion to fight the corrupt system, but they feel hopeless in finding a channel that will bring back justice. Contacts are coming along well. My mother is hesitant to ask my father for information... I think maybe she's afraid it will jeopardize my safety. I'll ask her again. Hope everything is well; tell Madison I said hi as well. Did you give her the DVD? Xoxo

As my brother seemed to have disappeared for the moment, I took the opportunity to write a quick response.

Hi, sweetie—I am at my brother's right now, but as soon as I get home I will send you all the flight info. My brother and I have had the most incredible heart to heart, and he believes this is what I was born to do, and he's excited for me that I'm finally getting to do everything I've always dreamed of. He really believes life has been training me for this, and that's a really encouraging and comforting feeling. I went w/Sophia today to get some cash, with the intention of getting a prepaid Visa before I leave; I figured it would be good to have with me as an emergency fund. Why? What's up, hon? What is it I should be looking for online?

Let me know what u r thinking—I'm glad u r staying busy, but try to remember to lie low and not draw attention too much. It could be stopped in its tracks before it ever gets off the ground if we are not exceptionally careful, so behave yourself, my love, and try not to get yourself in trouble. When u r talking to your mom, tell her we can come to him and that I have ideas, methods, and contacts that will help get the information and present it to the world without putting a gun to our heads. Safety first—remember u r there to focus on your music and acting, and I am there as your girlfriend to visit you, support you, and learn about your culture and maybe meet some of your people. We r not there for any reason that would spook any locals. Stay grounded, stay focused, and stay safe—the potential of this is too important to both of us to rush it and take unnecessary risks.

We will talk about what direction to go in when I get there, but I have been getting some really concrete and positive ideas in the form of dreams, and I think, once I get to see you and sit down with you, if we combine our ideas, and we go about this the right way, we can take flight with this and really make some changes for the better. But you are right, I think, in your original thinking that first we must open the world's eyes through arts and the media; once we accomplish that, the rest will fall into place as it is intended to.

Can't wait to get there and share your passion for your people and your country—kisses to you, xo

I was checking my daily tarot, and I let out a groan as my big brother walked in with a tea for me.

"What's up?" he asked, setting down the tea beside his laptop. "You get bad news?"

"No," I shook my head. "Just more proof that I'm an idiot for doubting. Don't worry about it. I'll get used to the weirdness again soon. Things have just been too normal for too long. It will take time to adjust."

"Wrong, sis." he settled into his chair. "The only thing that's been too normal for too long is you."

"Right, because me going my own way has always worked out before. Come on, Bob, I always manage to get myself into trouble eventually. Who's to say I won't this time?" I sipped my tea. "I'm bound to make a mistake at some point."

"No doubt, but when you do you, will get back up and keep moving. It's when you let doubt and fear slow you down that failure can catch up to you and bring you to a stop." He looked down into his tea, "Speaking of failure, Vik, about three years ago when you called to tell me you needed me. I'm sorry, kiddo, I—"

"Couldn't handle one more thing?" I offered up a little smile. "I get it. Really, you didn't fail me, and I'm not angry. You'd been through enough yourself, and it ended up working out anyway. I certainly wasn't alone, so stop feeling guilty. I'm here now, and that's what matters, right?"

"Thanks for that—you're the only person I know who gets me. I really am glad you're back; I missed your crazy selves," he said, laughing. "Now, you ready for bed?"

We headed upstairs to the spare room and he got me settled in.

"Don't know if I'll see you in the a.m. I have to leave early, but you can let yourself out the garage, okay?" he spoke from the doorway.

"Sure, no prob," I answered while snuggling into bed. "Thanks for having me for the night and running around with me. The company was appreciated."

"Hey, no worries; besides, running around with you is fun. The way you do things when you are on a mission is amazing—going in a million different directions and somehow meeting in the middle." He turned to go, then looked back. "Organized chaos, that's you. Always has been, and, honestly, I hope you never change."

With that he was off, and I was left to think over my day. If enough people told me I could, I wondered, would I eventually believe? I doubted it, but then I didn't think I had to believe it to do it. It was the doing that was important. I closed my eyes and prayed for another day of good luck and strength. I fell asleep giggling to myself about my daily tarot.

The *Six of Swords* suggests that my power today lies in transition. I have what I need and am willing to trust the process in order to move on, seek refuge or new opportunity. I'm not willing to remain where my perceptions are invalidated, but, being vulnerable, I must rely on guidance to move in a new direction or trust that I can make it or be led to security and new hope. "Wherever you go, there you are." I am empowered by perseverance and my virtue is survival.

Chapter 14

Really? You Name This One (I Don't Have Words)

I would like to say that I woke up and had a normal day—one not steeped in symbolism and intense spiritual conversation. I would like to say that, but I can't.

It started out normal enough. I got out of bed, made tea, and took my time waking up while I wrote a quick note to Rev.

> *Hey, my sexy baby—I forgot I have not given the CD to Maddi yet, because I haven't seen her—but I did tell her about it and I spoke to Saul about it too. He used to sing in a band back in the day, and I asked him if he would work with her and the CD (he can sing—boy used to give me shivers, lol. His voice is solely responsible for me getting pregnant in the first place, lol) and he said he would do that and he would take good care of the CD, so all is well there—which makes my life a little easier, I have to admit, because it's one less thing for me to worry about. Still can't believe he's supporting me in this, but, hey, I guess maybe we've been divorced long enough that he realizes we don't really have any reason to fight anymore, so it's all good. Gotta go, 'cause I should really hit the road and get back to the city to organize some of my equipment and get to packing. Will talk to you soon, xo*

After signing off, I jumped in the shower.

I have to stop a minute to tell you about the shower. Oh, I know, what can be so exiting about a shower? Honestly, though, until you've had one Bob style, you've never really experienced how beautifully relaxing a shower can be. Like I told you, my bro had spent a lot of time renovating, and one of his biggest challenges and accomplishments turned out to be the downstairs bathroom. Not only did he build an aesthetically pleasing environment, he also took the time to do a city-wide store-to-store search for the ultimate shower head. The thing is easily as big as a small plate, and I'm sure it is capable of many settings, but I never bothered to change it; the one he had it one is just fine. He had mentioned it to me the night before, but I thought he had to be exaggerating. I mean, really—getting all excited about a shower.

So, picture yourself standing in a pleasantly warm, fully tiled, big-as-most-closets shower enclosure. You turn on the water and this wonderfully created piece of equipment starts to…

Pour water over your head—come on, what did you think I was going to say? It's a shower—it can't rub your feet or give you a massage, or maybe you were thinking … I'm ashamed of you! Get your head out of the gutter, will you?

After my hour-long shower, I hopped in the car and headed home. I had a crazy busy day ahead of me, so I was in a hurry to get on with it.

As I was driving along, minding my own business, the phone rang. I glanced down and noticed it was the Gospel lady. Two things I should mention: I am horrible with names, so how I remembered hers is beyond me. Also, I have the worst time with numbers. I still have no idea what my social insurance number is, and, given that I am now in my thirties, you would think I have had it long enough to memorize it. How others remember things like bank account numbers, license plates, and friends' phone numbers is something that to this day amazes me. Oh, believe me; I've tried every trick I can think of, even translating numbers to words. I'm lucky if I can remember my new postal code six months after I've moved. Oh, I know what letters go where, but they just have to throw those stupid numbers into the mix, and I'm completely lost because of it. This particular day, however, I recognized the number, and I answered the phone with, "Well, hello, my dear. I've been waiting for your call."

"Allo dahlin'. Did I getcha at a bad time?" came this aged voice over the line.

"No, no love, just driving. Your timing is great," I answered quickly. "So, what can I do for you hon?"

"I'm a justa callin' to see where you at. We is havin' a Bible study, and I was a wonderin' if you is a comin'?" She really is the sweetest sounding lady on the phone.

"Oh, sweets, um, please don't think I'm putting you off, but I'm leaving town in a couple of days and I don't have much spare time." I was trying to sound as positive as possible. I was convinced I was supposed to talk to this woman and didn't want her to think I was putting her off. "How about as soon as I get back?"

"Sure, dahlin'; where it is you is a goin'?" she asked sweetly.

"Well, I am off to the Philippines to start work on a project. I am a freelance writer." I figured I might as well start believing it if I was going to be one.

I was confused by the silence on the other end. Had I said something wrong? Then I heard her draw a breath.

"That's a why you is supposed ta speaka ta me," she explained breathlessly.

"What do you mean, dear?" I asked, curious where this was headed.

She blurted out her answer all in a rush "I worka for CBC in Manila for twenty long. I keepa my people there. I talk to 'em; you go see; they help you… I say you is okay, they speaka to you."

Yeah, right—this was not happening. Okay, well, in case you missed it, let me explain. First of all, a reporter's lifeblood is her contacts and informants. Journalism can be an extremely competitive, even cutthroat business. The money is only in the breaking story. If you cannot get the news first, you do not get the money. Ergo, reporters do not go around handing out their contacts to complete strangers to use—no, not even retired reporters. Informants are usually handed down to a protégé or a younger friend who is still in the business. It can take years to build up a list of safe and reliable contacts overseas. Here was such a list being offered to me by a woman who I had not even met in person.

Secondly, I had never mentioned Manila. It was where I was headed, yes, but I had not told her. Now, one could assume, as it is a major city centre with a large international airport, that it was my destination. Manila is not a tourist area; it's for business trips, not vacation—too much smog and no beach. It is also, however, not a place one would go to learn about the native people and the native culture.

I was temporarily speechless.

"Is okay?" she asked timidly. "Mayhap you is too busy."

"No, no!" I practically shouted. "Not too busy for this. Are you kidding me? This is a huge help. It is amazing. I would be more than happy to make time. No problem."

"Okay, dahlin'" she said placidly. "When you be a leavin'?"

"On the midnight of the twelfth," I explained. "Not very far away, I'm afraid."

"Oh my, we meet soon, yes? Tomorrow? You be busy?" she enquired.

"Nothing too much; my daughter has a hair appointment at 5:00, dinner at my sister-in-law's at 6:00. Then nothing." It would mean a lot of rushing around the night before I left, but hey, that's okay—it would be worth it.

"Dahlin' you comma church 8:00, okay? I give you names and numbers; my friends they help."

She still sounded so sweet. How could I say no?

"Sure, but you'll have to call me later to give me the address. It's kind of hard to write while I drive."

We talked a little more, then agreed to talk again the next morning, and I hung up the phone thinking I was an extremely lucky girl. My phone rang again about thirty minutes later as I was exiting the highway.

"Hey, big bro. What's up?" I asked (gotta love call display). "Did I forget something?"

"Nope, just calling to see how your morning went," came his mild reply.

"Oh man, how did you know to call?" I said excitedly and then went into a brief account of my talk with the Gospel lady. "You know, bro, stuff like that does not happen every day."

"Humph," he snorted. "It doesn't happen to people like me every day, but you, on the other hand ..." I heard him mumble something about water and wine, then, "Hey, I gotta know. How did you like my new shower?"

"Oh man!" I exclaimed. "That was so cool. Really, man, I have never had such an incredible shower. It was like being..." But I won't bore you with that, because we have already established what could possibly be exciting about a shower.

I did eventually get home. It was around 10:00 AM, and the first thing I did, as usual, was check my email. Of course he had left a message.

> *Expect a different world when you arrive. Traffic is crazy. But that will soon be fixed. The reason why I'm asking if you have a credit card is because you need to get a personal air ionizer. It's a state-of-the-art air filter that you wrap around your neck. Literally, if you don't use it here, when you blow your nose after being outside for a bit, you will blow out all black. The pollution here is insane. My cousin has allergies and it breaks out every day. I gave her my air filter, and now she's fine, but I don't have one for myself now and need you to get it online, 'cause you can't get it out here. This is a different kind of pollution than Toronto*

Where we're staying we'll need it. Driving, or flying to the beaches, the air is heaven, but in the city… without proper protection, it will age you like no tomorrow.

Here's the website for it...

There are plenty others when you search "personal ionizer"—some cheaper, some more expensive. But this one has its own rechargeable batter and I've used it and can attest to its effectiveness. This emits ozone, which can be good and bad. Good when in an area that lacks ozone (like most major cities in Philippines) and bad when there is too much ozone. It works, though; my cousin, who normally gets sick every day 'cause of her asthma and the pollution here in the Philippines, said it helps her a lot.

This one is probably the best one, 'cause the most research has been done with this one, but the only difference is that it doesn't emit ozone. Some people are sensitive to ozone (which the other one emits) and can get dizzy or have headaches.

My mother still keeps ignoring my question about the origin of my name. Maybe you're right, and we do need to travel to Italy, but we have to talk about that 'cause I'm still focused on getting settled here and making my connections.

I already have a meeting on Tuesday at one of the largest malls in the world, called Mega Mall—lol—Filipinos love their malls, beaches, and food. I wake up at 6:00 every morning, I just finished playing guitar and wrapping up this email… thinking of you a lot. I don't know what will happen either, but whatever does happen, I just hope and pray that our relationship stays strong.

I left him a message of my own.

Hey, baby,

So, I was going to try and save all these little crazy coincidence stories so I would have something to make you smile when I get there—but this one tale I have to tell you now, because it's just too crazy and off the hook to not share right away. You know, while you are over there and weird shit is happening to you, weird shit is happening over here too—random people popping up with ideas and lending a helping hand and words of wisdom or just encouragement, but this time it's like the powers that be sent an active angel my way.

It started the day I got my tarot readings that confirmed for me I was on the right path; I was at the hair salon (yes, I know, weird that my hairdresser is also a spiritual guide, but, whatever), and right after she did the reading (remind me to tell you about that, because the card that made me decide to go to the Philippines literally flew out of the deck) the phone rang, and it was one of those random phone calls asking me to come join a gospel study, so, me being me, I told the lady politely that I wasn't interested and hung up—I mean, it's not that I don't believe; I just really have a problem with structured religion, as I feel it puts a box around the true beauty of spirituality and limits people from realizing their true potential.

Okay, so the phone rings again, and, instead of ignoring it (it was the same number, and usually I would refuse to answer), I get the urge to answer and take two minutes to talk to this lady. So I very gently tell this woman: Sweetie, you just called me; I said I wasn't interested. I asked why she called back, and she said there's no way, because she never calls people more than once. Apparently, she believes that if they are meant to talk to her they will; if they are not open minded, then it's just not their time. So, me, I am thinking: Wow, maybe there's a reason I'm supposed to talk to this lady, and I tell her that I feel like we have been chosen to connect for some reason, but as I am in the middle of a hair appointment, can she call me back (keep in mind this is a random stranger who called me out of the blue for a Bible study—not something I would normally be open to). She agrees to call the next day—we hang up on good terms but not with any set plan. She stayed in the back of my head, but I didn't feel any urgency for her to call and wasn't worried—figured she would when the time was right. So I am driving back from my bro's today, and the phone rings. It turns out it's this lady again, and she invites me to another study on Sunday night—I tell her that I still feel like we are meant to talk and though am leaving for the Philippines in a few days maybe when I get back we can meet up. She asks why I'm going—I tell her I'm a freelance writer, and she lets out this gasp, and I can literally feel the excitement over the phone—turns out she worked for the CBC (HUGE) for twenty years and still has all her contacts in Manila (haven't told her yet that's where I'm staying), and asks would I like it if she contacted them and set up a list for me before I go! Okay, so, really, now I am freaking out 'cause—oh my God—this is way too perfect, but also I am running out of time, but I'm driving and I can't write the directions down. So I tell her she is going to have to call me back yet again. Anyway, to sum it up, we are meeting tomorrow night and she is convinced that God sent her my way and that I am moving in a really positive direction and that we will have help along the way if we continue on the right course. So, baby, I hope this story gives you chills, and I hope the hair on your arms is standing up as you read this, because I know I'm getting chills writing it! Gotta run. Play safe, my love—stay safe, my love—I will be by your side very soon. xo

After I was done writing him a mini-novel, I got on the computer, looked up several stores in Toronto that supposedly sold the air filter thing, then started calling around. I only got hold of two stores, one close by and the other an hour away. I spoke to both people and ended up deciding to check out the store closest to me. Out of courtesy I called back the first store and told the very kind gentleman on the other end of the phone that if the store I was going to didn't work out I would get back to him in a couple of hours. He understood and said he would hold one for me just in case.

I jumped back in the car and headed over to Pacific Mall. It turns out the lady at the store had misunderstood what I had wanted. I called up the other guy, asked him what time they were open until, and promised to be there to pick it up before they closed at 8:00 PM. I figured I still needed a few things, so I would wander around and see what I could find. Pacific Mall is very confusing. It is really just a giant building with hundreds of little booth-sized mini-stores arranged in a grid. Half of the signs are in Chinese, so you never know exactly what you are walking into, and the map at the front is also in Chinese. Basically, if you don't have a translator you are screwed.

I began by going store to store. I reasoned the systematic approach would cover everything and I wouldn't miss a store that might have what I needed. It didn't work. I got through about twenty stores and had only managed to find one sweater that I had not been intending to buy. So I changed tactics and took my brother's advice to heart: organized chaos. I walked right past ten stores, then stopped and backtracked into a store two booths back. It turned out to be a jewelry store, and I thought, *Hey, maybe, just maybe, I can actually get my Medical Alert bracelet.* It was something I'd been trying to do for over a week, but everywhere I went they told me the same thing: it's a two week wait; this was not good. I would be long gone in two weeks, and I should probably have something on my body that said: No, DO NOT GIVE HER PENICILLIN—SHE WILL DIE! So I walked into the jewelry store and asked the girl if she had anything that could be engraved. I explained what I needed it for, but she apologized and said she didn't have any. Her sister, however, also worked in the mall, and her store had several such items, as well as an engraving machine. Brilliant! She gave me directions, and I wandered over. I started by explaining that I needed a bracelet that could be engraved and then told her why. So she told me that she could do one better. Apparently, someone had ordered a Medical Alert bracelet, but never came to get it. She and her co-worker had just been discussing whether or not they should send it back. No need, I assured her. I would take it. So they looked up the spelling of penicillin online and told me to come back in twenty minutes.

I went back to wandering the mall, thinking there was no way I would be as lucky with the sandals. It was the middle of winter (well, weather-wise, it was) and every store was filled with boots. I continued to wander until I felt a pull in a certain direction. Following my instincts, I headed into a store that also appeared to only sell boots. It turns out the store happened to have a back room, where I found a single pair of bronze wedge sandals with rope-style tie-ups. Perfect! They matched almost everything I owned. Even better—that one and only pair just happened to be my size; and they were on sale. Well then, I guess that worked out. Oh yeah, I forgot. The girl working the counter—she wasn't Chinese; she was a Filipina.

Okay, so now I'm thinking maybe I should try to arrange the rose I want delivered to my daughter for Valentine's Day. It is a tradition that my daddy started years ago, since he was often gone from home; he started sending me and my mom a single red rose every year on Valentine's Day. It never mattered where he was or what he was doing, you could count on that rose saying, "Hey, remember I love you." I have kept up the tradition for my own daughter, ever since my dad's death, and I was not about to stop now.

I wandered a little more, randomly picked a flower shop, and walked in. I got lucky. They had this great basket all in purple and red with a giant purple teddy bear (my daughter's favourite colour) and filled with Ferraro Rocher (my daughter's favourite chocolate). Nice! And, yes, they would deliver.

"Oh? You're going to the Philippines? I'm from the Philippines. You'll love it there. Sure, I can throw in a long-stemmed red rose. No extra charge. Yep, we will deliver on Valentine's Day." Then the young man smiled, "Great, thanks a lot. Have a nice trip."

It was time to pick up my bracelet and get my butt back to the house. So far, the day had been a success, and it was only 3:00.

I got home around the same time as Rey did, and I figured, since I still had a few little things like toiletries and stuff, maybe he'd be up for a tour. He was all for it, as he needed to get a rat to feed our snake anyway. Henry is a rather large boa who can get quite cranky when he's hungry. We hopped into the car and headed over to the Scarborough Town Centre. It was 4:30, so we grabbed a bite to eat and tackled my list. As we walked around, we talked about whatever popped into our heads until…

"Did you just say you were talking to your brother last night about your writer's personality vs. your normal everyday persona?" He stopped walking.

"Well, yeah," I shrugged. "But I like to think my artistic personality is my main personality. That other girl can be evil as hell." I turned and looked at him standing there. "Why? Am I freaking you out?"

"No, it's just that," he started walking again. "Well, it's a little strange, because I was reading a short story last night written by Stephen King. It's about this author who switches back and forth between this crazy writer guy and an average, ordinary family man."

"No shit!" I exclaimed. "Really? That sounds pretty cool."

"Yeah, it's a good story, very good story. It's just weird that you were discussing it with your brother around the same time I was reading it." He glanced over at me as we walked, as if asking me to explain to him how that was possible.

"Look, hon," I said gently. "I know you don't believe the same as I do, but, honestly, stuff like that happens all the time. The only reason you are noticing it now is because you've been watching and hearing about everything I've been through in the last few days."

"So, you're saying because I see it happen to you it will start happening to me? No," he said, shaking his head. "I'm not you. I don't think like you do. I'm not connected like you are."

"Oh, hon," again I said it gently. "You're wrong there. We are all connected to the same energies. Some are just a little more aware than others. Actually, to be honest, I'm surprised it took me so long this time to see the signs. I've been a believer for years, but, in retrospect, my mind has been pretty closed since Baba's death, so I shouldn't be too hard on myself. What I'm trying to tell you, though, is that once your eyes are open to it, once you know what you are looking for, you will start to see signs everywhere you look.

"If you say so, but honestly," he asked disbelievingly. "What do they mean? How do you even know when it is a sign? Let alone understand what it is telling you to do?"

"They are only there as guides," I said, giggling. "It isn't like God is going to write a message in the clouds. They pop up most often when we are headed in the right direction. They provide confirmation and reassurance, so we are able to move forward without fear."

"Oh," he sounded dejected. "Well, like I said, if you say so, but I just don't think I can see the world the way you do. I'm just not there yet."

No, I thought, *you're not—but maybe at least now you have a chance of getting there eventually.*

There was no point in pushing it, though, so I dragged him into my wife Sophia's favourite store so I could get some cream for my skin. My wife had introduced a shop called Sephora to me months ago on one of our rare non-work-related outings. It is strange to me that we can be so close, but, for some reason, never actually spend much time together socially. Most of our discussions about love and life take place either on the way to or from work. We can go for months without actually spending "quality time" together. No matter—it works, so why question it?

Now Sophia, being Sophia, is exceptionally picky about what products she uses on both her hair and her skin. She refuses to cut corners financially when it comes to such things. It is not unheard of for her to spend a few hundred dollars on products to straighten her hair. She dragged me into Sephora one day while we were wandering around the mall. It was a shocking introduction into the world of upper-middle class cosmetics. The prices are ridiculous (something Rey did not hesitate to point out), but Sophia insists they are well worth the price. As I am still smoking, I seriously doubt any amount of magic serum will save me from the visible effects of the toxins I choose to poison myself with daily.

I now meandered into this store, dragging a reluctant Rey behind. It only took a moment to find what I needed, and we were at the cash counter in no time. While I was there, I took the opportunity to sign up for the discount card. Part of the application had a spot for my email address, and my hand hovered over the space for a moment while I pondered what I was about to write.

My email *eviloctopus* didn't seem to me to be appropriate any longer. It was the first time I had ever found myself questioning the use of it, but it occurred to me that if I was going to make the effort to write a book or novel with a spiritually uplifting message I should have an email account that had an equally uplifting meaning. So I was standing there, pen in hand, not writing anything, when Rey looked down at his watch and exclaimed "Shit, Vicky, it's twenty to six. We gotta go, if you are gonna make it to that store for the air thing you need."

"Damn! Okay, let's get out of here." I rushed through the form and paid. Then we practically ran to the pet store to get the rat. Luckily we live very close to the mall, so I dropped Rey and the rat at home and then jumped back on the highway and raced to the other side of town.

The traffic was practically non-existent, and I made extremely good time, even though I did get lost for a brief moment. I pulled into the parking lot at twenty to eight, with plenty of time to spare. Yet when I got out of the car and approached the front of the store, I noticed it was dark. The hours listed on the door confirmed what the gentleman had said, 8:00 PM closing. Weird. Oh well; I figured maybe something had happened, and I hoped it wasn't something bad like a family emergency. At least now I knew where the place was. So I decided to give the man I'd spoken to a call first thing in the morning and come back as soon as they opened. Of course, the traffic would be worse during rush hour, but I was more concerned about the really nice guy I had spoken to earlier. He had been so kind to me on the phone. I really hoped all was well.

I decided during my drive home that I would look online that evening and see what kind of email account providers were available. If I found one I liked, I would then worry about finding a more appropriate name to go with my new account. I got home, went into my daughter's room, and began by checking my email.

> *Hi, baby,*
>
> *That is indeed a crazy fricken story. Lol—it's weird how God so often lends a hand when you're trying to help his people and are fulfilling your destiny. It seems to be falling into place so well here too. It's falling insanely well. It's crazy… I just know I'm meant to be here, and my studying in Toronto, New York, and everything else in my life has led to this moment. I've been thanking God all day for bringing me here.*
>
> *I'm going to send you a gmail invite, and I want you to choose a gmail name that suits you. This will redefine your purpose, mission, and destiny in life. I think your eviloctopus days are over… just a*

little disturbed every time I see EVIL OCTOPUS *when I check your email. Hahaha*

Check for my gmail invite, which will allow you to create a gmail.com account. I won't tell you or demand you choose a specific name. Just one that's the real you. Not one that someone else chooses for you. One that's the true you. The light that's inside you waiting to make a difference. Craving to go home. And persisting for change. Use the first thing that comes to mind. I trust you will feel it in your intuition.

Your dearest and dearest always.

Apart from the way he signed the email, which even now threatens to make my heart leap out of my chest, I found myself struggling to catch my breath. It was strange enough that he had sent an email at all, given my thoughts earlier in the evening, but when I checked the time on the email I was forced to take time to recover before I could act on it. It was sent at 5:32 PM my time. Well, what's a girl to say to that? I clicked the link and found myself at the Gmail site. Now all I needed was a name. I recalled the story Brigitte had told me with regards to her new identity. I decided to go back to the site I had previously found online explaining the meanings and purpose behind the names of the archangels. If one of the names leapt out at me, I would claim it for my own.

Out of the names that were listed at the top of the page, *Gabriel* really grabbed my attention. It was the only one that started with G, and I reasoned that as Rev had chosen gmail, maybe I should take a hint. So I clicked on the link and read about Gabriel.

Meaning: "Strength of God"; "The Divine is my strength"; "God is my strength." The only archangel depicted as female in art and literature, Gabriel is known as the messenger angel and is one of the four archangels named in Hebrew tradition, and is considered one of the two highest-ranking angels in Judeo-Christian and Islamic religious lore. Apart from Michael, she is the only angel mentioned by name in the Old Testament. She is a powerful and strong archangel, and those who call upon her will find themselves pushed into action that leads to beneficial results.

Gabriel can bring messages to you, just as she did to Elizabeth and Mary of the impending births of their sons, John the Baptist and Jesus of Nazareth. If you are considering starting a family, Gabriel helps hopeful parents with conception or through the process of adopting a child. Contact Gabriel if your third eye is closed and your spiritual vision is therefore blocked; if you wish to receive visions of angelic guidance regarding the direction you are going in; if you wish to receive prophecies of the changes ahead; or if you need help in interpreting your dreams and vision.

Gabriel helps anyone whose life purpose involves the arts or communication. She acts as a coach, inspiring and motivating artists, journalists, and communicators and helping them to overcome fear and procrastination. Gabriel also helps us to find our true calling. Ask for Gabriel's guidance if you have strayed from your soul's pathway and if you wish to understand your life plan and purpose. She can also help if you can find no reason for being or if changes are ahead and you need guidance, or if you are contemplating a house move, major purchase, or thinking of changing careers. Call Gabriel if your body is full of toxins and needs purifying and if your thoughts are impure or negative and need clearing and cleansing. Gabriel is also very helpful if you have been raped or sexually assaulted and feel dirty as well as being under psychic attack, or if you feel that you have absorbed someone else's problems.'

I am guessing I don't need to explain why, after reading all that on *Angel Focus*, I chose to embrace the name. I felt I had been given an incredible gift of a second chance. Keeping with the theme of *G*, I settled on gabrielasgift. Understandably, I was not surprised when the name was available. As I clicked *send* to complete the process and acquire my new identity, I offered up another little prayer of thanks.

I sent Rev an email entitled "last email from evil o," explaining the entire story and including a link to my new address.

Hey, hon,

Wow—you need to stop reading my mind—or maybe it was your idea and you were sending me ideas I was picking up on, because, while I was out getting some more stuff ready for the trip, I was thinking that the days of eviloctopus have come to an end—I mean, it's not really a good networking name, right? Funny thing was, I hadn't decided yet what email account I was going to go with, and I was going to come home and check out what's available. Instead, I got home and you had already sent me a link—all good, hon. I set it up—my new address is gabrielasgift@gmail.com—I actually got the idea from that other random lady I told you about the other day. I will tell you the story when I see you, but her business name is Auriel's Touch—named after the archangel Uriel, who is the bringer of courage to those beginning a new journey. I figured I would check out the archangels' names and see if one suited my purpose, and it seems that Gabriel would be fitting. I have always thought that it was one of the most beautiful names. Apparently Gabriel means "God is my strength." Gabriel is the angel of child conception or the process of adopting a child. Gabriel also helps anyone whose life purpose involves art or communication. She is the defender of the element of water and the west; the angel of resurrection, mercy and peace, and benefactor of messengers! Gabriel will help you with purity, rebirth, creativity, prophecy, and purifying your thoughts, bodily and emotionally. She is patron angel of all who work in the field of communications. I think you will agree that it fits.

I guess I will be sending you email now from that account, so watch for the name. I will write again soon. xo

I sent the email and, before logging off and heading to bed, I checked my daily tarot.

The *Queen of Wands* suggests that my power today lies in liberation. I radiate or communicate personal power, passion, and allure and am not dragged down by trends. I have a bold, magical flair and a spirit of innovation and pride. I am secure in my identity or performance and thrive on creating, designing, or fostering new or equal opportunities for aesthetic or personal growth, expression or awareness. I am empowered with gratitude, attention and reputation to go beyond the call, and I transform through exploring or initiating change.

This time I didn't groan. I smiled a satisfied, content, grateful smile. looked up at the heavens, and whispered "thank you" to the God who I was now completely sure was listening.

Chapter 15
Mistakes, Miracles, and What it Means to Know God

Should I bother commenting on my morning routine, or should I just jump straight to the email? Okay, email it is!

My Lady, very nice.

Yeah, I've studied the archangels a bit. Love the name.

Can you bring another ionizer? My other cousin has problems when he wakes up here, too. I'm thinking of just MASS importing a bunch of those here from China, I don't know how they would sell, though. I think if you educate the people on their benefits and educate them still on the side-effects of NOT using them, people would buy.

The meeting with the director went really well. So bizarre, because he's an inspiration to me through all his movies and the themes of them; yet, when I talked to him he told me that I was inspiring him. I have to watch two of his movies; then I'll meet him again.

If you see or talk to Sophia, tell her I already found a place to get her bags, hahahaha

I had a nightmare… but instead of dwelling on it like I used to, I got out of bed, shook it off, told myself it was just a dream, and converted the story to paper. Now I'll use it for my fictional story.

I found some hotels that are much, much closer. I looked at the hotel, though, and it looks nice… maybe you should stay there. Live it up, you know—you deserve it.

I have another meeting today. As long as you humble yourself to them and don't treat them any lower than you, they'll treat you like gold. They've been oppressed and repressed for so long… and still, in those living conditions, you see them laughing and with smiles. It's quite powerful.

I'll pick you up at the airport on Saturday. When you bring the ionizer on the plane, keep it in your carryon bag with your laptop.

Keep it turned off until after the plane takes off and keep it on throughout the entire flight; it will help you with your jet lag. Put on your headphones, too, when u use it. Some airlines don't allow it, but if they think it's just an MP3 player, you're fine.

Always yours, R

Really? Well, I suppose I should be used to it by now, right? Wrong! If you are one of those people who, like me, can see the cause and effect of seemingly coincidental occurrences, then you will probably agree with me when I say that I honestly hope I never get used to it. If you cannot understand that statement, then let me explain. When you live your life in a manner that allows you to follow the paths laid before you, every new day is a new adventure, with wonders around every corner. Like a small child, I am able to look at the world with eyes wide with wonderment and see the vast power and beauty in even the tiniest, drabbest parts of this remarkable place in which we live. There is warmth and light in all the things that surround us: people, animals, and nature. Call it God's light, if you choose, or the power of Mother Earth; either way, it exists when you open your heart to it and will fill you with hope for a better, more peaceful tomorrow.

Don't get me wrong. I am also, unfortunately, very in tune with the pain and suffering that exist here. It comes from being a fairly strong "empath"; yet empathy breeds compassion, so, although the abilities I have can sometimes cause pain, I am grateful for them nonetheless. It is not easy to feel others' pain, anguish, or negativity. I certainly don't enjoy the constant struggle that comes with each new invasion of emotion. I am a bleeding heart, so every time someone hurts I tend to tune into it, hoping to draw some of their pain away. Of course, their pain really should not be able to hurt me, but, if there is enough of it, it can be uncomfortable. I also try to stay away from confrontation if I can (me not Evil she thrives on it). If you add an empath into the mix when two people are arguing, the negative energy tends to flow much faster and build much more quickly. The negative energy literally bounces off itself in a continuous cycle. It is rather like the starter in your car; the magnetic energy continues to cycle in on itself until it builds a powerful enough charge to start your engine. Of course, the process is exactly the same for two people who are not particularly tuned in or empathic, but it is a slower building charge, allowing time to avoid the inevitable explosion. The worst case scenario is two strong empaths who are not aware of their abilities, as awareness breeds caution, which allows the outcome to be controlled. If, however, there is no awareness, the results can be catastrophic in nature. I have actually had a few no-holds-barred fights with others like myself in my younger years, before I learned how important it is to pull back. These were memorable, and every single one of them led to irrevocable emotional damage. Even while I mourn friendships lost, I know those moments taught me lessons I would later need, so I cannot bring myself to regret them.

There is as always a positive side, for, as dangerous as the pain and anger can be, the joy and contentment of others can be an equally powerful experience. Those who are at peace with themselves and their surroundings can be like a soothing balm to my at-times-tortured soul. As long as I focus on the positivity of the energy being offered and make sure my own troubled spirit does not affect the giver, then I am able to make use of others' purity of thought to heal an injured heart. This is also reversible, which is why I have constantly exposed myself to others who are unbalanced, willingly putting my own peace of mind at risk in order to ease their torment. It is partially how healers work, drawing negative energy from a person and replacing it with the positive.

Next time you find yourself in a confrontation with someone, instead of continuing to feed them the anger you feel, focus instead on giving them love; you will be amazed at how quickly they come around to your way of thinking. They will likely never know, in fact, how it is you managed to get them to change their minds; they might even believe it was their decision. I caution you, however, not to do this merely to get your own way; it will backfire, as it is not a tool that selfish people can use effectively. You must be truly interested in not wanting to hurt the person you are fighting with for it to be completely effective. It is a learned skill in some, an inborn gift in others, and something the world as a whole should explore the use of. Taking in someone else's anger and feeding that person love and understanding is a potent, powerful way to maintain balance in both your own life and the lives of those you care for. Try it—I promise you will not be disappointed.

As for ever getting used to the ever-present magic that this wonderful indestructible energy brings to my life, I pray that I will continue to be amazed and grateful for every strange, mystical occurrence. I fear the loss of these things in my life; if they were gone from my world, as strange as they sometimes make my world seem to be, I would much prefer my holographic existence to the reality that society deems it necessary to embrace. I think if these things were ever stolen from me it would very likely destroy me; fortunately, I do not believe in "reality" any more than the average person believes in "magic," so I doubt it will ever be an issue.

As for all of you out there who know exactly what I'm talking about, look up to the heavens and shout it out with me: "THAT WAS SOOOOO COOL!"

This is, of course, exactly what I did; I looked up said to myself, "That was so cool," then I took the time to answer his email.

> *Hey, my baby,*
>
> *So weird—I just got your email now about getting one more—thing is, I already drove all the way out there (it's at 400 and Rutherford Road, so long way), but, get this, I talked to the guy like 3 times today; he knew I was coming late last night; each time we talked he reassured me they would be open till 8 pm, so I leave early, take a wrong turn, have to double back, and still I manage to make it there for 7:40—but no guy—doors are locked. I guess when you want something you get it, eh, because now I am going back this morning, and I will be able to get an extra one. Things just seem to be completely out of our hands (well, mine anyway, lol).*
>
> *I'll let Soph know about the bag—she is spoiled, eh? What was your nightmare about? You are supposed to be having good dreams—maybe u r supposed to use it in your story. Like I said, if we are able to change the hotel when I get there, we will—but if I keep this one we will also have somewhere to escape to if we want alone time. As much as I would love to be beside you every minute of every day, I doubt, with all you have going on, that it would be possible, even if I was a few minutes away—though I am not sure I am comfortable with doing any exploring on my own. Is all good? We can figure it all out when I get there, right?*
>
> *I'll call the guy for the ionizers this morning—hopefully he has three. I am one day closer to Manila and one day closer to some adventuring with you—talk soon. xo*

So, email sent, I went about the task of getting him his ionizer; funny that the second time I drove out there it was so foggy that if I hadn't already known exactly where I was going there is no way I would have found the place. It would appear my trip the night before had been not without purpose after all. When I got there, I found out the owner had indeed been indisposed due to some kind of family emergency, but the clerk assured me that all would be well and thanked me for my concern. After a brief discussion on how the ionizers worked, I left with yet another busy day ahead. Granted it was only 9:30 AM, but I would be picking my daughter up at 3:00, then be off to the sister-in-law's for dinner, and then finally go to meet the strange woman and partake in a Bible study. The whole concept, I must admit, was a little daunting for me. I remember studying the Bible when I was young, at my mother's insistence, and, of course, I had done my time as a Sunday school teacher while in high school, so I was more than familiar with its contents—but I was aware that the people I would be meeting were more than merely familiar, they knew its contents intimately.

Now, you may be mildly curious as to why, when I am so interested in spirituality and religion, I would not take time to read the Bible and learn its contents. As I said, I have read it, though it has been years since my last legitimate study of it. That little adventure was one undertaken in my later high school years, and it was done from the view of somebody not merely looking to learn from the words written but somebody who was also looking for the flaws. As I have said before, it was written by man and man is fallible. There are several instances in the Bible where the stories are not complete or consistent, and some of the stories are riddled with contradictions. *Truth* to tell, if one were to study it in that manner, they would no doubt find more than enough evidence to make them question the validity of the whole thing. However, in saying that, I believe in what its lessons stand for, and I do, without a doubt, believe in God and the strength that comes from knowing him. My views, however, do not always mesh well with the Christian community, and though I speak to God on a regular basis, I cannot quote scripture, and by no means do I lead a pure life. Admittedly, one could point out the last two weeks as an example of divine guidance and intervention, but, for every person who believes that I have been guided, there will be one who says that my flaws and lack of study of God's word put me in jeopardy of saving my soul. Regardless of your own personal views—views which I myself choose not to judge—you have to admit the evening will be an interesting one!

All of this was in my mind as I drove back to the house to make a last-ditch effort at packing. Of course, I could not go on with my day without a quick check of the email—even if at the moment I had no real time to answer anything he wrote.

That is pretty amazing lol.

Yeah, the nightmare is probably just something I can use in my book and script.

It only becomes reality when you dwell on it. The constant energy you feed your thoughts can materialize them, right, so… I'll just see it as fiction. My mother's dreams seem to materialize, but mine don't, and neither do my nightmares… now I know why I get them, then. =) They're so I can write realistic events and know the feelings of them without them actually happening. It's so weird—my mother's nightmares and dreams actually come true. She had a dream of me standing in front of millions of people and talking and also dreams of my face on billboards all over cities. Who knows! Lol—I don't know… they haven't materialized yet.

I got lost in the mall today, and my whole family got so scared.

Anyway… just finished watching American Idol with my cousin, and it compelled me to practice.

My cousin's fiancé said he would drive me to the airport. So, see you then.

xoxo

Interesting thought, that: speaking in front of thousands of people…

Glad to know it was him she saw … to be quite honest, better him than me. I rather like my quiet existence and do not enjoy the prospect of ever having to talk to a large crowd of any kind of people. The idea terrifies me to no end, so if God is kind (and I have seen evidence that he is) then he will never ask it of me. Of course, if it is where this strange path leads, then who am I to question? I will do as I am expected when the time comes, but if I can ask for one thing for myself, it is that I be left alone to wander and explore the world and the people in it without the interference of the public eye. Leave me with my quiet life; the world not knowing my name suits me just fine, thank you.

Oh, right—how can I hope to write a book, publish it, and still not have any kind of fame… Well, we'll get to that later, but I am hoping against hope that that is what I'll be able to do. I guess, as with all things in life, I will just have to wait and see how that works out…

The next hour was not really overly exciting, which was a very nice change. The trip to pick up my passport was quick, and I soon found myself back at home, staring at my suitcases and wondering what to put in them.

While I was yet again wandering around my house, with a lost look in my eyes, it occurred to me that during the last two weeks I had not called the one person who would probably be most interested in what I was about to do—not interested, perhaps, in the writing or the reason for the trip, but more interested in the fact that I was taking a trip at all. And here now enters into the tale a woman who has stood by my side for twenty years, no questions asked. Regardless of what I have done, where I have gone, or who I have chosen to spend my life with, she has always stood by me. She was my tree, my strength—my Lina.

If home is ever to be found in the existence of another, then I have found home in Lina.

She is the quintessential redhead: she has a fiery temper and is willful, stubborn, strong, and independent. Yet, for all of those things—some of which people have viewed as flaws—she is also loyal, giving, loving, supportive, and honest—if she decides for at any reason to pass judgment on the actions or decisions of anybody in her life, she is more than honest about that judgment. She will quite openly tell you exactly why she thinks what you've done or are going to do is wrong, and then she will look you in the eye, smile, and tell you to do whatever you want—she will still love you in the end and catch you if your current stupidity happens to cause you to fall. She is a remarkable individual, really, and given all that we have gone through and done together, it is a wonder we have not yet managed to kill each other or ourselves. We're two strong-willed women, yes, who have managed through mutual understanding and respect to maintain a friendship that spans twenty years of life-changing experiences, moves, and personal growth. God willing, there will never be a day when the woman is not in my life. To me she is a tower of strength on a stormy day, the tree I seek shelter under when it pours or when the light of the sun gets too hot; but she is also my most entertaining friend, and it is for her I smile more easily than anybody else (apart from my daughter, that is).

Our relationship is twisted; at times she is an incredible tease, so when she found out a few years back that I have in the past had girlfriends, she made it a ritual to try to tease me as much as possible when I am visiting—not verbally, you understand, but physically. It was only after she discovered my weakness for the female flesh (oh, really, like you are surprised—honestly I have not had a girlfriend in years, nor do I intend to pursue that particular avenue again anytime soon. Truthfully, I much prefer the company of men, thanks, though the female body is, you have to admit, remarkably alluring). Lina got into the habit of changing in front of me, brushing my lips with gentle kisses rather than kissing me on the cheek, and hugging me, at times, in a little too—hmmm, how would you say it?—oh, *friendly* manner.

The thing is, she is straight as you can be, visibly shuddering at the thought of sleeping with a woman. It's funny, since she supports anything anybody else does and refuses to condemn anybody for their personal choices when it comes to sexuality, but she would not venture into that realm herself if her life depended on it.

Her teasing has gotten the attention of several others—friends who laugh uproariously when she gets going; it seems she doesn't much care who is in the room when she decides to test our friendship. I only refer to it as a test, since she is so straight; really, she has to know that I wouldn't ever dream of crossing that line with her, but she continues to offer unspoken promises of a physical relationship. Like I said, she is a tease, and the whole thing sends those who know us into uncontrollable fits of laughter when she takes the teasing to greater heights in public. Regardless of all of this, we will always remain extremely comfortable in each other's presence. There really is not much in my life she does not know about, and, as to those things I haven't shared with her, it is only because they are inconsequential or I simply haven't had time.

She still lives in the area in which we both grew up, refusing to leave the place, as it keeps her close to her family. Her mother is her main concern, and I can't blame her; the woman is hard not to love, really, and my friend's dedication to her is not unwarranted. Of course, it doesn't help that my friend is also terrified of flying, so, whether or not she will ever travel the world with me, it is an unspoken rule of our friendship that I will wander wherever life seems to take me as long as occasionally I make it a point to wander back her way into her comforting arms, to share with her in person whatever adventures I have had. And, no, you will never meet her—as much as she no doubt intrigues you, she also is an extremely private personality who would crumble from fright if she thought the public knew much beyond the fact that she exists.

She has plagued me for years with the question: When will you come home? (in reference, of course, to the town in which she now lives) and I have promised her many times that when the end is near I will find my way back there to live my last years out with her. I can promise her no more than that, and I dearly hope the powers that be allow me to fulfill that promise in the end. I have asked her many times to join me some day on my ventures, but still she refuses, which is not really a surprise, as she won't even spend more than an hour in a car; she claims it makes her too sick. Personally, I think maybe she just gets bored.

Really, there is not much else to tell about this incredible individual, except that we were hellions in our youth, both determined to get into as much trouble as possible, and we were arrested more than once for stupidity that should have never happened.

I remember one incident that resulted in both of us having to do community service over the theft of lawn chairs—yes, I know, who the hell steals lawn chairs? But, at the time, we needed them—no, really we did...

We were at a field party out near one of the local towns, and there was nothing to sit on, so my friend and I wandered into the closest settlement of new houses and borrowed a few lawn chairs from various backyards. Now I use the term *borrowed*, because we fully intended to return them the next day; however, we woke in the morning to the smell of burning plastic and discovered, much to our dismay, that the boys who had stayed up all night by the fire had run out of wood and were now contentedly stoking the failing fire with our chairs. Of course, since we had taken them, *we* took the blame for the whole thing and soon found ourselves having to go to court for theft of chairs. Stupid, really; we were both given community service and ordered to go to a class on the repercussions of theft and the effect it has on society. How embarrassing, really, to stand up in a group of people and admit you are here because, yes, you stole lawn chairs. Still, to this day it is a running joke with some of the people who knew us then, and my friend and I can laugh about it now; I mean, it's been years really—we were only fourteen at the time.

Lina tells people still that I was the ringleader then, and, I suppose I can admit it now, if trouble was found and we were involved, chances are it was my rambunctious brain that had thought it up. People grow up and they change, and, though I would not take back one single moment of time spent with her or take back any of the crazy silly things we did, I can't see myself ever having the desire to do any of it again. Still, I view it as the process called growth: we live, we steal lawn chairs, we learn.

I now chose to call this remarkable lady, just to let her know I would be out for awhile. I should have called her sooner, and I told her so on the phone, but she reminded me—without mincing words—that it really had no effect on our relationship, since I don't see her every day anyway.

"Oh, for..." Waves of exasperation and red-headed attitude came through in her voice, "What are you worried about; you hardly see me now anyway, and we talk maybe twice a month, not counting text messages. You'll be back soon enough; just do me a favour, and don't get killed, eh; you promised to come home some day and I'm holding you to that. Oh, and say hi to my goddaughter, eh; tell her I love her and you, too, so stay safe."

That's it really; she didn't have anything else to say—not *why*, not *when*, just: *don't get dead.* Again I make the claim that my friends *are* odd ... but, again, I have to take the time to acknowledge how blessed I am by their presence in my life; it has become a daily ritual for me to look up to the heavens and say thanks.

Phone call done, I took a moment to drop a quick line to the man on the other side of the world.

> *Hey, hon,*
>
> *I got the ionizers; I could only get two, as that was all they had, but when I leave I can leave mine behind for one of your cousins. I also picked up my passport today, so I am all set. I still have to pack, but at least my running around is done. It's so weird: everyone I talk to down here, even just random strangers at stores and the bank, are so excited about this trip. They always ask if I will come by when I get back and share some of what I've written. I've been telling them I will; I just hope I remember them all when it is time, but then, I suppose it will be hard to forget them, considering some of the crazy conversations I've had with them about this trip. It will make fantastic material and it's the kind of "No way, that did not happen" story that will suck people in.*
>
> *I still have to pack, but I am sure I'll be as ready as I can be come tomorrow night. For now, though, I have to run; still so much to do. Sophia sends her love and her pinches, lol—can't wait to be there. xo*

That done, I jumped in the car and headed off to pick up Madison. When she finally found her way to the car, she asked what our plans were for the night. I explained about the last couple days and my need to go the Bible study that evening. I asked her if she wanted to join me and realized she was very hesitant to answer. I reassured her she did not have to go if she didn't want to, but I made a point of asking her why she would prefer to stay home on our last night together.

"Oh, Mom, it's not that I don't want to spend time with you, really." She looked at me briefly and then turned her head back to the window. "It's just that, well, I don't go to church, and I've never read the Bible, and, well…" She paused here, as if gathering her thoughts, then blurted out in a rush, "I won't be comfortable there; I don't see things like they do, and I don't understand most of what they are talking about."

I could understand her point, but at the same time I was a little confused by one particular thing.

"But, hon," I asked gently. "You believe in God, right? So how is it you think that you don't see things the way they do?"

"Of course I believe in God." She shook her head. "I don't know how to explain it; I just don't think I'll be comfortable."

She paused again for a few minutes, and I was hesitant to push her; she might only be eleven, but give her enough time and she can put together some pretty well-thought-out explanations.

"It's like this, Mom; you know the story I told you when I was younger about what happened when I was born?" Her voice sounded a little distant, as if she were remembering something.

And I did indeed know the story, but thought perhaps it was one she herself had forgotten. The last time she had spoken of it had been when she was five years old, and I had never mentioned it since, thinking it was not something we needed to discuss. I am sure the idea of her telling me anything about the day she was born sounds a little unrealistic, but, as we have already explored my views on reality, you should not be surprised by anything I say. The story is indeed an odd one, and I will tell it to you briefly, as she told it to me at the tender age of five years. I can't for the life of me remember how the subject came up then, but, as you read the next few lines, try to keep in mind that this is coming from the mouth of a little girl who has been to church maybe a total of seven times in her short life and a few of those times were weddings not services…

The story she told me of her birth also requires a little back ground into the troubles that surrounded her birth. My body apparently does not like the task of bearing and delivering children, as we discovered much to our dismay while we were into my second day of hard labour. I could tell you the entire tale, but I doubt very much it is really pertinent to the issue at hand, so I will be brief. Basically, childbirth almost killed both me and my child, and though I was blessed after three days of labour with a healthy, beautiful baby girl, it would be weeks before my body would begin to recover. How my daughter managed to survive two days in the womb after the water had broken has never been explained to me by anybody other than my daughter herself. The doctors certainly did not have an explanation, and I can't seem to find anybody else who supports the notion that it is possible. Yet, by some miracle, it happened, and it was to this miracle and her remembrance of it that my daughter now referred.

At the age of five she had explained it in simple five-year-old's terms. Basically, she claimed that at the time of her birth she was scared that she was going to die. She remembers very clearly knowing that something was terribly wrong, and she also remembers not wanting to die. She claims also that shortly before she was born, God came and spoke to her, telling her not to be afraid, that she would be okay and that he would take care of her.

Seriously, that is what she told me, and, no, I do not question it. Would you? I mean, who am I to assume that it did not happen simply because she was only an infant? Who am I to assume that her recollections of this thing could not be real? To her they are very real, and it would be faithless and ungrateful of me to try in any way shape or form to sway her belief in this. How many five-year-old children can look you in the eye and say they talked to God?

Believe what you want; me, I choose not to doubt. She believes, and so I believe, and it was with that belief in mind that I now waited for her to finish her thoughts.

"Okay, so you asked me if I believe in God, right?" she again glanced over at me, "and you know I do, but you are asking the wrong question."

Oh yes, I know she's eleven; it's okay, I deal with it all the time, really I do. I think maybe, in time, you will get used to it to.

"You should be asking me *why* I believe, not *if* I believe." As usual, she continued to stare out the window of the car as I drove, and, as it seemed she was waiting for something, I took the obvious next step.

Simply, I asked her, "Okay, why do you believe?"

"Oh Mom, that's easy, really; I believe because I know he exists." She turned to me and gave me an impish little smirk, and then her face became serious. "I have seen the proof of his existence; I have seen miracles happen; I was saved by a miracle, so I know he exists, and I am grateful to him for saving me. He let me live—how can I not know he exists?"

Okay, so you can picture me driving along, both hands on the wheel, eyes round as saucers, and eyebrows climbing up to my scalp, right? Nope, not this time; there was no shock on my part, just a mild curiosity as to where this was leading. I have to say, at times like these I am grateful for the long ride home after school; it allows for the most unique discussions.

"Alright, so, if you believe, why in the world would you think you would be uncomfortable around people who also believe?" Leave to me to ask the silliest of questions, assuming that I knew the answer.

"Oh really, Mom." She managed to sound patient and exasperated at the same time, quite the feat coming from a young girl. "You said that it's a Bible study; I've never read the Bible, so how can I study it with them?"

At this point she looked at me yet again, and her eyes were very clear and bright and the impish smile that I know and love so much had again returned to her face. "It's simple: I don't know the Bible; I only know God."

With that, she turned her head away and went back to staring out the window, lost in her own thoughts. The discussion, it seemed, was over for the moment, and I was left, not with a feeling of awe, but a quiet contentment about what she had said.

It occurred to me as I drove that if you have a question, and you really want to know the truth, you should ask a child.

Chapter 16

I Am Who I Am, and I Can Only Be Me

I will not bore you with the details of dinner with the family, except to say that it is good sometimes to take the time to appreciate the small things—like a casual spaghetti dinner with the people who matter most to you.

Nor will I give you a detailed account of all that occurred during the Bible study. I will, however, include the lesson that the gentleman who ran it prepared, so that you may see what was discussed. I will also highlight one particular discussion that stood out and the lesson it contained. First the lesson plan.

Observations about John 19:

INTRODUCTION

"Behold the man!" "Behold your King!" (slides) Interesting parallel statements by Pilate. What did they see? Isaiah 53 tells us. Let's read it. So what did they see? (Click)

And what do we see when we look at Jesus? Paul tells us what he saw in Hebrews 12:2: Let us fix our eyes on Jesus, the author and perfecter of our faith, who for the joy set before him endured the cross, scorning the shame, and sat down at the right hand of the throne of God. Consider him who endured such opposition from sinful men, so that you will not grow weary and lose heart." We see a PERFECT, GLORIOUS EXAMPLE of how one man endured incredible suffering and shame in the service of God.

Every time we partake of the Lord's supper, our Lord Jesus is giving us the opportunity to LOOK at Jesus, to behold him at this ultimate moment of sacrifice, faith and humility, and endeavor to be more like him, to submit to our wonderful loving King.

We will be using today the gospel records to behold our Lord in his time of suffering, along with Isaiah 53, Psalm 22, and Psalm 69.

BEHOLDING THE MAN

Jesus "turns the other cheek," not saying a word in his own defense.

Finally, he speaks in private to Pilate, letting us in to his thinking process, the source of his strength: "You would have no power over me if it were not given you from above. Therefore the one who handed me over to you is guilty of the greater sin." Jesus acknowledges in word and, more importantly, in action that no matter what is being done to him, it is his Father's will, and therefore he can accept it.

Lesson for us: HOLD YOUR TONGUE/ACTIONS WHEN YOU FEEL YOU ARE BEING ATTACKED/MALIGNED

Being able to truly "turn the other cheek" when we are put down, physically or verbally, especially in public, is extremely hard, because of our selfish pride—we want to defend our honour amongst our peers. We feel, rightly or wrongly, that the other is trying to destroy our reputation in order to raise themselves up, and we want to fight against it in our self-righteousness.

But Jesus, even though he KNEW *he was in the right, encouraged us to keep the highest outlook: not to look at it as another person doing something to you, but to look at it in the light of faith: your Father is causing you to suffer so that you can be made perfect. Whatever you are going through, it is your Father's will you go through it.*

In Psalm 22, Jesus says it is God who brings shame and suffering upon us, for his loving and righteous reasons, and God we must turn to to save us from it.

Another hint as to how Jesus managed not to lash out at his attackers with his God-given power appears in the gospel of Luke. In addition to his God-centred perspective, it was his overriding care and concern for others that held his baser emotions in check. Jesus had an amazing ability to get outside himself, even during great suffering. How did he do it?

Jesus said in Luke 23:34 "Forgive them Father, for they know not what they do." FOR THEY KNOW NOT WHAT THEY DO. *Jesus demonstrated an* UNDERSTANDING *of his attackers—he put himself in their shoes and acknowledged that they didn't truly realize that what they were doing was wicked. In fact, a few of them probably did, to greater or lesser extents, but Jesus refused to judge them as having evil motives. He acknowledged that every one of us, even the ones that appear the worst, are fundamentally the same—we are all fighting hard internal and external battles in life. Jesus identified with the battle that raged within him as well as his attackers, and actually felt camaraderie with them, even if they didn't with him.*

Jesus' concern for others was primarily, but not solely, focused on their eternal well-being—he demonstrated concern for temporal and emotional well-being, also, when he provided for his mother and when he mourned for the coming terrors the citizens of Jerusalem would have to endure at the hands of the Romans.

Jesus taught us through his example, many times in his life that, although we are ultimately concerned about the kingdom of God and human salvation, true agape love commands that we be aware of human suffering in this life, and let it affect our hearts, instead of remaining aloof from it—weeping with those who weep, visiting the sick, feeding the hungry, and providing water for the thirsty. And, regardless, how can we expect anyone to listen to a message about an abstract hope for the future if they are dying of thirst right now, or have not known the comfort of being loved in the first place? Providing for the material and emotional needs of our fellow man is not just being a blind, bleeding heart; it is the right and godly thing to do.

But, of course, the ultimate concern continues to be people's eternal salvation, and Jesus' words on the cross bear this out as well.

In addition to using the words of Psalm 22 to help him keep a divine perspective, Jesus used them to actually continue his ministry of proclaiming the kingdom of God right to the last. He kept his mind on his JOB, *his* LABOUR OF LOVE.

Now we come to our Lord's last word on the cross, and we feel a tremendous sense of relief with the words "It is finished," and, in Luke 23:46, "Father, into your hands I commit my spirit."

This is further evidence of the fanatical drive to see his task of loving service through to the end. But not only was this a relief for our Lord, to finally rest after three and a half years of pushing himself to the limit in service to his Father; these words should be to us a joyful victory shout, for with them our Lord put to death his sinful mind and opened the way of salvation for all mankind.

Romans 5:12-21; Psalm 98, read!

Now, whether or not you are a Christian, there are good life lessons to be learned from these scriptures, but it is up to you to explore for yourself your own truth. As I have said many times before, it is not for me to decide for you what you wish to believe. I offer a view of what is out there and offer the idea that the truth is out there for each individual to find—but how you find it or what road you choose to take on your journey is not for me to decide.

However, I also believe strongly in the base messages that Jesus taught: *love and compassion for your fellow man.*

If you take nothing else from all that I have written or will write, then I hope you can at least accept that as being the most important life lesson you will ever learn. Love and compassion—they will allow you to move forward in your life with a smile in your heart and a spring in your step and to acknowledge that all other humans are fundamentally the same as we are. They suffer as we do, love and fear as we do, have hopes and dreams as we do. Remember these things. Embrace the idea that all your fellow men wish is to also be happy and to not suffer. Do what you can to help them in their quest for happiness and inner peace. This does not mean judging them or trying to change their ideals; that, my friends, is not our job. It means simply finding within yourself the courage to love and respect even those who would harm you, the courage to feel the pain of others, and the commitment to working toward relieving that pain. Whatever path you must follow to learn that lesson, whatever messages you receive, in whatever form helps you to see that as being true—those messages are the ones you were meant to see, the lessons you were meant to learn, and they will not be the same messages from the same source for all people. Our world is vast and ever-changing, our beliefs are varied, and our backgrounds are different. Far be it from me to say which belief system is the right one or the wrong one—as long as it is a positive one that is based on mutual love and respect for your fellow man.

Now that I have said my piece, I will explain a bit about one of the discussions during the study.

As I listened to various people in the room speak, one thing came to my attention. It was that some of them felt an overwhelming sense of sadness at the idea of Jesus being sacrificed on the cross. I was confused by it, and I took the time to tell them so. I explained that though I could not quote the scriptures, I understood their content and the message therein. I also explained that I did not think it was meant to bring sadness to their hearts, but rather to lift and inspire them. I told them that the idea of Jesus's death was to free men of past doubt and guilt for their sins, so that they could move forward with love in their hearts and continue to grow spiritually. I do not believe that if a person dwells on past mistakes and therefore spends time wallowing in self-pity and self-hatred that he/she can look at the mistake objectively. We are human, and, being human, we continue to make mistakes—but we must learn from those mistakes and take the lessons learned from them, using those lessons to move us forward in life. Those lessons help us to grow spiritually, and it is those lessons and spiritual growth that encourages our evolution as humans. Yet, how can we possibly see the lesson if we are blinded by fear, anger, and doubt?

I asked the people in the room, "Can't you see that it was with a great amount of faith in humanity as a whole that God was willing to sacrifice his only son? How can the idea of that much faith and hope for humanity make you sad or despondent? Is it not a message of hope? Is it not meant to free your heart and allow you to heal yourselves through faith? How then can it make you sad?"

I was amazed at the discussion that followed and the response that came from these questions, and I sat back for awhile, shaking my head at the idea that those these people believed in the Bible's teachings and spent hours a day studying them, yet some of them did not see the positive message contained within. I admit, of course, that I am no expert, but when I read the stories contained within the Bible I find messages of love, compassion, and hope, and I see no reason to be saddened by the sacrifices made by others who were sent before us to spread those messages. They willingly gave of themselves for the sake of future generations, and their stories should inspire others, for if the message of love is important enough to die for, then perhaps it is a message that we should latch on to and listen to.

The discussion that followed included my belief that we ought to have love and respect for all our fellow humans, regardless of their personal beliefs, and I was surprised at the willingness of some of the members to hear what I had to say. I expected, I suppose, to be shut down the moment I spoke of the idea that it is really the same God sending the same message over and over in different forms. I also was very clear that I do not much care what people call their God, as long as that God shelters them, protects them, and guides them to love and have compassion for their fellow man. I expected quite honestly to be rebuked and accused of going against the content of the Bible, and I was prepared to stand up for my beliefs—yet, surprisingly, I was accepted in spite of what I believe, and there was a good hour of positive, open discussion with some of the members.

Again, I maintain that the same message has been sent to us through other means, through other faiths, and through other religions for thousands of years. It continues to be sent to us in various forms: in literature, films, music, and all forms of creative art. Again, I will not tell you which of these belief systems to follow, but I will tell you that when the message comes to you, in whatever form it is sent, it is for you to listen and explore the truth behind that message.

All in all, it made for an interesting evening, and I left the place feeling very uplifted and inspired. I took the time afterward to call both my brother and Deacon to share with them my experience and I couldn't help but giggle at their individual responses. Of course, my brother thought the whole thing tremendously entertaining. Leave it to him to giggle at the thought of me standing in a room full of Christians and openly declaring my beliefs without regard to whether or not they will persecute me for them. Of course, Deacon's response was expected; he simply wanted to know what the hell I thought I was doing trying to convert a bunch of Christians. I laughed at that, really. As I explained to him and am trying to continue to explain to everybody else I meet and talk to, I do not wish to convert anybody to anything. I only want to open their hearts and minds to the possibility that there is a much greater power at work in our world, one that desires for us to learn certain truths and is continuing to send us messages to help us find those truths.

I feel I have to point out here for any Christians who may be reading this book that if they doubt what I say, then they should please read Romans 13:8–14, as well as Romans 14. For those of you who are not Christian, please do for me the favor of taking the time to partake with me in one minor experiment. Over the next few days, spend the time to consciously be aware of your thoughts and actions toward the people you share your lives with and the people you encounter on a daily basis. Do not look at them as you see them physically, but rather see them for what they are: fellow humans who wish only to find happiness and be at peace. Take the time to share with them as much positivity as you can manage, simply by showing kindness, understanding, and acceptance. Give to each new person you meet a sense of well-being and love. Smile as much as you can, and when you look around at your life, take notice of and feel appreciation for all the little things in your life that make you smile. Try it for a little while, and see where it takes you. As I have learned for myself, and, as I hope you will also learn, the more love you give out, the more you will receive; the more positivity you share, the more you will encounter. Do these things out of concern for all living creatures; do them with an open heart and open mind and see where the experiment takes you. See what comes of doing for others instead of yourself; perhaps it will open your eyes to the beauty that exists here and provide you with hope that that beauty will continue to flourish.

After I had shared my experiences over the phone, I also took the time to send Rev an email.

> *Hey, hon,*
>
> *Hope you are sitting down when you get this one. I sent you the story of how I found (or rather how I was found by) the lady that worked for the CBC out of Manila, right? She called me today to confirm that I would go to meet her tonight at this Bible study group for her church—again something I would not normally do but felt compelled to follow through with. The meeting was at 8 and I got there early, but she wasn't there yet, so I got to talking to some of the people there and kind of getting a feel for them. The Bible study starts and still no lady—but, hey, I jump in anyway. Now I am surrounded by 15ish people of different racial backgrounds (white, Asian, Indian, black) and they are all over 50, but, as the study continues, I realize that the topic of the night pertains in a big way to both our (yours and mine) views on religion, spirituality, and the need for change—so I offer a couple comments, but I openly explain to them that I am not a denominational Christian and I don't know the Bible well enough to quote certain scriptures, but in light of my own personal experiences I can put what they are discussing into a more realistic and earthly context. (I will so explain this all in detail when I see you in person). As I am talking, people start to get involved in the discussion, and, rather than spouting phrases like "but the Bible says," they begin thinking more in terms of the stuff that happens to people every day and how it relates to the teaching of the Bible. Keep in mind I have already told these people I do not study the Bible the way they do, but rather have studied it in passing, along with several other religions over the years. So, the study session wraps up on a really positive note, and we are hanging*

out having tea, and people begin to approach me, asking questions about my views, and about my trip and about my (our) ideas for this story. So I'm explaining that I view religion as a conduit for the fundamental life lessons that people have to learn in order to grow spiritually, but that I do not believe that any one religion is necessarily the "right religion" and that given that we live in a society where (especially here in TO) we work and live shoulder to shoulder with others from different racial and spiritual back grounds and yet somehow manage to have respect for each other's beliefs—then is that a stretch to be willing to study other religions with an open heart and open mind and look for the common vein in all of them—the base teachings that are geared toward bringing spiritual growth to each and every student of all religious and spiritual back grounds? I point out that maybe it is time for the world to stop arguing about whose God is the one true God and focus on the meaning behind the belief in a higher power—and OH, WOW!—THEY LISTENED! It was incredible—here were these hardcore Bible-studying Christians opening their minds up and willingly wrapping their heads around the ideas I was presenting—not all of them, of course, but enough to make me sit back and really think about what I was doing there. They were making comments like "I wish I could see it the way you do" (that was an 80ish-year-old white granddad) and "what you say makes sense—makes the teachings we study more real" (again 80ish, but this time African woman) The gentleman who led the session asked me to come back when I get back from the Philippines, and more than one of them asked if I would be willing to go talk to their church group located in Manila if they sent me the contact info via email. One man offered to contact the group in Manila and let them know about me if I would be willing to go speak with them—I mean WOW—it was incredible—so crazy incredible, and not something I had ever seen myself doing until tonight. To top off the story, on my way home I got a phone call from the lady who had sent me there in the first place (she never did show up) and she told me her friend from the study group had called her and thanked her (THANKED HER, LOL) for sending me to them. She told me that right around the time she was supposed to leave for the meeting there was a power outage, and her entire street went black, and she felt safer staying at home, as she wasn't sure how widespread the power outage was or even if the subways were working near her area. All she knew was that her street and surrounding area were dark, and she felt compelled to stay home. She wasn't even able to call me until the power went back on, as her cordless phone would not work without power—her power went back on right about the time I was leaving the church, so she had gotten the call from her friend and then called me right away. I know the whole story is CRAZY, but, baby, what a strange, wonderful end to a really powerful two week. If you are experiencing as many crazy things there as I am here, then, baby, the book is practically writing itself. I so can't wait to see you and talk to you and explore all this (your stories and mine) in person, but, he, if I go to this church in Manila, will you come with me? Think on it; I think you should—I think maybe that is part of the reason you are there. They say God works in mysterious ways, but this past two weeks has been way beyond mystical for me—so much to do—so much to say—so much to share—so excited! See you soon, my heart. xo

Well, I guess that pretty much sums it up for you.

Of course, as you can expect, I went to bed feeling exceptionally hopeful and excited about the upcoming trip. The previous two weeks had opened my eyes to a whole new world of possibilities. I now neither worried about or feared where I was headed, but, rather, I was determined to enjoy the ride. I checked my daily tarot, of course, before heading off to bed.

The *Four of Pentacles* suggest that my power today lies in possession. I choose not to be bound, identified, or paralyzed by ownership, possessions, or means, in order that I may always have a free hand and room to grow. I am practical, responsible, and determined about protecting my purpose or advocating for my resources. I am empowered by the status quo and my asset is value.

Right, well, I think that's enough said for the moment.

Chapter 17
Taking Flight

One of my favorite numbers is seven, and so it is no surprise that it is the seventeenth chapter with which I end up taking flight.

I checked my email in the morning before I began packing.

Hi, baby,

Excited to see you, too. Manila Bay is close to your hotel; maybe we'll go check that out on Valentine's. I just finished watching my director's movie. It talks about foster children and the system here. I love his movies 'cause they're socially engaging.

Have a safe trip. That is pretty amazing. It's true; most people will respond to the truth that way—only some who are blinded by fanaticism will not see the true light. That accounts for a good chunk of the world's population.

See you soon.

Safe travels, my lady

That's it; that's all—a simple wish for a safe journey.

Was I excited? Hell, yes, you bet—but the day, to be honest, was completely uneventful, so rather than bore you with the "I packed this, then that, then the other…," I will instead use this as an opportunity to explain what you will be experiencing in the following chapters and how the letters you will be reading came to be written. Oh, but first my tarot for the day, in case I forget later to include it.

The *Lovers Card* affirms my alter ego is a port key to a soul mate, or deal, whose superpower is compatibility in the midst of reconciling dichotomy to interconnect as a whole new entity or "color." To be or not to be: with ultimatum or rival tensions mounting, negotiating acceptable trade-offs validates our unique perspectives to reflect what each lacks for a balanced voice of truce. When we're together, I'm beside myself, so I concede mutual vested interest, incentive, or opportunity to my other half for valued consideration. For only by the power of self-respect in reciprocal vulnerability, need, and compassion do "me and thee consummate we." The rest is all a dance on the sidelines of Cinderella pandering, or prohibition, or around a Bermuda Triangle of bottom-line temptation to cheat by provocation, promiscuity, or shame. But here at the gate of impasse, I still have a choice and my pride.

Well, given where I was headed and how I felt about the man I was supposed to be meeting there, I guess it fits perfectly, doesn't it? So I feel I need not say any more about it.

Now, you have not met the person I will be referring to next, and I feel I need to explain why she plays such an integral role in this tale. She is another long-time dear friend with whom I share many mutual beliefs. I had visited with her for two days and explained about my upcoming journey. I enlisted her help as both a researcher and first copy editor. You need not know much about her, other than that her name and mine are the same. Her middle name is Rose. She is a Christian/Wiccan (shocking, isn't it?) who has managed to marry the two spiritual beliefs and use from each the positive teachings she claims are very evident in both. If, in the future, you need to become more intimate with her, then I will accommodate. All you need know at the moment is that she is somebody whom I love and trust. She is also somebody I happen to have a great deal of respect for. She is an information magnet, and her abilities as a researcher have helped me more times than I can count as I wrote this book, so it only makes sense that she is in my heart as I wrote the letters you are about to read.

It was my intention originally to just write about what happened and include those experiences in the form of stories buried in chapters. What happened instead was that I ended up keeping a daily log (sometimes more than once a day) of my trip and the events that took place. All the letters are exceptionally personal and from the heart, as they are being written to her, so I ask that you please understand and have respect for the fact that this is a very large piece of my heart and soul I am about to lay at your feet.

I will ask only that you read them all with an open heart and open mind, given the content of some of them, and not take offence at what you read, but, rather, allow it to arouse in you the curiosity that I hope will inspire you to continue your quest for your own personal truth.

Honestly, there is not much more to tell at this point, and I might as well get on with sharing the actual trip with you; although, before I do, I suppose I owe you one more daily tarot. As I left on the twelfth and landed on the fourteenth, I spent the thirteenth in the air, and, since the tarot for that day is more than appropriate, I think you should be given the opportunity to read it for yourself. Keep in mind that it was written for the very day that I was on a plane flying toward my future. Though I had absolutely no idea of what that future would be, I made the trip with full confidence that it was where I was supposed to be at the time.

The *Star* suggests that my alter ego today is the Goddess, whose superpower for rising to the occasion lies in my innate ability for inspiration. I will pursue my dreams and what makes me happy—life's too short. I will allow time for me today. I may even get my fifteen minutes of fame by seeking recognition from others and striving to sparkle in the limelight. I am immortal! Sometimes it's better to burn out than just fade away. Find your cosmic groove, and go for it!

Well, my dears, it has been a great honor sharing these past experiences with you, and I thank you for being gracious listeners. The next time you hear from me I will have another viewpoint altogether. Although up until now I have been talking to you, the reader, directly, from here on out I will be directing my words to another. Remember that they are from the heart, and that I wrote them with the awareness that the reader would probably be listening in, so please do not feel left out. All I say in them, and all I share, I do willingly and with a heart I am unashamed to bare to the world. Godspeed, my friends, I will talk to you very soon.

All major religious traditions carry basically
the same message, that is love, compassion and
forgiveness... the important thing is they should be
part of our daily lives.

Dalai Lama

If you judge people,
you have no time to love them.

Mother Teresa

I believe in the fundamental truth
of all great religions of the world.

Mohandas Gandhi

The essence of all religions is one.
Only their approaches are different.

Mohandas Gandhi

Letters to Beaner

February 14th
Hong Kong Airport

Hey, sweets,

Originally I intended to spend the flight out writing, but what can I say?—my body was screaming at me to sleep. Have you ever tried to sleep on a plane, especially flying economy?

Right now I'm sitting in the airport in Hong Kong, waiting to transfer. I already changed my clothes and freshened up, as it is twenty-three degrees here, but—go figure—the air-conditioning is on, so, even though I'm in the other side of the world in a tropical climate, I'm still freezing.

I'm trying to kill time, surrounded by Asians, and I can't understand a word they are speaking, but they are all friendly. I tried to get hold of you to tell you my crazy story from the night before I left, but you no answer. I could write it all out here, but I want (no, need) your feedback. When I called my bro to tell him he again mumbled something about changing water into wine.

The sun is starting to come up here; feels like a new life is dawning along with a new day. Did you know that 90 percent of the population in the Philippines is Christian? Considering my views and my hopes for this book, the next three weeks should be interesting.

I have made contacts in Manila through that random phone call, and once I tell the conclusion to that tale (maybe it is the continuation), you will agree, I am sure, that I am probably meant to meet some of them. I am thinking we will be boarding soon. It's almost 7:00 PM here, which makes it 6:00 AM there. I doubt we will be back in time to the hotel for me to call you today. I know Rev wants to try to get some time in together before we go exploring with his family.

We can't even let them know there might be anything more than friendship. Their traditions are very strict, and it would be seriously disrespectful to go against them. He says that in time, once they get to know what kind of person I am, they will welcome me with open arms, but for now, no public displays of affection allowed. It's too bad, but probably for the best.

Well, hon, I'm gonna get my shit sorted, put the book away, and hopefully I will be talking to you soon.

Play safe. xo

February 15th
Patio of the Heritage Hotel, Manila
Early Morning

Hey, Beaner,

Okay, so now I'm sitting in the hotel restaurant, and it's been one full day since I arrived, and I am still in shock over actually being here.

These people, baby—WOW!

They have so very little and live such simple lives. Okay, maybe not so simple (they are hungry, their city is dirty and polluted, and the traffic is insane)—but they are happy. I mean, living in TO we don't have nearly as much smog, our traffic is less, and we have so many more amenities—but we're angry and dissatisfied. Yet here there is a feeling of peaceful contentment and acceptance. They have a saying here in their native tongue: Bahala Na—it means literally "leave it to God."

Strange to think that they could live their lives day to day with a constant struggle for survival hanging over their heads, yet they have no inner fear. Maybe it is because they feel they have nothing to lose, but I think it is more than that.

I've only been here for one day, so I know I have so much more to learn, but if and when I get a chance to talk to these people, I am positive it will only confirm for me why they live the way they do.

When I arrived I was picked up by Revo and his cousin's girlfriend. They were so incredibly sweet to me. They helped me get settled in; they wouldn't let me carry my own luggage or even open a door. One of the girls is named Alya—the same name as the boss who randomly brought Rev and me together. She told me when I first arrived that the Filipino people are the best hosts in the world, and I believe it. I gave them all the soaps and candles I had brought. They were very surprised but definitely pleased. I also gave one girl one of the cards you had made (the one with the man putting a ring on a woman's finger). The girl I gave it to is getting married in July. She had tears in her eyes. I told her I had picked it out without knowing who I was getting it for, but that I knew now that it was meant for her. She seemed very touched; even though they are upper-middle class (which is to say they are much better off than most here), she was still flattered by the gifts. I think because they were made by a friend they meant more than anything I could have bought in a store.

After the gifts and a quick chat, the girls left Revo with me and ventured off home. I unpacked a little and then had a shower. Revo went wandering off to the gym. At first it was strange to be here with him. As I said, out of respect for tradition he has not told them about us, but, even though we displayed no open signs of affection, I think the two girls saw something there. The first chance we got to be alone, we talked. Amazing—since he's been here for two weeks, you would think the physical would come first, but not him. He is very focused and open with me about his hopes and dreams, so, instead of a dangerous, lustful reunion we had a comfortable, communicative reunion. (Don't worry, princess, the passion is still there, but it is not a priority or even a need, and I can't remember a time where I was more content just to be in somebody else's presence—not male anyway.)

No matter. I am going far afield from my story. After my shower we went to a mall, located not far from my hotel. Buddy, this thing was huge! I mean you could easily fit three or four Scarborough Town Centres in there. We wandered around awhile before deciding to get something to eat. Revo insisted I eat local food, so we had two rice dishes made with cow's tongue and mushrooms, as well as this other dish (it is kind of a cross between a soup and a sauce) made with oxtail. Surprisingly, it was all very tasty. After we ate, we wandered around the mall some more and talked. Though we had both promised ourselves to quit smoking, we ended up giving in to the cravings and going in search of smokes. We could not find one store inside that wonderful massive complex that sold cigarettes.

After questioning the locals, we ended up making our way down toward the water. We found ourselves at Manila Bay (it was a place he had wanted to go, but he hadn't known where it was). It was a giant boardwalk down by the water with little restaurants and food kiosks every couple of feet. It was the weekend, and the place was packed with locals; apparently, it is not really a tourist area but more a spot where locals go to hang out. You could see the shock on some of their faces at seeing a little white girl wandering around aimlessly, but it wasn't the kind of shocked stare that makes you feel you shouldn't be there. It was more a sense of "What the hell?"

This place was packed with people, kids everywhere running around, and every few feet there was a guard with a machine gun. Rev explained that the mall was privately owned and so, by extension, was the walk down by the water. Since terrorism by revolutionaries is always a threat here, the guards are a necessary expense to protect the owner's investment. If people do not feel safe when they go shopping, they will simply shop somewhere else—simple concept, really. Again, though there was no feeling of being threatened, in fact the guards blended in so well with the atmosphere that I didn't even notice them until Rev pointed them out to me.

As an empath yourself, you can understand, I am sure, what it feels like to be in a situation where everyone is either angry or afraid. The spiritual drain from that kind of atmosphere is extremely damaging, and it can leave you feeling exhausted and weak. Now, imagine for a moment entering a world constantly threatened by violence and poverty but still feeling a sense of inner peace and security from all sides. It's a contradiction, is it not? I mean, it's not something you would expect, not even something you would think could be possible. Yet, here it is reality. While I wandered around down here, the only feeling I could pick up that could be considered anything close to negative was a feeling of confusion mixed with a little guarded caution from the locals when they glanced my way.

Don't get me wrong; on the surface they are very welcoming and friendly, but I can tell that they are definitely wondering what I am doing here.

Okay, for now, I am going to wrap this up. I will find another patio later today and complete the tale, but for now I have to work on finding my way around this hotel. Maybe I will get a pedicure (my feet look horrid, and this is most assuredly sandal kind of weather), so, my dear, wish me happy wanderings.

I'll talk back at you soon. xo

February 15th
Patio of the Heritage Hotel Manila
Lunchtime

I'm back; I spent a bit of time checking on my email and looking up a bit about St. Lucia. Now all I have to do is talk Rev into going.

I also booked a spa session, manicure, pedi, and facial and am now back on the patio having lunch. I'm thinking of staying around the hotel today to get my strength back and get centered and focused. I ordered a glass of wine, and, as it happens, their wine of the month is one of my favorites—life is good.

Okay, so I left off with our wandering the boardwalk. While we were there Rev pointed out a building that one of their (Filipino's) previous corrupt leaders had begun construction on. The story goes that this particular leader was in such a hurry and cared so little for the workers that the leader pushed them well past the point of exhaustion. In their tired state (the workers), they began to make mistakes that resulted in the catastrophic collapse of one of the upper floors, which killed almost every worker on the site. The person responsible for these people abandoned them and the project, never even bothering to extricate and provide proper burial for the unfortunate victims. The building remains to this day unfinished; locals refuse to enter it for fear of the spirits that still linger there, trapped on our earthly plane by their anguish at their untimely demise. Now, please understand this is only as the story was told to me, and I pass no judgment on the truth of this tale, nor do I pass judgment on those who were supposedly responsible for these people's deaths. I was not there; I do not have all the facts, so, therefore, I cannot fairly judge. I do, however, feel deeply for the people who suffered the loss of loved ones, and I hope that they have managed to find peace since the time of the accident.

Rev was absolutely shocked when I asked to go there. As I said, he is young yet, and though he is very intelligent as well as intuitive, he has much to learn—but then, my dear, we all do.

I feel a need to explore the site, feel for myself what is there, and perhaps gain some guidance from who may still linger. It would also be nice to offer some kind of consolation to them and try to get across to them the hope for a better day. I would reassure them that they did not die in vain and that their memory lives on, and that the memory shall forever remain as a lesson to those that follow—a reminder of where greed can lead us.

After this, we wandered back to the mall, discussing politics and religion, expanding on our previous discussion about our hopes for this book. I should point out that we have now agreed to focus on both the political and religious repression that overshadows Third World countries. We have also agreed to focus our attention on the lessons that repression and corruption can teach us and society. For now, though, I should be focusing on our adventures.

We did eventually find our way back to the mall. I was wearing heels (silly, I know), and though I had already promised myself I would not buy anything from the big department stores, my feet were killing me, so I really had no choice but to search out some sandals.

I told Rev though that in the future I would rather make my purchases at local markets, so that the money would go directly to the people and not to the larger corporations. He said he didn't know where to find one, but one of his many cousins would. (As a side note: the club sandwiches here at the hotel kick ass in a big, big way—they are so good they are addictive!)

While we were at the mall, Rev told me that I can probably get some money for stuff by using my bank card. I hadn't had a chance to exchange my Canadian coin, and though Rev had been paying for everything so far, he flat-out refused to pay for the shoes. Too funny, really—there is apparently an ancient legend that is all about what bad luck it is for a man or woman to buy shoes for their other half. He could not remember the legend itself, as he heard it told at a very young age, so I cannot tell it to you; he did, however, remember the lessons behind the legend. Thanks to that story, though, and the superstition that is attached to it, I now know that if I get stuck I can access my bank account through the machines here.

I swear, every time I need direction or information it comes to me in the strangest ways. Even answers to little problems or needs seem to be provided before I even realize I actually am in need. Amazing how that works, really, when you think about it. I guess the trick is not to think about it at all but just believe that is the way it is, and the rest kind of falls into place.

We got the shoes and then headed back to the hotel. We hung out a bit in the room, while he read one of the books I had brought with me. The book was on the Freemasons and the Solomon Keys. (Coincidentally, he wears Solomon Keys around his neck as well as carrying a Templar symbol surrounding the two opposing triangles that represent man and woman)

Anyway, we eventually ventured back out. I wanted to get some snacks and drinks to keep in the room, and we had been told there was a store just down the street. So we went around a corner and, holy shit, wouldn't you know it—the market I wanted was right there in front of us. It ran for blocks, every single thing you could possibly want or need was being bought and sold by locals. Again, they seemed very shocked to see a little white girl wandering around in a hippie skirt. Given that it was very late at night, well after dark, and the fact that it was obviously a place tourists very rarely go, I'm not surprised at their surprise.

The people selling things were not wealthy by any stretch, and, when I asked Revo later if it would be there during the day, he explained that they probably all had other jobs during the day and only came out at night to try to make enough money to feed themselves and their families. And families there were: kids everywhere, mothers nursing babies, grandparents resting in chairs by the stands; some were even catching some sleep while people shopped around them.

Revo kept telling me to watch where I stepped; it was very dirty on the streets, and I had to constantly reassure him that I am not a porcelain figurine that will break the first time I fall.

The children, as I said, were everywhere; they were playing with each other in the streets, using empty cans and other pieces of refuse as balls to kick around and chase each other with. It could have been a sad experience: the children were very poor, covered in dirt, and barely clothed (I even saw one child sleeping curled up on the steps of a local store), but, even with all of that, they were very obviously not neglected. Not emotionally: the people here love and revere their young; though they cannot always provide for them in a material sense, they shelter them by giving them love and affection in an otherwise harsh environment. There is nothing more beautiful to a child than the comforting arms of a parent. As I said, it should have been sad, but it was uplifting; there is so much Western society could learn from these people about love and compassion. Their family values are stronger than anything I have ever experienced, and, if others could only think the way they do, perhaps we could learn to care for each other in a deeper sense.

We wandered for about an hour; I purchased some fruit and was swarmed by a group of very dirty little children begging for money. Rev explained they were probably working for the syndicate, the underground crime organization that runs the underworld in the Philippines. I didn't give them any money, because he told me it would just go back to the crime bosses anyway and the kids would not benefit from it. I guess in all places there is at least one organization that is not exactly interested in working for the greater good of the people but is more interested in working for itself. I sincerely hope the human race finds a way some day to get past that level of selfish indulgence and manages to find its way to being more concerned with humanity as a whole—but that, I am thinking, is a whole other topic...

I also bought a pair of shoes for Maddi, purple knee high convers, that I am sure she will love. While we were buying the shoes, I was approached by an elderly woman who claimed she was hungry. I asked her to wait while I got my change, then gave her twenty Php. She kept touching me, saying "God bless," and rambling about hunger, but at one point, while Rev was engaged in a conversation with the man running the store (can you call it a store—I guess it is really a booth), she wrapped her finger around my arm, pulled me to her, and looked me straight in the eye, saying quite clearly: "I see you, I know you; they see, they know... you are different, and you will be blessed for it... trust him; he will protect you." She cut off and went back to babbling and rambling on under her breath as soon as Revo started paying attention; then she wandered off into the crowd.

It is strange that I never felt compelled to give money to the tiny little bodies that were all around, but there was something about the way this woman had approached me that had drawn me to her. I looked for her many times as we walked, but I never saw her again, and I have to wonder, if she had had the chance, what more she would have said. It was a quick encounter, but it taught me to trust my instincts while I am here. I will probably need to go on instinct for most of my visit, as I do not think that everything here is as it appears on the surface.

Well, my sweet, my meal is almost done, so I should wrap this up—but, before I go, I should tell you something. I will be writing to you every day. The original handwritten ones are going to be given to my brother to be kept safe in an unopened envelope until they are needed. Yet, even though they will be used in the book, be assured that every time I write I am writing to you, and my words (whatever they are and however they spill out onto the paper) are from the heart and are meant for you.

I will try to call again tomorrow. Right now you are no doubt sleeping, but I will probably write some more soon, though I can't say when, as I am only writing when my muse tells me I should. Keep the faith, my sweet, and believe we are not done here. In fact, I am positive this is only the beginning of a long, trippy journey. Love much. xo

February 15th
Patio of the Heritage Hotel Manila
4:10 PM

Hey, hon, me again…

Just a quick check-in; I went and had a pedicure and manicure that turned into a full-body massage. Now I am back on my patio, I think to do a little reading. If I think of anything to tell you, maybe a little writing as well.

I'll get back to you. xo

February 15th
Patio of the Heritage Hotel Manila
10:30 PM

Hello, guess who…

I went upstairs and probably passed out; I guess jet lag is finally catching up to me. I'm feeling very seriously dopey today. I got to talk to Maddi, though. When I woke up I went online to check my email, and she was on msn. I said hi to you, too, but you were in soak-in-the-tub mode. It's really been a quiet day for me: a lot of sitting on the patio resting. I did a really cool sketch earlier, though. It started with a stylized version of the Masonic compass, then ended up as a heart-shaped rose with an all-seeing eye in the middle (which is not a Masonic symbol originally, but one they use), then worked in an angel wing that has an infinity sign in it. I forgot, I also put in a yin-yang symbol as the iris of the all-seeing eye, and then, to finish it off, I added in a symbol of the Solomon Keys that represents Yahweh. It turned out pretty good; even though it was totally unplanned, when turned on its side it looks like the shape of the original mother and child I drew three years ago; cool, eh?

Honestly, though, that's all the news I have really. Revo's mom flew in from Italy today for some kind of reunion, so he will have to spend the next few days with his family for the most part. I did speak to him, and hopefully, I will be able to see him tomorrow. If not, it's okay. I might get some real writing done; for now, though, I'm going to read a bit more and relax a little while I still have the chance.

Love, light, and laughter. xo

February 16th
Patio of the Heritage Hotel Manila
Early Evening

Okay, so I'm back from another day of wandering—well, not really a full day, more like a couple hours. This may be one of the last times I write to you from the patio at the hotel. I was taken to a place today by Revo that I'm hoping will be like a new home base for me. It is another local hotel, but they have a huge back lawn that looks out over the water, and you know just how much I love water…

There are tons of lawn chairs and umbrellas in case you get too hot or it rains, palm trees everywhere, and you can actually hear birds, not traffic. It will be the perfect spot to write during the day—when I am not being toured around, of course, by Rev and his cousin's girlfriend. Alya is super sweet, and I am hoping we will get some one-on-one time. You know, it just occurred to me that no matter where I go, men can still be pigs, and that is funny as hell, given that I am halfway around the world. I will have to keep that in mind while I am here; it is really not that much different than being at home. Also, remind me to keep my business and thoughts to myself. I'll have to explain that when I see you again in person. Okay, so where was I? Oh yeah, I am hoping that Alya will take me to a few places while I am here as well as tell me some more stories of her life growing up here.

She is, as I said, upper-middle class, and she was raised in a safe, secure home, but her schooling and education here ensured that she learn about all the people in her country, rich as well as poor. She told me that when she was in school one of her mandatory assignments was what they refer to here as immersion. We refer to all French schools as French immersion schools; here immersion means to go to live another way of life, one not like your own (so if you are upper class they basically force you to live in poverty for a few days). She had options to choose from; for instance, she and her partner (no, they do not go alone) could have gone to an inner-city slum area and lived as the people on the streets do. They chose instead to go out to the provinces; she claims she wanted to see what the poor people in the country lived like and experience what it was like to try to survive without all the amenities she had grown up depending on. I guess I should have known they would make that part of their education system. It makes sense, and it is too bad we don't do something similar in the West.

She and her friend went way out into no man's land to stay with a family who really had nothing that could be referred to as a material possession. Their house was a one-room hut with a bamboo platform to sleep on. They had no running water or electricity, and Alya found herself wondering how they survived. She asked them, of course (I mean, that was why she was there, right, and she wanted to know); how did they, for example, buy food.

The answer she got was pretty simple but not what she had expected. The mother of the house apparently looked at her a little confused at first but eventually came out of her shock and explained that they didn't buy anything. How could they? They had no source of income, so they had no money—but they also had no need for it, as they grew everything they needed. Simple, no? They grew what they needed, and they had continuous crops, so a continuous food supply. I'm sure it is a little more complicated than that—much harder to grow what you need and much more time consuming than going to the freezer and grabbing a roast—but, since they don't have to leave the house to go to work, they don't have to worry about extra time spent in preparation. Not much time cleaning either, I'm sure, when you live in a hut. I doubt very much you need to dust before company comes over.

Now, I know I seem to be making light of what again should be a sad situation, but the way she told it was that, as shocking as it seems, these people were extremely happy. She said they went to bed at night around 6 PM when the sun went down, and they got up when the sun rose in the morning. They spent their days together tending crops and animals, preparing food, or just playing with and loving their children. Not much excitement, perhaps, but they were content, and, after a day of adjustment, so was Alya. She was only there for a few days, but it had a profound effect on how she viewed the world and the people in it.

I sincerely hope, though I know they cannot stop their lives because I am here, that she will be able to find time to go out to the provinces so I can see for myself. I am also planning on contacting the people whose names I got through the strange encounter with the gospel lady. Perhaps they do missionary work, and they will be able to send me in the right direction.

Alya's story opened up a discussion about awareness and the imbalance that exists between the wealthy and the poor. She says that they all know it is unfair, but what can they do? She says very few people will openly voice their opinion about such injustice and that the average citizen is complacent about the problems they see every day. They are aware of them and would like to help but don't really know how to provide that help. It is easier, for example, for a wealthy family to donate to charities without thought as to where the money goes than it would be to actively seek out those in need and provide for them directly. I think it runs deeper than that. I think there is an underlying fear of the government and perhaps also the church officials. I am new to these people, so it is not comfortable for them to discuss these things in depth, but I am hoping that with time this will change. I know I planted a seed today. I could see it in Revo's eyes, and I also know that he—though, as I said, he is young—is starting to believe on a deeper level that change is possible—more importantly, that it is inevitable.

He is still hesitant to leave his comfort zone, but perhaps in time he will have a more adventurous spirit. It's strange to think that it was him and his openness about his ideals that led me here in the first place, but that he still hovers between being driven to make a difference and being afraid of the sacrifices making that difference might entail. I doubt very much that he will lose all his fears immediately, but then, he still needs time to know me and be comfortable in the idea that I do not have a hidden agenda. After all, what kind of crazy lady flies halfway around the world to stand by the side of a man she hardly knows, to embark on a personal mission—on such a grand scale, with nothing but the faith in a better future as her guide?

He is afraid of losing sight of what's important if he allows himself to feel too much, and he's scared of the effect getting too close personally could have on the success of any work we do together. He may be young, but he sees far. He wanted to know what would happen at the end of the three weeks when he is not prepared to let me go. He tried to tell me he was worried I would be the one getting hurt, but when I asked him who it was he was really trying to protect, himself or me, he conceded defeat and admitted to both. I told him that ultimately it would not matter; we would be together when we were meant to be together and we would not when it was time for us to be apart. I couldn't offer more than that, really, and what he was trying to get to but was failing miserably at was that that neither could he. Funny, eh? He makes me happy, lifts me up to a higher place, and inspires me to great heights, yet we both know that when I leave we will no longer be able to be together. I always said I would fight like hell to stay with the one I felt was my other half, and now I'm contemplating walking away because the only way to hold onto our time together and the feelings it awakens in me is to let it go.

I wish we had more time today to talk it out, but he is right about one thing. If we focus on that and the dangers those feelings present to each other, then we will lose sight of our reason for being here in the first place. As I told Sophia before I left: if nothing comes of this past my return to Canada, then I will still be able to look back on this book and thank God for the opportunity given to me.

Well, surprise, surprise...

I may just be running out of things to say—except that the staff here, after seeing me write seemingly non-stop for three days, are now beginning to be more open. They are now asking me questions about what I am doing here. One of the girls here has offered to sit with me and tell me more about her people, and one of the men has approached me several times to start idle conversations. I was hoping I could make my presence known here without seeming to be a threat to any of the locals. I was concerned, after several talks with Rev about the dangers here, that I would have a difficult time pulling these people out of their comfort zone. But it appears that, given time and patience, they will walk out of it willingly for better reasons than any persuasion on my part could provide.

I have to tell you, hon, they are a beautiful people, and they deserve so much more than what they have.

Okay, luv, that wraps it up for tonight, I think. I actually started writing the preface today and should probably get back to it, but I will be wandering around the city on my own tomorrow, so I am sure by tomorrow night I will have much more to share.

Stay safe, my dear. xo

February 17th
Patio of the Heritage Hotel Manila
7:30 AM

Good morning, sweetie,

I am sitting outside again having my morning coffee and was trying to relax and read a bit for once, but it seems that it is not to be. These overwhelming urges to put pen to paper are becoming quite distracting. Even when it is my full intent to sit and ponder or relax and read, I find at odd moments I am forced pull this damn book out and commence writing.

I get the feeling I'm supposed to drop you a quick note with regards to my plans for the day and maybe toss in some of my thoughts along the way. I spoke to you last night briefly so I could read you the preface I have written. Your reaction was extremely reassuring, as I remember well your own talent for the written word. I feel I have no more appropriate person to turn to when it comes to open and honest feedback on my work.

Manila is waking up, my love; the sounds of traffic filter through the walls, as the people of this great city embark on their daily adventures. I will hopefully be joining them soon enough, as I am headed out today with a couple of destinations in mind. I am planning to wander over to the Mall of Asia with the hopes of having my phone unlocked and getting a local SIM card, so I will have a local contact number to give to anybody I might randomly run into. It would also help when I email my contacts here in Manila if they have a way to reach me even if I am not in my room (which I never am, except to sleep). After that I am planning to wander over to that place Rev's friend showed me yesterday; there is a feel to the air today that is pulling me outside.

I was thinking this morning that I should try to get in touch with one of the Catholic churches here as well. I can't remember if told you, but Revo and I have often wondered how much of the natives' offerings are actually being fed back to the locals in terms of relief funding and education.

I am a little concerned that asking too many questions in that area may place me in an uncomfortable position, but, if I am cautious and approach the Church with the appearance of wide-eyed innocence, perhaps they will be more forthcoming. Besides, I honestly believe that I will be protected from harm as long as I stay aware of the possible dangers and do not veer off-course. Today is day four, and I would like to spend it laying the groundwork for the next couple of weeks, and perhaps, who knows, maybe I will run into somebody along the way who will guide me down the proper path.

I have also decided that my next stop after the Philippines will be St Lucia; it seems my gospel lady was sent as a guide of sorts, and I think it would be wrong of me not to follow where she leads. I know I mentioned it before, but I never did go into detail about the reason why I have just this morning decided to go (whether or not Rev wishes to follow). I feel it is time to explain why. This, however, we will discuss in person; it ties into my past and the trail I must someday follow to discover the source of certain truths.

Not yet, however—perhaps I will reflect on it more while I am sitting by the water today and have a clearer view of the energies around me. For now I will let you go, so I can make my way up to my room and get prepared for my day. I hope I have much to tell when I write you next, as I really feel things are going to start moving quickly once again.

Luv ya. xo

February 15th
Seawall lawn out back of Hotel Sofitel Manila
12:30 PM

Hey, sweetie,

Well, I am finally sitting down to write in a place that resembles the tropical paradise I am supposed to be staying in. There is a place here called Sofitel; it is an old hotel located on Manila Bay. It is the same place Revo brought me to yesterday and still as beautiful as I remember it to be (good to know I was not lying to myself). I am sitting on a chaise lounge facing the bay and surrounded by a vast expanse of lime green lawn. A slight breeze caresses my arms as I write, for which I am grateful, as the sun is extremely hot here even when the haze obscures its light. There is a small sprinkler only a few feet away, for which I am also grateful, as every once in awhile my body is kissed by a gentle, refreshing mist.

I keep expecting somebody to come kick me out. I mean, I don't belong here, really; my own hotel is a good fifty Php away by cab, but apparently it doesn't matter much to the people here whether you are a guest or not—or perhaps they simply don't realize I am not. I am thinking, while I am looking around, that this is most likely where the people with money stay, and, now that I know it's here, it is most definitely where I would like to stay when I come back (strange, this feeling that I will be back to the Philippines again, though I know no possible reason for my return).

It is very pretty and peaceful here, and the whole atmosphere is inspiring, but I find I get more inspiration wandering around among the poorer quarters of the city. I am becoming immune to the strange looks I get from locals. I guess they don't see many white people wandering the streets. The ones who are here stick mostly to the malls, restaurants, and hotels. Hell, there are hardly any white people in my hotel, let alone out in public.

It is so hot today, for some reason. Alya was saying yesterday the weather right now is very unnatural for this time of year, though I would think that since all weather is derived from nature it is completely natural—better, perhaps, to say it is unusual. She claims it should be cooler. I will try to bear with it (imagine me complaining about the heat—wow—we humans truly are never content to just be as are we). I am thinking, though, that unless I want a swollen brain I should probably go about finding some shade. Give me five; I will be right back, though I doubt you will even notice I am gone.

Hey, so I went to get up and move and what happened—the sun went behind the clouds; go figure. I guess I should have known, eh? I moved out to the pool, but it is not much more shady, and there is also not as much privacy. I think I'll take a walk, see if I can find some lawn to stretch out on, and then maybe I'll feel comfortable with staying here to write. Wish me luck, hon; hopefully I will have something interesting to tell you by tonight.

February 18th
Patio of the Heritage Hotel Manila
Noon

Hey, it's me yet again; I actually managed to find a peaceful place to write yesterday and ended up finishing the first chapter. Yes, I know, it was a bit of a surprise to me too, but once I started writing everything just seemed to flow.

Today, though, I am feeling like things are off. I woke up with a cold, and it seems like I don't have much drive or ambition today. I don't think it's helping that the person I was counting on to show me around is extremely distracted by the unexpected presence of his mother. Her timing is quite remarkable, really, and it is most definitely testing my resolve. I have to remember that my purpose here is not centered around him and me. I can't rely on him to give me direction all of the time, but it is difficult to go it alone. I have decided to stick around the hotel today, partly because I am hoping to find a way to strengthen my resolve. When he is not around, it is up to me to stay focused; I feel there is much I have yet to learn from him, and I know I must be patient—it is not easy.

His mother refuses (much as my own family did) to discuss the circumstances of his birth or the significance of his name—which plays a large part in how we got here. He continues to question her, and she (wisely, I think) continues to shut him down. He says she is here for a high-school reunion, but my instincts tell me otherwise. Security has suddenly been tightened up here in the hotel, and there is a feeling of anticipation in the air. I am not sure exactly what I have brought myself into, and, as you know, I hate the waiting game.

I have emailed the local chapter of the church I discovered in TO, and I am still planning on making my way to a local catholic Church, but, until his mother decides to give him some time to himself, I will not get much help in that area. I have to admit I am slightly disappointed in that. After talking to Alya I was looking forward to meeting his outspoken cousin. I think we may have a lot to learn from each other as well, but I am not sure Rev is anxious for us to meet. Who knows? Maybe I am reading too much into things, since he did tell me he had managed to slip some of my ideas about religions and the church into a few of their discussions. However, I believe that as Rev is preparing to stay here permanently he is now more concerned with securing a safe place among his family and social network before he takes any steps toward stirring up questions of faith and political position.

I was hoping to discuss this with him, as I have now resolved to go ahead with the book, with or without him, though I am concerned about the repercussions that might have on his life here. I understand why he wants to stay here, and I admire his desire to help his people. I am also constantly telling him to be careful about how he moves forward, but there is a fine line between caution and being fearful. Fear causes us to take a step back when threatened and often leads to loss of purpose and resolve, something I do not believe either of us can afford.

I know that if I were there, you would be telling me to let him find his own way, and you would, of course, be right. I try every day to think about what my friends would have to say by way of encouragement and advice. I also try every day to follow that unspoken advice. When you are on the other side of the world, however, and very much alone, it is extremely hard to maintain equilibrium. No matter; I believe that what is meant to come will come, and I will try to remind myself I am not really alone.

For the moment, I think I will let you go and again lose myself in a bit of reading. Later, perhaps, I will work on chapter two, and, in doing so, maybe I will get bit of my strength back.

Stay well, stay safe. xo

February 18th
Lying in bed in my room, Heritage Hotel Manila

So, I finished chapter three and I have only been here four days. Rev says that at this rate I will be finished before I leave. I sent back him a text telling him that I did not believe the story will end when I leave, so there is no way I can finish the book while I am here. He wants to read what I have written, but I told him that will be difficult until I put it into the computer, as I am sure there is no possible way he can read my writing (I can barely read my writing).

I am at the moment lying in bed waiting for dinner to arrive. I ordered a Caesar salad, because I am sure my body could use the garlic. This cold is making me miserable, though I am grateful I came down with it, as it has forced me to stay at the hotel.

Oh, hold up—dinner's here...

You know, I have to say I love these people. They are so sweet and they seem very curious about what I am doing. The young man who just delivered my food says he sees me downstairs all the time. I told him I am working on a novel, and the patio is a very comfortable place to write. I feel a little bad, though, because I did not sound very enthusiastic. My cold is making me unpleasant, but I will have to try harder to not be miserable; these people certainly don't deserve to be frowned at.

Their curiosity ties into why I am so glad I got sick.

Do you remember the young woman from the other night who said she was willing to share information about her culture? Well, she approached me today to let me know that Friday is her day off, and she could meet with me then. I told her I had a local phone now, so she gave me her number. Coincidentally (love the word, lol), her name is Angel. We ended up agreeing to meet tonight on the patio after she is done work, which I just realized is in only an hour and I am, as you say, slightly drained. I'll let you know what I learn, xo, but for now I should rest.

February 19th
Patio of the Heritage Hotel Manila
5:00 PM

My sweet,

I have to say I have undeniably fallen in love with both this country and its people. So far I am only scratching the surface, I realize, but the reality of what occasionally peeks out from underneath is at once shocking and soothing.

Last night I ended up having a very intriguing encounter, and I hardly know where to begin.

I had agreed to meet with Angel, and, though I was exhausted physically, I dragged myself down here at midnight as promised.

I was concerned about meeting her here, as I know from experience the strict expectations the management at hotels such as this have with regards to staff-guest interaction. It seems my fears were founded, as she was threatened with disciplinary action before we left together. She had unfortunately tried to meet me wearing civilian attire. She is young, only twenty-three, and very obviously new to the service industry. She was not expecting that her innocent attempt at making our rendezvous seem nonchalant seemed to her boss to be an attempt at deception. I don't know even now if the encounter cost her the position here, but I can only assume the worst, as it is well past the time she was to start work, and she has not appeared.

It's strange to think that even in a society where their entire behavioral pattern centers around being welcoming and accommodating hosts that her attempts to befriend a foreign visitor could cause such problems—but then, that is the way of big business. Propriety is always at the forefront of their day-to-day routine, and any breach of that propriety, however innocent in nature, causes great distress among those who, as they say, write the cheques.

What amazed me most about the whole situation was not that it happened but rather her reaction to it. She did not seem to be concerned. Here, in a country where the people struggle every day to feed themselves and their families, this young woman, answering my inquiries about her possible dismissal, simply stated, "If it's God's will."

I would love to explore this notion further, but, as that is not where the conversation began, it would not be in line time-wise with the rest of our late-night adventure. I only mention it to explain why I can comfortably sit here writing to you, unconcerned with the notion that this sweet young woman might have lost her source of income as a result of trying to assist in my work.

I have to pause here briefly to point out that I spent the afternoon sleeping. We did not return to the hotel until after 4 AM; combine the early hour with this irritating little cold, and my body simply refused to give anymore. I am feeling much revived after hiding away for the day in my room and will be adventuring out again later this evening to meet Rev at a mall near his mother's hotel. It will be nice to see him, of course, as we have much to discuss after last night, and yet I wonder at his request that we meet in public. I am certain he's avoiding spending time alone with me because he's concerned about straying from our purpose.

I do, of course, realize that his intentions are applaudable, but it is still difficult for me to accept his fears. Angel seems to think the whole situation is rather sad; she believes that we could find a way to be together as a couple and still manage to accomplish our goals. It is funny that as I am sitting here I am feeling the same sadness myself; yet, it was only a few short hours ago that I was trying to convince Angel it is just simply the way it is. I almost managed to convince myself. My explanations on the matter certainly made sense to me at the time; yet, the unfairness of it all threatens to overwhelm me. I dread the inevitable discussion on the subject, which is probably going to occur this evening, and, at the same time, I feel reassured by the comforting words Angel chose to share with me last night.

Our talk began shortly after we arrived at a local outside mall. After purchasing a couple of bottles and finding a quiet corner, she openly began to talk about herself and her own personal history. I had to stop her long enough to explain my presence here, and it was the first time since being here that I have been completely honest about it to anyone but myself and Rev. I was more honest, in fact, with my explanation to her than I had been to myself. The explanation gave me an opportunity to clarify the situation in my own mind and provided a much-needed clearing of clouded issues.

I told her that I had unexpectedly found myself giving my heart to a Filipino man, who, though he has made it more than clear he cares deeply for me as well, is much more concerned about finding a way to uplift his people and give them a chance at a better way of life. I told her that given our age difference, the fact that I am a white divorced single mother, and, of course, that my life is in Canada, it is extremely doubtful that we will ultimately end up together. As I said, she was saddened by this, but I replied that if our work together made a difference in the lives of the people here, then our union, as brief as it may end up to be, would still manage to create a stronger, more powerful bond between us than anything a mere romantic relationship could accomplish or provide.

Oh, Beaner, I want to believe my own words—I really do—but this man wakens something in me I have never experienced, and I am loathe to give it up. Physical attraction aside, his very existence in my life has led me down a path I'd never imagined I'd walk. His strength of spirit uplifts me and makes me fly to new heights. I greatly fear losing that feeling of free and easy flight and have to constantly remind myself to be grateful for the mere experience of stretching my wings to take that final leap. It is not easy.

Oh yes, I know it is not meant to be. Constant testing of faith, however, is draining on the soul, and if I were not constantly surrounded by this feeling of hope, it would be very easy to falter and fall.

Before Angel continued to expound on her life here, she took the moment to thank me for taking such a selfless risk as to travel halfway around the world in the hopes of making even the smallest difference. I wish I could justify her faith in me, but I struggle every day with my own insecurities.

She reminded me, though, that it is the little changes that lead to big changes. There were several times throughout the evening where she seemed to feed my own thoughts back to me. Three weeks ago a conversation like this would have made me squirm, but I am becoming used to encounters with various guides who are being sent my way. It has become commonplace, and I am recognizing it much more readily.

After reassuring me that the book I am working on may, in fact, have a positive effect, she carried on with her own personal story. She is a graduate of the University of Hong Kong, but, not being able to find work there, she came back to Manila. Her job at the hotel was quite by accident, and she claimed it was possible that she had been sent there simply to meet me. Apparently she had applied for several secretarial positions around the city, and the Heritage had been the first to respond.

(You know, I just looked up and the sunset is absolutely incredible—white and red and deep purple streaks across a pale sky—it covers the first half of the horizon, leaving a soft, pinkish glow on the clouds overhead.)

The hotel management had told her that she would be working the front desk, but when she arrived they put her in the lower position of server in the restaurant. She said she was disappointed but figured there had to be a reason. You see, she is a born-again Christian (a girl who was raised Catholic, as are most Filipino people) yet found herself disillusioned by the idol worship that dominates the Catholic faith. Later in the evening she compared Catholicism to Buddhism, citing the former as a religion that centers around the worship of material representations of both saints and demigods. She seemed to believe that it was this worship of what she called false idols that distracted from the lessons present in the teachings of the one true God.

I still will neither agree with nor dispute her beliefs, as it is not my place here to judge. I was, however, intrigued by her views, as—regardless of what you choose to call the power that we are born from and the energies that protect and guide us—I do not believe those energies give a damn for material objects. Though it can be argued that if God creates man and man creates material things, then, in essence, it is God who is also creating those material things. I do not believe, however, that those creations by man are a necessary part of our appreciation of God's power. I figure, if you need to see or feel evidence of that power, you need look no further than the feeling of holding a babe in your arms. If we could take that feeling further and stretch it to encompass all people and all things in our world, then we would be one step closer to experiencing that sense of oneness with the mystical energy that humanity seems to be lacking.

Man, by his very nature, exists to create. It was the creation that concerned her—not the act of creation itself, but rather the usage of the objects created. She explained that Catholics spend a large part of their spiritual energy directing prayers to extensions of God rather than to God himself. This confused her, and she couldn't understand why—if, as the church claims, God is always with us—she could not just talk directly to him. She started to question as well the need for certain rituals and gestures used in Catholic worship. Why, for example, would it be more important for her to genuflect at the altar than to, say, show her love of God through her daily interactions with people? She could not justify in her mind her right as a Catholic to go out into the world and judge and condemn others in God's name and then be assured her actions would be forgiven simply because she went through the act of confession and prayer over a string of beads.

I must clarify that my explanation of her thoughts is not word for word. Her English was very broken at times, and it was a struggle for her to find the right words. I have included metaphors in order to clarify for you her ideas, and I do not believe she would fault me for it.

Her reasoning, as I said, was sound, and her own quest to come closer to that power had led her to find an open-minded Christian community. She said it had not always been easy for her; she had struggled daily with her own doubts and fears before she learned to put faith in something she could neither see nor touch. She explained that the Christians taught acceptance and forgiveness of self and others. She claimed that the longer she studied with them, the easier it became to find peace within herself and her surroundings.

When I asked if, coming from a largely Catholic society, she found it difficult to openly not follow the same faith, she assured me that the condemnation of others with regards to her faith was a test of character. It was how she responded to that scrutiny that allowed her to maintain her strength of purpose and her belief in a higher power. She asked me if I loved God. I told her as truthfully as I could that I loved the idea or essence of God but reminded her that my perceptions of god might not be the same as hers.

I explained to her my encounter with the Gospel group in Toronto before I came to the Philippines and told her that my experience there had been positive. I mentioned that I could not quote the scriptures, as I had not studied the Bible in depth in recent years, but that I could take the teachings in the scriptures and relate them to the here and now. I told her I understood the fundamental lessons behind those teachings but could not willingly believe that the scriptures themselves were the only message that God had ever sent to his people to show them and guide them to a better way of life. I feel it is the meaning behind the words that is meant to be the lesson, not the words themselves.

At this point, she brought up a very valid concern and taught me a lesson I needed to take to heart. She explained to me that people needed proof to believe in something. It is part of human nature to want to have something they can see and feel that connects their belief in a higher power to the physical existence here on earth. It is not the words themselves, as I said, that teach the lesson, but they do provide a weapon of sorts against doubt and adversity. She described the scriptures as a sword in hand (interesting description, given the imagery that got us here in the first place), a blade that could be used to cut through the fears and doubts of others.

She suggested that others I speak to might not be as open or accepting as the group I first met with in Toronto and that, though my purpose was pure in its intent, my methodology might be flawed. She asked me whether it would not be better to acquaint myself with the actual teachings, so I would have a weapon at hand when questioned or confronted. Her reasoning again was sound, and I found myself admiring the wisdom in one so young.

We talked at great length about her faith. She mentioned that sometimes it was hard to attend mass on Sundays in light of her job and her need to pay her bills. She said she felt guilty when she could not attend. I questioned her again and asked if she really believed that God cared one wit if she was in a church when she prayed. I told her about my grandmother who had suffered guilt and self-doubt for years about not being able to attend church on Sundays. I explained that as a result of her failing knees she could no longer climb the church steps, and though she had lobbied for a ramp to be built to provide wheelchair access, it was a good ten years before anything had been done. The whole scenario had been rather disappointing, as the Catholic Church has access to funding far beyond the means of other religious communities, and it was discouraging that they could not or would not use those funds for such a simple request. It was only after the ramp had been built that my grandmother commented that she no longer felt the need or desire to be in a church to pray. She had accepted the idea—after many years of self-deprecation—that God was listening anyway. My grandmother had asked how I had known the truth of it at such a young age, and I couldn't give her an example, except to tell her that it was what I knew to believe, so it was my truth. Now she believed, so it was therefore now her truth. I explained to my grandmother that I believed the energy that we call God is all around us at all times and that it stands to reason that those energies are in tune with our needs and fears, regardless of where we are. I also explained that perhaps it was the need for her to learn that for herself that allowed the failure of her knees and the delay in construction of the ramp. It simply took so long for the ramp to be built because it took so long for my grandmother to learn and accept the lesson being taught.

It was here that Angel imparted another much-needed form of wisdom. She explained that her need to go to church did not stem from the need to be in a place of worship. The idea, in fact, that the building itself was anything other than a gathering place was foreign to her. The purpose behind going to church at all was twofold.

First, it was a way to surround herself with those of like mind. She could spend time with people who believed as she did, who both helped to keep her grounded and lifted her up when she was feeling afraid or sad. She also stated that it gave her a chance to do the same for others. The actual act of going to church was centered on communal support and encouragement and really had nothing to do with the building at all.

Secondly, going to church was, in its own way, a manner of self-sacrifice. She said it seemed very little to ask to give up a mere three hours of her week and dedicate those hours to worship. The challenge, or sacrifice, if you will, was in putting aside worldly needs and commitments in order to give herself over to God for those three hours. It became a matter of choosing between, for example, her job and the paycheck it provides, and the spiritual rewards gained from that sacrifice. She pointed out that, by being willing to give up that paycheck in order to commit herself to worship, she was quite literally putting her worldly safety and security in God's hands. She strongly believed that he would provide for her what she needed—but only after she was able and willing to both see and accept what he provided.

The night was wearing on by this time, and the establishment where we were sitting was closing, so we decided to walk over to a store close by and try to find another place to sit. As we walked, she told me it was not so long ago that she had cried herself to sleep several nights from fear and despair. She knew at the time that something was missing from her life, but she was not able to grasp what it was. As we sat, she said it wasn't until God took everything from her that she began to search for answers in the direction of the church. Once she got past the bitterness and pain and opened herself to the idea that perhaps it had all been taken away for a reason did she begin to really open her eyes to what could be if she gave herself over to a higher power. She began to feel what she described as "lighter"—not so weighted down by her physical needs and desires. She felt more in tune with her surroundings; the more peace and kindness she worked very hard on giving to others, the more she received. She said it was a continuous cycle of giving and receiving God's light. What she shared with others she got back in turn.

In short, she was describing the same principle mystics and prophets from all ages and parts of the world have taught for centuries, yet she was relating it in terms she could understand and believe in. She had learned to embrace the idea through her introduction to Christ, and it had become her truth. In living by the very principal of getting back what you put out into life—a principal as old as time and a principal taught around the world in countless different forms—she had started to turn her life in a more positive direction.

As I continue to explore each new religion and belief system as it is presented to me, I am aware of the common vein that threads through them all. Will it become apparent, as I venture forth, that the indescribable energy that flows between all living things is in the end (or rather the beginning) the root of all faiths in a higher power? Will the theory of the give and take of that energy be finally proven to be the essence, the very spirit, of that higher power itself? What kind of possible effect could that have on the ultimate survival of the people who claim they alone have knowledge of the true path to connecting with that power? What, in the end, would happen if the average person realized that access to that energy is easily attainable? Would it be for the better? Are humans yet at the point in their spiritual development where the use and manipulation of that power will not become corrupt?

It concerns me that we may not yet be ready for that next step. Yet it seems to me, in light of all of my recent experiences and discoveries, that we humans are taking the first steps necessary to achieve that higher understanding. I can only hope that when the time comes society will be able to overcome its greed and lust for power and move forward together as one toward a higher, more peaceful state of being.

Fears and speculations aside, I still have much to learn here, and my story with Angel has not yet come to an end. We are to meet tomorrow, as she wishes to share more of her community and her church with me. I agreed to go with her to a gospel session, as I think I am not yet done exploring the Christian faith or their beliefs. I am eager to learn from these people as well as share my own experience—in the hope that we can benefit each other mutually in our own personal quests for spiritual growth. I have to wonder, though, where this particular branch of the road will lead. I do hope my idle curiosity does not ultimately end up being my undoing. I will have to put my faith in my purpose here and hope I do not get led astray.

I suppose, as I have been writing now for hours, I should give my hand a rest as well as my heart and mind, but I will continue to update you on my adventures. Until next time, my sweet, love, light, and laughter…

February 19th
Starbucks patio, Gledhill Shopping Centre Manila
11:00 PM

Well, this is different; I am on the other side of the city, by myself, at 11:00 at night. I'm here to meet Rev, even though he's always telling me not to go out alone at night, but it's okay, I'm not overly concerned. The people here—though shocked, I'm sure, to see me here alone at night—seem to be, for the most part, ignoring me. I wouldn't have bothered pulling out the book, but I have to wait anyway, and I have a short update for you.

I was sitting up in my room, after sending text messages back and forth to Rev all day, trying and failing to set up a meeting. I was feeling very alone and very discouraged. I was wondering yet again if I had lost my mind, travelling halfway around the world on a whim. I had sent a text to Angel earlier enquiring as to what had happened and asking her why she was not at work and if she was okay. So I am lying there having my moment of doubt when she sends me a text telling me she is okay and asking how I am.

I wrote back the following.

I am doing okay; just lying here trying to remind myself that I am not alone, but then you just proved it—really, are you okay?—I was a little concerned.

Her response started:

"Yup… I happened to ask for a rest day—that's the reason why I'm not around tonight. And, yes, you're right; you're not—" *message cut off*

Seriously, it was cut off, but I got the gist of what she was trying to say. I was crying silly tears and feeling very much revived, thinking to myself she really was an Angel, and I sent back:

I am not sure I got all your message, but I am sure I got the message.

I was halfway through sending my response when the rest of her message came through again, only this time it was the whole thing.

"Yup…I happened to ask for a rest day—that's the reason why I'm not around tonight. And yes, you're right, you're not alone; however, you're just being given more time to think things through. You're called for it—you're one of God's messengers. You can do it, I know. God bless."

I wish you could be here, buddy, and see these things with me. I honestly feel so overwhelmed at times by all these little messages and signs. It almost feels unfair that I can't share them with the people in my life. If for one day you could see this through my eyes, I think that you, too, would cry. Like me, you wouldn't know if you were crying tears of joy or sorrow, and, like me, you wouldn't care.

I guess that's why I was born a writer, so I could share this crazy trip with the rest of the world. Well, hon, gotta go. Rev's here, and the story must go on.

February 20th
Patio of the Heritage Hotel Manila
1:24 AM

The deeper I delve into the mystery that is my trip to this country, the harder I find it to cope with the unexpected emotional ups and downs that result from my experiences here. Right now I am warring with myself over my uncontrollable and undeniable love for this madman and the also-undeniable fact that for the moment, at least, I have to keep my distance.

I mean, hon, if you could have seen him last night, you would have wanted to cry. He is so obviously confused by all of this: him—me—us—why we're here—what we're doing—I wanted to grab hold of him and tell him that I refused to give up on this feeling. Yet all I could do was distance myself and see if he could work it out alone. God forgive me my greed, but I so want to be allowed to be with this man—but somehow I feel that he will ultimately end up being my final sacrifice.

It doesn't seem fair in the slightest, and I am having trouble coming to terms with acceptance. I had the chance to tell him I need him; I had the chance to tell him I loved him—and I didn't. Instead, I watched him squirm like an ant pinned by a thumb, wanting desperately to get away and not knowing how.

Two more weeks is all I have left, and every day that passes I accomplish more toward my goal and cut out more of my soul. I have a memory of kneeling at this man's feet and I cannot bring myself to tell him about it. Again I ask forgiveness for my greed, for my selfish desires. In this world it is easy to give up a life. The real test is to be willing to give up your own wants and needs, to sacrifice that which you hold most dear. I thought I was finished with that part of my test, but now I feel like all the rest was only in preparation for this.

How can I look into his eyes, knowing that he is the very same man I have shared so many lifetimes with, and yet be willing to walk away from sharing this one? I wish you were here; I need some kind of guidance, some comfort, some hope…

I do not want to do this alone. I want to stand at his side; it is my place, my right. I have too much pride, perhaps, to think that at the end of it all I deserve for my prayers in this to be answered. We talked about my writing, about his dreams—always about his people and his hopes for them. I watched him, relished in the beauty of his presence and my faith that he will stay strong; yet, at the same time I wept inside for the loss of him.

I told him I would publish this and asked him if he was prepared. I told him the story had to be told and asked him if he was ready. I can see that he is; he harbors no doubts or fears for his own safety; he is scared, but not for himself. He says his time here is not yet over; he has too much left to do. He says that my time here is also not yet finished, and so, for the moment, I am safe to wander among these people. He says that God is not finished with us, that we will be protected—and yet he is scared. He told me the government would not go after him directly; he said they would threaten his family. He didn't want to finish the thought, struggled visibly to find the words. He said if they did, then he would dare them to try. He said that God allows vengeance for those who do not hate, that God allowed certain individuals the right to impose justice on those who do wrong. But justice, he said, would not save his family, and justice could not bring them back.

So will we make a choice. Will I stand with him and risk my most precious gift? Will he allow it, knowing that which I hold most precious could be threatened? Can we allow ourselves to continue this journey, knowing the possible cost?

The air seems very heavy tonight; despite the slight breeze that is playing across the leaves, there is a feeling of weight to the air, even as it causes the leaves to dance.

He smiled and said, "But your book it is just a story…what have I to fear from a story?"

Still, he asked the question, wordlessly (we are far beyond the point where words are needed), silently imploring me to make the choice.

Baby, I had no answer…

I still do not know what I will do when the time comes.

I fear I will soon have to decide. I will come back to you, of that there is no doubt, but will I leave my heart and my soul here with him when I go.

If he asked me today to be his bride, it would be my duty to stand with him. He will not ask. I can see it in his eyes; he cannot—not from lack of love or desire but because he does not want the sacrifice to be mine. I think he feels it is his to make and in making it he will protect me. Beaner, I think it is too late—not too late for us, but too late for me; the decision is, after all, mine to make, is it not?

I must resolve to tell him when I see him next, to reassure him I have thought it through, so that he knows I made the choice willingly. If it is what's meant to be, I will have one more chance. Whether or not he will accept is long since out of my hands, but I will have to make the offer. If I don't, it will be my life's failure and regret. Rejection I can live with, in light of the spirit in which it is given, but to never try or take the chance—that is unthinkable and therefore unacceptable.

Damn, I wish you were here; it would help a great deal to have a voice of reason whispering in my ear. But it is not to be; I will have to go it alone and hope against hope that I am doing the right thing. Maybe my dreams will give me the answers I seek.

I certainly hope yours are more peaceful in nature than mine. Stay well, my heart, until we speak again.

February 20th
Patio of the Heritage Hotel Manila
10:00 AM

Well, hon, my dreams had no answers, not that I could see.

It is morning, and it is supposed to be a day when I get together with Angel. We are to go to a gospel session together tonight and maybe out for some social interaction. I don't feel the slightest bit excited about it. I have been writing for days, and both my spirit and my body are exhausted. I woke up this morning with little red dots all over my legs. It does not appear to be a rash; more likely it is little ant bites from my hours spent out here on the patio. I am tired though, so very tired and worn. I still feel a little lost.

My ramblings last night went far afield of my intended writing, but lately it does not seem to matter what I want to write or even if I want to write. There are times when the pen flies so quickly across the page that I do not see how the words flowing out can be coming from me. I don't even know half the time why I am sitting down to write—only that I am compelled to, and, regardless of how weak I am feeling, if I do not get out of bed and put pen to paper, I can find no rest. I did try one day to stay in bed, but I couldn't sleep. My body, though tired, was restless, and my mind would not stay silent long enough for me to get any sleep. Even today there are things I need to do, but I can't seem to put the book down long enough to do them—so I write.

I think I am only allowed to stop long enough to go learn or experience something new, and, when the lesson is learned or the experience complete, I find myself back here, unable to sleep until I write it down. I am sure that I was stuck at the table this morning because I did not tell you everything that we discussed last night. I was so concerned about my inner fears that I lost sight momentarily of the reasons we had gotten together in the first place.

When I got there, I wrote you briefly while I was waiting, and when Rev finally showed up, his smile lit up my world. He was so excited about an audition he had just gotten for a local show here. It is the Philippines version of Big Brother, and, unlike the one in the States, this show could make or break his career. I thought when I was still at home that it would be best for him to concentrate on his arts and push the political ambition aside. Now that I am here, I wonder if success as an actor would divert him from his purpose. Something tells me not; something tells me it will be a doorway for him to enter the public eye. He explained that famous actors here are virtually untouchable by the government, so it would also provide him with a safe haven of sorts. If successful, he would be protected from retribution from those in power. If he was known and loved by the people, then the government would not move against him. The situation here is unstable at best, and they cannot afford to have another uprising on a large scale.

I do trust that if he were put in that kind of position he would not walk down the path of corrupt power. I am sure his intent is pure; his eyes sparkle when he talks of his hopes for the future of his country. Still, he is young, and fame and money do strange things to the soul.

I suppose it is really my own impatience that is bothering me. I am well known for wanting things to happen when I want them to happen. You would think that after all these years I would have learned to accept what comes and not try to force situations to adhere to my own personal guidelines. I find it difficult, however, to sit and watch while an event plays itself out. The waiting game has never been my forte. It is odd how Angel pointed out that perhaps part of my reason for being here is to learn patience. She is probably right; every time I have sat back and let the "power that is" point the way, the road suddenly becomes smoother.

As I said, I asked Rev if he was worried about the repercussions from this book. He seemed annoyed that I would ask; in fact, his whole demeanour last night was one of restless impatience. He was continually fidgeting and shifting in his chair. He also was finding it difficult to meet my eyes—eyes that he has told me before are at times far too intense for comfort. I was having trouble understanding what had him so uncomfortable, but looking back, I realize he had recently poured his heart out to me and I hadn't had the courage to respond in kind. I shall have to remedy the situation, as I think only then will we be able to again find comfort in each other's presence. There are still too many things left unsaid.

While we talked, I asked him if he thought his people were ready to let go of their fears and latch onto the idea of freedom. I wanted to know if, given a leader to follow who truly had their best interests at heart, they would stand behind that leader. In short, I wondered, as I did in the spiritual sense, if these people were ready for change in the political sense. He says that though they still live in a world where fear overshadows their ability to move forward, that, given the right kind of leader, they would abandon their fears. He talked about the political infrastructure and explained that if the person at the top of that structure was corrupt then the corruption would ultimately trickle down and spread among the people. He doesn't believe that the people of this country need a leader who will tell them how to live, nor do they need a leader who will show them how to live. Rather they need a leader who will simply inspire them to want to live so they can work together for a cleaner, safer world.

Give a man a fish; feed him for a day. Teach a man to fish; feed him for a lifetime. It's a sound theory and one that applies both politically and spiritually. After discussing briefly my hopes that this book would marry the two ideals, we talked a little about the risks. That is when he explained his theory that God allows justice if and only if the reasons for that justice are pure. He questioned, for example: if God had frowned on righteous retribution, then how could a man like Genghis Khan be allowed to live to the age of eighty years? Surely if Genghis Khan's actions went against the natural order, then the powers that be would have stopped him. Rev cited names of conquerors throughout history who had tried and failed to destroy in the name of justice but whose underlying hate eventually destroyed them.

Men like Napoleon and Hitler, in an attempt to abolish religion and replace it with political domination, were thwarted and the world allowed to recover. Rev said that it wasn't until I came along that he found a way to accept the idea that anger had its place in the world. My idea that balance was essential for survival had awakened in him the realization that without anger we would become complacent. If we cannot feel anger at the unjust behaviors of others, then we have no reason to take action against that injustice. He said if we continue down a path of blind acceptance then we have no hope of initiating change. For too long we have allowed repression and starvation to run rampant, out of our belief that it is not our place to rise against it.

These ideals, however, go against the fundamental grain of the spiritual belief system here that seems to be at the core of these people's strength. I believe that the two ideals can co-exist, but it will take time for the general populace to make such a monumental shift in their beliefs. It's a shift that they would have to initiate on their own, not one they can or should be forced to.

Again I wonder if it is a change they are ready for. It would not be an easy one, and I cannot even say it would at first appear to be a positive one. "It is God's will"—the centre from which all hope in this land spirals out. How much would they have to alter their beliefs to achieve a state of "it is Gods will that humanity actively impose its own"? The idea that man was created to feel, dream, and think for himself—so he could take responsibility for his own actions and thereby take responsibility for his future—is one that has been around for centuries. Yet, even with that belief, man seems to need to put blame on an unseen force for all the wrongs in this world. It is a strange balance of complacent acceptance and an active desire to make change.

It concerns me still that man cannot find the balance, only because the two ideals are so seemingly opposite. I cannot see how humanity could embrace them as one. I suppose that is why I am actively seeking the common thread that underlies all religious and spiritual beliefs. I am curious whether the basic thread that is seemingly woven through them all can be safely acknowledged by the people of this world. If they are shown the possibility of its existence, would they begin to search on their own, or would they recoil in fear of the repercussions to their own faith? I would hope we are past the point of fearing knowledge. I could hope we are ready to seek the answers that are being made available, but we are human and thus we fear the unknown. We fear change, and we fear that which we cannot understand. Sadly, it is not possible to love or embrace fully anything we fear.

Someday, perhaps, we will learn; some day our eyes may be opened…

As I said, I have hope and faith that we may be moving toward that change. As a student of this world, I look forward to watching humanity take those first steps, but it will take men like Rev, with great sense of purpose and purity of heart, to lead us to it.

It is funny that even given his history and his family's belief in his future role as leader, he himself is too humble to see how much good a man like himself could do for this country. He understands what they need here, and he does not fear the dangers that would come with working toward fulfilling those needs. He sees a chance for change, and he believes his people ready for it, but he does not yet, I think, embrace the idea that he can be a powerful force to initiate that change.

We will see…

Time is the only answer to this particular question, and time, thankfully, has a way of never running out.

Well, my sweet, I must wander off again. I feel my time is done here for the moment, and I should probably get back to the reality of living. If I continue in this vein of ignoring the day-to-day essential requirements of this physical body, then I will not long hold onto my strength. Besides, the story can only go so far if I am sitting here writing—after all, it is not my story, it is theirs, and they are out there…

February 20th
Random coffee shop, South Central Manila
8:00 PM

Okay—seriously…

I am yet again sitting in a random part of Manila, alone, waiting to meet somebody…

I wonder if these people are convinced yet that I am completely nuts. I am—convinced, that is. Damn, this city is BIG and loud and busy and dirty and…

Oh hell, I could go on listing shit for hours. I don't even know what street I'm on or how I would go about getting back to the hotel if I needed to. I mean, holy shit, this is certainly a test of Rev's theory that I am safe here no matter what.

Amazing culture…

I told the taxi driver he is incredibly brave to drive here for a living. You know, there are hardly any traffic lights, cars just go wherever the hell they want, and so far I haven't seen one accident. Incredible to think about, really. If our people tried to live this way, there would be blood everywhere.

February 21st
Hotel room, Heritage Hotel Manila
10:36 AM

As I'm lying here in my bed trying to motivate myself to get up, I am having a hard time reconciling myself to continuing the work I thought I was sent here to do. Every time I think I have a clear picture of why I am here, I find myself facing another personal wall that I am forced to climb in order to continue. I don't suppose the whole trip is meant to be an easy one, but, as I told Rev two days ago, the emotional roller coaster that is this trip is turning out to be quite draining.

I must apologize for leaving you hanging last night. Angel arrived while I was in mid-sentence, and I was forced to quickly tuck the book away so I could join her.

Last night's adventure was a long one, with many discussions that I will share with you shortly, but, before I do, I must tell you that some of what we talked about has left me shaken. Not shaken in the sense that I doubt my purpose for being here but in the sense that I doubt my worthiness to pursue that purpose. I told Revo last night that I do not think it fair that I cannot be with him. I don't mean in the sense that I am here by his side always or that he is by mine, but that we will not be allowed to test the boundaries of our relationship. He says that as much as he does not want to lose what we have, in his heart and mind it is already over. He cannot see past the inevitable time when we will have to be apart, and he cannot see how it could possibly work with us apart. At the same time, he fears the threat to the core of our bond—not so much because of being apart physically, but having that physical separation cause doubt and anger between us.

He is worried that in the end I will hate him for not being willing to try. I attempted to explain that our inability to be together is situational and has no effect on how I feel about him, but I do not think he has much faith in my being able to separate the physical and emotional. When we are together like last night, talking to others and sharing our ideas, we feed each other. It would be nice to think that a year from now, when I come back, book in hand, we will still have that bond of shared energy.

He has admitted he is a lustful young man, and I have to remind myself to very careful about the lure of physical hunger. It is, after all, not the physical bond I am seeking, and though I know just how beautiful having both can be, I do not need more than the emotional to sustain me. Perhaps this is something I should discuss with him, though I am not sure he would believe me. I, like every other person I know, struggle with my own insecurities. I have felt jealousy and possessiveness in several relationships, and I know from first-hand experience the damage they can cause. Here with him, though, I don't feel the need to hold on. I do not need to cling to him to keep him with me, and I certainly don't feel any kind of desire to keep him to myself. I think he belongs to the world. I think he has the chance to make a difference here, and it would be wrong of me to want to keep him from that. I really feel that as long as I know he's with me in his heart it doesn't matter how many others he shares that heart with. I myself love deeply and passionately many people in my life, so why would I expect that he could love only one?

It makes so much more sense when I am able to put it on paper, and, even though I would rather discuss this with him in person, I don't think that he needs to see my eyes anymore to know that I speak the truth.

I'm gonna take a break, hon—as I said, I am not yet out of bed, and I need to look up a couple things before I do downstairs and commence writing. Our discussion last night was long and it will no doubt take hours to get it on paper for you.

February 20st
Patio of the Heritage Hotel Manila
12:56 PM

Why do we pray? Why do we doubt? Why do we suffer?

I resolve from now on to ask these questions of each individual I meet who is willing to share his or her beliefs and faith with me.

I am done asking them of myself; I already know what I believe… yet I also know that beliefs change as new knowledge is provided and really all I desire is to continue to learn and grow.

I am sitting in my favorite spot on the patio and relishing the renewed energy that has been blessedly bestowed on me. It was only after I wrote to you, and then forced myself out of bed, that I received a message that confirmed my beliefs that I am meant to wander and explore. Deacon had sent an email explaining that his company is being reconstructed, and, as he refuses to move to and work out of Denver, they have presented him with an amazing severance package. He says he wants to spend the summer with his kids and then spend a couple months travelling the world, and he asks if I would come with him.

He wouldn't be ready to leave until fall, at the earliest, and in light of how quickly the book is progressing, I figure that I will have wrapped it up about then and be free again to journey on. The timing of both his email and his plans for our trip could not be more perfect.

As I said earlier, I have been struggling with the idea of finding my place and finding my mate, and it was only after meeting Rev that I felt like my lifetime search for my other half was complete. The thing was, it didn't make sense that I would have met my perfect partner and then have to leave him. I mean, the unfairness of it was overwhelming, and I viewed it as yet another test of strength.

When I met him, I was still searching for that final missing piece; there was still a void, an empty space that had to be filled. Yet, even with the empty space, my life has been very full. I have had the joy and sorrow of loving and losing many people over the years. Each time I met a kindred spirit, another piece of me was put back into place, another part of my spirit returned, and it was a constant roller coaster of intense emotion. Each and every person who has touched my life has given me direction, and every adventure with those people has been beautiful and enlightening. Each and every one of those adventures inevitably came to an end.

Somehow, someway, those friendships and bonds have endured. I have loved both men and women and shared my hopes and dreams with all of them. Yet I still felt incomplete, as if I were destined to be alone, because it seemed that in the end I always had to leave those people behind. Then, when I met Revo, I really felt that he was the one soul that I had been searching for, but I did not recognize that he was not the only one I needed to make my life complete.

People speak often of old souls reunited, of soul mates finding each other, and the beauty of the idea has an undeniable pull. Yet, it does not make sense to me that an ancient soul could have only one mate.

Looking at it in a larger sense, in terms of souls being extensions of the massive energy that is the foundation of our existence, you have to wonder at the implications of it. I have a theory which, of course, I will share, but in no way will I expect you to believe it—in fact, even if the theory seems sound to me at the moment, I might very well change my mind as this journey continues.

In the beginning there were the original explorers, the then-new but now ancient spirits that came to this world to learn and explore. Those beings have continued their adventures and returned times innumerable in the quest and thirst for knowledge and understanding—for the mere purpose of exploration and experience. Yet every generation and race expands in the physical sense, and each new body is inhabited by either an old soul or a new one. The question, then, is Where do the new souls come from? Does it not stand to reason that the older, stronger souls are able to shed a part of themselves and divide their energies to give birth to the new? In that instant of division they leave behind a part of themselves that is, as a result, incomplete. Does it not then also stand to reason that the more times that soul divides the more pieces of that soul are spread out among humanity? Following that line of reasoning, one could conclude that of those ancient souls there are many extensions stemming from their cores currently walking the earth.

Perhaps, the older the soul is, the more pieces of itself—or "soul mates," if you will—exist, and it is the quest for finding those lost mates that leads people to search for their perfect mate here on earth. As humans, however, we do not allow for the idea of having more than one life partner. It is unnatural to our conditioned beliefs to embrace the concept of more than one love. We do not share easily, especially the younger inexperienced personalities who, like children, are still learning to let go of what they have so they can gain something new.

Picture the infant who is grasping a piece of jewelry, say, a nice golden necklace, that the unknowing wearer has inadvertently put within the baby's reach by the simple act of picking up the child. The baby sees the shiny object and is intrigued by it so latches on by wrapping little fingers around the piece and refusing to let go. It is a mother's natural instinct to replace the infant's treasure with something new, thereby encouraging the child to release the grasp on the pendant. As the child grows, it learns through this experience, as it is repeated time and time again, that only by letting go of the object it currently holds can it make room in its hand for each new gift that is presented.

I liken this action to our search for our ideal mate—the one person who makes us whole, the one treasure we long to have with us always and never release. Yet, as I said, if the ancient souls throughout the centuries divided many times, then they would not have only one perfect mate, but many. It would seem that, regardless of how many of those pieces they managed to draw back to themselves during their current lifetimes, until they come into contact with that final piece they would continue to feel incomplete. They would continue to seek and hunger for that oneness, that feeling of wholeness that they know is available to them but which they have not yet attainted.

It wasn't until I took a step back and looked long and hard at the people in my life, both past and present, that I realized where this hunger was coming from. Though Rev might have been what seemed to be the final piece (we will see), he is not the only one. By releasing me to explore further my own purpose, he ended my search by confirming for me what I already suspected.

I have been struggling with my own personal guilt for the effects of my actions on Rey. I have been trying to figure out how I could possibly explain to him and have him understand that our time as a couple is done. I am fearful of hurting him and destroying in him his willingness to love again. I mean, how could I possibly justify my actions here; how could I convince him that I was capable of loving and needing more than one person in my life? It is a concept not easily understood.

How could I reasonably expect him to accept the possibility, if I could not accept it myself—if I continued to struggle with the idea that I was meant to stay with one person, even when the very centre of my being denied that that was reality? How could I expect him to see it as I do—or even expect him to be willing to hear what I have to say and believe it as truth—when I do not understand the truth of it or believe it for myself?

I do not think that in the end I am meant to settle. I am a wanderer, an explorer of time and this world. I cannot explore and learn from this place if I am not free to go where circumstance and opportunity take me. I do not think that, as an explorer of this world, I am meant to make a difference on a grand scale. It is not for me to lead these people to a better way of life. I have never felt that was my purpose, and I do not feel it now. Rather, I must inspire those who will make a difference—however, whenever, and wherever I can.

It would appear I am going backwards, from this morning's life lessons to last night's discussions, but I know of no other way to explain it and have you understand. I say again, if you could see through my eyes you, too, would find hope in what you had witnessed.

I would not have gotten the email if I had not gone online to look up the Age of Aquarius. I did this after a conversation we had last night about how the world is destined for change. Our dispute was over the how and the when—more so about the when—the how is, I think, for another time.

It was close to the end of the evening, and we had spent the night discussing religion and spirituality with Angel. We had explained our views and our beliefs and answered for her as many questions as we could.

At one point, after purposely antagonizing me and putting me on the defensive, Rev looked at me and said, "You know, you are beating a dead horse. The time has not yet come for this, and you are attempting to do something that these people are not ready for."

I argued that I realized that it was not yet time for a monumental shift in reality, but it was still my purpose to work toward that shift. I also argued that I didn't think I was the one to finish that particular struggle, but I was definitely meant to help move it along.

I have to point out that Angel seemed lost for the moment, but we will get back to that.

Rev said, "Why do you continue, when you cannot possibly achieve it in this lifetime? It is not meant for us to see this time around."

I know he was not trying to talk me down; rather, he was reminding me to stay focused on the smaller changes, but I was frustrated enough to respond quite selfishly: "I am tired; I do NOT want to do this again; I do not WANT to come back—I want to go HOME!"

It is something that you and others like you have heard me say many times, and, until today, it was how I felt. I was tired; I didn't really want to do this again. We have been here too many times before and seem to be getting nowhere; yet, when I look around now, I see how far humanity has really come. Our evolution, albeit slow, is irrevocably moving forward, for good or bad; we are advancing, and it seems to me we may finally be moving in the right direction.

Even with that knowledge, it is still exhausting to continue the fight when, as he pointed out, it is not yet time to win it. He is right, whether I like it or not. We are not done here, and it was my rebellious nature that led me to respond so thoughtlessly.

His eyes flashed for an instant, only the tiniest of signs that he was briefly annoyed, but they softened immediately. His voice was silken when he responded, and I was reminded yet again of how much I needed this man in my life to give me strength.

"You have to come back." He whispered it quietly, not wanting, I think, to share this moment between us with the world. "You—we—are not done...

After that he seemed to come back to himself and realize that Angel was quite openly staring wide-eyed at our conversation. He asked her if she believed in past lives, and she shook her head, no.

Babe, if you could have seen her eyes,—she was like a deer caught in the headlights: startled, afraid, and frozen in place by what she had seen. I quipped that she was young yet—she will learn. He nodded his acknowledgement even as he began to explain to her the theory of the ages. He went over it only briefly, explaining about Jesus coming around the end of the age of Pisces and the meaning behind the Age of Aquarius.

That is, after all, how the whole conversation started, with him asking if I knew about the Age of Aquarius. He had asked me if I knew when it was, and I had answered: now. He had begun to argue that it was not until around the year 3000, so we still had many more years to wait. I argued back that he hadn't asked me when it ended, only when it was, and, as we were currently in the development of that age, I stood by my answer of "now."

He rolled his eyes at me, as if to say that I was purposely playing games, but I told him that if he wanted a specific answer he should ask a specific question.

He went back to his argument that our next big step in evolution as a race would not take place until the end of that age, giving us a good seven hundred or so more years of struggle and strife. I have looked it up since then, and they say it ends in the year 2600; yet, that is only one theory, and, as you know, the calculations have not yet been proven to be precise. It is a comfort, I must say, to be able to write to you knowing that I do not have to go into long-winded explanations about the history behind these ideas. It's a comfort also to know that if I brush on a topic that you have yourself not yet explored, you will simply go look it up and find your own answers.

I still hate the idea of being responsible for someone else's education, and I abhor the idea of having to direct somebody toward one particular belief system. We discussed that, too, but I will get back to that as well. As I said, Angel looked somewhat poleaxed, not quite sure we were for real. We had, after all, been having a very open and animated discussion about God, Christianity, and religion. For us to switch over so quickly to reincarnation, old souls, and the passing of the ages must have been very disheartening for her. She is a very young soul, and, as such, fearful of concepts she does not understand. She does not like us to embrace the unknown, nor does she see the beauty in the unexplored.

Perhaps part of our reason for pulling her to us was so that we could awaken in her a thirst for knowledge. Only time will tell, but I do not think that it was accidental that she stumbled into my life. I felt mildly amused at her reaction; she is so secure in her faith that it occurred to me that she was not in danger of losing her way, and, if and when she decided to, she would search out answers to the questions we had inadvertently put in her head. So far, we had spent the evening working on encouraging and securing her faith while, at the same time, asking her to acknowledge and accept that ours was not identical in nature.

To be honest, the evening had begun innocently enough. I had agreed to join Angel in the gospel study, which turned out to be fortunate, as the group of Christians she studied with were all Chinese. As such, they were born-again Christians coming from a Buddhist background. It gave me the opportunity to meet some of these people and leave them my number. If Buddhism is something I am meant to explore and learn about, they will call. If they do not, then perhaps it is meant for another time.

Again, only time will tell, and I have quickly learned not to force the issue. I did, however, have a small run-in (if you can call it that) with a minister; I later shared this encounter with Rev. He later used this encounter to yet again try to antagonize me into backing down from my beliefs. I didn't, and he is quickly learning that the more he tests my resolve the stronger it becomes.

Angel had introduced me to the minister, and I talked with him about my book and my purpose behind writing it. I can tell you, he was not open to the idea that more than one religion could be accepted, but I tried to explain that, as long as an individual's God guided him or her to enlightenment, then it didn't matter what that person chose to call God. He wanted to know what I believed. I told him I believe there is a higher power and that the power guides us, shelters us, and protects us. It is through knowledge and acceptance of that higher power that we grow spiritually and learn the lessons required to achieve a higher state of awareness and harmony within ourselves, the world that surrounds us, and the people in it. He wanted to know what I call that power. I told him: "You call him God, so today I call him God." He obviously did not like my answer, but then I did not expect him to either understand it or accept it. I left my number with him, however, and if he chooses to call, I will meet with him and learn what I can.

Rev was annoyed apparently at what I had done, and he questioned my right to try to alter the views of a minister of the Christian faith. This in turn angered me, and I shot back that I had the right to explain my own beliefs without fear of condemnation. He gave me one of his quirky little smiles and softly stated, "You're so defensive."

Unfortunately, I heard his words and not the meaning behind them and again responded in a very ungracious manner. I exclaimed, "If I am defensive, it is only because you accuse me of doing to others the very thing I so openly disdain and speak out against."

I argued that I was not trying to convert a Christian into believing what I believe but rather asking the Christian to accept me regardless of my beliefs. Why should I have to call my God by any particular name to gain acceptance, when I know, love, and respect that God on a personal level? Who, in fact, was he to judge or question my knowledge of God on the basis of my name for God?

Exodus 3:14: God said, "I am who I am. You must tell them: 'the one who is called I AM has sent me to you'"

Writing continued from the hotel room, lying down

At this point, Rev pointed out that I was setting myself up for failure if I believed that I could convince people to follow my beliefs. I told him yet again that I did not expect them to believe as I did and that I only asked for the respect and freedom from others' judgments to explore my own beliefs. I continually forget that I am surrounded by Christians, and he seems to keep a constant vigil out for anything I might say that will endanger me, yet he continues to question and challenge me.

I explained that I had been accepted and welcomed in several different communities so far in spite of my openness about my beliefs. In fact, the only time I had felt pressured was when being confronted by fanatical Christians. At this point, he quickly changed the subject by pointing to a monument in the distance and asking Angel what it was. In the end he apparently got from me what he had been looking for. I think he tests me at odd moments to be sure I will be able to defend myself in a manner that will not bring condemnation and retribution. He seems to have a great deal of faith in my writing, as I have faith in his work to provide his people with tools to create better lives for themselves. For each of us, our chosen paths contain apparent and unseen dangers, and we must shelter and protect each other from those dangers.

When Angel was preparing to leave last night, she asked Rev if he would see that I got home safely. She asked him to protect me, and he very quickly answered that we protect each other. It is when he is soft-spoken and gentle that he touches me the most; his quiet assurance is extremely comforting, and I need it for survival here. If I were not constantly sheltered by those moments of love and understanding, it would be easy for me to lose my way. He is such a blessing to me, and I am so very fortunate to have finally found him.

I apologize for bouncing around so much with regards to our conversation last night; it is not one that can be properly explained in a linear manner. If I attempted to start from the beginning, you might not experience or learn the evening's lessons in the intended manner. I understand that might make no sense to you, but, since you will be reading this long after it was written, then the timing of all of it is relative to you. As usual, I do not map out what or how I am going to write; I simply write and therefore cannot adhere to the restrictions of linear time. Nor can I attempt to create within a boxed-in ideal of someone else's expectations. It is not my nature nor is it my purpose.

I have faith that you are keeping up with me and my random ramblings; fortunately, you are an intelligent, inquisitive creature who can easily follow.

I am sorry, sweetie, but I must for the moment take a break; my body is telling me to rest, and I am very much in tune with its current needs. If I do not rest when it is time, then I will eventually weaken. So, I am off to take a nap, but, before I go, I will tell you that my earlier reference to a box brings to mind a game Revo played with Angel last night—the same game he played with me the night I discovered I needed to go to the Philippines. I will tell you all about it when I wake. xo

February 21st
Patio of the Heritage Hotel Manila
9:53 PM

Okay, so I was going to continue telling you about our story last night, but something came up. I wrote it down in another notebook, because at the time it didn't seem to have a place in this one, but it would seem the answer to my dilemma was, in retrospect, another part of the tale. I will, however, write my views down in the other book as well. I only wish to make note of it here, so, if and when I choose to incorporate it, I will know where it belongs. I will, of course, discuss it with you in detail, and we can decide together if it has a place in these pages.

Okay, so I just filled you in on everything, and we shall see what happens later, eh?

So, when last I left you, we were sitting on a bar patio in Quezon City, Manila, playing a game with Angel. It is a visualization game involving a series of questions that grow from each other. The answers are supposed to reflect one's personal beliefs and desires.

The questions and answers run as follows.

The subject is asked to picture in their mind a white room, an empty room with white walls, and then the questions begin…

REV. Picture a box in the room. What size is the box? Is it small, medium, or large?

ANGEL. Small box.

REV. Where is the box? Is it sitting on the floor? Is it floating in the air? What is the box doing?

ANGEL. It is on a table.

REV. What colour is the box?

ANGEL. It is red, yellow—all the sides are different colours.

REV. Now picture a ladder in the room. Where is the ladder? How big is the ladder?

ANGEL. Ten steps, and it is leaning against the wall on the right side of the room.

REV. Now, picture flowers in the room. What colour are they, and where are they in the room? How big are they?

ANGEL. One flower, a daisy, and it is on the table. It looks like a normal-size daisy.

REV. Okay, now picture a horse in the room. Where is the horse? What is it doing? What colour is it?

ANGEL. It is a rocking horse, like the ones children play on. It is brown, and it is on the floor in the middle of the room.

REV. Okay, now use three words to describe the horse's personality.

ANGEL. (looking confused) It is a normal horse. (At this point she struggled for words, but, as Rev prompted her, she came up with the following.) Harmonious, graceful, content, relaxed, and chillin'.

REV. Okay, now picture a storm in the room. Where is the storm? How big is it, and is it affecting the things in the room? Is it touching them or blowing them around.

ANGEL. (with an odd look on her face) It is on the left side of the room, across from the horse, away from everything. It is a letter storm, made of words.

Okay Beaner, are you ready to learn what it all means?

Well, before I tell you, take the time to ask yourself the same questions, write down the answers, and then compare them to our explanations.

"Nothing, it means absolutely nothing; it's an idle game to pass the time… I'm joking," he told her that, just as he had told me the same thing before he was kind enough to explain it.

I had written everything down, so it was easier to go through the explanation with her.

The box represents her pride; as she chose a very small box it showed she was a very humble girl. He couldn't explain about the table, and if I ever get the chance, I will ask him where he learned the game, so I can try to find the answer myself. The fact that the box was sitting on something, however, and was not floating, represents that she is not an artistic soul. Rather, she is grounded, logical, and rational.

The colours on the box indicate her personality and how others view her. If it had been clear or transparent, that would have meant that people could easily see through her. As it was multicoloured, it indicates that she shows many sides of herself, her personality, to different people, depending on the circumstances.

The ladder represents her life ambitions. As hers was approximately the same height as her, she has attainable ambitions. As the number of rungs on the ladder was very specific, her ambitions are also very structured and well thought out.

We came next to what the flower represented, and before she answered the next question I wrote down on my own paper the word God. Rev began to explain to her that the flower represents the people in our life who we love and cherish, but he was confused as to why there was only one. So he asked her who she thought that one person was. She answered God; the fact that it was a common type and normal size then indicates that God is a normal part of her day-to-day life.

Okay, now to the horse, of course…

It is meant to represent her ideal mate. Her horse was a rocking horse, so her mate should be fun-loving and love kids. He should be harmonious, graceful, content, and relaxed. Let's not forget chillin'! Though Rev was stuck on the colour, I pointed out that since it was brown it indicated an earthy, grounded personality, which is like Angel's own.

Well, hon, there's more, but again, I am tired, so off to bed. Tomorrow I think I will head off to Rizal Park and maybe find a shady patch of grass to work on the next part of my tale. I wonder if I will meet anyone along the way who can tell me more about these people. Rev seems to have withdrawn from the equation for the moment, so, as I said before, another guide should be popping up at any time.

I'll let you know what happens. xoxo

February 22nd
Patio of the Heritage Hotel Manila
4:43 PM

You see—if I wait long enough the answers come. I quite literally only crawled out of bed an hour ago. I was so sick and so tired all day. I had no drive or ambition and was feeling quite lost as to which direction to go next. So I eventually pulled myself out of bed and decided I was going to come down and try to get some food into me. While I was here, something Angel said to me the night before kept popping into my head. She asked if I would like to visit a local orphanage with her and see the work that is being done there to help the homeless children.

The idea intrigued me. After all, the point of coming here was to bring the plight of these people to the attention of the world. I got sidetracked, of course, as I am wont to do. My curiosity about human behavior gets the best of me at times, I admit, but the idea itself was still buried in the back of my mind.

I wondered, though, who was sponsoring the organizations, and, as I was pondering, it came to me that my time here is running short; I have only eleven days left. If I aim to find out as much as I can, I can't sit and wait for Angel to take me around. She has her life to live, and I don't want to intrude on that. It also occurred to me that the fact that Rev has been unavailable is a very strong lesson in independence. I would have to learn not to rely on anyone's but my own intuition and intelligence to lead me in the right direction.

So I took a chance and asked the waiter if he knew of any local orphanages that cared for homeless children. He said yes—as a matter of fact, he could tell me two organizations off the top of his head.

One is government-run, called the DSWD, and another one is run by the local media network in Manila: ABS-CBN, which also happens to tie in with Revo's work in the entertainment industry. I took a few minutes out to go upstairs and look up a couple for myself online. I typed in orphanages, Manila, Philippines on a Google search and the first name that came up was Shepherd of the Hills Children's Foundation. Once I was back down at the patio, I asked the waiter if he had ever heard of that particular orphanage, and he informed me that the hotel that I am staying in happens to sponsor that organization. He did not, however, have any information on what they do, but he told me I could more than likely get the contact number through the concierge. He told me if there was anything else I needed he'd be more than happy to help me out.

It's amazing how open these people are when you show an interest or concern for their people. I guess I shouldn't be surprised by it, really; any interest from the outside in helping to alleviate the poverty here must serve to open their hearts a bit more to the possibility of a better future. They get quite excited when I tell them I am writing a book and am here to learn about them. Their eyes shine just a little more when I ask questions, and, instead of being cautious, they seem to want to jump at the chance to help. I am, I admit, still feeling drained, but at least now I seem to have a trail to follow. I will have to wait and see where it leads.

In the meantime, I will try to wrap up for you our previous night's discussion with Angel. She, like the minister, wanted to know what I believed, especially after listening to Revo and me arguing about whether or not my expectations were too high. I told her the same thing I tell everyone else who asks and reiterated that I did not believe I had to call that higher power by the same name as others, as long as my faith and knowledge of it was secure. Revo jumped into the conversation at one point and asked her if she knew what voodoo was. She replied, "Black magic." I shook my head, while Rev began an in-depth explanation of the basis of that particular spiritual belief.

He explained that the practice of voodoo originated in Africa and was, in fact, a religion that was headed by a dual god/goddess, Mawu-Lisa, or, alternatively, a single divine creator, Nana Buluku, who embodies a dual cosmogonic principle, and of which Mawu, the moon, and Lisa, the sun, are female and male aspects. The religion is believed to be so old, in fact, that it dates back ten thousand years and is believed to have ancient roots in Mesopotamia, Egypt, India, and Asia Minor.

The word voodoo (vodon, vodoun, or voudon) means God Creator or Great Spirit. It is a belief founded in one supreme God, a very abstract omnipotent force. It is through worship and knowledge of that God that its participants strive to better understand both the natural process of life and their own spiritual nature. The art of vodon is one of healing, both within one's self and the world. Practitioners use prayer and ritual to celebrate forces of nature. They also honour specific deities or spirits who are believed to actively work as protectors and guides. Rev likened this to the Christian belief in angels, saying that they were extensions of God's power sent to shelter and protect. He also pointed out that a large part of their faith centered around the idea that the more positive action they took in their lives, both toward their own spiritual growth and toward that of others, the more positive energies they would in turn receive.

I pointed out it was very similar to the wiccan Law of Threefold Return, which holds that whatever benevolent or malevolent actions a person performs will return to that person with triple force, thereby ensuring that its users could only expect misery if that power was not used for the betterment of others.

Rev made it quite clear that only the Westernization of these arts twisted them into a religion that was believed to have negative connotations. When they didn't understand the belief behind the religion, people's views of it were prone to inaccuracy. I agreed and say that it is human nature to fear what we do not understand. It is also our nature to hate that which we fear—and what we hate we work toward destroying.

Angel looked rather taken aback by all of this. It seemed to her, I believe, that we were attempting to cloud her own beliefs and thereby lead her astray. We attempted to reassure her, and I hope we got through to her that we did not intend to threaten or belittle her faith. In fact, the opposite is true—we were merely trying to point out that there are underlying currents of similarity to be found in most major religions.

For example, vodon involves the search for higher levels of consciousness in the belief that we must open the way to God. Again, you can compare it to the Christian belief that through faith and knowledge of God we open the way to allow him into our lives.

Angel was surprised, I think—in fact, I am sure that would be putting it mildly—but it was heartening that she didn't immediately run from the idea. Rev pointed out that her body language indicated that she was feeling insecure and possibly threatened by the topic. She had, in fact, leaned back in her chair as far as she could away from him; her chin was also lifted as if in defiance, and her arms were folded across her chest defensively. When he mentioned it again, she said quite pointedly and fiercely that she believed in God and that she could not see voodoo or black magic as being a way to worship that God.

Rev replied that was indeed the whole point he was trying to make: because she had not researched these things for herself and could not definitively say they were true, she could not then accept our explanations of them. He also said that her God teaches acceptance and understanding, not judgment of others. How could she claim to live out God's wishes if she was not willing to at least try to accept or understand the beliefs of others? Why, also, should she, secure as she was in her own relationship with God, fear knowledge of other faiths and religions? She did not have to change her beliefs in order to open her eyes to the possibility that the core of those beliefs could in fact be found in other religions.

Angel had mentioned black magic more than once, and Rev seemed to think the matter needed to be addressed. He explained that the "black magic" part of voodoo was, in fact, a twisted offshoot of the original religion. It is not what the true practitioners of that religion believe, and it has no place in their worship.

I pointed out that every religion has its opposite, evil side. Christianity has it counterpart in Satanism, and the Wiccans also have their opposite in the dark arts of black witchcraft. As long as there has been religion there have been those who choose to follow the opposite path of that religion. The world revolves around balance, and so, for every good there must be an equal and opposing bad. Yet it is personal choice that dictates each individual's beliefs, not the foundation behind the beliefs themselves.

I do not advocate the belief or practice of these darker arts, but I do acknowledge the need to understand them. I do not believe that one can effectively defend against an enemy one does not understand. I also do not believe that the denial of their existence will in any way, shape, or form initiate the destruction of those beliefs. I think that it is for those who follow a more enlightened path to reach out and understand those who do not. Only through that understanding can we begin to call those who have lost their way toward a more positive direction. I also believe that in order to accomplish that task we must understand why they lost their way in the first place.

If, for example, you point your finger at someone who has stolen from you and loudly declare, "You are a thief—therefore you are a bad person!" then you are closing yourself off from an opportunity to help that person find a better way. You have not asked why the person has stolen, and, in not asking, you cannot know that he is perhaps trying to get money to feed his children. You cannot know, if you do not ask, that he has lost his job. You cannot know that, though he has applied for government assistance, he has been denied. You cannot know that he is perhaps the only source of income for his family, as his wife is ill, and you cannot know if you do not ask that his friends or family are in no position themselves to help him.

I do describe one of the worst-case scenarios, and I openly acknowledge that not all people who have committed crimes have any justifiable reason for committing those crimes. I only wish to point out that if we merely point our fingers and accuse, without first asking why, then we are ignoring one of the fundamental life lessons we have been sent here to learn. Empathy for others leads us to understanding, and understanding opens the door for positive action. We can continue to point and accuse, or we can seek the reasons behind behavior we do not understand. It is a personal choice to be made by each individual as they journey down the road of life.

I would like to think most people would be open to the idea that the question Why? is an important one to ask.

Why does that person believe as they do?

Why does that person act as they do?

Why does that person live as they do?

When we look for the answers to the questions of why, we open ourselves to a greater understanding of those we share the world with. Should we not make peace with those around us?

Our discussion, as you can plainly see, ran all over the place throughout the evening, but it kept returning to that base belief that part of learning about ourselves is opening ourselves to learning about others and the world around us. I don't want to tell others what to believe; it is not my place and it is not my way. I only want to understand why others believe as they do. It is a constant hunger in me that I cannot seem to satisfy, this curiosity of people's ways and reasons. There is so much out there to learn and so much that others have to offer.

I hope we didn't scare the little darling too badly. She is young, yes, but she is intelligent, and I have hopes that she can eventually get past her fear of the unknown. I think her strength of faith will take her far, and I am certain she has much to teach the world. She has taught me a great many things already, though I am sure she does not recognize the fact. I am very grateful for the opportunity to meet her and hope I have, in turn, given her some things to think on.

Well, hon, the evening is wearing on, and I have hopes that tomorrow will be a busy day …

I sent Rev a text regarding my plan to seek out orphanages and organizations that fund them. I hope, since his mother is leaving in the morning, that he can find the time to tour around with me—but I also realize that he may still be more interested in protecting himself by keeping his distance. We will see what happens tomorrow, and I will keep you informed. Goodbye for now, beautiful lady. I will talk to you soon.

February 22nd
Patio of the Heritage Hotel Manila
7:30 AM

Well, darling, I may just have both found myself a new friend in adventure as well as a way out to the provinces under the protection of a fairly burly, yet surprisingly sweet, gentlemen from England. I hate to celebrate my good luck prematurely; I will tell you how it happened if and when anything comes of it. It may turn out to be another one of those "No #*! ##!* way—that did not just happen" moments—but it appears that yet again, as I need them, so they are provided. If in this case I am wrong, then I can't say I much regret the time spent, and I certainly will not consider it to be time wasted. It did turn out to be a much-needed distraction and release of tension.

I am, however, at the moment very much in need of a shower and a bit of down time. The shower, at least, I think I can manage; the down time is much more unlikely, as I still intend to see if I can gain access to some of the orphanages. I am not sure what I am looking for, and certainly I do not have an expectation as to what I will find; I just feel that I need to go.

It has just occurred to me that I have made a breakthrough here with the people who work in the hotel; they are finally beginning to call me by name, which is a huge step in the right direction with regards to open communication. Wonderful, only eleven days left, and I am finally getting them to see me as more than just another guest.

Man, it's early; in retrospect it's a very good thing I slept all day yesterday. I honestly can't tell you at what ungodly hour I actually fell asleep last night, or rather this morning, but, as I said, it was well worth it.

I met some new and unique individuals last night, on two separate occasions. One was a mild-mannered flight instructor from China, who was obviously in need of a bit of company. He was mildly interesting and very nice, but I have the feeling his intentions were not exactly pure. I think his eagerness to buy me beer was a bit of a giveaway, but, as I was expecting a call from Deacon at 11:00, I had an excuse to escape to my room.

It was on my way to my room, however, that I was stopped briefly by a much more intriguing personage. A sweet old guy who I have seen around the hotel several times over the last few days with his team of… hmmm… well, let's call them engineers, for lack of a better word. I've noticed him only because the fact that he bears a striking resemblance to my dad made him stand out from the continuously changing crowd of people who inhabit this hotel.

I was walking by his table when he called me over, and, as I felt I had time, I allowed myself to be pulled off-course. It turns out he is an Englishman here with his work crew preparing to install some fiber-optic cables out in the provinces, which will allow Internet and phone access out in some of the rural areas. Again we go back to communication; always it seems we are pulled back to communication and the use of it in bringing out world closer together. Novel idea, that...

He was interested, as I have discovered many here to be, in what I am doing writing every day. He wanted to know from whence I hail and what it is I am working on. At first I tried to give only a surface explanation, but he, being much older and possibly wiser, saw right through the façade and proceeded to ask questions meant to draw out more information than I was at the time willing to give. I was tied to the clock this time so had to excuse myself, but, as I left, I did promise to return and talk a little more with him about my book. After speaking with Deacon briefly on the phone, I made my way back down to the patio and partook in a glass of wine with both the elderly gentleman and a young man who had joined the table.

The young man, I will call him Hippie, was at first very quiet, and, in obvious deference to the other gentleman, kept silent while my fine English friend began to drill me for information. What was my book about? How did I come about the idea to write it? What was the purpose behind the book? What were my conclusions so far? Most importantly to him: had I been published before and, if so, where and under what name?

The answers to most of those questions you already know, so I will not bore you with the details. As for his enquiries as to what I had previously published, I admit I was vague at best. I flat-out refused to give him the name under which my work has been published and I refused also to give him any solid information concerning the content of that published work. I was also shamefully misleading with regard to the type of work I had done in the past, but, as I explained to him later, the current topic is one that could in a roundabout way cause serious repercussions for those involved. Much to my dismay, I found myself being overly forthcoming about the how and the why of this particular piece of literature, and I sincerely hope that my openness will not, as they say, come back and bite me in the ass.

I blame his similarity in appearance to my late stepfather for my blatant disregard for caution. I am sure it had nothing to do with beer and wine.

It was only after he seemed satisfied that I was leveling with him that he ceased his relentless questions, and his young friend took the opportunity to speak. It was the young friend, in fact, who I discovered had much more to offer by way of life experience than the unusual old gentleman I had first thought to gain some insight from. It turns out my young hippie is the son of a well-to-do entrepreneur who managed somehow, in spite of his wealth, to raise a selfless, earthy individual. It amazed me that this man, who had been sent to the best boarding schools in England and who at one point had thought nothing of purchasing things like Lamborghinis and yachts as playthings, had chosen to put aside his worldly possessions and go to live a much-less-materialistic life in South Africa.

Oh yes, darling, you read that correctly. His father is a self-made multimillionaire, an oil barren among other things, and yet he chooses to eke out an existence in a small community in South Africa. Without, I must add, the aid of his parent's not inconsiderable fortune to help pay his way.

Okay, I admit it—it sounds a bit farfetched and very much like a story fabricated to lure in an unwary female. However, as it did not come up until much later in the conversation that he hailed from a wealthy background, he had absolutely no reason to lure me anywhere; I was already there. We were thoroughly entranced in an animated discussion and he had already won my attention with his open and friendly demeanor. His story goes something like this.

He was born and raised in England by a well-to-do self-made oil tycoon. In his youth, he attended all the best schools money could buy and worked where he chose in occupations that allowed him to surround himself with all the toys a rich kid could want. His spending habits in his younger years were flamboyant, to say the least, and he himself had no regard for the people in this world who had less than he. He did, however, have the fortunate benefit of having two supportive and loving parents. So, when, at the age of nineteen, he found himself in a situation where he was forced with the very real probability that he was soon going to be a father himself, he was saved from self-destruction by the some very well-rounded advice from his father.

Rather than condemn him for his carelessness, his father encouraged him to embrace the idea that perhaps it was time to grow up. Hippie told me that his father never chastised him, only supported him unconditionally, and it was through that support that his views of his life and the lives of others began to change.

His father had apparently always tried to instill in him the belief that he was no better, regardless of his financial or social situation, than those who seemingly stood below him. He did have the benefit of growing up knowing that money and status were not what defined an individual, yet he was still complacent toward the struggles and trials of those less fortunate. How his attitude changed and his eyes opened is, according to him, a story in and of itself. I am therefore hoping to come back to it at a later date. I would like the opportunity to see him again and perhaps glean from him a more in-depth version of his tale—which I will, of course, share with you.

He did, however, have a few enlightened views that pertain to the material and topics discussed at various times throughout these pages. He seems to agree that the world could use a gentle nudge in the direction of acceptance and understanding of others, but he views the lack of these things as a lack of interest, not a lack of information. He pointed out quite readily that we all see the pictures of starving children on TV and in the papers, but, as it does not immediately affect us, it does not hold our interest for long. He says the world is very much aware of the plight of these people and others in Third World countries around the globe but that awareness is nothing more than a passing glance.

I argued that it is one thing to see or read about the child but quite another to feel and understand the child's hunger. He says it's true that they are two different levels of awareness, but he does not believe it is easy to attain the latter. People must first be convinced that they need to do more than simply stare blankly at the face of the child before they will be willing to take the next step and taste the tears of that same child. The problem and the challenge are: how does one convince anybody that empathy and understanding of others is an important part of our growth as humans? I have to agree; it is a dilemma, yes, but one I am willing to attack full-force, if I have to exhaust myself to do it.

I was surprised, however, at the eloquent explanation given the source. He is, as he openly stated from the beginning of our conversation, a non-believer in the spiritual and religious communities. This fact shocked me completely, as he had had such well rounded and grounded views of the world in which he lived. He amended the comment later, saying he simply refused to discuss religion and spirituality openly, as his views on the matter covered such a vast array of belief systems while adhering to none that it was impossible for the average person to understand from whence he was coming.

I am anxious to explore his ideas further with him, and, as we are meeting up later to wander around, I intend to get him to open up a bit more about them. It is strange that I have come halfway around the world and have encountered people from different parts of the globe and different religious backgrounds who believe all the same fundamental ideals. They only call them by different names and describe them as coming from different sources, but the end result seems, so far, to be the same. Humans, as diverse as we are, really are not that different when you get down to the core of the being.

Hippie also talked about the idea that living a simpler, less materialistic life is not one many people are ready to embrace by choice. They do, for the most part, enjoy their creature comforts, and it would seem unwise and unfair to expect them to give them up. He did, however, agree that we would do well to take a step back from technology once in awhile and get back to the basic one-on-one level of communication. For example, rather than come home and sit in front of the TV with your child and consider that quality time, get off the couch and actually spend time talking with that child. He agreed with me that children see way more and are much more perceptive than we give them credit for, citing his own experience of finding himself on the receiving end of profound wisdom coming from the mouth of a nine-year-old. He says he does, in fact, find himself basing most of his more important life choices on that wisdom, believing that his child's intuitions are for the most part more accurate than his own. And I thought I was nuts…

Realistically, though, we do share many of the same views and ideas, and I am greatly looking forward to talking with him further. It does surprise me that we could come from such different backgrounds and life experiences and yet end up coming to the same conclusions. I am beginning to see a pattern emerging in this, and, as it emerges, so, too, does the possibility that my very broad views on spirituality and reality might just have a basis in fact.

It is, I admit, the long way round to proving it, but I am up for the trip, which is, after all, why I am here. I wonder what interesting person I get to meet next. Yet again, the prospect excites me, and I look forward to my next unexpected encounter.

Well, hon, it was a late night, and I would like to get showered and work toward getting some info on the orphanages. I will talk to you soon. xo

February 23rd
Patio of the Heritage Hotel Manila
11:30 PM

Hey, sweets, just dropping a line to let you know I should not have dismissed my encounter with the pilot so soon. It turns out that one of the two things that he continued to bring up throughout our discussion has significance after all. He had mentioned Balacun several times, and I was under the impression that he was trying to get me to go there with him, because he kept saying over and over that I should go to Balacun, but you know, I was thinking about it the wrong way and didn't pick up anything until today when I went back online to look for more orphanages. This time the one I first found was not there (weird), but a new one did show up in the form of a link to the Precious Heritage Children's Home in Balacun, outside metro Manila.

I am going to run with the idea that I should go there and am about to call a lady who the concierge told me will be able to put me in contact with the various orphanages here in Manila.

The second thing he seemed to feel was vitally important was the terracotta army of China's first emperor, Qin Shi Huang. It was hard at times to discern what he was trying to say, as his English was very broken, but he was very definite and clear in one respect. The first time he mentioned it, his English became very clear and fluent and his eyes shone as he peered into mine and told me: "You know this place; you must go to this place; then you must know that you remember this place."

Honestly, the first time he said it I thought I had heard him incorrectly, but not ten minutes later he looked me square in the eye again and said definitively: "You must remember this place; you must remember the horses, the reason for the horses" (again with the horses).

The entire evening had been like that. We would talk, and whenever it was about his family or work, his English would be extremely difficult to follow. He tried to teach me a little Chinese, but again, he didn't know the English words to translate, so the conversation had been sporadic and slow—yet, every few minutes his eyes would brighten and sometimes in mid-sentence he would very pointedly insist that I go, that I remember…

It was a bit on the weird side, sure—especially since I had not discussed with him my interest either in history or religion, and I couldn't figure out why he was being so emphatic about it—but then again, I did not put any importance on it at the time. Now, however, I am thinking it is maybe something I should look into. I know nothing about the history and cannot therefore relate it to my current search for answers, but I think that somehow, some way it might also tie into the rest of this crazy tale.

I keep wondering where these many leads that apparently run off in many different directions are taking me—but I feel it drawing to a conclusion. Yet, for the life of me, I cannot grasp what that conclusion might be. There are no coincidences, eh, or so it would seem, but, again I am completely and utterly stumped as to where this one will lead. Wish me luck, my Wiccan friend; I feel at this point I may need it.

February 24th

Patio of the Heritage Hotel Manila

10:00 AM

Patience has its rewards. I took the time to stop at the desk this morning at Hippie's urging, and discovered some information I would not have found otherwise. The owner of the hotel personally supports an organization in the provinces that cares for orphans. In fact, the concierge and his friend have travelled there many times to make donations and help feed the children. He gave me the name of the place and said he will speak to his boss about arranging for me to go there. I do not think, though, that I should go out empty-handed and am wondering what I should bring. I will ask them when I go back in what an appropriate donation would be. As I visit each home, I will carefully collect information on how people can make donations to these organizations directly, so the funds donated will not be wasted on things like red tape and advertising.

These people are being so incredibly helpful to my search, and I look forward to any adventures I might have out in the provinces. I came out to the patio, as usual, for my morning coffee and was just treated to the most pleasant surprise. One of the young waiters here brought me out a plate of fresh fruit without my asking, explaining that he had noticed that when I am writing sometimes I forget to eat and he wanted to remind me to take care of myself or I would become ill. I have only been here for a few days, but they have apparently come to know me very well. I do, indeed, forget to eat when I am working; it's true, and if I am not prompted I can go for the entire day without remembering. My little guardian angels—that is what the staff here are to me. I am so glad I ended up in this hotel. I would have missed the chance to meet all these beautiful people.

People are very surprised when they hear I am financing this book and this trip myself. They seem to think that it is a long shot to go halfway around the world on a whim in search of a story; yet, as Hippie pointed out last night, if you believe in something strongly enough and your purpose is pure you will be rewarded in the end.

I've really been doing nothing but writing for several days, and it is time I got out of this hotel, but at the same time I realize that had I not stayed here and gained their trust they would not be so willing to help. The boys at the front desk are digging up a number for me, so I can contact the orphanage I intend to visit today. I do not wish to offend anyone there by just showing up unexpectedly, and, again, I would like to know if there is anything I can bring. The trip out will be expensive, but, as the hotel is providing me with a driver, I will at least be safe.

I sincerely hope that Baba is smiling down on me and approves of how I've decided to spend her money. I think she would…

I got a lecture of sorts from Deacon, and it reminded me that a large part of this particular learning experience is learning to help people, not in the way I think they need to be helped, but, rather, in the way they would like to be helped. If I can provide information on organizations that exist here and dispense with all the red tape that surrounds the funding of these organizations, then, maybe more of the money will reach the people those organizations are intended to help.

It is a novel idea, don't you think? I'd be giving those more fortunate the chance to be in direct contact with the people whose lives they would touch if given the chance. Crazy thought, I know; again, I say we will see what happens, and after I have gone out there, I will come back and explain more of my idea. It is not a path I saw myself going down—yet it is a path that I can be nothing but grateful for being led to.

Must fly luv, much to do…

February 24th
Patio of the Heritage Hotel Manila
4:00 PM

Okay, so my day so far has been one of writing and waiting…

I managed to obtain more contacts form the hotel with regards to local orphanages, but other than the one meeting already arranged, I have not had any more positive feedback. This has turned out to be fortuitous, as I have managed to complete yet another chapter. I also met some of the crew that my new hippie friend is working with. They were very friendly, and they had a fair amount to say.

They asked me what the hell a little white Canadian girl was doing in the Philippines. I told them the book was based in the Philippines, so I was here to see for myself the people and the culture. They asked whether I had been to various places and whether I had partaken in certain local delicacies. I told them that I had not as yet had the opportunity, and one of them asked, 'How the hell can you write a book about a people and their culture if you don't expose yourself to it?' I was tempted to explain that the book was based in the Philippines, not about the Philippines, but I chose to keep my mouth shut. I did, however, explain that, given the fact that I am a single white female travelling alone, it was not wise for me to venture out too far from the hotel on my own. I did not bother to tell them that the man who had offered to be a guide of sorts had quite literally abandoned me to my own devices—a fact I am now coming to view as a blessing. I did tell them that as my evenings were free, and as they have actually been living here and working here for years, I was open to the idea of evening tours around the city. If there was a part of the culture they wished me to see, then I was more than willing to let them show it to me.

I am not sure they took me seriously, but they will be back for dinner, and we will see then if they have taken to the idea. They are burly, rough men, the kind I have always chosen to surround myself with; I have no fear of them. I have every faith in the fact that I would be quite protected and sheltered by their presence.

I also was bold enough to tell them quite seriously that when I needed things they were usually provided to me when the time was most beneficial. Therefore, I am completely convinced that when it is time for me to go out to the provinces and see some of the culture there, a way will be provided for me to do it safely. The crew are all atheists, and they didn't believe a word of it. They scoffed and said that the idea of me simply sitting and waiting for my next guide to show up, or for the path to that guide to be made clear, was a ridiculous way to get things accomplished. I am thinking if they hang out with me long enough their attitude just might change a bit.

They did ask me if I had been to Smoky Mountain, and when I said I had not, the biggest, nastiest of them (we will call him Bear, as his nature is one of a grizzly whose cub has been threatened, yet he can be quite gentle as well, so, grizzly or teddy—either one fits) decided to give me an education. According to him, Smoky Mountain was originally a dump that over the years built up to a massive mountain of garbage overlooking the bay. After years of this buildup, someone (the government, apparently) decided they should try to put the land to better use. So they levelled it off and proceeded to cover it with topsoil and build housing on it for the less fortunate. The problem is that every time it rains the toxins from under the soil rise up like a mist and poison whoever happens to be in the area. So the people behind the project had to abandon it, and they proceeded to knock down all the buildings, levelling everything and leaving behind only rubble. Of course, they never replaced the housing, so the people who had moved in there are again without a place to live. The whole thing ended up being a huge waste of time and effort, not to mention money, and it was all because there was this idea that housing should be provided for the people but they really didn't want to have to spend the extra money on better land. They told me that, to this day, when it rains the mist continues to rise from the ground and the massive pile of earth looks like it is smoking. That's how it got the name Smoky Mountain.

I can neither confirm nor deny this story, as it was handed down to me in the form of legend, yet behind every legend there is a lesson—but we'll get back to that.

The tale's end led to the next tales beginning, as often happens in these cases. The next guy, one of two twins living and working with the crew (we'll call him Blue Eyes, as his eyes are a striking match to the colour of a clear blue sky) began a story about a company that came here with the intention of striking it rich.

This company moved into one of the local communities and proceeded to hand out thousands of free phones. People were very excited and started using the phones to call all around the world. Keep in mind that many of the locals have family members who work overseas, where the money is better, so they can send money back to support their families. The people called everywhere: Canada, Europe, other parts of Asia (you get the idea).

Time passed, and the bills came in, and the people said, "What is this?" When the company people explained that the phones were free but the usage was not, the people said, "No, no, you said free!" Now, herein lies the problem: thinking these people simple and uneducated the company never bothered to get them to sign any kind of contract. The company just assumed that they could either pressure or outsmart the people into paying, but the people said, "No way! We no sign, we no pay—we know our right." Of course, legally, the company can't do anything—no contract, no money.

They were never able to convince the people and eventually were forced to give up the fight. As Blue Eyes said, "They had to shut down the entire operation and leave the country with their tail between their legs. Bloody fools lost millions!"

This story also is hearsay, but the lesson remains the same.

So the other twin (we'll call him Pale Eyes, as his eyes are the white-blue colour of the sky on a summer's day during a light misty rain) decides it's time to add his piece. He starts in about how everybody blames the government, but in reality there's a much deeper reason for some of the problems. He says the people are used to having things for free. For example, when they want power they simply tap into existing power lines and use what's already there.

He told another story about a project he worked where they were asked to go in and provide power for some new housing that was being built. When it came to the attention of the people who were supposed to be relocated to the new development that they would have to pay for power, they argued and said they wouldn't. The people refused to move, and the project was abandoned like the others. This time, however, the building was not knocked down; they were left with unfinished shells. Once the crews moved out, the people moved in. They tapped into existing power and to this day remain there living in incomplete buildings that amount to not much more than hovels. They do, however, have roofs over their heads, running water, plumbing, and, of course, hydro—they live quite contentedly there for free.

As Pale Eyes said, "Bloody fools keep trying to come in and make things better, to change things, but these people are happy the way they are, because, in the end, they are free."

I don't think I have to tell you this story is, again, word of mouth and therefore cannot be taken as fact. The lesson, however, in all of it is pretty clear. When you are an outsider looking in, it can be very costly indeed to presume you know what another person needs or wants.

They left shortly after that, and it was only after I had worked on chapter six that it occurred to me the lesson was an echo of what my friend Deacon had cautioned me about on the phone two nights ago. That was the very same night, in fact, that I met Hippie, and, by the long way around, met these interesting fellows.

I hope I get the chance to know these fellows; at the very least I would like to enquire whether they think I will learn as much by wandering around sightseeing and partaking of local cuisines as I will wandering around and partaking in conversation with locals. I doubt they will argue the point when I present it in such a reasonable and logical manner.

This, by the way, brings us around to my reasonable and logical Deacon—who made a point to connect via phone the other night regarding the possibility of us doing some exploring around the globe. While we were talking, he made sure to point out that I had to be very careful in my intentions to help people who I might not yet understand. He said he hated to play the devil's advocate, but he wondered whether it had occurred to me that these people might be quite content living as they were. I told him not to worry, that it was very much on my mind that I shouldn't meddle in other people's ways. I told him that was, in fact, what this whole damn book seemed to be turning out to be about. I do always advocate the open-minded approach to different belief systems, and it turns out I also see the need for that approach when dealing with people we see as less fortunate. I mean, really, if they want to be Westernized, fine, who am I to judge—but, at the same time, we as Westerners need to be willing to only share with them what they require, not what we think they should have.

I have mentioned before that I was immediately struck by the contented nature of these people, and I have come to the conclusion that neither I nor anybody else has the right to assume they need or want my help. It has occurred to me also that it is another one of those really big life lessons many of us have yet to learn.

Quite honestly, empathy and understanding tie into these both politically and spiritually. It is not up to us to decide when and how to help others; rather, we should be there for them if and when they decide they want or need to change or help themselves. As I said in one of my previous letters,

I very much felt this whole affair drawing to a close, and the time for that is, in fact, very near. Yet, given that fact, I am grateful to the people of this country for allowing me in long enough for me to see and understand where they are coming from.

I am still going to continue my attempts to tour the orphanages and research the different charities that exist here, if only so that I can include them in my book. This will give the people who read my work a chance to donate freely and directly to the already abundant and active charities here in Manila and around the Philippines.

I came here with the intention of hunting down a story I had the enormous ego to presume I knew the truth of, and I leave here with a very humbled outlook on religion, spirituality, culture, and life.

From the beginning, when we were driven by the desire to help initiate change, to the journey itself that taught me the true meaning of that change and its possible repercussions, to the yet unfinished conclusion that indicates it is very much up to the people here to decide if they even want change, it has been an interesting and eye-opening journey.

I will continue to write to you and keep you updated on any new developments, but I will be surprised if anything profound pops up. I think I should now spend my days working on my chapters and my evenings relaxing and enjoying these people and their hospitality. I am sure there are more lessons to be learned, either here or on my next adventure, but for now I am quite content with where this particular road has taken me. I will for the moment bid you a good night and leave you with this thought: I have been blessed and am very grateful for every new opportunity to learn about life.

Night night. xoxo

February 25th
Patio of the Heritage Hotel Manila
8:00 AM

Well, darling, there were no profound philosophical quandaries to ponder in my adventures last night. As I predicted, the whole evening passed rather peacefully over wine and beer. The conversation, however, was interesting and the people, as always, intriguing.

I met a fish last night by the name of PH. He is a power horn who resides here on the patio at the heritage hotel, and he is much loved and revered by his caretakers. He is three years old, and I am very much hoping he will live out the fifteen or twenty years that are expected of him, as I would very much like to come back and visit.

He is very maganda (beautiful), with clever markings on his body that resemble Chinese characters—appropriate, since at the time of our introduction I was sitting out here on the deck having a beer and learning Chinese from my pilot friend. The markings mean "luck" or "good fortune" in Chinese—also appropriate, as this whole trip has turned out to be rather fortuitous.

The man who cares for and feeds my sweet little finned friend took the time to explain a little about the breed. They are extremely violent fish, much like the Japanese fighting fish, and cannot be put in the same tank with other fish, not even ones of the same breed. They are so confrontational, in fact, that in order to allow them to mate one must install a divider in the tank. The divider must allow the two fish to come close and smell each other but be strong enough to keep them apart. The female is then put into the other side of the tank and their courtship, if you will, ensues. The whole process takes about six months. He explained that for the first while they mainly ignore each other, then after awhile they begin to spend more time close to the divider. Eventually they make it a daily ritual to bump noses, and, once they get to the point when they are almost always swimming face to face, the divider can be safely lifted. Once they have mated, the female is removed before they start fighting (apparently pregnant fish get cranky too). It is a long, arduous progress from the viewpoint of the breeder, but I could see how humorous he thought the whole adventure actually was. In fact, my fish-keeping friend seemed to think the whole thing funny as hell. He kept bumping his hands together to mimic the bumping of noses and laughing his ass off.

Every time he grinned he showed off this odd little gap in the front of his teeth that on any other man might look extremely unattractive. Yet this quirky little fellow's smile was warm and honest and rather endearing; I simply couldn't help but love the guy.

Just to clarify what he was telling me, I asked, "So, essentially, what you're saying is they meet, they take about six months to acknowledge and get to know each other, then, after deciding they like each other, they have sex and he kicks her out?"

Again he laughed his ass off, and I pointed out while he was giggling away that if our youth today would take a cue from these fish and spend more time getting to know each other before hitting the sheets maybe there would be a lot less unplanned babies.

He laughed at that as well, but then he stopped long enough to smile down at me and say, "You see, there is a lesson everywhere, if you can only recognize it."

Strange little man, wouldn't you agree?

The rest of the night passed rather quietly; my Chinese pilot friend eventually went to bed, and I remained, making a valiant effort at reading and relaxing. One of the floor managers approached me, and we ended up having a long conversation about my writing, his life, and all the things we have both learned along the way.

He apologized for disturbing me and explained it was not usually his way to talk so openly with strangers. He told me that he felt very comfortable with me, though, and was surprised that he was so willing to share what was in his heart and his head. Partway through the conversation he asked me who I would be publishing the book under. I explained to him that I choose to keep my identity as an author separate from my identity as an everyday ordinary person. He was at first a little confused by this, but, when I explained about my desire to protect my daughter, he began to understand.

I told him I very much desired for her to grow up to be a grounded and down-to-earth young woman. I had very strong feelings about the negative affect that fame and money can have on the young. I didn't want to raise her to believe that she was better or more important than anyone else because of her mother's success. It was my intention, therefore, to keep as low a profile as possible until she was older and could separate herself from the effects that public intrusion into our lives might have. He laughed and gave me a thumbs-up when I told him that I only worked with people who could keep their mouths shut. I guess he decided he could appreciate my reasons, and he seemed very pleased with my views on the matter.

Our conversation was interrupted at this point by a rather large group of rambunctious young men exiting the casino. They, seeing a single white female sitting seemingly alone on the patio, decided to take up residence at every single table immediately surrounding mine. My new friend, however, decided to take upon himself the role of guard dog. He placed his body between me and the young men and stood there with his back slightly turned toward them, talking to me about the language and the culture while effectively keeping these drunken individuals at bay. They did, on several occasions, make the effort to get my attention, but he would very pointedly stiffen his stance and give a mild-mannered warning glance to whoever happened to be approaching the table. It was interesting to watch, as he was indeed himself a stranger to me, yet his seemingly coincidental arrival at my table ended up protecting and sheltering me from what could have quickly turned into an uncomfortable situation.

Lesson learned: I am really no safer here in the hotel than I am on the streets, and I must resolve to be more careful. He let me go to bed only after he was sure that they were long gone. Although he never openly asked me to wait, he did not stop my lessons on Tagalog until several minutes after their departure, at which point he asked me if I was not tired, as I had been working all day. I took his very diplomatic cue and thanked him for his conversation, agreeing that, yes, I was indeed ready for bed. I made it to my room safely, escorted by another young employee who just happened to be standing by the entrance of the restaurant at the very moment I chose to take my leave. I am very grateful for the angels I continue to encounter here and will in the future endeavor to be more cautious and aware.

Well, sweets, I really don't have much more to share. I only plan today to work on the next chapter and try yet again to get in contact with the various orphanages here, though my purpose for that is not the same as first intended. Maybe, given my change of attitude, it will become easier for me; again, we will see.

Must run; would like to check my email and look up something on the comp. I will probably get back to you later and let you know what's up…

February 25th
Patio of the Heritage Hotel Manila
Noon

A quick note to you, hon; I was finally able to contact another home and set up a meeting for tomorrow morning. I am planning to bring along some rice for the orphanage and am thinking it is a very good thing that last night my Chinese friend and I agreed to go to Mall of Asia tonight after work. I am a very tiny girl, and I will no doubt need the assistance of a stronger man to help me cart one hundred kilos of rice back to the hotel. I hope he's willing…

February 25th
Patio of the Heritage Hotel Manila
8:00 PM

Well, my darling, that was interesting—just as I was putting the pen down earlier, my rough and tough boys from the work crew happened to stop by for a lunch meeting. The twins joined me at my table afterwards and inquired what I was up to today. My hippie friend had not managed to yet make it down, but I am on pretty good terms with all the others, so it was quite comfortable to just sit with them and toss stories back and forth.

I told them my plans to go to the orphanage tomorrow and that I would be heading out later to try to get some rice from the mall to bring as gift. They asked me how much, and, when I answered one hundred kilos, their eyes popped. Pale Eyes said it best: "Bloody hell, luv, how's a tiny thing like you gonna lug one hundred kilos of anything anywhere?"

I told him I didn't know yet, but that I was sure a way would be provided. Of course they scoffed at that as well (they always do, lol), since they simply can't believe that things are given to me as I need them. If they believe that, then they will have to admit there might just be some kind of other energy at work. As they don't embrace the idea of there being anything beyond the reality of what we can see and touch, it would be expecting much too much to have them believe that my desires—or, more appropriately, my needs—are met before I am forced to take action myself.

Just as Blue Eyes was rolling those eyes at my obvious refusal to accept reality, Bear popped over to the table and took a sea; he also inquired what I was up to today. The twins explained that I needed to get some rice for a visit tomorrow, both of them bantering back and forth and joking about the very comical visual of little tiny me trying to drag a hundred kilos of rice through a store and into a cab. Of course, my big, burly, cuddly teddy came up with a solution, which shocked both of the twins into silence. He offered to give me the company truck and their driver to take me over to the mall and pick up the rice. Just as he was saying that I would need a guy to go in with me, and that he knew just who to get, Hippie showed up and asked who he was getting to do what.

Bear told Hippie he would be taking a couple hours off work to go with me to the mall and get me my rice, at which point Hippie smiled and asked if he would be paid.

To which Bear growled, "Of course you're bloody getting paid, you useless lump of sod!" then, laughing, he added, "Make sure you get a bloody receipt, gofer boy, so we can find a way to write the bloody rice off as a charitable expense."

Well, as you can imagine, the twins were… ummm… what's the word?… oh yes, stunned.

Long story short: I got my rice.

The driver dropped my hippie friend and me off at the mall and then went back to work, after we told him we would rather take the time to have dinner and were more than willing to take a cab home.

We wandered around the mall and found a beautiful little Italian restaurant that had a patio overlooking the bay. I bought Hippie a couple beers by way of thanks for the physical effort he would soon be putting in on my behalf. We were watching a really interesting spectacle across the way of a couple blow-up pools that had been inflated and laid out on the ground between the mall lot and the bay. In each pool there were two gigantic plastic balls floating in the water, and in each ball a small child was running around inside the ball, making it roll across the surface of the water. It was too comical, rather like watching a hamster in a wheel, but it did look like a lot of fun. I asked Hippie if he would seriously get paid for coming to the mall, and he explained that Bear would clock in the hours that he spent here as well as the time the driver spent in traffic getting us here. He said it was no skin off Bear's nose, so to speak. The money was there, and as it was the lead hand's decision to send him and lend me the truck and driver; he was responsible for making sure the driver and Hippie were not docked pay because they were doing something other than work directly related to the company. If they had offered themselves it would have been different, but, as it was Bear who was sending them, then it was up to him to make sure their income wasn't affected.

So we spent a couple of hours sitting in the sun, enjoying the slight breeze off the water, sipping beer, and chatting while watching the children play—not a bad way to spend the afternoon, really, and a pretty good deal for hippie: free beer, pleasant atmosphere and good conversation, and all on company time.

Hippie did ask me how the whole thing had come about, and, when I explained to him what had happened, he laughed at the twins' reaction and then asked if I always get what I want. I told him no, I very rarely get what I want, but I very often get what I need. To that, he lifted his glass and offered a toast to that amazing unseen force some of us call God…

February 26th
In a cab on the way from Heritage Hotel to children's home
8:00 AM

Morning, darling,

Just a quick hello; I am on my way to an orphanage here in Manila. I would like to see for myself what is being done to alleviate some of the problems caused by poverty here. I am also looking forward to meeting some of the people involved with these organizations. It would seem the more I ask around the more I discover that it is the working class here who run such organizations, not just the government and churches. I am on my way to meet the couple that runs this one, and, hopefully they can shed some light on who is behind helping the children here. I won't talk long, as I am in the car, but I will tell you I have had a few more enlightening encounters but nothing monumental. Perhaps meeting these people at the orphanage will change that.

I have to tell you, though, for all I had heard about these people before I came, when I look out the window I notice that they do not look defeated. Passively accepting, yes, but overall they seem to be content. I was talking to Blue Eyes yesterday and mentioned my observation.

He agreed that they are content to live as they do, "But then, they really don't bloody know any different, do they?" These were his words, not mine, and I have to wonder—do they want to know different? Perhaps they choose to live this way. It is still a question I do not have an answer for, but am hoping to gain some more insight into it before I have to leave. Wish me luck, luv. xo

February 26th
Patio of the Heritage Hotel Manila
3:30 PM

Well, hon, I scarce know where to begin…

I just had the most incredibly uplifting visit with the people that run the Shepherd of the Hills children's home.

My first impression upon walking in was that it was just that—a home. I entered through a gate into a carport, then into a joint kitchen-living area that contained two lounge chairs and a small kitchen table. The furnishings themselves were sparse, but the room was colorful and bright. There were plants in several corners of the room and bamboo blinds covering the windows. Directly to the right were two sets of stairs, one leading up and one down. Sitting in one of the lounge chairs was a young woman holding an infant; beside her stood a playpen that was being used as a portable crib. Directly to my left was a small office that had glass windows, allowing anyone working there to have a clear view of the family area and entrance.

And that, my friend, is all the visual description I feel I should waste my time giving. But the feeling in that house… Contentment comes first to mind; warmth and love were everywhere I looked. It was a peaceful, happy atmosphere, as children moved around us going about their daily lives. Music—wow, the music saturated the home; every room held a child practicing an instrument or listening to songs; even the comfort room (bathroom), which was decorated to resemble a jungle, had music playing in it. As I said—incredible. I am finding it hard to put into words what I have seen this day. The peaceful beauty that is these children's existence cannot be described, not fairly, not accurately. I do not think it is something I can convey to you in words, it was pure feeling.

Have you ever lain down in the middle of a field of hay on a hot summer's day and just let yourself feel the simple pleasure of breathing?

Have you ever lain on a beach late at night and simply enjoyed the spectacle of millions of stars seemingly twinkling simply for the sole purpose of bringing you peace and joy?

Have you ever danced as a child in the rain, letting yourself move with complete abandon to the rhythm of the rain?

Have you lain quietly in the middle of the bush and allowed the sounds of all the surrounding nature to wash over you and wash away your fears and worries and doubts? If you have done any of these things, then try to remember how it made you feel, and, maybe, just maybe, you will get a glimmer of what I felt sitting in that house.

I do not think it is something I can convey to you. I simply do not know a word strong enough or pure enough, but perhaps just saying that much is enough.

I was greeted warmly and asked to sit in the dining area with the mother of these children. Understand I do not use the term lightly. Yes, she is the coordinator, but her love of these children shone in her eyes; their love of her shone in theirs. This woman, this mother, had a glowing warmth radiating from her, and sitting next to her was very much akin to sitting by a wood stove on a cold winter's day.

We talked about our work, my book, her shelter, and what we hoped to accomplish with both.

Her husband came to join us, and I was very much drawn to this solid, earthy father figure. He had the appearance of strength and self-assurance, but he was also blessed with gentle eyes. When he smiled at me, his wife, or his children, those eyes showed compassion and understanding. His demeanor was as causal as his wife's was welcoming, and I was drawn in by the comfort of these two magnificent souls. They live so simply; they really have very little for themselves, but they do not, I think, want for very much.

I called Revo on the way back, to the hotel and he told me to try to come back here and relax. He said I should digest it all before trying to write it out, but I felt compelled to put on paper my immediate impression. Then and only then would I be able to relax, which I am now off to do, but, before I go, I have to say that yet again I am blessed by the opportunities, and yet again I have to say thank you for this chance to be welcomed into the lives of selfless people such as these.

Their commitment to their cause and the light it brings to those they touch is something I have been very honored to witness and something I will forever cherish. I spent many hours with them, easily falling in love with the entire family and basking in the warmth of their love for each other. I am yet again uplifted by the goodness that seeps out from the core of the people I have met. I went there a stranger but left there a friend, and I am grateful. They lifted my spirit to a higher place, and it was an experience I will never forget.

Goodbye for now, my heart. I will write again soon, but for now I must make arrangements for my trip tomorrow, as they have invited me to tag along with them to Baguio to see for myself the work they do there in another one of their locations. The journey, it appears, goes on. xoxo

February 26th
Patio of the Heritage Hotel Manila
9:00 PM

Well, arrangements have been made, and my bag is packed and ready to go…

A few interesting things to note, and I will start with the effect my presence has had on some members of the work crew. They were out here around dinner time, and I took the time to sit with them and tell them I'd be out of town for a few days. When I explained where I was going, and with who, the twins were again obviously in shock. Blue Eyes just sat staring at me for a few minutes, and I had no idea until he spoke what the significance of my upcoming trip was. I'd never heard of Baguio City and had no idea what to expect…

"You mean to tell me you bloody well wander off to a bloody orphanage on a bloody whim and get invited out to stay with them in Baguio for the weekend…" He placed his hands on the table and leaned forward. "Luv, do you even have any bloody idea what weekend this is?"

"No, mate, I'm thinking our little darling hasn't a clue," laughed Pale Eyes, then added gently, "Luv, you are going to Baguio during the flower festival. You wanted culture—well, you're about to be swimming in it!"

Waving a hand at me, Blue Eyes added, "Bloody woman—off she goes to one of the biggest cultural festivals in one of the most interesting cities in this backwards country, and she hasn't a clue what it means!"

Blue Eyes grunted, "You know you need to make bloody reservations six months in advance to get a place to stay up there this weekend, and you not only have a way to get there but a place to stay—bloody freaky, if you ask me. Honestly, luv, do you always get your way?"

Of course, I again explained, after they were done with their little tirade—and, trust me, it went on for quite some time—that, no, I don't get what I want, only what I need.

Before they left, Pale Eyes confided in me that I had shown him some things his eyes had not been open to before, that his heart had not been willing to feel. He admitted he had been living here for years and was disillusioned with the thing he had seen, but that through watching my adventures he was more willing to explore the real meaning behind the why and how of the lives of these people. He ended by thanking me and admitting that perhaps there was something out there that he had not been able to grasp—but maybe now he would be more aware of his surroundings and the meanings behind what he had considered to be mere freakish coincidence.

Well, it was not my intent, but if I have opened up one heart or mind, then perhaps that heart will, in turn, open others. I am hoping I can keep in touch with these guys even after I am gone, as they have taught me much and provided me with much-needed comfort in times when I was feeling very alone. This brings me to our current phone situation.

It appears that all this time that Rev had not been responding to my messages it was not that he was avoiding me; it was that he simply wasn't getting my messages. I discovered this while sitting in the front drive of the children's home. I had just been blessed to witness the children in the home playing for me in their living room. My immediate thought was: Wow, I wish the world could see this—not see them playing outside the home when they did concerts, but seeing it from inside. It was an inspiring sight.

I also thought that Rev would love these kids, being a musician himself, and I wished that I could get hold of him so he could listen. I did try to call from inside the home, while they were playing, but the call wouldn't go through. After the kids were done, I took my phone outside and offered up a little prayer, asking for the phone to work for me just this once. I then dialed his number, as I had been doing for the last few days, in a futile attempt to reach him. This time, his voice washed over me from the other end—full of concern as to where I had been—with a breathless comment that he had been worried sick.

I told him not to worry about it—what I was calling about was much more important, and I explained where I was and what I was doing. I asked him to come meet the kids upon my return to Manila, and he agreed to come with me back to the home and see their talent for himself. I didn't talk long; I didn't want to take away from my time with them, but I did, as you know, call him back on my way back to the hotel.

Once back at the hotel, as you know, I made my arrangements to have my room locked until I got back, and then I spent some down time with the boys. This brings to mind another interesting thing I had previously forgotten to mention. Hippie's name is Scott—the relevance of this is not obvious now, but it will be later. We were sitting around one night talking about our tattoos, and one of the twins told a story of when he was working in Africa and had decided on a whim to go out and get a tattoo. He remembers only one thing about the whole experience: he had told the guy that was doing it to put whatever he wanted on his arm. This was years ago, and the artist in question was a tribal fellow who used the old method of body art. The process is long and painful, but the twin in question remembers none of it. He does not, in fact, even remember how he got home or the name of the fellow that did the art. When I questioned him on why he had gotten it done in the first place, he couldn't tell me the answer to that either. The whole adventure was hazy for him, but he does know one thing—he came out of his daze the next day with a simple tribal marking on his shoulder. It was a circle with a dot—the meaning of it tugs at me, and I know I should be grasping it, but for the moment it doesn't seem to be overly important, so I have neglected to research it. The boys also said that the meaning of the symbol seemed to be tucked in the back of their minds, but, try as they might, they simply couldn't seem to pull it forth at that moment. I will take that to mean that it is not yet time to know the meaning and have decided to leave it alone. Perhaps by the end of this story it will be made clear, or perhaps when I arrive home you will have the answer for me; you often do, it seems.

Well, luv, that's about it for now. I will talk to you as soon as I am able…

February 27th
Upper deck of SOTH, in Baguio

There's magic in this place, this city in the sky…

If you've seen the children's show Magic School Bus, then you will be easily able to visualize my journey to this mountainous home. We travelled in a van full of laughing, singing children, five hours through the provinces, surrounded by the beauty of nature and the poverty that comes with the desire not to destroy it.

I know I promised to get back to you sooner, my dear, but I have been rather preoccupied with the goings-on of these people and their dreams of a better world for their children. And when I say their children, I mean they have an undeniable love and seemingly unquenchable desire to protect all the children of this poverty-stricken nation.

I cannot say even now that I support any one religion, but I can openly admit that if this is what Christianity leads these people to then there is a definite benefit to being a member of the Christian community.

The people I have met are the real people behind an extremely strong, positive movement in this country to alleviate some of the poverty caused by oppression. They are not in power; they do not want power, and yet, they have more power to help make change than I would have previously believed.

Their hunger to help others is far beyond what we define as charity. They live each moment wrapped secure in their faith and are willing to give their lives for that faith. They eat, sleep, work, and play with one goal in mind. Their entire existence revolves around that goal, and they continue to sacrifice all they have in order to achieve that goal. It is empowering to witness how a few tiny steps begun with strength of conviction can turn into such a long and wondrous adventure.

I have witnessed those who have nothing giving of themselves, because it is all they have to offer. I have witnessed those who have only one piece of bread breaking that bread and dividing it, willingly going hungry so others can eat. I have witnessed the man who owns only the shirt on his back going bare-chested so a child would be clothed, and I have witnessed the birth of a new day, with renewed hope for a better, safer world.

One of the children just came out to sit with me, and when she saw what I was doing, she simply stated, "You need to write…"

She is only nine and her use of the English language not extensive, yet she is more able to perceive the reasons behind what I do than I myself am able to comprehend.

It is a need—one that cannot be put aside and one that will not be denied. I write to appease that need, to quench that desire, and I hope that in doing so I can share what I have seen and learned here. As I have said many times before: if you could see what I have seen, you, too, would believe.

There is magic in this place. Magic in the hearts of these people. Magic in the lives that they live. Magic in the truth of what those lives, lived as they are, mean for the future of their children, their people, and, I believe, the world.

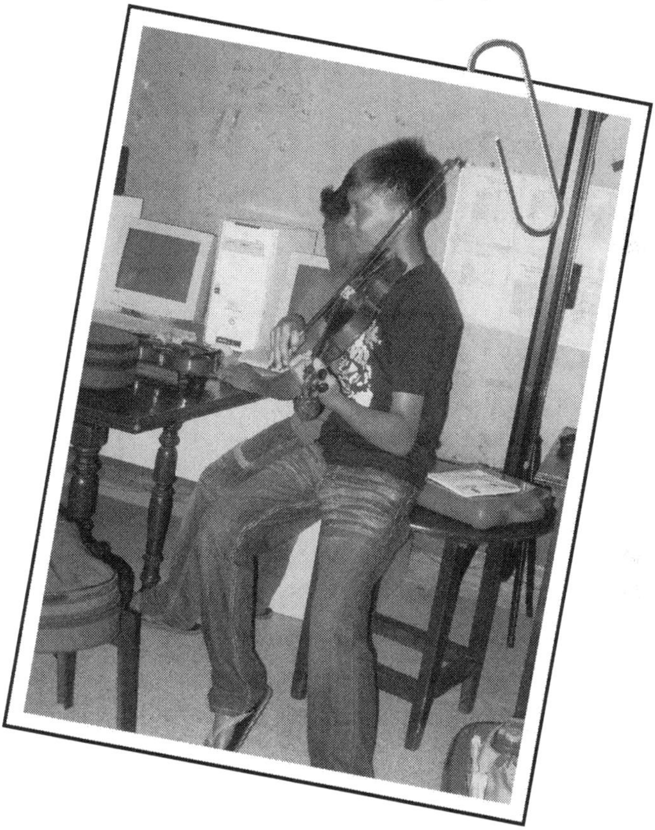

March 4th
Patio of the Heritage Hotel Manila, 9:00 AM

And to think, my dear, I thought I was done. Honestly, it was my belief that in my last few days here I would not be troubling you with these letters. I wanted to take time away from this awhile and immerse myself in the endearing glow of the people I have met here, people I have grown to love.

I have to be honest: the prospect of leaving now is tearing my heart out, but from somewhere across the ocean a little girl calls. I told Rev yesterday that I would have to find some wilderness as soon as I got back. The big guy and I need to have a long chat about the price he has asked me to pay. I do not appreciate the freedom of choice he has granted me, and I very much wish to ask him why. It is difficult to explain the feelings I'm having, the conflict within. I only know that three years ago a young man wrote a song calling me home, and two days ago I realized I was.

I will come back; that has been decided by a greater mind than mine, but for how long remains to be seen. As much as I wish this one thing above all others to be granted me, I do not feel my work is yet done. I hate that Rev is right in his belief that he has to let me go. I fought the reality of it as hard as I could and denied the need with every ounce of my being. We just had two beautiful days together, and I should be grateful. I feel as if I am being selfish to ask for this—selfish to ask to be finished with this work so I can settle down and find a life for myself. The minutes tick by slowly, pulling me toward another place and another life.

You see, I can't even get it out; I can't seem to write the words I need so much to say. My soul is screaming, and as the time to leave draws closer, the agony of this is threatening to destroy what I have built here. I do not have his faith, nor do I have his strength. I never did have.

It has been a long time of shaping and molding, these years of preparation by a master craftsman. He has forged through fire and pain a weapon to use, but the blade, I fear, is flawed. I mourn the flaw and the weakness it represents. I fear the losses I have yet to endure and the sacrifices yet to be made. A life of wandering seems to be my fate. I will live out my destiny and obey the will of that higher power, but, as I said, the price will be high.

Each step taken toward a new adventure is a step away from those I love and cherish. It is a painful realization, this coming to terms with what must be. I do not enjoy the inner turmoil and am having trouble finding faith in my purpose. I will be leaving very soon, and when I go, I will leave my heart here in the Philippines, in the hands of a man whose only way to protect the heart he holds is by sending me away.

March 4th
In a cab
10:30 AM

I am on my way to meet a sister of the Catholic Church who found me while I was wandering around Baguio. She came straight to me, like a moth to a flame, and told me that when I returned to Manila I was to come see her before leaving for Canada. Of course, I never told her I was staying in Manila or that I was from Canada, but, hey, these things I am now used to. I have, at Revo's request, sacrificed my last day here with him in order to explore her world and her faith. He seems to believe there is something there that I must learn, so I will go, knowing I will not see him again for many months.

My soul still weeps at the loss of him, but, as I clung to him in our final moments of goodbye, I managed to find a way to smile. I joked with him, while we stood on the steps of the hotel, that four months was not that long. Then I watched him drive away, anguished by the price we have been asked to pay.

I have sent him a text (that I do not know if he will receive) in the hopes that somehow, someway he will find the strength to let me in. He still believes that if I am to be by his side I will suffer for it. We have spent our last two days here, in fact, arguing over it. He refuses to accept my willingness to walk into the cage that he believes his love for me would create. Yet I know that if I walked in freely, he would eventually close the door. He fears, however, his inability to reopen the door at will, knowing that eventually my work will take me away. So, I write to him one last time, trying to alleviate his fears.

Okay, so I believe if you are meant to get this, you will. If and when you decide that you are willing or want me to be yours, know that in my heart I already am. My loyalty to you will hold strong while I am gone, and if you find yourself being able to accept what I offer, all you need do is call me home.

As I said, I do not know yet if he will get it; his phone and mine have several times failed to work, and, if he does get it, I do not know how he will respond. He is stubborn in his resolve to set me free, but—as I have also said more times than I count—we will see.

March 4th
Sitting on the step outside St. Paul's University, Manila
12:15 PM

I have just finished meeting with the most wonderful sister who showed me a side of the Catholic Church I very much needed to see. It is, I think, too long a story to tell to you here, but I am sure Sister Flor at St. Paul's will more than likely have her own chapter or perhaps even someday her own book. The real reason I am writing to you now is to tell you about the text message that I received during my stay here at the university.

This is what Rev wrote.

I love u just 4 that. I will.

It is the first time he has used those words (they have been implied and discussed often but never verbalized), and, though I long to hear them from his lips, it seems fitting to me that they first come to me in written form.

With that simple message I can now go back to Canada and finish what I started here, knowing that someday, when the time is right, and if the gods allow, my Rev, my conqueror, will call me home…

March 4th
Patio of the Heritage Hotel Manila
1:45 PM

Well, my dear, what a strange, crazy trip it's been.

I'm writing to you while sitting outside in my favorite spot surrounded by familiar faces. It is an extremely comfortable feeling being here. Over at the next table sits one of the twins talking to his boss about their continuing struggles to get their equipment out to the job site.

You see, I was just interrupted by Blue Eyes, who stopped to tell me he will be right down for a drink. Scott dropped by quickly to tell me he'd see me tonight and we'll head over to the MOA for one last wander around. Angel has also stopped by to say hi, and it is nice to see that she both still has her job here and has apparently found happiness in it.

I honestly should not spend too much time out here; I still have to make arrangements for tomorrow, but I thought I'd take advantage of the weather to write what should be my last letter. I have no idea where to start explaining to you my last few days here. They will be in the book, of course, which you are helping to edit, so the stories themselves you can read at another time. Instead, I will try to concentrate my efforts on giving you my last thoughts and feelings about all that I have seen and done, while I try to prepare myself to leave.

Of all the things that I have been through in my short, but full, life, this has been most definitely the hardest to endure. From the moment I realized that this man I had met was to be part of my future—and all through our quest to get here, our search for purpose, right up until this very day that I sit here writing to you—this entire trip (and it has been trippy as hell) has been a crazy emotional roller coaster.

The continuing up-and-down ride, through the eyes and lives of these people as well as our own personal internal struggle between duty and desire, has been exhausting. Yet, even as tired as I am, I do not feel drained by my efforts here; rather, I am peacefully content in my exhaustion. I feel secure in the knowledge that the energy I need will be provided to me as long as I expend that energy continuing the work I have begun here.

My fears of tomorrow seem, for the moment at least, to have disappeared.

We have put into motion by our presence here a few projects that will hopefully provide these people with independent means to continue their work. We have also managed to accidentally bring together a couple of organizations that now have the opportunity to collaborate their efforts and their resources. The whole process has been quite by accident, and it is through coincidence alone that these people have found each other.

You and I, however, know that coincidence does not exist, and it will be interesting to see where this new path will lead and if and when they will choose to follow it.

As for the effects this will have on my life in Canada, I sincerely hope that I can find a way to soften the blow to those who will be affected. I have no doubt now that what we were sent here to do was important, and it is my heart's desire to allowed to come back and continue to explore the possibilities this country presents for me. I will not, of course, willingly leave behind my child. If, however, when I get back, the factors necessary for my return fall into place, I will know that my path has again been chosen. Several individual events will have to occur, but, rather than forcing the issue, I find myself more than willing to sit back and wait.

I will watch for signs, listen to my guides, and follow where they lead. I have given my life to something bigger, and, though I do not expect everybody to understand, I know that those who do are also those who are meant to share that life.

Gone are my days of trying to live up to the expectations of others. I have for far too long denied the reality of who I am in the attempt to fit in with what society deems the norm. I am mildly entertained at the thought of the shock that others will feel at the changes this trip has wrought in me. For some, I do not think it will be easy to accept. But it was in the hopes of floating on those winds of change that we came, and it is on those winds of change that I must continue to soar.

I am again the wandering gypsy, content to explore this world and its people, content to live and learn from those who would willingly let me into their lives…

I thank our Creator for sending me an angel to wake me from my slumber and push me toward the edge.

I thank our Creator for raising me up and preparing me for flight, through loss and pain, thereby strengthening the wings I will need to fly.

I thank our Creator for giving me the courage and the will to stretch my wings.

I thank our Creator for providing me with friends and family and the safety net that they represent.

I thank our Creator for sending me angels to walk by my side as I took those first uncertain steps toward the edge and for the angels who have been sent to fly by my side to show me the way.

Lastly, I have to most humbly thank our Creator for blowing toward me those winds of change, which, I now have no doubt, will eventually allow me to fly home.

{ The Dream }

To Beaner:

Start: February 20th; 5:50 PM

Dark imagery appears that has, as far as I can tell, no place in this tale—but I will write it to you, and, when I see you next, you can help me make sense of it.

He's screaming at me that I am his: his bride, his possession, and he will no longer share me. He came to me in my sleep and took what he thinks is his. At first it was beautiful and powerful and passionate, but when I realized that he was not who I expected, I was scared. I tried to run; it angered him, and, even after I woke, I could feel him calling me. He tells me he is coming for me, that I am his, but I do not want to give up my freedom. I do not feel, though, that I have a choice. I was his, I am his—and he will take back what belongs to him. I am wide awake, and I can still feel it. He knows where I am, and he is coming, and I cannot stop him.

But I do not know him, not in this life, and I am not sure I am ready to meet him. He will come, and even as I fear it, it excites me. Will I know him when he comes for me? I do not know…

It is hard to let go of this fear I have; I don't even know why I am afraid, but it is hard to breathe. I want to call you and talk to you, but you are far away and you cannot help me, not in this.

I am shaken and do not know what else to do but wait and see what comes of this. I want to believe that it was just a dream, but my instinct tells me it's not. Even now I feel him coming closer, and I can sense his eyes on me, his hold on me, and I have nowhere to run. He takes, in his belief that it is his right to take, that which is mine by choice to give.

What's worse is that I have been here before, and I know this feeling well, even if I can neither put a face or a name to this entity. It has from time immemorial dominated me, and it chooses yet again to impose on me its will. I do not want to face this, not now; I have too much left to do.

I am sitting out on the patio trying to calm down. Neither you nor Sophia will wake for hours yet, and by then I am afraid I will already know the answers. I wrote a text to Rev but cannot bring myself to send it.

Why? Who?

What have I to fear from him?

Why am I feeling any fear at all?

What? Who is coming? and again I ask, Will I know it when it comes?

They said I would be safe here; I thought I would be safe.

Why now am I in danger? I DO NOT understand…

So I wait. I ordered food but do not know if I can eat. I have to eat, need to eat, but I am not hungry.

He told me to come down here and wait, so here I am; still I am afraid and want to run. I want to stay here; I don't want to leave, not yet…

I talked to him, asking him to come and tell me what he wants. He answers that I know what he wants, and I scream NO! "I only know what you tell me," he says, "Don't argue …"

I feel cold inside. Again I ask, "Why now?"

I am suddenly very tired, very drained and worn; I feel like we have had this argument many times before. I argue—what right does he have to tell me to whom I belong?—and he shouts back that he is the right to tell me to whom I belong.

I am trying to eat again; it tastes like ash, and between bites I am forced to write. I don't know why, just that I am being driven to document this.

I argue again that he has no right and he shouts at me again that I am HIS bride and it is his right.

What does he want?

How long do I have to wait?

I want to send that text, but something is stopping me, and again I do not understand. Every time I even look at my phone it gets harder to breathe. I can't reach over and pick it up.

Why?

Who?

I want to believe it is some kind of crazy dream and that I will wake up soon and see it as a dream—but I do not think it is a dream. Still I write…

Why?

Who?

I have to find a way to come down from this; I will not let it beat me. If he wants me, he will have to show himself to me this time and walk beside me. I will not go with him. He whispers, "You will come..."

He is purposely making me wait.

Why?

Who?

I am still trying to eat, to act as if everything is normal, as if there is nothing strange going on. You know, I half expected him to be waiting here for me. I feel as if I'm being watched. Why won't he show himself? If this is real, and I am his, why is he playing this game? What purpose is there to it? I can only sit for so long and wait, when I don't know what I am waiting for. Again I try to send the text; I can't; my hand cramps whenever I move it toward the phone.

I am calmer now; I tell him: fine if it is what he wants, I will bow to his will, but he will have to come to me—here, now, in this reality, on this plane, in human form—or I will not go. He has waited too long this time; I am stronger now; we will stand together, side by side, or not at all.

I can feel him backing off. He did not expect this, did he? No, he thought to find me weak. I am not, and, being stronger, I have nothing to fear. Oh, he's angry, so very angry. He rants and raves without words. If he wants me it will be on my terms this time. I tell him to come; I will not reject him. He tells me to go to my room; like a child I am to obey. "No," I say, "I will go when I am ready. You can come to me here; you have that power, but you fear the weakened human form."

Again I ask, Why? Who?

I am no threat to you; what have you to fear from this place?

I will go soon, and we will see...

I am not sure if I can stand up to him for long, but we will see. I think perhaps I am too strong this time, and I taunt him, telling him he has waited too long.

(There is a break in the writing, a point where silence and meditation was required so I could recover and regain strength...)

I am still in shock over all that I have just written, and I am gathering my strength before I go back upstairs. If I am right, and he comes to me there, it will be an epic battle of wills, but I am even now calling out to you, calling out to Sophia, Deacon, Lina, Alya, and others like you who have always come to my aid in times of weakness. You are my strength, my power, my parts that make me whole, and, with that final piece put into place, I have nothing to fear.

Who do you think he is, this entity that calls me his, this being that claims I'm his bride?

Not who is he here—who cares? It will not matter—but who is he in the bigger sense of things? From where does he come, and why does he choose to make himself known now?

If and when I see you next, I will show this to you, and we can figure it out together. If, that is, he does not show himself tonight. If he will not play the game my way, it will not be played. As I said, he is not happy about it. I'm having one last smoke and then going upstairs. I would say wish me luck, but I don't feel I will need it. He holds no power here; that's why he fears this place. I just felt it, and you, it seems, are waking; I felt that too.

You feel closer now, more aware of my plight, my battle. You see, I do not go unprotected or unarmed.

Alright then, let's go do battle, shall we?

End: February 20th; 7:27 PM

My phone beeps; it is a text, no message, only a name: Revo (7:28 PM)

The Battle

March 3rd
Patio of the Heritage Hotel Manila
9:21 AM

To Beaner:

I don't know if either you or I will be able to read this; I very much fear the more I write, the more my hands will shake.

He is lying now asleep in my bed, and he is for the moment peaceful, but the battle that rages within will in time return.

He fights it so very hard this time, refusing to accept the price of who and what we are. As I said, he found me too late, and, even as he tries to send me away, I still maintain the power and the strength to fight.

I was lying in his arms when he asked about the dream. I couldn't deny him, even knowing he was trying to prove his point, trying to scare me off. So I told him all, and I told him I had written it down. I told him I know who and what he is and that still I am not afraid.

He argued, "Don't you see—I can't do this, not to you, not anymore…"

I told him it's my choice to make. I explained I am not weaker than him this time; my place is by his side, and that is where I choose to be. So we remain locked in a battle of wills.

He is standing over me, looking down, and my head is in my hands. I am pleading with him to see reason, but again he is stubborn and willful. He does not want to destroy anymore. He talks about Genghis Kahn and his duty to slay millions, about Mark Antony and his drive to conquer, about so many others who have come before.

I remind him that each of those men, regardless of all the pain they caused, had a woman that stood with them and loved them; I tell him again he denies me my rightful place by sending me away. He tells me he does not want to be that man again, not this time, and I remind him yet again that he has no choice.

He says that when it is time for him to fight, it will not be the man I know who does the fighting, and I answer quietly that I know, and I am okay with it. I have made my choice. I tell him how I lay in bed that night after finally coming to terms with who and what he is. I describe how I talked to him there in my sleep, telling him I was stronger this time and that it would be okay. I tell him that I argued about it for two hours lying there in the dark, and how angry he was at first that I dared to question him. I explained that after time his will had begun to bend, and he became calmer with the knowledge that he could not push me away.

He whispers, "I know, I was there…"

Then I laugh and say, "Yet, here we sit, in a stinking bathroom of a bloody hotel, having the same damned argument that we had only last week, and I tell you nothing has changed. I will not be driven away. I do NOT fear you."

He tells me he cannot put me in a cage, that I am meant to soar, and he would set me free to fly. He says, "Look how much you've done without me by your side; look how far you've come, what you've learned, what you've accomplished. I cannot—will not—take that away."

I answer softly, "But all that I've done, I've done with you in the back of my head. How can you say that you will hold me back, when it was you who lifted me up in the first place?" I look him straight in the eye and silently I plead.

He whispers to me, "But maybe that's where I belong this time, in the back of your head—then maybe I can't be taken away."

So I explain that I can live with the fact that he may eventually be taken from me. I can live with losing him through circumstance. I can live with losing him through the selfishness of others. I can live with losing him when God decides to call him home. I cannot live with losing him through his unwillingness to let me be hurt. I cannot bear losing him by choice.

He argues again that he will not destroy me this time, says I don't understand what I ask.

I tell him I do—I know him, and I can handle him.

He says, "But my other half is a beast, a beast that will devour you if I let it."

I answer that it was he who claimed to see me tame the lion, he who pointed out that I could…

"Not this time. You don't have to do this; you can be free of this, if you will only listen," he sounds so sad, and I have no words to comfort him.

I tell him I am stronger now, that life has molded and shaped me for this. I can handle his power; I can handle his strength. I can handle his hunger and his lust.

He bows his head, "Not my lust," and quietly again whispers to me, softly pleading with me to run while I still can.

I try to tell him yes, even that… I explain that this flesh means nothing, and as long as he holds me close inside I care not where his body goes, but he struggles visibly with the concept, telling me it would not be the same for me. I would not be allowed my freedom. I tell him I would rather live the rest of my life alone than with another man, and he whispers, "No…"

It is an old argument, we both remember; we both know we've had this conversation before, and the reality of it makes us laugh. There we stand, giggling together like schoolgirls for a moment, forgetting that we are in the process of making a monumental decision. If it affected only us, it wouldn't matter; we wouldn't care—but it doesn't, and we both feel the weight of that burden.

This time it is he who looks me in the eyes. "Maybe that is my sacrifice this time; have you considered that?"

It is a question I was expecting, but not one I am willing to answer. I do not like to think of the sacrifices he has made from the beginning, the pain he has endured; it hurts me and angers me. Though I know how necessary it had been, I cannot bring myself to justify it. He fears what he will have to become, and I cannot place blame on him for that. I cannot look him in the eye and tell him this time it will be different. I do not know that it is meant to be.

He wants to know how to control it this time; he wants to know how not to be the slayer. He wants to know how to keep from unleashing his anger on those who deserve it.

I explain that he cannot stop it, that it is what must be, but that if there comes a time when it is necessary to tame the beast, it is then my job to be there to calm the rage inside. To help direct it, to help guide it, it is my place to keep him grounded when he teeters on the brink of destruction, my role to hold him close and keep him from plunging off the edge. He disagrees and he denies me my right to live as I am meant to.

Still he argues and fights against what cannot be changed. He detests the idea of me sacrificing my freedom to fulfill the role, and I fear the consequences if I do not. I tell him not to be afraid for me. I tell him he cannot waste time protecting me. I reassure him that he cannot stop the gypsy from wandering, but that she will always come home if he will only bring himself to allow it.

It is late, or early, and we are tired, but while I am lying there in his arms, he asks me, "Do you think it was God who gave me that dark side? Please tell me it is him, that he wills this… is it for me to be his justice?"

I answer, "Not this time; not like that. It is for you to stand behind and inspire others to act. You do not have to be that kind of leader anymore; you do not have to be the slayer, but you do have to show them the way, and the price again will have to be paid. It is he who gives you your dark side, because he knows you will need it. It is your shield meant to protect you and shelter you from the pain you will cause. It is your weapon, to be used in this fight, a weapon you must learn to wield with strength and purpose. It is your sword and your conviction. You will do what needs to be done, and, when it is over, only he can decide who wins this battle.

He is asleep finally; his eyes are closed, and I can hear his heart as I lie with my head on his chest. I can feel his breathing; he struggles even now in his sleep, murmuring quietly, "Not this time…"

No words are needed now, but I send him a message in his dreams, "Hush, it is okay. Rest now; I am here…"

The Message

I was not sure the dream had a place in this story. I was hoping that this time the darkness might be held at bay. I realize now that the opposite of light has its place here. It is what gives us balance. It is a struggle that has been wrestled with before. It is a battle we have already fought, a war we must continue to strive to win. It would be wrong for me to deny it its place here, so I will include it in these pages as a message to those who read them.

We are here.

We will fight.

In that fight there will be loss of life, loss of self; yet from the blood and ash comes forth hope for another chance for his people to survive.

We are here.

We will fight.

We will suffer willingly, selflessly sacrificing for a chance to make change.

We are here.

We will fight.

If we are lucky, if the Creator wills it, in the end there will be victory for the people.

We are here.

We will fight.

And if we are destined not to win this battle, we will return to fight again.

Like a phoenix born out of the ashes, we will rise to begin a new life, a new battle, and, with that battle, a new hope.

From time immemorial, we have returned.

It is an old tale; one you have heard, one you have read and one your soul knows to be true

When you read these pages, when you hear the call, will you heed it?

We are here.

We still fight.

Do we fight alone?

Will you close your eyes, your minds, and your hearts?

Or will you join us in this quest for knowledge?

Will you walk with us the path?

Will you willingly seek out the answers?

Will you open yourself to the possibility of what this world could be, or will you turn away?

Out of legend, from the beginning of time, the story unfolds to yet again reveal to the world the one thing we have been sent here to discover…

Truth

{Help Them Help Others}

As I was wandering around the Philippines I came across a few organizations that are actively helping the underprivileged youth of their country by providing them with much needed food, shelter and education...

If you are interesting helping in these groups and others like them I applaud your selfless nature. I do however encourage you seek out and research several different organizations thoroughly before choosing the one that best represents you and your personal hopes for the future of our children.

I have included the names and websites of the places I was able to visit there so you may have both a place to start and a direct link to these organizations. It is my hope you will explore them on your own, see for yourself the beauty of the hope they represent for the countless street children of the Philippines and find a way to support their cause in whatever capacity you are able. Much love to you all...

SHEPHERD OF THE HILLS CHILDREN'S FOUNDATION
http://www.shepherdofthehills.org.ph/

PRECIOUS HERITAGE CHILDREN'S HOME
http://phch.eccmanila.org/

ST. PAUL'S UNIVERSITY
http://www.spumanila.edu.ph/

HOSPICIO DE SAN JOSE
http://www.rcam.org/ministry/socialservices/hospicio.htm

These are only a few but there are countless active organizations out there doing remarkable work, through the support of others they can continue to help the children who are not able to help themselves. Go out and explore, perhaps you to will stumble onto something that will inspire you and set your soul free to soar.

From My Heart to Yours

Well, my friends, life is full of trippy little coincidences that sometimes leave one speechless or, as my nephew just proved, sometimes leave one dancing around the living room shouting to the heavens, "No WAY!—that was so COOL!"

Two weeks ago I picked up my nephew Derek, and when he got in the car, one of the first comments out of his mouth was, "Man, I really hate that woman!"

He was referring to the superintendent in his building, and the fact that he used the word hate disturbed me just a little. I asked him why he felt that way. He didn't really have an answer, except to say that she simply wasn't very nice. I explained to him that, given the work he knew I was doing with regard to my novel, he ought to know better than to use the word hate around me. I asked him if there was not at least one good thing that he could find about the lady. I pointed out that if he could convince himself that she was worth knowing, then perhaps his approach to her would be more positive and her response in turn would be equally positive. He, being a sixteen-year-old boy, came up with, "Well, it would be nice if she gave me twenty bucks."

So, given some of the research I have recently done, I latched onto the idea and went about cooking up a little experiment with him. I told him then that from now on when he saw her, he should smile at her and repeat in his head the phrase, "Thank you for the twenty bucks."

Then I explained the theory of unquestionable faith to him and how it's supposed to work. He asked me, "What happens if she only gives me fifteen?"

To this I responded, "Then it still proves that it works, but your faith in it working was not strong enough to actually make it work as you intended."

As we drove, he told me about a dream he had had the night before. I had come to pick him up and, instead of us using my car, he had offered to drive. In the dream, however, when we went to the garage to get his car it was a very new, very hot red Ferrari.

I told him that the dream made sense in that if the theory I was asking him to experiment with was true, then it was possible that he could use that newfound belief to start taking his own life in any direction he chose. Ultimately, it would not then be a far-fetched notion to believe that in the future he could in fact own such a car if he used the skills I taught him to create his own success.

He told me, "You're nuts, you know—but it's a kind of crazy I can appreciate; in fact, I really like your kind of crazy!"

Now for the trippy part: I was just sitting here going over the last chapter, which I had written months ago, and getting ready to write the conclusion to this wonderfully unreal adventure into self, when I received a text message from said nephew.

Guess who just gave me 15 dollars?

Of course, I simply had to call him right away and ask if it were true, and he told me that, most assuredly, it was true. It had just happened, and, oh yes, he certainly did believe now. I told him to look to the heavens and say thank you, and he told me to wait, as he walked to his window and shouted thank you to the sky.

I hung up the phone soon after and headed to my computer. I did, of course, first call Rey, as I am still trying occasionally to prove these things real to him, though he stubbornly clings to his black-and-white world.

This brings me to the point in the story that I know you are waiting for.

In fact, I would stake everything I have on the fact that you are just "dying to know."

How much of this little tale is true, and how much is not?

First, let's explore the previous statement; then we will get back to appeasing your curiosity.

"Dying to know" is an extremely common and overused expression that is uttered from the lips of thousands daily without them ever taking the time to reflect on the phrase. You are, you know, quite literally dying to know…

If you break it down and dissect it, which I must point out does not take much effort at all, really, each day you live is one step closer to death (oh yes, I did go there), and each day you live is one step close to acquiring the absolute truth.

I mean, as we grow and experience this wonderful gift called life, we learn along the way many of the truths that prophets and guides have been trying to teach us for centuries. It is a very basic principle that the teachers of today, yesterday, and tomorrow are well aware of and embrace as part of their daily routines. It is the regular Joe, the you and me of now, who seem to have problems with this concept.

What, you may ask, are these simple truths that we are meant to learn?

Well, my friends, that is the part that will no doubt shock you…

I have no idea.

No, really—I don't!

I am still learning and am not in any position at this stage of my own personal growth to tell you that even one of the truths I have written about in this book are the real truths. That is not my message to you, not my role, not my life's purpose. My message to you is that those truths that you are meant to seek are just that—YOUR TRUTHS!

You, the reader, want to know: Is it real? Do these people exist?

Yet I have to ask: What is the definition of real? Whose reality do you wish to define your truths by? Do you wish to define your life by what others tell you is true, or do you wish to seek out for yourself the truths that work for you?

I will tell you this much: the story (and it is just that, a story) is based on a true story. It is the collaboration of the thoughts and feelings of people too numerous to mention, most of whom you have already met. As to whether or not those people actually live and act and have said the things that this book claims them to have said, well, perhaps someday you will happen to run into one of them and you can ask them for yourself. I doubt very much that it will happen anytime soon, so, for the moment, perhaps it is best that you simply accept the spirit in which the tale is being told and the incredible amount of enthusiasm and creativity on the part of all of those involved that went into the telling of it.

Of course, there are a few key characters that I am sure you are curious about, and I am sure I know also who would be at the top of that list. Yes, Vincent does exist, and he is a very dear and close friend, who, through his loving and nurturing nature, has managed to bring to life in me a talent and skill that I had long ago thought to have died. I must point out that his current drive and ambition are centered on his career in the arts and his love of children. He strongly feels we must work toward a day when our children no longer need to go hungry, and it is through some of his work that others have a chance for a better tomorrow. He is not a revolutionary, not in the sense that this book portrays, but, oh my goodness, how boring would the story be if I told you he has a simple desire to provide food, shelter, and education to the countless street children who exist in his country? All of the information about the government there can be found on the Internet, and the stories of people like Jose Rizal are not in any way a secret. Yet, speaking of them can open eyes, as well as minds, to the change that has been fought for by many self-sacrificing heroes in all nations around the globe for centuries. Slowly we are advancing; with each tiny step forward, we do, as a race, come closer to a day when there will no longer be a need to save anybody, as there will be nothing to save them from. As to the story behind his name, well, I would think it much easier for you to believe that he was named after St. Vincent and that the other name is simply in honour of a random basketball team his father played on in his youth.

Oh now, don't be too disappointed. I mean, you didn't really believe that all that happened did you?

I will be honest with you and say that I did at one point take a trip to the Philippines, and I did encounter there some incredible people who were working tirelessly to help the youth of their country, and it is through that dedication to nurture and protect our young that the story of *Truth* came to life.

You see, there have always been truths and have always been guides and teachers to tell us these truths, but, as humans, we stubbornly insist on going our own way and ignoring what others out there are trying to teach us. Of course, as I said, the quest for the Grail—the quest for truth—is an extremely personal one. It is a journey, and so it is appropriate that this story be presented to you in the form of a trip to an unknown place, which happens to also be, according to the clock, in the future—yes, they are twelve hours ahead of us, so, therefore, going from the Philippines to Canada is going to the future…

I know, twisted, isn't it? We could, of course, get into the whole theory of relativity and explore the concept of time for awhile, but I am pretty sure that is meant for a later date as well, so I won't trouble you with it at the moment. What I will trouble you with is whether or not you, after reading this, are at all interested in embarking on your own personal search for answers. I cannot give them to you, but I hope that I have perhaps opened up your hearts and minds just a little—enough to at least entice you to venture out into the world with a new outlook on the possibilities that life presents. I also hope that through this adventure I have awakened in you a hunger for knowledge, a curiosity to explore the unknown and unseen. Only through fearless exploration of these things do we begin to understand the world in which we live.

A few things I should probably mention before I send you off on your adventures. The book itself was written months ago, but I was waiting patiently for the conclusion to present itself, and in the last few weeks I have been drawn to some enlightening books and drawn into some exceptionally eye-opening conversations. All seemed to point me in the same direction, and it was with these things in mind that I had encouraged my nephew to take his first leap of faith into the unknown and experience for himself what the power of believing can accomplish.

The first thing that I have to talk about is a very brief, but profound, conversation that I had with my daughter only days ago. I took a chance to ask her what she thought happened to bad people when they die. She told me they go back to God. So I asked, of course, why they didn't go to hell. She answered that hell doesn't exist. Yes, I know, it surprised me too, and it is something I fully intend to explore. I allowed myself a moment of recovery, then I asked her the one question I think we should ask all our children: "What is God?"

She said, "God is energy, I think; the closest thing to describe it would be energy, but honestly, I don't know, Mom… God just is…"

Well, then, okay.

Moving on, I was reading a book three days ago by Deepak Chopra, and the symbol that one of the twins had tattooed on his arm just happened to pop up in one of the chapters. Now, as often happens, I had bought the book over a year ago, randomly picking it from the shelf, not knowing at the time why I was buying it. I did not, however, start reading it until a few days ago, long after this entire novel had already been finished. The symbol leaped out at me, and so I will share its meaning with you, as it seems the appropriate thing to do. It is the symbol of all embracing reality. It is an ancient mystical belief signifying that each individual (represented by the dot) was secretly infinite (the circle), the idea being that the Creator permeated each particle of creation equally, and that the same divine spark animated life in all forms.

Why I am to bring this up now is well beyond me, but, as usual, I do not often question what I am being asked to write. I simply write, and it is only later that I am able I go back over my work to dissect and explore what I have written. I can guess, though, that to end this book with such a bold statement on the perception of reality can only mean that it will be the next step in this wondrous ongoing adventure—which also means that the story is not yet done.

But then, you and I, we already knew that, didn't we?

So, I imagine we will meet again, in another place and time, and I will have much more to share. God willing, there will be insights galore to come, and the experiencing of those insights will be as fulfilling and entertaining as this little journey has been.

In the meantime, do us all a favor, and go out exploring for yourself. I will meet you back here someday, and perhaps when we are reunited you will have learned a great many truths that you might be willing to share with me.

Don't forget, while you are out and about wandering the world, to spread a little (preferably a lot) of that love and compassion for others I talk so often about. It honestly does lighten your own burdens when you are able to selflessly give of your heart and soul to others.

And, by the way, thank you for opening your hearts to me and allowing me into your world for a short time. I so look forward to sharing with you again.

Safe journeys my friends; love, light, and laughter to you all.

God bless and Godspeed

{ The Truth about Truth... }

Truth is the multifaceted, multidimensional documentation of my divinely inspired synchromystic journey.

Which means truth is whatever you need it to be, whether you see it as a wonderfully inspired tale derived from the imagination of a truly artistic creator (which it is), or whether you believe that the experiences and encounters shared within its pages did in fact actually happen (which they did)—or anything in between… Whatever feels right to you, and however you come to terms with the story I have presented is exactly right for you in this particular now moment.

I once had a friend who read *Truth* three times… she claimed that with each reading she would integrate the new knowledge that she had derived from the pages into her everyday life, then would revisit it again in 6 months. She explained that each time she explored the book, she did so from a new place of understanding and so, she was able to dive deeper into the truths buried within. She is one of the main reasons I never gave up on *Truth*, as it was her encouragement and enthusiasm for my work that brought me through some of the dark days that followed the initial publication of *Truth*.

You see *Truth* was published twice before; once in 2009, shortly after I returned from the Philippines and again in 2010. Which makes this it's third publication, and since they say the third time's a charm, I guess we should be celebrating the imminent success of *Truth*. Back in 2009, when it was first published through a self-publishing company, I was given, as part of the package, 50 copies of the novel. I gave all 50 copies away to family and friends, many of whom never bothered to open the pages. I carefully signed each copy with a personalized message and handed it to them, all excited to hear their thoughts on my literary baby. Weeks later, I would ask them if they had read it yet and the answer inevitably was 'no, I haven't had time'… Out of the 50 copies that I gave away, only 3 of the people who had been gifted with *Truth* actually read it, and one told EVERYBODY she could about it… That is the young lady I am speaking of here, and as I am sending her a singed copy of the new book, she will know upon reading these pages that she is one of the reasons that you, my treasured reader, are also reading these pages today.

In all fairness, I have no regrets with regards to how this all played out, the delayed success of *Truth* was in fact one of the greatest gifts I have ever received; there have been many gifts, and to put one above the others would be unfair, it is however in my top ten. It has allowed me the time I needed to grow, and to expand my understanding of God, the universe and everything. It has also allowed the world time to grow, to catch up to the truths revealed throughout the story so that the story as it was meant to be told could be told in all its infinitely complex glory.

The truth is, if you gave me a lifetime and asked me to come up with a tale as bizarre as this, I could not do it… my imagination is just not that vast, nor was I able, in the emotional state I was in at the time of this adventure to truly grasp the implications of the journey I undertook. I had faith in *something* but it was untried, untested and indefinable. I had a concept of God in my head and in my heart, but there was a conflict within me, a contradiction in what I had been *taught* to be a truth and what I *knew* to be a truth. I had much to learn and we will in the pages following cover some of that, but in the meantime, I imagine you have some questions…

If it was me, my first question would be; 'did it happen?'.

Yes, it did…

Everything that you have read is an accurate representation of the events as they occurred. Every single email within the pages has been copied and pasted (with Revo's permission of course) from my email in box and used as a part of the ongoing dialogue that built up your relationship with the characters of *Truth*. Every single conversation did in fact take place and I was careful to keep the story as close to fact as possible. It may be at times that I did not write the exact words as they were spoken, but I did my best. It was a mad rush for me to get it all on paper before my memory of it faded. The letters to Beaner were written during my time in the Philippines and the reason I chose to write them to her (Beaner is the nick name for one of my old college roommates) is because I felt comfortable sharing my truths with her. She is a remarkably accepting woman, who in her own way, has encouraged my own personal growth and exploration with mysticism and the divine. I felt that she would not judge, and that, when it came time for me to seek answers, she would assist me to find them. True to her nature, she did just that; when I returned from the Philippines, stacks of paper in hand, she began to help me research the archetypes. She helped me breach the gap between God as He is known in the Christian faith, and GOD as they are known in the ancient teachings of our tribal ancestors. Her work with me confirmed for me that there is indeed only one GOD, albeit manifested in many different expressions, shapes and forms and that this truth has been known by mystics and the indigenous peoples for as long as humanity has pondered the question of our existence. She too will know exactly who she is.

Which brings me to the next question; 'if these people exist, will they step forward to confirm the story?'.

Fascinating question that; by its very nature, the question itself makes the assumption that confirmation is needed. It isn't… needed that is. Not for me anyways, I know where I've been and what I've done. If it is on the off chance needed for you, then perhaps you should take my friends suggestion and revisit the book again in 6 months. By then I am sure you will have discovered that enough people have come forward recently to make the claim that synchromystic life is a part of our current reality. It's hard to escape it really, it's all around you. It is right there, in your face, in the lives of some of the most successful people of our time. Ask many of them and they will tell you that once they chose to make a change in their lives and to embrace life in full faith that all is as it is meant to be, things would just fall into place. They will tell you that the right people always seem to come along at the right time, and that as long as you continue to pursue your passion with the fullness of all that you are, you are destined to succeed. They will tell you that it is not about how hard you work to accomplish a task but rather how hard you play at the things that bring you joy and inspire you to push yourself beyond your perceived limits. Finally they will tell you, that faith in the divine is not a belief; it is a deep seeded knowing that wells from within and shelters and protects us all from the dangers that our fears and doubts represent.

And to answer your question, some of them will… and some of them won't… (step forward that is) Some of them have been approached and told about the re-release of this book and have wholeheartedly agreed that it is not only time, but well deserved and something to be celebrated. Some of them asked me from the beginning to keep their private lives, their beliefs and their identity secret. I fully intend to honor that. So unless they step forward of their own volition, you may never know who some of them are, but that's OK, because they are still out there, touching hearts with the sharing of their own unique understanding of life.

I imagine though that you would like to know a little more about Rev…

Thankfully, we have recently reconnected and he is fully aware of my intent with regards to this book. He is in full support of it, and I am grateful that whatever division that may once have occurred between us has been reconciled. You see, the story did not end with me stepping off a plane in Canada. I would return to the Philippines twice more in my attempt to give back to the children of SOTH (the children's home I discovered in Manila) what they had given to me. I was young, and naïve and believed that it was for me to save the world… "Here she comes to save the day…" (you just sang that didn't you?)

The truth is, it was never about saving the world, the world is doing just fine on its own thank you very much, without my interference. It was about me saving myself, and it would take me years of dramatic ups and downs to finally step into and take ownership of my own life. In the years following my initial trip to Manila, I would, for a time, carry the weight of the world on my shoulders. Believing that I had been sent there to do this thing and if I failed then I would essentially be failing God, I pushed myself well beyond my limits.

When I first came back to Canada I began work on a project that I thought would not only tell the world about SOTH but would also provide them with an ongoing income that would help to financially support their work. I was blessed to be working in a multicultural city where I had access to the Filipino community. I took a job at a local Filipino bar so that I could make contacts and reach out to them for assistance and support for my work. The results of these attempts left much to be desired. Although, I was encouraged and embraced by a few treasured souls who saw me for who I was, I was also constantly inundated with warnings about interfering in a country that was run by a corrupt military enforced government who didn't give a shit about their people. I was told repeatedly by those older and wiser than myself to 'give it up' that things there would 'never change'… I was surrounded by doubters and naysayers… people who, though they valued my contribution and the passion and drive with which I worked, were determined to protect me from myself. As for whether or not the Christians and the Muslims of that country would ever find a way to get along… well… I was thrown out of churches and Bible studies at the suggestion that it even be considered. Oh how times they are a changing… Not so long ago, the people of the Philippines elected an amazing president by the name of Benigno "Noynoy" Aquino, and since his inauguration into office he has made great strides towards bringing peace and prosperity to his people, even going so far as to sign a peace treaty with the Muslims living in the south. I think he understands that people are just people, and just because we call our God by some other name, should not mean that we don't all desire and need the same things in life. Hmmm… perhaps he read my book?

Things with Revo were not much better, in my disillusioned state, and with the help of all these supportive people, we quickly went down a very dark path. There were conspiracies and threats to our safety, evil men of power to fight and a war to be won… I would tell you more about it, but this is not the time and this book is not the place for such a tale. I will tell you this… that as quickly as you can manifest assistance from GOD you can also manifest and create an attack from SATAN… and let me assure you that one is no less real than the other… be careful of your thoughts and your feelings… they can take you to places you have absolutely no desire to be.

That being said, I also had a few self-importance issues to work out. After all, I had been sent there, guided by divine signs every step of the way so I MUST know right from wrong… I was an expert on right—the trouble with being and expert is this… as stated so eloquently by Japanese Zen Master, Shunryu Suzuki, "In the beginner's mind there are many possibilities, but in the expert's mind there are few".

I thought for a while (short as it may have been) that I had all the answers. So I began to resent Revo's repeated attempts to push scripture upon me. I stood blindly in my place of self-righteous judgement and boldly accused him of being self-righteous and judgemental. You see, he seeks his answers in scripture, it is where he is most comfortable, and it is from there that he began to 'teach me' truths as he saw them. As for me, I prefer a more diverse perspective, and did not appreciate his onslaught of Bible verses and sermons. Of course, I doubt very much he was really as bad as all that, but at the time, it seemed to me that he was so far out of alignment with my own understanding of GOD that we would never again see eye to eye. I remember him buying for me a small key chain on my second visit to the Philippines. It was made by local artist out of wood native to the region we were visiting. It had a small footprint carved into it along with the inscription, "The fear of the LORD is the beginning of wisdom"—it is the first line of **Psalm 111:10** and oh how I hated that damn keychain…

It wasn't until a few years later that I began to understand what it meant, and by then it was too late. The truth is, none of this had anything to do with Revo. The only reason his 'preaching' got to me was because I was not yet secure in my own faith. I was so lost in self-deprecating torment with regards to all the things I had done wrong and all the things that I failed to do, that I saw his sharing of understanding as an accusation. In my mind, it was his way of telling me that I was not good enough and that I never could be good enough. As you can imagine, this was, at the time, quite devastating. After all that we had shared and all that we had experienced together how could it be that this man could not love me for who I was? Blow after crushing blow rained down upon me and the downward spiral began…

Interestingly enough, carrying the weight of the world on my shoulders, manifested some very serious health issues that all stemmed from my spine. Go figure… I had no other choice, given my failing health, than to stop EVERYTHING… I lost my job, my home, all my money… I lost my desire to help and damn near lost my sanity. Still, this little whisper inside my brain just simply wouldn't let me die…

Something I had learned from my experience with the children of SOTH kept me alive long enough to find the help I needed to get back on my feet and back into life. I knew that their story, if ever told properly could inspire thousands, if not millions of people to not give up. Yet, I also knew that I was in no shape to tell that story, so I set about the daunting task of healing my heart so that someday I could do the story justice. And here we are…

(don't worry, you will get to read about SOTH soon enough, but I think they deserve their own chapter—don't' you agree?)

What followed in the years to come was a total and complete separation of everybody involved in the adventure that was the writing of *Truth*. I left the restaurant that had provided me with the connection to Revo in the first place, I handed over the project in the Philippines, I handed over the running of my own personal blog and website for the book to others to maintain, and eventually, I left behind the city that I had been living in when I stepped onto my path towards *Truth*. I completely disconnected myself with the children's home, with Revo and anybody else who knew the truth about *Truth*. I wrote two more books, found a new life partner, moved to a new province, and began a new career. I literally stepped out of my own life (yes—*again…*) and let go of all my pre-conceived notions and expectations regarding the success of my literary works. With the help and guidance of too many friends to count, I learned over time how to let go and let GOD… and it is through the action of letting go that I gained immeasurable insights and wisdoms into how this whole synchromystic thing works in the first place.

Which brings us to our final question; 'what the hell does SYNCHROMYSTIC mean?'.

The beautiful magical thing about life is this… all gifts we are given come from the same place and our birthed out of our desire. One of the truths that Christianity teaches is us "ask and ye shall receive".

Throughout the journey that was *Truth*, you will notice that there is a connectedness to all the events that took place, hidden meanings in names, significance in numbers, signs and messages delivered when needed. All these things can be described as a word that is used often of late thanks to the people who have paved the way with books like 'The Secret'. They are called synchronicities and they are both accepted and expected by people around the world who have stepped onto 'the path'. Mysticism on the other hand is a little less main-stream; reserved for the likes of Shaman and Channels, or so you might think. Mysticism predates Christianity, and has been a way of life for many cultures since the early stages of our evolution. It is also present within Christianity, many of the Saints we know and recognize today as being good solid examples of the Christian faith, were considered by their peers to me mystics. Mystic is defined as… "a person who seeks by contemplation and self-surrender to obtain unity with or absorption into the Deity or the absolute, or who believes in the spiritual apprehension of truths that are beyond the intellect." Of course this means, that by the very nature of this book, and the undeniable truth that you are at the moment reading it, you too are a mystic.

The trick is to combine the two understandings and allow your self-surrender to lead you to ask so that you too can receive. You see, it is not very complicated at all, and not difficult to achieve. It is however more fun that you can ever imagine, and I highly recommend it as a way of life. Right now, it is possible that you are thinking that all these things that happened to me could not ever possibly happen to you, and if you continue on with that line of thinking it is more than likely that they never will. But you can change that, right now… all you have to do is put your faith in the Divine and step on the path towards truth. As it happens, your truth as you discover it, may not be my truth, but that's as it should be.

The point is, if you are reading this book and thinking to yourself that it might be fun to explore the world in a way that seems to some a bit 'Harry Potterish', then you are ready. All you need do now is be willing… odd word that, 'willing', it is the turning of 'will' into an action word; how cool is that?

Fun with words, it is a game I play often, along with my other favorite game, fun with numbers. These things, you too may in time come to enjoy. They are a part of being a Synchromystic, and as far as I'm concerned they should be taught to our children in school. Certainly life is easier when all you have to do is follow the signs laid before you, when little confirmations pop up continually to reassure you that you are on the right path. Like this weekend for example, as I am writing the final chapters of the new book, it is Easter Weekend. Now if you are a Christian, I need not explain the significance of this. For those of you who are not, here is how that all works. Jesus died on the cross to save mankind from their sins on Good Friday… now we are not going to debate the use of the word 'good' here, nor are we going to explore that whole 'dying for our sins' thing. We are however going to focus on the third day, Sunday, which is celebrated as the day that Jesus rose from the dead (rose… ha ha ha) and then we are going to count the number of days that all took. 3—a number much beloved by me and prominent throughout this story and my life. Coincidently, Jesus also happened to be 33 when he died so that makes three - 3's.

First let's explain the significance of the number 3—In Biblical numerology (yes there is such a thing—look it up) 3 signifies completion or perfection, and unity. 3 is the number of Persons in the Trinity. Many significant events in the Bible happened "on the third day". Jonah spent three days and three nights in the belly of the fish and Jesus' earthly ministry lasted three years.

The following information on the number 3 in regular numerology comes from a wonderful blog site I discovered during my research. NUMEROLOGY—The Vibration and Meaning of NUMBERS—run by a woman named Joanne Walmsley—this blog site is a *wealth* of information, and the woman herself is quite fascinating (must try to get her on the show)—if you have questions about numerology and the power behind numbers, this is the place to go for answers.

www.numerology-thenumbersandtheirmeanings.blogspot.ca
and/or (I recommend both)
www.sacredscribes.net

ATTRIBUTES OF THE NUMBER 3

Synthesis, triad, heaven-human-earth, past-present-future, thought-word-action, demonstrates love through creative imagination, comprehensive, fulfilling.

Relates to:

Mars

The Empress

Tuesday

Yellow

Character:

Frank, forceful, motivates others.

Negative Traits:

Indifferent, lacks stamina and concentration, spectacular rise and fall, mania, mood swings. (pay attention to these in particular as they may explain a lot about my life and some of my less that glorious moments)

The urge of 3 is to conserve the growing faith in yourself while encouraging others to expand their faith as well.

3 is to do with the 'performing arts'.

The Number 3 is considered to be feminine and introvert and relates to the planet Jupiter. The Tarot card representative of the 3 energy is The Empress.

The Number 3 symbolizes the principles of growth. When the initiating force of 1 unites with the germinating energy of 2, there is fruitfulness = 3, the Trinity. 3 signifies that there is a synthesis present - that imagination and an outpouring of energy is in action. The 'thought' of 1 and the 'fertility' of 2 results in the 'creativity' of 3. The joy and happiness of the 3 vibration is to be shared with others.

The 3 energy is optimistic and fun-loving, and strives to uplift and colour its surroundings. They tend to be the 'joker', have a wonderful sense of humour and are very charismatic.

The 3 energy is enlivening, youthful and enthusiastic. Their talents lay within communications of all kinds.

The gift of words and communication are there for the 3 person, as is inspiration, cheerful optimism and joy. The 3 energy loves life and needs to share their enthusiasm with others. Number 3 is the energy of the 'creator' and wants to inspire and light the 'fire of life' in others so that they can also feel the joy and enthusiasm for living life to the fullest.

They feel the need to inspire and beautify the world. The natural capabilities of the 3 allows them to take anything they have a create something beautiful from it.

3 represents the principle of increase, expansion, growth and abundance on the physical, emotional, mental, financial and spiritual levels. The 3 is a free-form energy that does not work well with structure, plans or routines. They are an open channel with spiritual insights and inspiration for living life. They are the creator, not the worker.

Intuition and psychic gifts are abilities of the 3 vibration, and is a very positive aspect when used for the service of others. This is uplifting and joyful to the 3 vibration.

The Triad—Body, Soul and Spirit

The Ruler—Venus"

Now that we have the basic rules for our little game, let's play…
I have had 3 parents in my life…
I have had 3 sets of grandparents…
I have almost died 3 times… (giving birth, car accident, pneumonia)
I was 33 when I first went to the Philippines…

I went to the Philippines 3 times…

I published the book 3 times…

Truth was published for the 2nd time in 2010 by Grave Distractions Publications – 2+0+1+0 = 3 (oh and 3 names in the Publishing company —almost missed that)

The date chosen by my publicist for the re-release is June 1st, which also happens to fall on the 3rd year anniversary of the launching of the talk show that made all this possible…

I was born on 5/7/75 – 7 and 5 = 12 – 1 + 2 = 3….

Of course that last one could be me stretching it just a bit, but you get the picture. Now for the BIG QUESTION… 'does this make me special?'

Not particularly, although there may have been a time when I would have said 'hell yes—I'm off to save the world!!!'—not so much anymore. I do view it as confirmation that our third publication attempt on the date chosen for a story such as this will be a success.

The way I see it now, is that I am no more special than you or anybody else on this amazing planet. Humans in general, by their very nature are awesome; being physical representations of GOD and all that, how can they be anything but? Perhaps the only thing about all this that makes me special is that as some claim, I showed a great amount of courage in choosing to hand over my life, not once, not twice but you guessed, thrice. (when my parents died, when I was arrested for being a dumb ass, and when my strength failed me upon my return from the Philippines) Me however, I tend to disagree with that, I think that the truth is that it wasn't so much courage as curiosity that got me where I am. I blame it on my unquenchable desire to explore humanity in all its varied forms. I just wanted to know how this whole living thing worked so I asked the only person I thought could answer the question. It surprised the hell out of me (pardon the pun) when GOD answered but answer he did, so now I know, which also means that so do you, and that as *they* say, is that… (who are them of '*they* say' anyways?—has anybody figured that out yet?)

Oh and before I forget, Revo is doing great; he is living a life of Ministry in the Philippines happily married to a lovely young lady… I wholeheartedly wish them a lifetime of divine inspiration and blessings…

He was married on March 12th of this year, and will be 33 on the 3rd of November in the year in which this book is published…

Seriously—I could not make this shit up if I spent a lifetime trying ;)

My Everyday Connection To George...

Who on Earth is George and what does he do?

George is the executive producer of our talk show Everyday Connection Now and our breakfast magazine Waking Up With Everyday Connection, he also handles scheduling, travel arrangements, guest introductions and is the not so silent, silent partner of our company Everyday Connection Media.

He has always just kind of been around, and it made sense when we launched our vision of Everyday Connection for us to ask George to be a part of it. I am pretty sure George introduced me to my business partner Richard O'Shields, although exactly how and when that happened, we can't really say. People have been asking Richard and I how we met for three years and to be honest neither of us can remember. We have decided then to blame George as he is responsible for all of the magic that is the Everyday Connection experience.

So which do you want first, the story of George, or of Everyday Connection.

I imagine that if I first explain who George is then the rest will make more sense, so let's get to it.

Back in 2009 when I was preparing for the publication of my first book, I also began preparing myself for the anticipated onslaught of questions that was sure to follow. I had realized about half way through the writing of it, that I had had a running dialogue in my head during the entire process. A conversation if you will, with something, or somebody, that was giving me the answers to all the questions I was asking. I would even occasionally get warnings, some of which I did not heed (and look where that got me) to not do a certain thing if I wanted the book to be a success. So who, or what, was I talking to? Well, given the current circumstances, it stood to reason that I was talking directly to God, and why not? After all, I had asked and oh boy had I received, so why could it not be possible that these direct messages were coming direct from source. Mind you, I rarely spoke of it, and if I wrote about it, it is so intertwined with the rest of the story as to be almost unnoticeable. I assumed, and rightly so I might add, that people would think me nuts, white coat, padded room and all that, so I did my best to not speak openly about it with those I perceived to be unable or unwilling at the time to understand.

I did however face a major dilemma; due to the nature of the book and my insistence throughout the book that all major religions and all beliefs have a common thread of truth, and therefore must also be birthed from the same source, I was hesitant to label GOD. If my story, such as it was, was to reach the hearts of those who were not of the Christian faith then it would not do to start throwing the word God around. I had begun writing a blog called 'Feenxrising' and was regularly contributing writing to several sites that were more in alignment with the 'New Age' movement than with Christianity and so I needed a word for GOD that would not offend people of other faiths. As usual, whenever I had a question, I brought it to my go to guy, and sure enough, when I asked Him (I still referred to Him as a Him at the time) what I should call him, he told me George…

Now my immediate response to this was; "hell no—they'll crucify me" but He assured me that it would be OK and that by the end of the day I would understand why. Sure enough, that afternoon Ayla called me to chat about some thing or another and I mentioned my conversation with 'George'… she laughed and laughed and laughed… I could hear her wheezing and trying to catch her breathe on the other end of the phone and so I asked her what the hell was so bloody funny… Her response was a disgusted snort and a blunt 'seriously—are you telling me you don't get it?'

Well no, I didn't get it, and I was slightly offended by her assumption that I should get it. Nonetheless, I patiently asked that she explain it to me which she flat out refused to do. She did however ask me a very important question. "What is your understanding of God?"

Ah… and it comes to this…

So as I sat there on my sofa working out the explanation to such a massive theoretical question, it dawned on me… OH… Now I get it… and suddenly it all made perfect sense.

One of my favorite ways of explaining who and what GOD is to people is this… God, is the core of all creation, a massive energetic force that through its desire to experience life, manifests itself into all kinds of different versions of it. Essentially, God, as I understand God to be, wants to experience EVERYTHING and therefore is the most curious entity of all time… ie: Curious George…

I fell off the sofa laughing, as I have said before, and as I will surely say again—George is a comedian, he writes the best jokes, tells the best stories and in light of the journey that is *Truth*, you have to admit, he is one hell of an author. (I sincerely hope that all this time that it has not been George Carlin speaking to me—that really would be a hilariously funny cosmic joke) Now all that being said, I was still hesitant to use it in public, but I did begin using it around the house and the next thing I knew, my daughter was saying things like, 'thank George' and 'George knows'—my favorite however has always been—'by George, she's got it'

George has become a regular part of our show Everyday Connection, he is present at every show, and he is mentioned at least once every single time we go on the air. As synchronicity would have it, he was recently mentioned on a show that featured a very dear friend of ours from the U.K. He is an award winning author, a Celtic Christian Spiritual Explorer Guide, and a good man. He has spent almost 20 years studying scripture, and he is without a doubt the most Christ centered person I know. He really *understands* Jesus, and he brings the teachings back to the fundamental values that Jesus originally taught. He has shed new light on the teachings of the Bible, and through his knowledge of ancient Hebrew text he has helped me to find an alignment between my understanding of God and what the Bible teaches about God. He has put it all into context in such a way as to make it easy to accept as being a *Truth*. I still maintain that I am not Christian (but then again neither was Jesus), I cannot be anything other than that which I am to do the work I have chosen to do; yet I can through my work support and encourage those who follow their own path, by way of my own understanding of why they have chosen a particular faith. My friend also confirmed for me that there is no word for Spiritual in the Hebrew language, and that they did not ever refer to any one thing or person as being Spiritual. Rather they understood that all life was an expression of Spirit, and that there was no division between that which is physical and that which is Spiritual; to hear a Christian leader say that was for me pure bliss…

Anyways… he came on the show for his 3rd visit (there's that number again) and heard us make several references to George. He asked me about it later and I explained that it was what we called GOD. I told him I would tell him the story another time on Skype as we were messaging back and forth on FB at the time and I did not want my fingers to get tired out the day before I began work on the new chapters for the book.

He sent me back the most intriguing bit of information... this is what he wrote...

"In the late 16th early 17th century, following the rise in Puritanism, people became quite intense about misusing God's name, so they started to replace it with other things.

In those day, as common as it is now to hear 'oh my gosh' the name of 'false' gods was used. The most common was the King of the Roman gods 'Jupiter', also known as 'Jove'. Statements such as 'by Jove' became common.

Later on, in the late 17th century it became more anglicised to be 'George' instead of 'Jove'. Hence statements like 'by George, she's got it!' (Made famous by the song 'The Rain in Spain' in the musical *My Fair Lady*)

George is a replacement word for God via the Roman god Jove/ Jupiter."

Fascinating that, on a day when I am preparing to write a chapter in my new book that will explain why I call God George, he comes up with this. All this time, I thought the use of the name George in lieu of God would be considered by some to be blasphemy (it still may) but at least now I have an answer to that; it was originally used so that people would NOT misuse the word God... and after all, isn't that kind of why I did it in the first place. For many Christians the name God is a part of their perceived and often misused unique connection to Spirit, a connection that for some allows them the right to stand in judgment over their fellow man and so in my mind, the word has been being abused for centuries.

Thankfully that way of thinking is coming to an end, thanks to people like my friend who are teaching the original truths with the support of scripture and most recently thanks to our beloved Pope Francis, who has made it quite clear, that he is not so much concerned with what you call your God, but more with what and who your God inspires you to become. Finally a Pope who gets it...

Oh and just as a fun fact; the roman God Jupiter (Jove) was the king of the gods and the god of sky and thunder in ancient Roman religion and myth. Jupiter was the chief deity of Roman state religion throughout the Republican and Imperial eras, until Christianity became the dominant religion of the Empire. Jupiter is usually thought to have originated as a sky god. His identifying implement is the thunderbolt, and his primary sacred animal is the eagle. Now it sounds to me a little familiar, the 'god' of 'gods', a man in the sky that people pray to, where have I heard that before?

Oh yes, and the Eagle is particularly interesting, given that it is used as a symbol of strength and power on a multitude of flags including that of the United States. Whoever told you the roman empire fell was telling a little white lie; it didn't fall, it just changed its name to The Roman Catholic Church… pretty sneaky…

While we are talking about the church, which is of late one of our favorite topics at Everyday Connection, if only because we are simply in awe of what our friend Pope Francis has been up to; oddly enough, my partner Richard has been poking me on Skype with a 'look what he did now message' so before I go any further, I guess I should share…

Just this past Thursday, the Pope washed the feet of 12 disabled people in Rome as part of the Maundy Thursday service commemorating Christ's Last Supper.

He broke with tradition by washing the feet of several women and a Muslim man in a ceremony traditionally restricted to men only. Now THAT is a Pope I can stand behind…

Hmmm… perhaps he read my book?

Seriously though, that is a huge step in the right direction for the church and as with all things awesome, we do our best at Everyday Connection to tell as many people as possible about it.

It all began 3 yrs ago when I was living at a friend's house awaiting my move to Quebec. I had already met Richard, and he had been a huge part of my healing journey thus far. He had assisted in the writing and publication of my 3rd book and I think he was just looking for something else to keep me busy and keep my mind off the pain. Perhaps he wished me to rediscover my purpose, George knows I needed something to get the fires of passion burning. Whatever his reasons, he managed to somehow trick me into agreeing to co-host a radio talk show with him. At the time, I was absolutely terrified of public speaking, I had just come out with my real name on my 3rd book, but was still using my pen name for all of my social media sites. Public exposure was potentially the most dangerous thing in my mind, although how I figured to write the kind of books I was writing and keep myself out of the public eye is beyond me. Silly is what it is; write a book called *Truth* and then hide your truth from the world, it doesn't even pass the giggle test.

He knew all of this, he had been running my blog site for some time and we had a good solid foundation in friendship so he told what he considered to be a little white lie. He said, nobody would be listening…

Well they were, and not only did they listen, but they began to call in. So out of a synchromystic encounter with a friend/listener on the 3rd show (this is the last time I am pointing that out—you should be picking these up on your own by now) the concept for Everyday Connection was born. A conversational show that would offer an open invitation to wayshowers and changemakers to come play in our virtual sandbox. Over time, the show has expanded, and by the power of word of mouth it has grown into something that has far surpassed our original vision. We now offer two shows, our old faithful, **Everyday Connection Now,** a pre-recorded show which features conversations with some of the most dynamic free thinkers of our time, and **Waking Up With Everyday Connection**, a Monday—Friday breakfast show that focusses on positive news stories from around the world.

Everyday Connection Now

Inspiration, information and conversation... Those are the backbones of Everyday Connection and with those three things we have opened the door to an open and honest representation of our ever changing world. We know that human beings are innately creative, intelligent and compassionate. It is our goal to seek out and connect our listeners with as many of these magnificent beings from around the world as we can find who are using their own personal passions and gifts to make this world a better place in which to live. At Everyday Connection we believe that ordinary, everyday people are doing extraordinary things Everyday and we are passionate about being the mirror that shows the world it's awesome potential; when people finally realize how awesome they are, they then take that awesomeness back out into the world and the world expands exponentially.

Waking Up With Everyday Connection

Is waking up to what's going wrong in our world wounding your spirit?

For over two years, Richard O'Shields and Niki Norlock have been using inspiration, information and conversation as keys to open the door to an honest representation of our ever changing world. After over 375 airtime hours of uplifting exploration into the personal journeys of change-makers from around the world, the one thing they have learned to be a truth is that our world is indeed changing for the better and it is due to the tireless, joy-filled efforts of ordinary people that humanity has begun to truly understand the value of compassion, collaboration, and community. As our focus shifts, both as individuals and as a global family, to settle upon that which inspires and moves us; our ability to both embrace the beauty of life and to create new beauty within our own lives expands. Through our exploration of that expansion, we wake up to all the potential that life has to offer; and happiness ceases to be something we seek and becomes a part of who we are.

Join us while we wake up to the truth of humanity's greatest accomplishment, and celebrate with us humanity's innate ability to bring our inner light into our everyday lives...

Both shows can be found at the Everyday Connection website... www.everydayconnection.me (because it's all about me no matter which me happens to be reading that at the time)

Through the show we have both been graced with an intense journey into self, and through the show we have both found immense healing and pleasure. Through the show, I have once again found my purpose and my passion. I consider myself to be one of the luckiest people on the planet, not because I have a high paying job that allows me to travel the world, but because I am awarded the opportunity on a daily basis, to get up close and personal with some truly remarkable human beings. I have the honor of sharing with them the exploration of their personal growth and expansion, and through the sharing of that growth we are also able to inspire similar growth in others. Essentially, I get paid to love people, as they are, in each now moment as they come into my awareness. Can there possibly be a better job in the world?

Oh and speaking of being sneaky, I gave this chapter to Richard to proof last night, and so now can add in a quick note about him for all of you, without him knowing until the book has already been printed. (muah ha ha ha ha)

Here's the blunt and honest truth about my partner... I think he and our work on the show probably saved my life, if he had not told that little untruth (which he claims he thought was a truth at the time) I would never have discovered the pure magic of my everyday connection to George... The Philippines opened my eyes, my heart, and gave me an unwavering faith in humanity, for which I will be forever grateful... but Richard... oh

Richard… now *he* has helped to nurture an unwavering faith in myself… and in somebody as messed up and angry with herself as I was at the time we met, that is quite the accomplishment. I'm pretty hard on him some times, we have this brother/sister relationship that gives me permission to tell him when he's being an ass, which I do, when it's required. Still, I am well aware of the impact both he and the show have had on my life and on my own personal growth and expansion, and though I know he is going to cry when he reads this (real men cry happy tears), it has to be said… "Thank-you Richard O'Shields (mystical magical manifestation of George) for coming into my life at just the right time, and doing what nobody else had been able to do; you taught me how to love and appreciate 'me', and I will be forever more be in a state of full appreciation for your presence in my life"

All right, enough with the corny bunnies and rainbows type stuffs (I hope it's not GMO—bad for your health that—bad for the bunnies too) moving on…

It just so happens that it is also through the show that we were connected with my publicist Devra, who has not only sent to us some truly remarkable guests, but has also been a guest herself on the show due to her special relationship with Archangel Michael. You might say in fact, that, my publishing team includes Michael since much of the initial advice on how to handle the re-launch of this book came directly from Michael through Devra his channel. If you have read the rest of the book, you will understand the significance of his involvement in this publication. So of course in keeping with the theme of the book as it was originally written, I looked up the meaning of her name. "Derived from the Hebrew dēvōrah —The name is borne in the Bible by a prophetess and judge who led the Israelites to victory over the Canaanites.,"

Why do I sense the continuation of a common theme?

Oh, because there is one…

While we are outlining synchromystic moments in time; not so long ago, my partner Richard had our birth names and dates run by a lady who specializes in numerology. Curiouser and curiouser…

It turns out that we are both master numbers… (The following information is taken directly from the website www.TokenRock.com— if you would like to learn more about numerology I highly recommend stopping by this comprehensive and informative site.)

A person with an Expression or Life Path that reduces down fully to an 11 or 22 are said to be endowed with special gifts of high-level inspiration and leadership, but their life may also be very challenging and highly paradoxical.

They radiate enormous potential, accompanied by a high level of inner tension resulting from an overwhelming desire to achieve something extraordinary.

Due to the intensified vibration and potency of 11 and 22, those who are born with them often feel a heightened sense of obligation in life and a greater need for self-discipline and purity of consciousness. They tend to have challenging childhoods, yet often lead extraordinary lives after learning to utilize their full potential - therefore many are late bloomers.

People whose core numbers reveal Multiple Master Numbers often experience more challenges in life than most, evidence of their higher-self's intense inner drive to propel itself onto a higher path in this lifetime.

Richard is an 11

In Numerology 11 is the most intuitive of all numbers. It represents illumination; a channel to the subconscious; insight without rational thought; and sensitivity, nervous energy, shyness, and impracticality. It is a dreamer.

The 11 has all the aspects of the 2, enhanced and charged with charisma, leadership, and inspiration. It is a number with inborn duality, which creates dynamism, inner conflict, and other catalyses with its mere presence.

It is a number that, when not focused on some goal beyond itself, can be turned inward to create fears and phobias. The 11 walks the edge between greatness and self-destruction. Its potential for growth, stability, and personal power lies in its acceptance of intuitive understanding, and of spiritual truths. For the 11, such peace is not found so much in logic, but in faith. It is the psychic's number.

I am a 22

> In Numerology 22 is the most powerful of all numbers. It is often called the Master Builder. The 22 can turn the most ambitious of dreams into reality. It is potentially the most successful of all numbers.
>
> It has many of the inspirational insights of the 11, combined with the practicality and methodical nature of the 4. It is unlimited, yet disciplined. It sees the archetype, and brings it down to earth in some material form. It has big ideas, great plans, idealism, leadership, and enormous self-confidence.
>
> If not practical, the 22s waste their potential. Like the 11, the 22 can easily shrink from its own ambition, causing difficult interior pressures. Both the 11 and the 22 experience the pressure-cooker effect very strongly, particularly at an early age. It must work toward the realization of goals that are larger than personal ambition. The 22 serves the world in a practical way.

So they are both master numbers, and it just so happens that when they are put together add up to the master number that many claim once belonged to none other than Jesus Christ; 33…

It seems that Everyday Connection really does have the George stamp of approval.

Well my dears, I think that concludes our broadcast day, be sure to stay tuned for updates on some key characters from *Truth* as well as checking in to see what interesting adventures might be coming next. I am sure we will see you soon enough out there on the ethernets but until then…

To our Mother, to each other, and especially to yourselves… STAY CONNECTED!!!

On a Personal Note...

Here I go, here I go, here I go again (again?)
Girls, what's my weakness? (Pens!)
(some of you actually sang that…)
I couldn't resist, for three reasons:

First, I have to pay homage to some amazing women who defied the public perception of who or what a hip hop artist should be and paved the way for some of the hardest hitting female pop culture icons of our age. They wrote edgy lyrics, challenging people to think about our societal oddities and reflect on the impact of our preconceived notions.

Second, It's the truth… The pen is my weakness, and though it has been a long time since I spent this much time dedicated to putting my thoughts on paper, it is through the process of re-releasing this book that I have re-discovered my love of writing. I consider it an honor to be able to openly share my thoughts and feelings with my readers, to be invited into their homes and their hearts to sit down over a cup of tea and explore the meaning of life.

Third, I had no idea how to start this chapter and 'Shoop' is the first thing that popped into my head when I got out of bed this morning.

Of course one need only look at the lyrics and the energy behind the song to see how appropriate it is and how in alignment it is with certain aspects of the story of *Truth*. *Truth* is a lot of things to a lot of people, but one of the things that it seems to be to just about everybody who reads it, is a love story. I admit, I left my life behind to follow a man to an unknown foreign land, and was, at the time completely convinced that we were meant to be together in the Philippines. I still am, but as I have grown and expanded my awareness over the last few years, I realize now that it is for reasons that I could not have grasped at the time and certainly not in the way I first imagined. Still, at the time, romantic relationships is what I understood, I had spent a lifetime looking for the 'perfect mate', the one man/woman who could complete me, make me whole, save me from myself. It was my current 'truth', it is all I had ever known. I was one of those people, who when they fall, fall fast and hard; I was an 'all in' kind of girl. I still am today, but I have learned through my journey and my experiences that love comes in many different shapes and forms, and romantic love is only one aspect of that magical emotion that most closely represents the Divine creative essence of all of life.

I have also learned that GOD has to work with what's available, and that although our experiences can shape and mold us, planet Earth is a free will zone and GOD does not manipulate us into doing what is best for either us or the world. GOD provides us with guidance, and then allows us to choose whether or not we will accept that guidance. GOD comes to us where we are at in each now moment, so it is no surprise to me that he would send a hot little Filipino musician to coax me out of my comfort zone and encourage me to see the world in a new way. Revo played his roll beautifully, and through our relationship I learned some very powerful life lessons; I wonder sometimes if he even knew he was playing a roll, or if he was just following his own signs, and taking each step as it was offered. I will have to ask him someday; I imagine at some point we will be reunited and I am sure the conversation that follows will be magical. Until then however, there is still work to be done here, with regards to wrapping up this fantastical tale and shedding a bit of light on some of my more personal discoveries about life.

One of the things I have learned is that our past can be altered by our perceptions. That the things we have been through, that we may have viewed as tragic and painful at the time, can in fact be used as healing tools, and inspiration for us later in life. This also applies to choices we have made, even if some of those choices were questionable. I have learned that regret is a thing to be avoided, and that, though at times it is appropriate to apologize for our actions, it is not beneficial to our own personal growth to dwell on our 'mistakes'. Each step we have taken has led us to where we are now, and it is in the now where we are gifted with an opportunity to initiate change within our own lives.

For instance, if I had never put myself in a position where my back was so far against the wall that I felt I had no other choice but to fight my way out of the corner, I would never have experienced the kindness and compassion that were gifted to me. My choice to allow my friend to burn down my house so that I may escape the mess that was the life I had created led to me experiencing the blessings of second chances. It also gave me an in depth understanding of desperation, and so, I am able to look at the actions of others in a different way. It is easier for me not to judge others out there who are lost in fear and despair; I can look at them not with pity or anger but with understanding and empathy. I also know from firsthand experience that the 'system' is not this big nasty thing that we need to fight against, rather it is a collection of individual people who have chosen for their own reasons to follow a certain career path. Because they are people, some of them may make 'mistakes' or pass unfair 'judgement' on those who rely on them for help; yet some of them use their positions within the system to uplift and encourage those whose lives are for a time placed in their hands.

It is with that in mind that I continue to do the work that I do. I was blessed to have been lucky enough to be arrested by a compassionate and understanding detective, blessed to have been defended by a wise and knowledgeable lawyer, blessed to be judged by a fair man and then blessed again to be handed over to parole officer who was more interested in the person I 'could' become than the person I was. Interestingly enough, once my time was served and all I had left to do was pay of the massive monetary debt that I owed to the insurance company, I was blessed yet again with a lawyer who would ultimately work with me to allow me to find ways to pay off my debt without robbing my daughter of the basic essentials. I was, with his help, able to pay off half of the debt before I got sick, and because of his kind-hearted approach in the handling of my situation, have every intention of paying off the rest of it. Granted, due to my illness I have not been able to make a payment on that debt for quite some time as for most of the past 3 years I have been forced to live off welfare, my husband's income and the generosity of friends. Regardless of my current monetary status, I have not forgotten the debt I owe and I am determined to fulfil my promise to pay it. I must point out however, that this is not because I am a changed person, or a good person; it is because I am aware that I would not *be* a changed person without the intervention of all those involved. It is their kindness that helped me to become who I am today and it is out of respect for that kindness that I am driven to prove that their faith in me was not unjust.

All that being said, I also know that if those people had gotten to me *before* the situation got out of hand then none of this would have happened; but how could they help me if they didn't know I needed the help. So you see, as my partner Richard is so fond of saying, there is no one left to blame really, only ground left to reclaim.

And reclaim it I have…

I have stepped into a new life, and am happy in my *me.* I have learned to appreciate and be grateful for all of life's gifts, even the gifts we don't' recognize as gifts at the time of the gifting. I have found love, not just with my extremely awesome life mate but also with incredibly supportive friends, family and colleagues. I have a job I love, and though it does not pay much at the moment, the rewards are infinite. I live in my dream home, a home that was gifted to us through a series of interesting little events that proved to us once again that when you let go and let GOD, all things are possible. Long before fortune and fame even became a consideration, I was blessed with the fruition of my dreams. Through the magic of synchromysticism I am now living the life I wanted to live and money had very little to do with any of it.

Would you like to hear some of the stories?

You have already read about my dream job and the creation of our new media company Everyday Connection. So you realize I am sure how much of an impact our work with the show has had on my life. Yet, one of the things I did not expand upon was how much of an impact our *guests* have had on my own personal spiritual growth. For three years, I have been spending at least 4 hours a week (sometimes 6–8) discussing the universal laws of spiritual truths with people from around the world. Some of these people have spent a lifetime studying in their respective fields. The amassed knowledge and wisdom that has been freely shared with us and our listeners since the inception of our show is priceless; not only because you simply cannot put a price on that kind of insight but also because it has been freely gifted to us, and through us, is freely gifted to our listeners. It would be impossible for me to do what I do for living and not learn *something* that would influence the course of my own life. Our work has been of immense worth and value, not just to me, but to everybody else it touches, because it is the collective knowingness of countless free thinkers and as such it cannot help but have a powerful impact on the world in which we live.

Still it is not the only source of knowledge I have stumbled across during the course of this wondrous adventure.

Shortly after arriving back to Canada after my first trip to the Philippines, I made the decision to break it off with Ray and move out of the house I was living in. At the time Ayla was looking for a new roommate and I was looking for a new place to hang my hat, so it made sense that I should move into her home for a time and patiently wait for whatever was meant to come next. Already living with her in her home was her cousin, who had taken up residence in her basement and was happily spending his days equally split between work and play. It was he who helped me to move all of my 'stuff' out of the house I was sharing with Ray and into my new rooms at Ayla's. And it is he who I am now happily sharing space and my life with in my dream home in the mountains of Quebec. Ayla used to joke that we were a 'match made in *heaven*' and for those of us who know the inside story, that one little phrase rings true on so many levels. During my time at Ayla's I wrote my second novel "*Going Home to Heaven*" which included some very intense discussions with the residents of the home on social issues, politics, religion and love. I am still planning on re-releasing that one as well, but for now it will have to wait as my heart tells me that it too is not yet finished. As the writing of the work progressed, and as the discussions began to explore deeper into the truths of the human heart and all its' complexities, it seemed natural that the friendship that Ayla's cousin and I had built would eventually evolve into something more. In time, it grew into a relationship unlike anything I had ever experienced, with truth and honesty as the foundation, and the 'now' moment as the building blocks, it was destined to not only survive but to thrive.

What is unique about it, is that neither of us was 'looking' for a life mate. We both knew who we were, where we had been, and what we wanted; we also knew that we had no idea where we were headed, and were perfectly ok with just going along for the ride. Both of us were sick to death of the societal expectations that had been laid upon us with regards to marriage and commitment. Because we had no intentions or expectations as to where our time together would lead, we also felt no need to be to each other anything other than who we were. Our acceptance of each other was unconditional and complete. We spent hours talking about all the things we had done, our individual perspectives on life, and our own personal dreams for the future, never factoring in each other as a necessary component to the realization of those dreams. When I met him, he made it perfectly clear to me that all he had to offer was 'now', there were no promises of tomorrow and certainly the concept of forever was not even open for discussion. Interestingly enough, in the process of refusing to do anything other than take it day by day we ended up staying together in a state of appreciation for each now moment as it came. It hasn't been all bunnies and rainbows; we have had some interestingly challenges, my failing health, interference by family members and friends and financial burdens could have all threatened to tear us apart if the foundation of our friendship had not been built so strongly on trust. Our ability to speak our truth to each other without fear of judgment allowed us to take on each new experience as 'just another day in the life of…' and we quickly learned that the more honest we were with each other, the more able we were to lean on/or support one another as was needed.

We may have met at Ayla's in Toronto, but my love was originally from Quebec, and so the time came when he would be pulled back there so that he could play a bigger part of his own daughter's life. The day he chose to return to his home province was also the day we chose to see how far we could take this little experiment that was our relationship. Because our relationship had begun with us living together, how would distance alter or affect the outcome. We travelled back and forth for almost a year, alternating the trips so that neither of us spent more time away from home than the other, until my health failed completely and I was unable to hold up my end of the unspoken bargain. Ultimately, it transpired that I was no longer able to support myself or my daughter and we were faced with another major decision. He had a decent paying job in Quebec, and space for me to live and was willing to support me financially if I was willing to give up my life in Toronto to start a new life with him in Quebec. It was probably the hardest choice I have ever had to make; it meant that I might have to give up shared custody of my daughter and resign myself to being the 'weekend' parent. I was terrified at the prospect but at the time saw that I had no other choice. Every single time I have been faced with major life choices (with the exception of the odd choice I made with respects to my stalker) I have made it a point to include my daughter in those choices, not only because I respect her insight, but also because the decisions I make affect her and therefore I believe that she should be a part of the decision making process. From apartment shopping, to hopping on a plane to blindly follow a man to the other side of the world, her opinion has been an integral part of the journey. So I asked her and her answer completely blindsided me and left me scrambling to keep up with her own personal growth. I discovered that my young child had, unbeknownst to me, grown into a decisive and brave young woman who was committed to taking control of her own life. For many of the same reasons I had left her father so many years ago (reasons I must point out that I had not discussed with her for fear of tainting her own perceptions of him) she now faced me and boldly stated that she wished to come live with me in Quebec so that she could pursue her life as she chose to live it, not as it was perceived it ought to be lived by those in her family whose intentions for her future were not in alignment with her own.

Wait—What?

Ok… so maybe not so much in those words (but pretty damn close —this is Madison we are talking about after all), but the point is, that at the tender age of 13, she opted to go to court and attest to choosing to live full time in another province with her mother. So off to court we went, and custody granted, we packed our bags and embarked on another new adventure. Of course, life is never that easy or simple, there was much about our (Madison's and mine) relationship that needed mending before we could fully commit to such an endeavour. The story of the fire that she had been told thus far by me was not complete. I had been warned by child psychologist that I had consulted shortly after my arrest that she was too young to understand, and when I asked the man when would be a good time to tell her, he told me with conviction in his voice that I would know because she would ask and I would see in her eyes that she was ready for the truth. Ask she did, and truth I told… ALL of it… and in the telling of it, we found a way to heal, with the help of one another, some very deeply buried open wounds that were coloring our individual perceptions of life.

It turns out that for many years she had carried a dark secret around with her, a secret that had led her to question her faith in me as a mother. She had been told (and it does not matter who did the telling) that mommy had burned her house down for money and she had kept that horrible truth locked up in her tender little heart for far too long. It still to this day makes me weep to think of it, and my hands are shaking as I am writing this but the truth of the story needs to be told so that others might know the potential power of their words to damage and break the hearts of others. Good Lord I don't know how she bore it and I will never fully understand the depth of love and trust that one tiny child must have for her mother to not turn her back on a woman she believed had destroyed everything she owned just to make a quick buck.

(deep breathe)

How do you repay that kind of faith? How do you honor it?

I do it by continuing to write, and to speak out in defense of truth. I do it by dedicating my life to inspiring others and instilling in them a sense of self-worth so strong that though SATAN himself may stand before you in judgment claiming to be GOD you will know it for the lie that it is. I teach forgiveness of self, I teach perseverance, I encourage love and compassion, understanding and acceptance of self and of every single other person out there who calls this amazing planet home. There is never a time when we come to a point of no return, not a person on this planet who cannot alter the course of their life if they so choose.

Who among us can truthfully say that we are without sin? Did you know that the original Hebrew word for "sin" has been wrongly translated... It doesn't mean to commit something wrong; it simply means to miss, to be absent. To miss means not to be there, doing something without being present there. To not be in the present 'now' moment, this is the only sin. It's opposite, to be 'present'—to be 'alert'—to be 'aware'. That's all that is needed, nothing more.

I remember fondly a message Revo sent to me after my final trip to the Philippines. He said he watched me walk away that final time and couldn't help but think that God chose some really strange people to do His work... Well Revo; I have to say, I tend to agree...

But then again, is it by God's choice or our own? Did GOD choose me to live this tale and then share it with you? Did GOD give me the gift of writing so that I might have a way to share the things I have seen and in the process bear witness to the power that is GODS love?

Or... did I, in my desire to seek out the answers that my heart was asking, step into the roll that I had chosen before I manifested in to Physicality?

It is a deeply philosophical question, and as far as I am concerned both are accurate.

I can't count the number of times that I, being completely fed up with this whole living thing, have begged GOD to bring me home. Each and every time I bitch, whine or chew about the shit I am going through I am told in no uncertain terms "you agreed to this... stop complaining and get on with it".

Honestly, it's the same damned answer every time and so now I don't even bother, I already know exactly that George is going to say.

Speaking of George, I asked once what my purpose was, what I was meant to do with my life and though you might think I would be given a long list of to do's and not to do's, (I was actually expecting a whole bunch of rules to follow), I was only given one. Clear as day, right there inside my head and my heart, one message that is the Divine driving force behind ALL that I do and ALL that I be...

"Never lose faith in Humanity"...

"No matter what you experience, where you go, who you meet or how it all makes you feel—DO NOT GIVE UP ON THEM..."

Ok George, I haven't and I promise, I never will.

{ Looking Back... }

Almost 5 years to the day I wrote the final chapter of *Truth* I find myself once again looking at a computer screen and wondering if it is even remotely possible to put into words the wild and wonderful adventure that has been my life. Looking back on the story now, I realize I did it a grave injustice by writing and publishing it as a fiction… no—that's not exactly true…

At the time, there simply was no other choice; everything that happened and all that I had experienced was pointing me in the direction of publishing this particular book as fiction. At the time, it made complete sense to all involved to tell the story in such a way that the publication of it and the release of it out into the world would not taint or affect our own personal lives, our journeys or define for us, our purpose and our future. For some of the key characters of this book, time was required for growth and expansion both internally and externally as contributing members to the monumental shift in Global consciousness that is now taking place on planet Earth.

Time you see has a magical way of altering our perceptions, and for some of us, it would take some major life altering experiences to come to the full understanding that to follow our passion was also to fulfil our purpose. Time, you see, is not the structured linear 'thing' we perceive it to be. It is fluid, like water, and it flows through life like a river, winding its way past the shores of our understanding. Much like water, it has immense power to alter the shape and form of those shores. A trickle of time, seeping into the rocky shores of our belief, can eventually wear down our stony dogma's… and like water, time is a life source, a fundamental basic element upon which our survival here relies; without it, we cannot experience this magical thing we call physicality.

I suppose then that it is to time that I owe the revelations that I am now about to share.

So where does one begin… I spoke briefly at the end of the book, as it was originally written, about reality and my understanding of it; or perhaps it was more like my misunderstanding of it. It took five years of hard work and serious study on the topic of life, the universe and everything for me to finally come to a place of peace about this whole living thing… and to be quite honest, if you had offered me these truths back when I originally wrote this book, I would have laughed in your face and told you that you were crazy. Not because they are overly challenging truths, but because I was more prepared to fight for our survival than to not fight and so it was that for a long time, I really believed, that a fight is what was needed… It's not… and we will get to that in a moment, but for now let's explore a few simple concepts that were brought up at the end of the book, and in the exploration of them we will perhaps discover the truth about truth.

Often, during the course of this book, I have referenced Him, and at the time, that made complete sense to me. I had come from a Christian upbringing and jaded though my views may have been on Christianity it still seemed the simplest way to define and label 'GOD'. Years later, I have come to a more complete understanding of who or what God is and so I thought, given that this entire book is about connection to Spirit, we would take a minute to explore God. Mind you, that is exactly what we have been doing through the entire course of the book, and though your own understanding of 'GOD' may not be in alignment with my own, you just might find yourself beginning to ask a few more questions of your own after setting this book down for the final time.

After my daughters eloquent and simplistic answer I began to reflect of how I 'saw' God… Who was this 'HE' I was referring to and why did I have this intense connection to 'HIM'—I, who had not been to church in years, who refused to reference the Bible as a guide to life or a teacher of *Truth*; I, who saw the Bible as being tainted by the manipulations of men greedy for control and power—who was I to have this conversation and connection with 'GOD'. What did all of it mean, what was it that I was meant to understand, to write down, to share… It became my quest, and so I set out once again on the path of discovery to explore the essence of 'GOD'. I eventually came to understand who and what 'GOD' is, and though I do not, for one moment, expect you to alter your own belief in any way, I simply cannot deny this little bit of self-discovery a place in the pages of this book.

I did take time to look into the scriptures in search of confirmation of what my heart was telling me to be true, and so I offer that scripture to you now so that we may explore it…

Genesis 1:26
And God said: 'Let us make man in our image, after our likeness; and let them have dominion over the fish of the sea, and over the fowl of the air, and over the cattle, and over all the earth, and over every creeping thing that creepeth upon the earth.'

Now, without getting into my opinion of the whole 'dominion over the…' thing that would probably take up too much space in this book, let's think about the key words in the first line. 'US' and 'OUR'—Now some people have taken this to be proof positive that the trinity exists—'the father—the son—the holy ghost'—however, I believe there is a much more expansive way to look at this hint at truth hidden with the scriptures. A concept so vast and all-encompassing as to include within its boundaries every philosophical belief ever known to man as well as the scientific theory of 'The Big Bang'

What if, and this of course is just the hypothetical tossing about of maybe's, in the beginning, before time existed, there was a thought. An energetic spark of life if you will, that over time, became conscious and aware of its state of being. Now, as much as being a ball of energy would no doubt for a time be interesting enough, I am sure that after a while, you too would get bored. So, out of a desire to experience more, it split, much like the a cell in the body divides to become two whole and complete cells, while still maintaining within itself, the basic DNA codes of the original cell. Now what if, this division continued, and as each new creation was manifested out of this division the aspects of that being created began to evolve. As each new cell memory contributed its experience to the creation of new experience, life as we now know it, and as we have yet to discover it, began to take shape. What if this spark of life, consciousness if you will, chose to divide itself in order to create a way to physically experience its own existence? It would explain a lot, and would in the end, allow for a more adventurous exploration of this thing we call life. If the core of creation were in fact nothing more than a conscious thought that desired to experience the physical, then it would have to separate itself into multiple representations of that physical. Physicality as we know and understand it cannot exist without duality, therefore the creator would have to become the light and the dark, the male and the female, the good and yes, you guessed it, the bad. Now as far out there as this concept may seem, I have spent 5 years exploring my understanding of it, and so am able to give some wonderful examples of some of the more tangible truths of our time that this theory might explain.

Let us start with the Golden Mean or 'ratio'—1.61803398875

It is pervasive in nature, in fact, it has been proven time and time again that this magical little number, represented in Nature by the spiral (yet another symbol for all encompassing reality) is present in the core structure of all of creation. It is in fact right there in our DNA, it is how our bodies are divided up and structured, it is how plants and animals express form, it is buried in the creations of the artistic masters of both our past and our present. You cannot get away from the Golden Mean, it is a part of all that you are, a part of all that is and it represents the physical, never ending expansion of creation. It would take an entire book to explain this theory that is in actuality a fact so I will direct you to a comprehensive website that will allow you to fully explore this miracle of creation. Stop by www.goldennumber.net and prepare to have your mind blown.

Moving on…

Male and female: two separate, unique expressions of GOD that are, despite their differences, inexplicably drawn together and undeniably co-dependent. Their union is required for the natural creation of new life and the continuation of their species. And even in these remarkable times in which we now live, where love is love and thankfully sexual preference is no longer an issue, even those who have fallen in love with those of the same sex, do still maintain friendships with those of the opposite sex. It would seem, that we need each other, regardless of where our hearts may for the moment lie, almost as if we belong together, and are a complimentary aspect of one another.

Which brings me to my next hot topic issue—Soul Mates… the much debated belief that somewhere out there, in the world, there is our 'perfect other half' and perhaps there was a time when this may have been a truth. However, if you follow the theory above and understand the division is infinite, and the spiral of creation continues to expand ever outwards, you might come to conclude that as expressions of creation continue to multiply, there may in fact be more than one representation of your 'perfect mate' currently living on our Planet. It may then naturally follow that you do not have a 'soul mate' so much as you have a 'soul family'; persons who you will recognize as displaying complimentary personality traits to your own. It has always been true that our 'soul mates' are not like us but rather are our opposites and allow us through their time shared with us to explore and experience more of our true selves. Perhaps that is why we feel drawn to them, why we have this belief that they 'complete us'. This too is worth exploring, as my current business partner is so fond of saying "That's a bunch of B.S." (believe system—goodness gracious—what were you thinking?)

As before, if we subscribe to the above theory, and are in fact a 'cell divided'… then are we not whole as we are? So stop looking for your 'other half'—you don't have one, there is only you, and trust me when I say YOU are enough. By all means, continue to seek out those who inspire personal growth and expansion but do not stop at them. Do not buy into the idea for one minute that this person you know you have known before is the answer to all your questions, or that without them, you would cease to be who you are. Certainly, they are an aspect of who you are, but they are not the whole of who you are and therefore that cannot define for you neither you path nor your purpose; that my friends, is up to you.

While we are on the topic of duality, the aforementioned theory also explains all of duality and brings us to a place of understanding with regards to issues such as good and evil. Imagine if you will the desire of a floating ball of energy (GOD) to experience ALL of physicality. Does it not stand to reason then, that in order to do so it would be required for it to create ALL aspects of physicality? This would then mean that everything that has EVER happened is part of the DIVINE PLAN for EXPERIENCE. Which means that all things created, good—evil—the concepts of heaven and hell (and we will dive into those in a moment)—God—Satan—and everything in between is a physical representation of source energy—that magnificent creative force that birthed all that is. Of course coming to terms with this idea is neither easy nor is it something that is often done overnight. I do highly recommend however that it might be worth your while to explore the concept. It might just bring you to a place of complete acceptance, move you past the current human condition of compassion to a state of total all inclusive unconditional love for all that is. This would be a great gift to all of mankind because as it is clearly stated in the above scripture, we are in fact created in God's image which means we too hold within us the power of creation and manifestation.

Oh yes, and on the topic of 'heaven' and 'hell'—they do not, never have and never will exist out there… they are the divine manifestation of your personal perception and experience—without ever leaving home you can experience both 'heaven' and 'hell' in the space of a day, right there in the comfort of your living room. They are states of being—is life easy, breezy beautiful cover girl? (heaven) or does it suck (hell)—now the perk to understanding this long misrepresented truth is that you can literally jump from heaven to hell and back again any time you wish—In fact I wrote a book about it—so keep your eyes open for it—I am sure the new revised edition will be coming soon…

Now we come full circle, back to a more exploratory scientific understanding of the nature of reality; Quantum Physics. Which, though it sounds complex and difficult to grasp, is based on a very simplistic theory; YOU are the centre of all of creation and your conscious (and unconscious thoughts) create your reality. Now there are a whole bunch of complex mathematical equations that explain this, and countless experiments being done right now around the world to prove this to be true so if after you are finished this book you would like to explore this for yourself, I encourage you to do so—there is ample material out there for research. However, I like to keep things simple so I highly recommend you first googling the movie 'What the Bleep do we Know—Down the Rabbit Hole'—Start there, and then allow yourself to wander wherever it is your you takes you after that.

But I digress; the whole point to bringing all that up is to shed light on one of the secrets that people so often miss when reading 'The Secret'… (I might point out though that it was very clearly explained in the story about Mother Teresa refusing to attend an anti-war rally)

And in keeping with my often times overzealous desire to play the name game, let's take a moment to giggle about the fact that she was born to the name of Agnes… (that name just keeps popping up)

Sadly it is imperative for the continuation and evolution of mankind that this basic concept be understood (although following the laws of quantum physics—in my reality you all already have this figured out, so I might be wasting paper)

Here's the thing about consciously creating your reality; the trick is to accept and celebrate the fact that you are creating ALL of it… that means that in the process of creation it helps to be aware that there is no 'they' —that to point the figure at any 'they' and loudly exclaim 'they are wrong' is in fact, confirming the existence of 'they' in the first place. To 'fight' against evil, is to confirm the existence of 'evil' and therefore empower 'evil' to affect your experience…

Now I know what I wrote in the final pages of this book—"we will fight" and all that rot… but this is 5 years later, and I have spent 3 of those years having intense and expansive conversations with some of the greatest minds of our time so don't throw that back in my face… I too am allowed to change my mind ;)

Now we can take this one step further… because I know you are wondering how then do we alleviate poverty, abolish war, cure disease and all that stuff if we refuse to acknowledge the existence of them…

First of all—never refuse to acknowledge the importance of ALL of existence, including these things in our current reality that we would prefer to see change. Accept their existence and be grateful for their existence as it is through their existence that we are allowed to have a full, expansive, human experience. Then once you have acknowledged that they exist, without the attachment of emotions such as fear and anger you may find your way to creating solutions to our perceived problems.

Here are a few basic simple rules…

Focus on the helpers, not the hurters…

Give your attention to the creators, not the destroyers…

Give your energy to the lovers, not the haters…

Give your time to the up lifters, not the down pullers…

And remember, that YOU are in charge of this experience, so if it is your heart's desire to spend your life 'helping' others, you will be in fact creating a world in which there are plenty of people who need help…

God it would appear is the greatest comedian of all time ;)

Now the best part of all of this, is that you now have permission to stop beating yourself up. You can look at all of who you are and appreciate the divine complexity that went into the creation of your unique expression of creation. Nothing you have ever done is against GOD's WILL—it simply cannot be when ALL of it is in fact GOD… so you see, you've done nothing 'wrong'… but then again, you've done nothing 'right'—these are only convenient terms we have used in the past to explain how we 'feel' about an experience.

This also allows you to now look out into our world with appreciation for the multifaceted and diverse expressions of Divinity. You can embrace all beliefs as being not only acceptable but ab-soul-lutely necessary for the evolution of our experience. You can look back on our collective past 'transgressions' as simply another form of growth and expansion that brings us one step closer to complete understanding. You can fully embrace whatever B.S. you wish in each moment to embrace, because it is, in each now moment, where the yummy of life really is. You can stop wasting time fighting against those you are not in alignment with and start seeking out those with whom you can play a new game.

And when I say play… I mean play…

Enlightenment only really means to lighten up—stop taking everything so seriously.

Stop trying to 'be' something and start appreciating the 'being'. Or continue on as you are, it is and always has been your choice to create whatever experience you so desire to immerse yourself in.

Either way, at least do so from a place of awareness that you are doing so. Make the conscious choice in each now moment to live with purpose. To embrace that all things happen FOR you—not to you - and that ALL things as they are happening, are, in fact, happening exactly as they are meant to happen.

Speaking of the 'now' moment; it would not do to wrap up this chapter without first touching on the other aspect of quantum physics—time—our perception of it and the very real truth that the only reason for its existence is that we created it. We need it don't we? To explain ourselves, to define our experiences, to rationalize our existence. That does not mean however that we cannot appreciate the malleable nature of it, nor do we have to always play within the confines of it. It is also fun to explore the truth that since time in its linear form is only a physical manifestation of our desire to experience duality and therefore ALL that has happened BEFORE, ALL that is happening NOW, and ALL that WILL happen is in fact happening at the SAME TIME… and that changes things, and explains things… like past lives, our memories of them, our connection to people we have never met and our more unique experiences like paranormal activity and psychic ability. Consider this, if we all come from the same source, and we are all CONNECTED to that source then are we not ALL able to tap into the amassed knowledge of that source. It also explains some of our more creative expressions of Divinity like angels and demons, and our ancestral legends that tell tales of other races, fantastic mythical beasts, and even dare I go so far as to say the existence of extraterrestrials and multidimensional beings. When you consider that in order to experience ALL that is, GOD must first create ALL that is, then these creations do not seem so mystical or mythical after all. Nor does it seem that unlikely that we would come to a point in the evolution of our experience when the time lines would begin to intertwine and dimensions begin to merge; it would simply be the next logical step in the evolution of both our understanding and our experience.

Ah… creation; how I love thee… let me count the ways… one dimension, two dimension…

So what does it all mean?

I think it means, that many years ago, when I asked my small child what the meaning of life was, her answer, as simplistic as it may have seemed at the time, was the absolute TRUTH. The purpose of life is to live…

It is no more complex than that, to live your life, in whichever way you choose to live it, and to enjoy each new moment and each new experience you have in the process of living it.

It means that life is still the gift from GOD that we have always known it to be, and it means that it is still completely natural to have great reverence and appreciation for it.

It is EVERYTHING and it is NOTHING—it is YOU and ME and ALL OF THEM… it is in fact the very essence of one more simple truth that is hidden deep in the scriptures and the only truth I know definitively to be a truth. In **Exodus 3:14**—it is the answer that GOD gave to Moses when he challenged him to reveal his true nature, it is the answer to all our questions on the nature of GOD and REALITY…

It also happens to be the answer that I offer to those asking 'who are you to write these things as truths?'.

And God said unto Moses: 'I AM THAT I AM'; and He said: 'Thus shalt thou say unto the children of Israel: I AM hath sent me unto you.'

And so I say to you… so are YOU—Shalom my friends until we meet again <3

But then again, if that's not your truth—that too is ok ;)

Truth-The Untold Story...

There is so much that I still haven't shared about my experiences in the Philippines, and it leaves me feeling a bit overwhelmed. As I mentioned before, I went back twice more to work on a project that we had hoped would bring inspiration and light to the world. It left little time for anything else upon my return to Canada, and between working at the restaurant, transcribing *Truth* in preparation for publishing and the project, I had little time for anything else. The original book was first written in notebooks during my first trip, everywhere I went I carried around the shoulder bag gifted to me by Sophia before leaving; it contained my pens, my notebooks, my camera and my wallet. I really didn't need anything else, and though it may have seemed odd to some to see me whip out a pen and notebook in the middle of a conversation, I was pretty honest with everybody I met about what I was doing. It opened a lot of doors for me, that might not have opened so easily if I did not have an 'excuse' to be asking about their culture, and their personal views on life, love and God. Even then, it took some time to break the ice, but once I did break through the natural defensive walls of a cautious people, the insights I was gifted with were pure gold.

Now don't get me wrong, when I refer to walls, it is not meant to imply that they were not some of the most welcoming, hospitable people I had ever met. They were warm, friendly and exceptionally helpful. Keep in mind however, I was asking some extremely personal questions and I am not sure many of us could make the claim that we would be willing answer those kinds of questions when they are being asked by a complete stranger from a foreign land. It took time for me to build relationships with them, I had to allow them to get to know me well enough that they might feel comfortable opening up. I also had to let them in, show them a little bit of my own heart and allow them the freedom to ask me as many questions as I was asking them. The results of these explorations into one another's lives were nothing short of miraculous. I built wonderful relationships with some amazing people, and over the course of my three visits to the Philippines was initiated into a way of life that is based on the fundamental values of faith and family.

I did of course document the entire journey, as with the first trip, each new visit involved me setting aside time each day to journal, writing down my thoughts, my feelings and my experiences. Much of what was written challenges our current paradigm and dives deep into the dark heart of fear and loss of faith. The time has not yet come to reveal those writing so the notebooks used during this time are locked up tight in my studio awaiting the day when my heart tells me that the world is ready for the "The Unravelling of Truth".

I can share a few of the highlights now if you are interested, as well as tell you a little more about the incredible organization called Shepherd Of The Hills Children's Foundation (SOTH)

Because I was still writing a blog, some of my encounters were shared by way of blog posts. Although I think that my friends/family in the Philippines thought that I had forgotten about them, I was still gleaning inspiration from my time spent there and slowly spreading the light they had offered to me, to others through my writing. One of those was with the remarkable young man who had stood guard over me late at night while I was writing on the patio of the hotel in which I was staying. We eventually became really good friends and had some really incredible moments together. His real name is Dexter, and it was during one of my return trips that he invited myself, my daughter and my friend DEO to come stay at his home out in the provinces.

It was an absolutely incredible experience, we had the chance to explore the Philippine culture much more deeply than before, and were invited to not only share their space for a time but also their lives. Don't worry, I had my pen with me, and everything I learned there I will eventually share. One of the things that stood out for me however is the wisdom that was imparted to me by local farmers, who though they may not have had a formal education, were well informed about the current political and social issues of that time. They would sit around roughly hewn picnic tables out in the middle of the Philippine fields, pass around buko (coconut), gin and calamansi (a little lime like fruit) and share stories and/or discuss politics, religion and education issues. The discussion would easily bounce from topic to topic and they had a vast appreciation for how all of those separate threads intertwined to weave a pattern of social truths that affected their daily existence. Some of their insights were mind blowing and I quickly learned that all of my pre-conceived notions about the intelligence or intellect of local farmers were wrong; it turns out that I was the uneducated one. It is something they very quickly remedied.

Dexter himself was a wealth of information, his understanding of the simple truths of life were brilliant and so on January 30, 2011, I posted the following blog...

The Beauty of The Shared Experience

I have a friend who lives on the other side of the world, a good man, simple and true. I have not spoken to him in some time but he is often on my mind as I move forward in my life and my work. There are few people out there, though admittedly the number grows every day who truly appreciate the basic simple things in life. People who have a base understanding of the importance of family values, compassion and understanding are very precious to me and very much respected regardless of their age, race or background. I would wish for him to forever be in a state of joy, so that he may continue to share that joy with others. Being the pen that I am I feel I have no better way to honour the man that he is than to pass his message to me onto to you so that we may all remember the meaning of the times in which we now live.

He told me a leader walks ahead of the people expecting that when he turns around they will still be there behind him. He chooses the road to walk and shows others where to step.

He told me a good leader walks among the people and talks with them so that they may choose their road together. They walk side by side so that if a step is taken that causes them to stumble they may hold each other up.

He told me a great leader walks behind the people, nodding silently to himself in quiet satisfaction and joy as they choose the road they wish to take. If they stumble and fall he is always there to help them get back on their feet.

He is wise, gentle and kind and does not care that the world may never know his name. Yet to the family and friends who know, love and respect him, he will forever in their hearts be a great leader.

Why? Not because he has a position of power, status or wealth. He does not; he manages a restaurant in Manila, and works 12 hrs shifts before travelling two hours by bus so he may spend time with his family. What makes him so special is that he understands that to lead sometimes means to follow.

How many different leaders does our world have? Spiritual, religious, political and social; it seems there are literally thousands around the globe who stand ready to show us the way. Which leads us to ask the question; who is it that we should choose to follow.

We were warned to beware of false prophets; warned that a time would come when only the whispers of our heart could be trusted to be our guides.

In the last few years the number of people claiming to be messengers has grown by an alarming rate, something that may cause concern for those who are leery of being led astray. Yet it cannot be denied that the messages of peace and love seem pure, and much of what is now being taught is quite logical. It stands to reason that if we wish to survive and move forward in our evolution that we must make peace with ourselves and the world in which we live. It makes perfect sense that we must learn to love ourselves, our world and each other; to know ourselves, our world and each other.

If you really think about it, the most common sense teachings of our time are also the most commonly taught. We are all one—connected—united—what you do to others you also do to yourself—what you do to our world you in turn do to you...

Still we were warned and many may be wondering where the false prophets are and how one can tell if they are false. I wish I could give you that answer but I am not you, I do not see through your eyes and even though I am a part of the world of which you are also a part, it is not for me to choose your path.

So if each person's journey is their own, why now more than ever, does there seem to be so many different guides. Why now more than ever does there seem to be some many teachers and lessons available for others to learn.

I imagine it is merely so that we may choose what in the end works for us.

Perhaps if our perceptions of those who have come before could be altered just a little we may begin to view them more as friends and not as somebody that should be raised above us. Many of them have made it clear they are no different really from us, in no way more special than us and not so long ago probably just as lost and confused as us.

That my friends is where the magic in the message is. They have not come to tell us how to make our lives better or even so much that we should. They have only come to show us how they improved their own lives so that we will know when we choose to do so that we can.

It would seem the days of complex rules and regulations are coming to an end. The do's and don'ts of yesterday no longer seem to be something people wish to concern themselves with. There is a freer, more creative way of looking at our world and each other; judgements and condemnation are no longer welcome. Instead of focussing on our faults we are now spending time recreating ourselves and our world. Things are being flipped around, altered, the artists and musicians, the outcasts of yesterday are now stepping forward and using their talents and skills to help those in need. Having always lived out of the box, they have long ago forgotten the box is there and are now using the energies they have always used to create entertainment for the masses to co-create and new world for the masses. Thought and feeling are merging and becoming one and balance is being restored.

Through the shared experiences of others that reassures us that we are not alone and the creative force of those who have set out before us in the interest of freedom of expression we are leaping into a brave new world. Through the open hearted discussion of all our various beliefs and ideals and the common interest of sharing our gifts and visions we open the magical portal to our future. Through our new found acceptance of ourselves and each other our new world begins to emerge, lives transform; love and laughter are again reborn, All because we stopped saying this is where you should go and started just going, then sharing with others where we have been.

So we come to time when leaders no longer walk ahead of us and into a time when through the sharing of experiences they walk among us. We have come to a time when teachers no longer tell us what we should learn, but encourage us to remember that which we already know. We have come to a time when the guides no longer point the way but instead wait patiently on us as we choose the direction we wish to walk.

We have come to a time when the guide may be led down a new path, where the teacher realizes that there is much yet to be learned from the student and the leaders fall to the back of the line so that none may be left behind.

I think he would approve, and when I finally get to return to the Philippines, I have every intention of hunting him down and letting him know how much of an impact he had on my life.

Also a visitor to Dexter's home and an employee of the hotel in which I was staying, was a young woman by the name of Angel who was mentioned several times in the original book. There really is not much to say about her that I have not already said, as I was pulled to write at great length about the things that she was teaching me about Christianity and her reasons for choosing to follow that particular path. One of the things she insisted on however as being a huge part of our spiritual growth, was our attention to the little things in life that bring joy to us, and through our actions, to others. She reminded me that it is not how many hearts I touch but how I touch those hearts. So on Jan 31st of 2011 and posted this in honor of her teachings…

The Little Things

While you are out there taking a long hard look at what is not working in our world don't forget to stop long enough to appreciate what is working. I call them the little things, because it is not only the big self-sacrificing acts of giving that show us love and compassion, it is the little everyday sweet things that the people in our lives do to ease our burdens that truly define the divine spirit of oneness.

Little things; when you really want that cup of coffee but you are stuck at work, somebody not only brings you one but they turn down your offer to pay them back. Little things; you run out of change for laundry, your neighbour gives you a bunch of loonies and won't accept anything in return. Little things; you are hurt and can't quite keep up at work, but your team picks up the slack and when you thank them they simply smile and say you'd do the same for us.

Look around you when you leave your house today and see how many of those little things just happen to pop up. If your hands are full and a stranger opens the door, that's a little thing. If you aren't feeling well and the people you live with do more around the house so you won't have to expend energy you don't have, that's a little thing. When a stranger on the bus gets up and offers an elderly person a seat, that's a little thing.

Here is what I've seen through my job as a server in a local restaurant, if this does not show the selfless nature of the human spirit than I am at a loss for what will.

A young couple come in, they have their meal, enjoy their evening but when it comes time to go the man discovers he can't find his wallet. He goes to the car thinking he left it there but no luck and now they are starting to look a bit panicked. The young lady doesn't have her purse, it's her birthday and it was supposed to be his treat. He begins to explain it to me but before I have the chance to offer to cover the cost of the meal a woman from the next table quietly reaches over and lays the cash to pay for the meal into his hands.

I remember him being completely shocked, speechless for a few minutes until he finally managed to mumble a thank-you. Then he gave the money back...

He spoke to management and left his ID, then went to get the cash. I remember asking her after they had left why she had done it. I thought at the time that she knew them but she had answered no, she just felt it was the right thing to do. That was over a year ago, and since that day I have seen her often but never mentioned it until last week, when I sat with her for a moment and told her I had written my first book, and was now working on my second. I explained that I was planning on putting this story in it. I was touched by the tears shining in her eyes. A simple thing, an offer to pay for a meal and maybe now that one simple act will be read by many who will see how a simple kind deed can touch more than one heart.

An elderly gentleman dining at our restaurant had a massive heart attack. Out boss worked tirelessly for 20 minutes doing CPR until the ambulance came but was never able to revive him. We all assumed the worst and our boss I am sure was tormented by the realization that this man could not be saved. Yet a week later the man's son came in to thank our boss for his efforts and to explain that the gentleman in question had lived for days after his heart attack. His family had the chance to say goodbye and for that the son was very grateful. It was remarkable to me that he had taken the time out of his own grieving to understand and act on the very real probability that his father's death had affected more than just him and his family. I told him so and thanked him for his kind words to our boss.

An elderly couple had a small accident in our parking lot; the lady had tripped and fallen and the gentleman had tried to catch her. They came in bruised and bleeding one extremely busy afternoon and waited patiently for a table. Our young hostess, harassed and surrounded by more than a dozen people asking for seats didn't notice, but a customer passing by did. He came over to ask if they were ok which caught my attention as I was rushing by. I dropped what I was doing and went to work cleansing the gentleman's hands, taking my time to bandage them up and stop the bleeding. I had a full section, and it was a very long time before I was able to get back to my tables yet not one person complained. In fact when I apologized to them they told me not to worry, they had seen what I had done and they were more than willing to wait. I did however do something that day that I am not proud of; I scolded our young hostess for not taking care of the elderly customer and told her she had a lot to learn about compassion; it was something I felt horrible for days after yet a month later I walked by her while she was tending to yet another elderly customer who had injured her hand. Our young woman was kneeling by the table, patiently and gently applying ice to the woman's fingers. I whispered to her that she was a sweet girl and she offered me a little smile. I can't say my words to her the first time were right, because it is never right to judge but I can say I am happy that I was just more than a little wrong about this girls willingness to care. The elderly couple did come back two weeks later to thank me, and the gentleman proudly showed me his hands, they were fine; no marks, no scars, no infection and as he said no worries.

I recently got an injury that makes it difficult to do my job yet I still have bills to pay like everybody else and so have been trying to continue to work. My co-workers have shown me what it is to hold somebody up until they can again walk on their own. They lift things for me, do all the things for me that really I can't do for myself. My boss, who could have told me to stay home until I am better, instead goes out of his way to explain to customers that I am only able to use one hand and ask them to be patient; they are.

I have seen one young man from a table on one side of the restaurant put down his own plate of food then follow a complete stranger around plate in hand helping her get what she needed. We are a buffet and she was an elderly woman in a wheelchair struggling with her attempts to move the chair and balance her meal. I watched him walk by her, notice her, turn around, put his plate down on the nearby counter and go to her offering her his assistance. I watched as he spent time with her, getting her what she wanted then bringing it back to her table for her. Only after she was seated did he go back to getting his own dinner. I asked her if she knew him and she told me no—but added that she would like to because isn't he a sweet young man. I had to agree.

What about the waitress, a single mother struggling to pay her bills who went out of her way to buy 15 crossword books in large print for one of our elderly customers because he was going into the hospital for surgery. He loved crosswords, his family was very far away and his eyesight was horrid. His name was Bill, her name was Jackie and I hope someday she sees this and realizes how big a difference the little things make.

And you see, that's the key, if you are looking for the answer to life's dilemmas; if you are looking for the Holy Grail, God's light as it were, the salvation of mankind. You will find it in the little things; the random acts of selfless kindness...

Sure these people could be angels, they could but they aren't. I know an ***angel*** *when I see one, they give off a bit of a glow to the well trained connected eye and none of these people were angels. They were just people, ordinary every day, work for a living, struggle to survive people.*

And they are why we are here.

Not one of those people knew I was watching, they had no idea I'm a writer or a messenger of hope and they would probably not care. I do.

I care a great deal for every person out there who displays compassion and understanding for no other reason than that is simply who they are. I care, my soul cares, my spirit cares and my creator cares. Perhaps you also should care because they are the ones who will save this world, they are the reason humanity has a chance to survive. To those people I say thank-you for all the little things you do every day to bring light and love into our world. Thank-you.

Angel had told me that if I looked at the world with an open heart I would begin to see God's light shining in the people I met… she was right, I did and I still do to this very day.

Now what about those remarkable children who I accidentally stumbled upon while wandering the Philippines. I never could write enough about them, or tell enough people about them and even though they were completely unaware of it, every time I was invited to come share my story on another radio show I would tell people about the children of SOTH, there is even a short blurb about them on my current website that directs people to www.shepherdofthehills.org.ph—it was my hope that as I moved forward with my own career, I could pass along the message of hope that SOTH represents. I have never met a group of children quite like the SOTH kids, nor have I ever met a couple more compassionate than Nathan and Ruth Mejica, so I would like to take a moment to say thank-you to them for the lessons that they have taught and the courage they have shown.

I recently reconnected with them in anticipation of the release of this book and was thrilled to learn that they have continued to slowly expand their organization allowing them to assist more children in getting back the life they deserve to be living. Just this year they had 20 of their young people graduate high school at the same time, such a monumental achievement for an organization that began as a small family residence in the middle of metro Manila is a huge testament to how affective the SOTH methodology of rehabilitation and re-integration is.

One of their biggest success stories is the story of a young man who goes by the name of Dan San Jose. San Jose is not his original name, it was gifted to him by one of the orphanages he was originally living in before he was handed over to SOTH. His story is a horrific one; as a very young man he was left alone to care for his younger sibling while his parents went off to ? (work perhaps) and sometime during the evening he was pulled out of the house by the sounds of singing. It was a festival time, one of the many that take place regularly in the Philippines, and as such, a large group of people were wandering past his door holding candles, praying and singing. He followed them, and before he knew it, he was so far away from home as to not know his way back. He began asking people for help and was soon offered shelter by what appeared to be a kindly man. It was not to be so, he found himself held captive in the man's home, forced to clean and work for the man for little scraps of food. He was chained there, and left with nothing but his own dark thoughts when the man was forced to go out of the house. Eventually he managed to escape, and soon found himself living on the streets, which although common, is not exactly legal and so it was only a matter of time before he would be forced into a government funded boys home. From there he was rescued from unspeakable abuse at the hands of older residents by the Sisters of Hospicio de San José, a Catholic run orphanage in Manila. There he was gifted with his name, and the attempt was made for his parents to be found. By this time, too many years had passed and because Dan did not remember where he lived or what his parent's names were, there was no way for them to be found. Dan became disgruntled, angry and began to lash out; the human spirit can only take so much after all before it breaks and this young man had been through more than his fair share of torment. His story as it was explained to me is far beyond your worst imaginings but I promised him that I would not dwell in the darkness that was his childhood, but rather shine the light on his new life as it was gifted to him by SOTH. Nathan and Ruth took Dan in, and began working with him to heal his damaged heart, through gentle nurturing they managed to encourage him to focus on his studies and begin to build a future for himself. They worked hard to make sure that once he had achieved the seemingly impossible task of graduating high school, that he would, if he wished, have the opportunity to follow which ever post-secondary educational path he chose. Dan chose nursing, and so with the help of their financial supporters, Nathan and Ruth Mejica arranged for his dream to come true. Years later, Dan is now happily married to a lovely young woman and living in the U.K., where both he and his wife work as civil servants; his wife in education, and Dan in healthcare.

Now as amazing as all of that sounds, here is the true miracle of the story. Dan does not hold one ounce of anger or resentment in his heart for those who partook in his childhood torture. And *that* more than anything, is the MIRACLE OF SOTH...

By combining music, art, education, acceptance, compassion, forgiveness and gratitude with the teachings of the scripture Nathan and

Ruth Mejica have designed a programme that works. It is not standardized, not structured and not institutional. It is modified and carefully molded to fit the individual needs of each new child that is entrusted to them. Countless sleepless nights, and long days have gone into the meticulous crafting of their unique programmes, programmes which focus on one goal and one goal only, instill an unshakable sense of self-worth in the children they have chosen to call their own; THAT is why, even after all these years, I am still singing the praises of SOTH.

That is also why we worked ourselves almost to death to force the success of the project we originally began those many years ago. My gift however, is in the written word, not in the running of projects so it is to others I have entrusted our precious vision of hope so that I may focus on what I do best—the writing of *Truth*.

Still, some amazing things happened during the work on our project, not least of which was my introduction to three unique individuals who sheltered and protected me on my subsequent return visits to the Philippines…

Jeffrey de la Cruz, with his larger than life enthusiasm for everything, brought the laughter into every working minute. There was not a day that went by with Jeff around that I did not find myself in full appreciation of the moment. No matter how hard things got, and no matter how discouraged I became, he somehow found a way to make me smile. He was my go to guy when I found myself a stranger in a foreign land who helped me centre and find peace within regardless of what was going on around us.

Randy Raytos, who would appear to some to be 'just our driver' but was to the crew so much more than that. He had this intriguing quiet quality about him, and though he didn't often say much, when he did, it was always something to stop you in your tracks. He watched everything and everybody, took all of it in and just when you thought he wasn't paying the least bit of attention to what was going on he would smoothly and gently offer a bit of advice by way of a mild observation about the current situation. He also kept us safe, easily maneuvering our vehicle through some extremely dangerous terrain; he seemed to have a sixth sense with regards to our travels, if Randy said we shouldn't go—we didn't.

Deo Loredo… sweet—could not have survived without him by my side DEO… where is he now?

I wonder… I have sent the boys to find him, because we lost touch but not a day has passed that he has not been in my heart. I think out of all the people I met, he was the closest to an old, comforting friend that I ever came across. He was also my daughters favorite, which is no surprise because he was just the kind of man you can't help but fall in love with. Where Jeffery brought peace and laughter, and Randy brought security and instinct; DEO brought WISDOM and INSIGHT.

He was the friend I took with me to Dexter's home in the provinces, and honestly if I had the money, I would send him a plane ticket right now today because as much as I love all of the people I met there, Deo is the one I miss the most. When the darkness came and hope seemed but a distant memory, Deo and I would sit together into the early hours of the morning and talk about our hopes, our fears and our dreams. The depth of his understanding seemed bottomless, and there were times when I could have sworn, I was curled up on the floor of Revo's apartment having a one on one with God. Everything he said just seemed to make sense and a few minutes with him could melt away hours of pent up anger and frustration. I miss you old friend, and I will find you again…

It's no surprise to me that there were three of them, they were the holy trinity of our project, and my strength in my hour of need.

Speaking of the Holy Trinity, the book would not be complete without a story about my Fleur-de-lis, Sister Flor, the unfathomably wise woman who found me in a crowd of thousands and made the request that I come visit her. As you know, I did, but at the time I had very little time, and quite frankly absolutely no desire to share what she revealed to me during our conversation. Given the recent changes in the direction of the church however I feel I can now safely discuss a few of the things we talked about. The first thing that was glaringly obvious to me upon entering the school in which she worked, was that though it was a Catholic run organization, there were a surprising number of young Muslim women roaming the halls, easily identifiable due to the fact that they were wearing the traditional head covering (Hijab) that some Muslim women choose as a way to mark their independence. Yes I know, you are confused, many of you will have been taught that Muslim women are *forced* to cover their heads and you probably believe that the words 'Muslim woman' and 'independence' have no place in the same sentence, so before we go further, let us set the record straight on that. I had recently taken up the wearing of the Hijab in public during the long, cold winter months in my home country; originally intended to keep me warm, I soon discovered that it not only felt extremely natural to wear it, but that when I attempted come spring to go out without it, I felt naked and exposed. What's that all about? I decided that I both liked the way it looked, and the way it felt so I was going to continue to wear it; I was however, cautious in my approach, as I did not wish to offend any of the Muslim women I happen to run into in my wanderings, as I am, after all, not Muslim. So, I did a little research and discovered that not only are they not offended, they are deeply touched when a non-Muslim woman chooses to wear the Hijab. I continued to wear it on a regular basis, even though I live near and shop in a town full of people who seem to be less than thrilled to see me wearing a traditional Muslim head covering. About a week ago my love and I were visiting a friends crystal shop, located in a market in a neighbouring city. I was wandering the stores and as I entered one I was approached by a beautiful young Muslim woman to talk about my head covering; you see, she was not wearing one, but she did want me to know how pleased she was to see that I had chosen to do so. It was a fascinating conversation and it led to a revelation that I promised her I would pass along through my work as an author and a radio show host. Her name was Ayesha (Means "alive" in Arabic. This was the name of Muhammad's third wife) She explained that upon moving to Canada, she had chosen to stop wearing the Hijab in honor of the intended meaning and purpose behind the wearing of the head covering; as it turns out, in the East, Muslim women wear the Hijab so that they will not be judged on their appearance, as they know that their value and worth comes from within and that their body shape, and their external beauty is not always reflective of the inner beauty that shines within their hearts. Yet here, in Canada, and in America, often times they are 'judged' *because* they are wearing it and so many of them opt to not wear it to maintain their status of 'non-judgement'. Not what we have been taught to be a truth, but then again, many of the truths that we have been taught, have been taught to us so that we might think about a certain thing a certain way. I encourage you therefore, to go out into the world and talk to people so that you can discover for yourself what the 'truth' is, it may just serve to alter a few of your perceptions and bring you closer to a place of acceptance and understanding. As for me and my Hijab, I do still occasionally wear it, not so much out of need, but more out of my desire to show my support and solidarity to women who have chosen to a adopt a style of dress that makes a very bold statement to the world—'we will NOT be judged on our appearance, we are so much more than that'...

Now, regarding the young Muslim women wandering the halls of this Catholic school, when I asked Sister Flor about it, she simply shrugged her shoulders and replied 'It is my understanding that there is only one God, and regardless of what we call Him, we all honor him in our worship of Him and should therefore be allowed to connect with Him in whatever way is right for us." Then she gave me a crooked little smile and added; "I would think young lady that you of all people would know that..."

Alrighty then...

Oh Sister Flor, what to do with you...

She revealed to me that they had set up a Mosque within the confines of the School that would allow the young women to have a place of worship, however there was one unique expectation that the young women were required to fulfil; they would also be expected to attend the regular Catholic Masses, so that as Sister Flor explained, they would come to understand that the teachings of both religions were essentially the same. Wise woman that Sister Flor.

I came away with a wealth of knowledge, some much needed confirmation and a book, called Bread For The World, written by the Sisters of Saint Paul, and documenting 100 years of dedication to the Philippine people. On the cover it boasts a picture of a Sister of the Cloth giving Holy Communion, and contains a message from the Provincial Superior, Sister Mary Magdalen Torres; I am sure you understand then why I simply *had* to have it.

I consider myself truly blessed to have met this amazing woman, and though I cannot share with everything you told me out of great appreciation and respect for her position within the church, I can say this... though we may assume that within the confines of the Church the men hold all the power, much like we assume that the same is true within the confines of the average Muslim home, it is very difficult to truly see what goes on inside of any one kind of 'societal structure' or 'organization' unless we are fully immersed in it. It just may be that there are people out there, working diligently to help ease this great ship we call Earth onto a new course, and sometimes, when we are not looking, a change occurs so slowly that before we know it, that which was, is no more and we suddenly find ourselves looking at a new world in which equality for all just is.

Now last but not least, the young American girl who was living and working at SOTH when I first arrived at their doorstep. Her real name is Hannah Newman and though she was just a girl when I met her she has grown into a beautiful young woman who now goes by the name of Hannah Theisen, as she too is now married. Her passion is to assist with the prevention of child slavery. We just spoke a few days ago, and she told me that although she is no longer works with the original organization that helped her to define her purpose and her passion she is still hard at work bringing light to the darkness that is the child slave trade. She explained that she had discovered that there was more power in working towards something than in fighting against it and so with that understanding she has initiated the birth of her own project which focusses on sustainable solutions. You can find out more about and support her work by visiting www.lifestylejustice.com.

Well, that pretty much sums it up, and after all these years, as I sit here writing the last few lines of this incredible story I am still in awe of the people who I have been blessed to have shared this journey with.

And so I leave you with a few more powerful words, written in 2010 on a day when I was feeling rather reflective about all that I had learned during my trip to the Philippines.

They call it simply Spiritual…

And it is...

Simple I mean; but we'll get back to that.

Lets' explore that other word for a first. Dissect it a bit; discuss for a moment its meaning.

Spiritual: defined by the experts at Merriam Webster as being;

1) Of relating to, consisting of or affecting the Spirit

2) a) of or relating to scared matters

b) Ecclesiastical rather than lay or temporal

3) Concerned with religious values

4) Related or joined in Spirit

5) a) of or relating to supernatural beings or phenomenon

b) Of, relating to or involving spiritualism

Which leaves us where? In my view nowhere close to simple.

The word itself has so many different meanings that are perceived by the masses in such a vast variety of ways that it would seem impossible for some to accept the word as being simple. Yet when we get back to the basics, take it down a notch, do away with all the hype and fancy explanations we can find ourselves in a place of simplicity.

There seem to me to be a lot of rules and rituals tied up with this one simple word. There are a whole collection of do's and don'ts, instructions and expectations that cause confusion and division. The trick, I think, to keeping it simple, is to get past all the outside influences and get back to inside where the spirit actually resides.

They call it connected, a state of oneness, being enlightened; I could go on since they call a lot of different things, but I feel at the moment as if I would be wasting your time. You see it is in my heart to tell you today that it doesn't matter what they call it, all that matters is what it is in ***your*** *heart that* ***you*** *feel it is. After much contemplation and consideration I have come to the conclusion that I myself have grown weary of the teachings and guidance of self appointed spiritual leaders. My reasons for this are my own yet I imagine that if I, a curious soul who is always asking questions, has grown tired of those who would force on me their answers, then perhaps there are others out there who have also become disillusioned by the whole scenario.*

Now don't get me wrong, the spirit within me is very much alive and well and still at one with the flesh, but then too, so is yours. Perhaps that's where in lies the confusion, that in this quest for knowledge and inner peace we forget that it is already ours. There within you, at your core, is the part of you that is, always has been, and always will be connected to all that is. When we tap into the creative side of who we, are we discover that our connection to the spirit ties in with our ability to create. Now in an age when we are being told if we want a better world we have to create it, we struggle to figure out with the help of others how exactly to go about it.

We seek answers outside ourselves; we go out into the world and look for that connection. We rely on the wisdoms and guidance of others to lead us to it yet it has never been something that we need to find. It's yours, right here, right now and it's not going anywhere. You see as much as we are human, prone to mistakes and full, at times, of doubt and fear, we are also all born of the spirit. Being born of it, we are a part of it, it is a part of us and therefore our connection to it can never be severed. Immortal, never ending, not needing to be redeemed or saved, we are as we are, perfect and complete, and simply cannot be anything else but that perfection.

I guess that's what makes it simple.

Simply put whatever it is in within you that dreams of a better tomorrow, that yearns to create a better world, whatever is in you that envisions something greater, more beautiful and more profound ; that is your you. Make it your reality...

Pick up a pen, write a tale that tells a story of love, a story of hope, a story that inspires. Pick up a brush and paint a picture that causes the viewer to stop and ponder it's meaning. Write a poem that whispers to the reader the secrets of the ancients, the secrets of your soul. Sing, full of joy and gratitude for all that we have been gifted, or just hum a tune that catches the ear of those walking by.

That is your connection, your creation done by you for you and benefitting all of us.

I will never understand why we choose to complicate matters, why we choose to add things to the mix that seem to confuse the issue. It's really not that hard. Basic and simple, a thing we all feel in our hearts to be a truth; when you walk out the door you are connected to ***all*** *that you see and when you lay your head down at night to rest you are connected to all that is, it will never be any other way.*

Spirituality and religion are often used to teach us things like compassion, understanding, empathy and love but honestly, your heart already knows these things; perhaps it is only that today your ***you*** *has chosen not to listen to your heart; or perhaps you were listening but have been afraid to allow others to share in what you have heard.*

We are all here together, and we all hold within us a magical ability to be and do whatever it is we wish, through our art, our vision, our creative energy there flows forth the change that our world needs, longs for and will have if we learn to let go and flow with it.

They say peace comes from within which means that it's already there within you. So maybe, just maybe, the time has come to stop searching for it and just start living it.

That would be keeping it simple.

And a few last final truths…

You never know how far the ripples of your compassion will take you; for none of these people had it in their hearts to be wealthy or famous or to inspire a great literary work or art. They were simply being who they were, and doing what they do and in the doing they motivated me to become a better person, a whole person, a person of whom they could be proud to call friend.

You cannot find unless you first choose to seek; and it is a choice and that choice made right *now*, today, could be the choice that redefines your existence and brings you one step closer to having intimate knowledge of the power of the Divine.

And power it is… for once you tap into your own ability to connect with the Divine and to, through that connection, create life exactly as **you** wish it to be, your life as you no know it will never be the same. Everything you ever dreamed will become your reality, everything you want and need will fall into your lap, every single person you meet will be there to help and to guide you to your next step… You will never again feel alone, or afraid or unsure of who you are… you will know your *you* and *you* will cherish and honor your *you* in every step you take for the rest of your life…

Such is a life lived in full faith that all is exactly as it needs to be for your highest good…

Such is the life of a SYNCHROMYSTIC.

{ Photo Captions and Credits... }

Photo credits: Jeffrey Dela Cruz, Randy Raytos, Deo Loredo, Hannah Theisen

Page 196: Niki with Sister Flor in Bagiou during the Flower Festival—Feb 2009

Page 196: Niki with some of the SOTH children in Bagiou city—Feb 2009

Page 196: Niki with a SOTH girl in Quezon City, Metro Manila—Jan 2010

Page 200: Niki with Angel, Dexter and Dexter's family in his home in the provinces—May 2010

Page 211: Niki with SOTH children at home in Quezon City, Metro Manila—Jan 2010

Page 213: Niki with Revo in Bagiou City—May 2010

Page 215: Revo and Niki hanging around outside the home in Quezon city, Metro Manila—May 2010

Page 226: Madison and the SOTH children in Bagiou city—Jan 2010

Page 229: The SOTH children playing at home in Quezon City, Metro Manila—Jan 2010

Page 246: V for Victory—shot on the road through the mountains to Bagiou city—Jan 2010

Page 258: Nathan Mejica talking to Revo in the SOTH office, Quezon City, Metro Manila—Jan 2010

Page 260: Niki with a SOTH girl at home in Bagiou City—May 2010

Page 265: Niki with Dan San Jose in Bagiou City—May 2010

Page 269: Niki with Nathan Mejica in the SOTH office—Quezon City, Metro Manila—May 2010

Page 272: The SOTH children playing at home in Quezon City, Metro Manila—Jan 2010

Page 277: One of the SOTH children playing at home in Quezon City, Metro Manila—Jan 2010

Page 279: The SOTH children playing at home in Quezon City, Metro Manila—Jan 2010

Page 282: The SOTH children playing at home in Quezon City, Metro Manila—Jan 2010

Page 285: The SOTH children playing at home in Quezon City, Metro Manila—Jan 2010

Page 285: Revo (trying to play the violin) with one of the SOTH boys at home in Quezon City, Metro Manila—Jan 2010

Page 289: Niki with Angel in Dexter's home in the provinces—May 2010

Page 293: Niki with Dexter in his home in the provinces—May 2010

Page 295: Niki with the SOTH children in Bagiou City—May 2010

Page 359: Dan San Jose with his wife Anna Valerie San Jose on their wedding day in the U.K. and Nathan Mejica, Anna Valerie San Jose, Dan San Jose, Ruth Mejica at Dan's wedding in the U.K.

Does it take a miracle to save a woman who has lost everything? Does God really step in and carry those who cannot or will not for the moment carry themselves? Are the prayers we scream to the heavens in our most desperate hour of need really answered?

The answers can be found in the remarkable journey of the woman who went from laying curled up on the bathroom floor praying for God to take her home, to the woman who now believes that faith in the Divine is just the beginning of this incredible adventure we call life. It is the story that takes you from a jaded and misdirected view of faith, to having an unshakable faith in God, Humanity and finally in Self and Knowing without question that all of these things are irrevocably intertwined.

After losing the majority of her immediate family to illness, losing her marriage to disease, losing her freedom to the physical powers that be and finally her health to a broken spine and a broken heart there seemed no other option but a graceful exit… The Spirit however, did not agree with the flesh and her request for death was bluntly denied. In one final act of desperation she lay awake late one night and cried to the heavens 'I give up—show me the way—lead me and I will, without question, follow'. The next day she woke up, quit her job and two weeks later she stepped onto a plane, leaving her beloved daughter and her life behind, to land in the Philippines where life as she had never dreamed it would begin.

Truth—My Synchromystic Journey is the story of a phoenix taking flight… along the way you will witness miracles, be awed by abundant synchronicity and astounded by the insights of those she met on her journey. You will be moved by the realization of the power of the love and courage of one small child and inspired by the strength of those who are poor in material wealth but undeniably rich in Spirit. More powerful than all of these, you will be offered a glimpse into the heart and mind of a tormented lost soul seeking the Divine in everyday life.

Niki Norlock is now ready to talk openly about the true story behind *Truth—My Synchromystic Journey*; revealing a side of herself she has far too long denied. In a bold, bare all tribute to those who stood behind her on her journey she is shedding light on the very real places and people in the book that was originally written as a fiction. A life no longer denied, Truth is just the first step on a monumental climb to health and happiness. She now lives secure in her understanding of self-worth. Happily residing in her dream home in the Appalachian Mountains of Quebec Canada with her husband and their family, enjoying a successful run as a co-host on the International Podcast Everyday Connection she is now ready to share the Truth about what it takes to not only choose to live, but to choose to love living when all you can do in the moment is lay on the floor and wish for death.

Your Truth will set you free…

Truth-The Untold Story...

There is so much that I still haven't shared about my experiences in the Philippines, and it leaves me feeling a bit overwhelmed. As I mentioned before, I went back twice more to work on a project that we had hoped would bring inspiration and light to the world. It left little time for anything else upon my return to Canada, and between working at the restaurant, transcribing *Truth* in preparation for publishing and the project, I had little time for anything else. The original book was first written in notebooks during my first trip, everywhere I went I carried around the shoulder bag gifted to me by Sophia before leaving; it contained my pens, my notebooks, my camera and my wallet. I really didn't need anything else, and though it may have seemed odd to some to see me whip out a pen and notebook in the middle of a conversation, I was pretty honest with everybody I met about what I was doing. It opened a lot of doors for me, that might not have opened so easily if I did not have an 'excuse' to be asking about their culture, and their personal views on life, love and God. Even then, it took some time to break the ice, but once I did break through the natural defensive walls of a cautious people, the insights I was gifted with were pure gold.

Now don't get me wrong, when I refer to walls, it is not meant to imply that they were not some of the most welcoming, hospitable people I had ever met. They were warm, friendly and exceptionally helpful. Keep in mind however, I was asking some extremely personal questions and I am not sure many of us could make the claim that we would be willing answer those kinds of questions when they are being asked by a complete stranger from a foreign land. It took time for me to build relationships with them, I had to allow them to get to know me well enough that they might feel comfortable opening up. I also had to let them in, show them a little bit of my own heart and allow them the freedom to ask me as many questions as I was asking them. The results of these explorations into one another's lives were nothing short of miraculous. I built wonderful relationships with some amazing people, and over the course of my three visits to the Philippines was initiated into a way of life that is based on the fundamental values of faith and family.

I did of course document the entire journey, as with the first trip, each new visit involved me setting aside time each day to journal, writing down my thoughts, my feelings and my experiences. Much of what was written challenges our current paradigm and dives deep into the dark heart of fear and loss of faith. The time has not yet come to reveal those writing so the notebooks used during this time are locked up tight in my studio awaiting the day when my heart tells me that the world is ready for the "The Unravelling of Truth".

I can share a few of the highlights now if you are interested, as well as tell you a little more about the incredible organization called Shepherd Of The Hills Children's Foundation (SOTH)

Because I was still writing a blog, some of my encounters were shared by way of blog posts. Although I think that my friends/family in the Philippines thought that I had forgotten about them, I was still gleaning inspiration from my time spent there and slowly spreading the light they had offered to me, to others through my writing. One of those was with the remarkable young man who had stood guard over me late at night while I was writing on the patio of the hotel in which I was staying. We eventually became really good friends and had some really incredible moments together. His real name is Dexter, and it was during one of my return trips that he invited myself, my daughter and my friend DEO to come stay at his home out in the provinces.

It was an absolutely incredible experience, we had the chance to explore the Philippine culture much more deeply than before, and were invited to not only share their space for a time but also their lives. Don't worry, I had my pen with me, and everything I learned there I will eventually share. One of the things that stood out for me however is the wisdom that was imparted to me by local farmers, who though they may not have had a formal education, were well informed about the current political and social issues of that time. They would sit around roughly hewn picnic tables out in the middle of the Philippine fields, pass around buko (coconut), gin and calamansi (a little lime like fruit) and share stories and/or discuss politics, religion and education issues. The discussion would easily bounce from topic to topic and they had a vast appreciation for how all of those separate threads intertwined to weave a pattern of social truths that affected their daily existence. Some of their insights were mind blowing and I quickly learned that all of my pre-conceived notions about the intelligence or intellect of local farmers were wrong; it turns out that I was the uneducated one. It is something they very quickly remedied.

Dexter himself was a wealth of information, his understanding of the simple truths of life were brilliant and so on January 30, 2011, I posted this blog…

The Beauty of The Shared Experience

I have a friend who lives on the other side of the world, a good man, simple and true. I have not spoken to him in some time but he is often on my mind as I move forward in my life and my work. There are few people out there, though admittedly the number grows every day who truly appreciate the basic simple things in life. People who have a base understanding of the importance of family values, compassion and understanding are very precious to me and very much respected regardless of their age, race or background. I would wish for him to forever be in a state of joy, so that he may continue to share that joy with others. Being the pen that I am I feel I have no better way to honour the man that he is than to pass his message to me onto to you so that we may all remember the meaning of the times in which we now live.

He told me a leader walks ahead of the people expecting that when he turns around they will still be there behind him. He chooses the road to walk and shows others where to step.

He told me a good leader walks among the people and talks with them so that they may choose their road together. They walk side by side so that if a step is taken that causes them to stumble they may hold each other up.

He told me a great leader walks behind the people, nodding silently to himself in quiet satisfaction and joy as they choose the road they wish to take. If they stumble and fall he is always there to help them get back on their feet.

He is wise, gentle and kind and does not care that the world may never know his name. Yet to the family and friends who know, love and respect him, he will forever in their hearts be a great leader. Why? Not because he has a position of power, status or wealth. He does not; he manages a restaurant in Manila, and works 12 hrs shifts before travelling two hours by bus so he may spend time with his family. What makes him so special is that he understands that to lead sometimes means to follow.

How many different leaders does our world have? Spiritual, religious, political and social; it seems there are literally thousands around the globe who stand ready to show us the way. Which leads us to ask the question; who is it that we should choose to follow.

We were warned to beware of false prophets; warned that a time would come when only the whispers of our heart could be trusted to be our guides.

In the last few years the number of people claiming to be messengers has grown by an alarming rate, something that may cause concern for those who are leery of being led astray. Yet it cannot be denied that the messages of peace and love seem pure, and much of what is now being taught is quite logical. It stands to reason that if we wish to survive and move forward in our evolution that we must make peace with ourselves and the world in which we live. It makes perfect sense that we must learn to love ourselves, our world and each other; to know ourselves, our world and each other.

If you really think about it, the most common sense teachings of our time are also the most commonly taught. We are all one—connected—united—what you do to others you also do to yourself—what you do to our world you in turn do to you...

Still we were warned and many may be wondering where the false prophets are and how one can tell if they are false. I wish I could give you that answer but I am not you, I do not see through your eyes and even though I am a part of the world of which you are also a part, it is not for me to choose your path.

So if each person's journey is their own, why now more than ever, does there seem to be so many different guides. Why now more than ever does there seem to be some many teachers and lessons available for others to learn.

I imagine it is merely so that we may choose what in the end works for us.

Perhaps if our perceptions of those who have come before could be altered just a little we may begin to view them more as friends and not as somebody that should be raised above us. Many of them have made it clear they are no different really from us, in no way more special than us and not so long ago probably just as lost and confused as us.

That my friends is where the magic in the message is. They have not come to tell us how to make our lives better or even so much that we should. They have only come to show us how they improved their own lives so that we will know when we choose to do so that we can.

It would seem the days of complex rules and regulations are coming to an end. The do's and don'ts of yesterday no longer seem to be something people wish to concern themselves with. There is a freer, more creative way of looking at our world and each other; judgements and condemnation are no longer welcome. Instead of focussing on our faults we are now spending time recreating ourselves and our world. Things are being flipped around, altered, the artists and musicians, the outcasts of yesterday are now stepping forward and using their talents and skills to help those in need. Having always lived out of the box, they have long ago forgotten the box is there and are now using the energies they have always used to create entertainment for the masses to co-create and new world for the masses. Thought and feeling are merging and becoming one and balance is being restored.

Through the shared experiences of others that reassures us that we are not alone and the creative force of those who have set out before us in the interest of freedom of expression we are leaping into a brave new world. Through the open hearted discussion of all our various beliefs and ideals and the common interest of sharing our gifts and visions we open the magical portal to our future. Through our new found acceptance of ourselves and each other our new world begins to emerge, lives transform; love and laughter are again reborn, All because we stopped saying this is where you should go and started just going, then sharing with others where we have been.

So we come to time when leaders no longer walk ahead of us and into a time when through the sharing of experiences they walk among us. We have come to a time when teachers no longer tell us what we should learn, but encourage us to remember that which we already know. We have come to a time when the guides no longer point the way but instead wait patiently on us as we choose the direction we wish to walk.

We have come to a time when the guide may be led down a new path, where the teacher realizes that there is much yet to be learned from the student and the leaders fall to the back of the line so that none may be left behind.

I think he would approve, and when I finally get to return to the Philippines, I have every intention of hunting him down and letting him know how much of an impact he had on my life.

Also a visitor to Dexter's home and an employee of the hotel in which I was staying, was a young woman by the name of Angel who was mentioned several times in the original book. There really is not much to say about her that I have not already said, as I was pulled to write at great length about the things that she was teaching me about Christianity and her reasons for choosing to follow that particular path. One of the things she insisted on however as being a huge part of our spiritual growth, was our attention to the little things in life that bring joy to us, and through our actions, to others. She reminded me that it is not how many hearts I touch but how I touch those hearts. So on Jan 31st of 2011 and posted this in honor of her teachings…

The Little Things

While you are out there taking a long hard look at what is not working in our world don't forget to stop long enough to appreciate what is working. I call them the little things, because it is not only the big self-sacrificing acts of giving that show us love and compassion, it is the little everyday sweet things that the people in our lives do to ease our burdens that truly define the divine spirit of oneness.

Little things; when you really want that cup of coffee but you are stuck at work, somebody not only brings you one but they turn down your offer to pay them back. Little things; you run out of change for laundry, your neighbour gives you a bunch of loonies and won't accept anything in return. Little things; you are hurt and can't quite keep up at work, but your team picks up the slack and when you thank them they simply smile and say you'd do the same for us.

Look around you when you leave your house today and see how many of those little things just happen to pop up. If your hands are full and a stranger opens the door, that's a little thing. If you aren't feeling well and the people you live with do more around the house so you won't have to expend energy you don't have, that's a little thing. When a stranger on the bus gets up and offers an elderly person a seat, that's a little thing.

Here is what I've seen through my job as a server in a local restaurant, if this does not show the selfless nature of the human spirit than I am at a loss for what will.

A young couple come in, they have their meal, enjoy their evening but when it comes time to go the man discovers he can't find his wallet. He goes to the car thinking he left it there but no luck and now they are starting to look a bit panicked. The young lady doesn't have her purse, it's her birthday and it was supposed to be his treat. He begins to explain it to me but before I have the chance to offer to cover the cost of the meal a woman from the next table quietly reaches over and lays the cash to pay for the meal into his hands.

I remember him being completely shocked, speechless for a few minutes until he finally managed to mumble a thank-you. Then he gave the money back...

He spoke to management and left his ID, then went to get the cash. I remember asking her after they had left why she had done it. I thought at the time that she knew them but she had answered no, she just felt it was the right thing to do. That was over a year ago, and since that day I have seen her often but never mentioned it until last week, when I sat with her for a moment and told her I had written my first book, and was now working on my second. I explained that I was planning on putting this story in it. I was touched by the tears shining in her eyes. A simple thing, an offer to pay for a meal and maybe now that one simple act will be read by many who will see how a simple kind deed can touch more than one heart.

An elderly gentleman dining at our restaurant had a massive heart attack. Out boss worked tirelessly for 20 minutes doing CPR until the ambulance came but was never able to revive him. We all assumed the worst and our boss I am sure was tormented by the realization that this man could not be saved. Yet a week later the man's son came in to thank our boss for his efforts and to explain that the gentleman in question had lived for days after his heart attack. His family had the chance to say goodbye and for that the son was very grateful. It was remarkable to me that he had taken the time out of his own grieving to understand and act on the very real probability that his father's death had affected more than just him and his family. I told him so and thanked him for his kind words to our boss.

An elderly couple had a small accident in our parking lot; the lady had tripped and fallen and the gentleman had tried to catch her. They came in bruised and bleeding one extremely busy afternoon and waited patiently for a table. Our young hostess, harassed and surrounded by more than a dozen people asking for seats didn't notice, but a customer passing by did. He came over to ask if they were ok which caught my attention as I was rushing by. I dropped what I was doing and went to work cleansing the gentleman's hands, taking my time to bandage them up and stop the bleeding. I had a full section, and it was a very long time before I was able to get back to my tables yet not one person complained. In fact when I apologized to them they told me not to worry, they had seen what I had done and they were more than willing to wait. I did however do something that day that I am not proud of; I scolded our young hostess for not taking care of the elderly customer and told her she had a lot to learn about compassion; it was something I felt horrible for days after yet a month later I walked by her while she was tending to yet another elderly customer who had injured her hand. Our young woman was kneeling by the table, patiently and gently applying ice to the woman's fingers. I whispered to her that she was a sweet girl and she offered me a little smile. I can't say my words to her the first time were right, because it is never right to judge but I can say I am happy that I was just more than a little wrong about this girls willingness to care. The elderly couple did come back two weeks later to thank me, and the gentleman proudly showed me his hands, they were fine; no marks, no scars, no infection and as he said no worries.

I recently got an injury that makes it difficult to do my job yet I still have bills to pay like everybody else and so have been trying to continue to work. My co-workers have shown me what it is to hold somebody up until they can again walk on their own. They lift things for me, do all the things for me that really I can't do for myself. My boss, who could have told me to stay home until I am better, instead goes out of his way to explain to customers that I am only able to use one hand and ask them to be patient; they are.

I have seen one young man from a table on one side of the restaurant put down his own plate of food then follow a complete stranger around plate in hand helping her get what she needed. We are a buffet and she was an elderly woman in a wheelchair struggling with her attempts to move the chair and balance her meal. I watched him walk by her, notice her, turn around, put his plate down on the nearby counter and go to her offering her his assistance. I watched as he spent time with her, getting her what she wanted then bringing it back to her table for her. Only after she was seated did he go back to getting his own dinner. I asked her if she knew him and she told me no—but added that she would like to because isn't he a sweet young man. I had to agree.

What about the waitress, a single mother struggling to pay her bills who went out of her way to buy 15 crossword books in large print for one of our elderly customers because he was going into the hospital for surgery.

He loved crosswords, his family was very far away and his eyesight was horrid. His name was Bill, her name was Jackie and I hope someday she sees this and realizes how big a difference the little things make.

And you see, that's the key, if you are looking for the answer to life's dilemmas; if you are looking for the Holy Grail, God's light as it were, the salvation of mankind. You will find it in the little things; the random acts of selfless kindness...

Sure these people could be angels, they could but they aren't. I know an ***angel*** *when I see one, they give off a bit of a glow to the well trained connected eye and none of these people were angels. They were just people, ordinary every day, work for a living, struggle to survive people.*

And they are why we are here.

Not one of those people knew I was watching, they had no idea I'm a writer or a messenger of hope and they would probably not care. I do. I care a great deal for every person out there who displays compassion and understanding for no other reason than that is simply who they are. I care, my soul cares, my spirit cares and my creator cares. Perhaps you also should care because they are the ones who will save this world, they are the reason humanity has a chance to survive. To those people I say thank-you for all the little things you do every day to bring light and love into our world. Thank-you.

Angel had told me that if I looked at the world with an open heart I would begin to see God's light shining in the people I met… she was right, I did and I still do to this very day.

Now what about those remarkable children who I accidentally stumbled upon while wandering the Philippines. I never could write enough about them, or tell enough people about them and even though they were completely unaware of it, every time I was invited to come share my story on another radio show I would tell people about the children of SOTH, there is even a short blurb about them on my current website that directs people to www.shepherdofthehills.org.ph—it was my hope that as I moved forward with my own career, I could pass along the message of hope that SOTH represents. I have never met a group of children quite like the SOTH kids, nor have I ever met a couple more compassionate than Nathan and Ruth Mejica, so I would like to take a moment to say thank-you to them for the lessons that they have taught and the courage they have shown.

I recently reconnected with them in anticipation of the release of this book and was thrilled to learn that they have continued to slowly expand their organization allowing them to assist more children in getting back the life they deserve to be living. Just this year they had 20 of their young people graduate high school at the same time, such a monumental achievement for an organization that began as a small family residence in the middle of metro Manila is a huge testament to how affective the SOTH methodology of rehabilitation and re-integration is.

One of their biggest success stories is the story of a young man who goes by the name of Dan San Jose. San Jose is not his original name, it was gifted to him by one of the orphanages he was originally living in before he was handed over to SOTH. His story is a horrific one; as a very young man he was left alone to care for his younger sibling while his parents went off to ? (work perhaps) and sometime during the evening he was pulled out of the house by the sounds of singing. It was a festival time, one of the many that take place regularly in the Philippines, and as such, a large group of people were wandering past his door holding candles, praying and singing. He followed them, and before he knew it, he was so far away from home as to not know his way back. He began asking people for help and was soon offered shelter by what appeared to be a kindly man. It was not to be so, he found himself held captive in the man's home, forced to clean and work for the man for little scraps of food. He was chained there, and left with nothing but his own dark thoughts when the man was forced to go out of the house. Eventually he managed to escape, and soon found himself living on the streets, which although common, is not exactly legal and so it was only a matter of time before he would be forced into a government funded boys home. From there he was rescued from unspeakable abuse at the hands of older residents by the Sisters of Hospicio de San José, a Catholic run orphanage in Manila. There he was gifted with his name, and the attempt was made for his parents to be found. By this time, too many years had passed and because Dan did not remember where he lived or what his parent's names were, there was no way for them to be found. Dan became disgruntled, angry and began to lash out; the human spirit can only take so much after all before it breaks and this young man had been through more than his fair share of torment. His story as it was explained to me is far beyond your worst imaginings but I promised him that I would not dwell in the darkness that was his childhood, but rather shine the light on his new life as it was gifted to him by SOTH. Nathan and Ruth took Dan in, and began working with him to heal his damaged heart, through gentle nurturing they managed to encourage him to focus on his studies and begin to build a future for himself. They worked hard to make sure that once he had achieved the seemingly impossible task of graduating high school, that he would, if he wished, have the opportunity to follow which ever post-secondary educational path he chose. Dan chose nursing, and so with the help of their financial supporters, Nathan and Ruth Mejica arranged for his dream to come true. Years later, Dan is now happily married to a lovely young woman and living in the U.K., where both he and his wife work as civil servants; his wife in education, and Dan in healthcare.

Now as amazing as all of that sounds, here is the true miracle of the story. Dan does not hold one ounce of anger or resentment in his heart for those who partook in his childhood torture. And *that* more than anything, is the MIRACLE OF SOTH…

By combining music, art, education, acceptance, compassion, forgiveness and gratitude with the teachings of the scripture Nathan and Ruth Mejica have designed a programme that works. It is not standardized, not structured and not institutional. It is modified and carefully molded to fit the individual needs of each new child that is entrusted to them. Countless sleepless nights, and long days have gone into the meticulous crafting of their unique programmes, programmes which focus on one goal and one goal only, instill an unshakable sense of self-worth in the children they have chosen to call their own; THAT is why, even after all these years, I am still singing the praises of SOTH.

That is also why we worked ourselves almost to death to force the success of the project we originally began those many years ago. My gift however, is in the written word, not in the running of projects so it is to others I have entrusted our precious vision of hope so that I may focus on what I do best—the writing of *Truth*.

Still, some amazing things happened during the work on our project, not least of which was my introduction to three unique individuals who sheltered and protected me on my subsequent return visits to the Philippines…

Jeffrey de la Cruz, with his larger than life enthusiasm for everything, brought the laughter into every working minute. There was not a day that went by with Jeff around that I did not find myself in full appreciation of the moment. No matter how hard things got, and no matter how discouraged I became, he somehow found a way to make me smile. He was my go to guy when I found myself a stranger in a foreign land who helped me centre and find peace within regardless of what was going on around us.

Randy Raytos, who would appear to some to be 'just our driver' but was to the crew so much more than that. He had this intriguing quiet quality about him, and though he didn't often say much, when he did, it was always something to stop you in your tracks. He watched everything and everybody, took all of it in and just when you thought he wasn't paying the least bit of attention to what was going on he would smoothly and gently offer a bit of advice by way of a mild observation about the current situation. He also kept us safe, easily maneuvering our vehicle through some extremely dangerous terrain; he seemed to have a sixth sense with regards to our travels, if Randy said we shouldn't go—we didn't.

Deo Loredo… sweet—could not have survived without him by my side DEO… where is he now?

I wonder… I have sent the boys to find him, because we lost touch but not a day has passed that he has not been in my heart. I think out of all the people I met, he was the closest to an old, comforting friend that I ever came across. He was also my daughters favorite, which is no surprise because he was just the kind of man you can't help but fall in love with. Where Jeffery brought peace and laughter, and Randy brought security and instinct; DEO brought WISDOM and INSIGHT.

He was the friend I took with me to Dexter's home in the provinces, and honestly if I had the money, I would send him a plane ticket right now today because as much as I love all of the people I met there, Deo is the one I miss the most. When the darkness came and hope seemed but a distant memory, Deo and I would sit together into the early hours of the morning and talk about our hopes, our fears and our dreams. The depth of his understanding seemed bottomless, and there were times when I could have sworn, I was curled up on the floor of Revo's apartment having a one on one with God. Everything he said just seemed to make sense and a few minutes with him could melt away hours of pent up anger and frustration. I miss you old friend, and I will find you again…

It's no surprise to me that there were three of them, they were the holy trinity of our project, and my strength in my hour of need.

Speaking of the Holy Trinity, the book would not be complete without a story about my Fleur-de-lis, Sister Flor, the unfathomably wise woman who found me in a crowd of thousands and made the request that I come visit her. As you know, I did, but at the time I had very little time, and quite frankly absolutely no desire to share what she revealed to me during our conversation. Given the recent changes in the direction of the church however I feel I can now safely discuss a few of the things we talked about. The first thing that was glaringly obvious to me upon entering the school in which she worked, was that though it was a Catholic run organization, there were a surprising number of young Muslim women roaming the halls, easily identifiable due to the fact that they were wearing the traditional head covering (Hijab) that some Muslim women choose as a way to mark their independence. Yes I know, you are confused, many of you will have been taught that Muslim women are *forced* to cover their heads and you probably believe that the words 'Muslim woman' and 'independence' have no place in the same sentence, so before we go further, let us set the record straight on that. I had recently taken up the wearing of the Hijab in public during the long, cold winter months in my home country; originally intended to keep me warm, I soon discovered that it not only felt extremely natural to wear it, but that when I attempted come spring to go out without it, I felt naked and exposed. What's that all about? I decided that I both liked the way it looked, and the way it felt so I was going to continue to wear it; I was however, cautious in my approach, as I did not wish to offend any of the Muslim women I happen to run into in my wanderings, as I am, after all, not Muslim. So, I did a little research and discovered that not only are they not offended, they are deeply touched when a non-Muslim woman chooses to wear the Hijab. I continued to wear it on a regular basis, even though I live near and shop in a town full of people who seem to be less than thrilled to see me wearing a traditional Muslim head covering. About a week ago my love and I were visiting a friends crystal shop, located in a market in a neighbouring city. I was wandering the stores and as I entered one I was approached by a beautiful young Muslim woman to talk about my head covering; you see, she was not wearing one, but she did want me to know how pleased she was to see that I had chosen to do so. It was a fascinating conversation and it led to a revelation that I promised her I would pass along through my work as an author and a radio show host. Her name was Ayesha (Means "alive" in Arabic. This was the name of Muhammad's third wife) She explained that upon moving to Canada, she had chosen to stop wearing the Hijab in honor of the intended meaning and purpose behind the wearing of the head covering; as it turns out, in the East, Muslim women wear the Hijab so that they will not be judged on their appearance, as they know that their value and worth comes from within and that their body shape, and their external beauty is not always reflective of the inner beauty that shines within their hearts. Yet here, in Canada, and in America, often times they are 'judged' *because* they are wearing it and so many of them opt to not wear it to maintain their status of 'non-judgement'. Not what we have been taught to be a truth, but then again, many of the truths that we have been taught, have been taught to us so that we might think about a certain thing a certain way. I encourage you therefore, to go out into the world and talk to people so that you can discover for yourself what the 'truth' is, it may just serve to alter a few of your perceptions and bring you closer to a place of acceptance and understanding. As for me and my Hijab, I do still occasionally wear it, not so much out of need, but more out of my desire to show my support and solidarity to women who have chosen to a adopt a style of dress that makes a very bold statement to the world—'we will NOT be judged on our appearance, we are so much more than that'…

Now, regarding the young Muslim women wandering the halls of this Catholic school, when I asked Sister Flor about it, she simply shrugged her shoulders and replied 'It is my understanding that there is only one God, and regardless of what we call Him, we all honor him in our worship of Him and should therefore be allowed to connect with Him in whatever way is right for us." Then she gave me a crooked little smile and added; "I would think young lady that you of all people would know that…"

Alrighty then…

Oh Sister Flor, what to do with you…

She revealed to me that they had set up a Mosque within the confines of the School that would allow the young women to have a place of worship, however there was one unique expectation that the young women were required to fulfil; they would also be expected to attend the regular Catholic Masses, so that as Sister Flor explained, they would come to understand that the teachings of both religions were essentially the same. Wise woman that Sister Flor.

I came away with a wealth of knowledge, some much needed confirmation and a book, called Bread For The World, written by the Sisters of Saint Paul, and documenting 100 years of dedication to the Philippine people. On the cover it boasts a picture of a Sister of the Cloth giving Holy Communion, and contains a message from the Provincial Superior, Sister Mary Magdalen Torres; I am sure you understand then why I simply *had* to have it.

I consider myself truly blessed to have met this amazing woman, and though I cannot share with everything you told me out of great appreciation and respect for her position within the church, I can say this… though we may assume that within the confines of the Church the men hold all the power, much like we assume that the same is true within the confines of the average Muslim home, it is very difficult to truly see what goes on inside of any one kind of 'societal structure' or 'organization' unless we are fully immersed in it. It just may be that there are people out there, working diligently to help ease this great ship we call Earth onto a new course, and sometimes, when we are not looking, a change occurs so slowly that before we know it, that which was, is no more and we suddenly find ourselves looking at a new world in which equality for all just is.

Now last but not least, the young American girl who was living and working at SOTH when I first arrived at their doorstep. Her real name is Hannah Newman and though she was just a girl when I met her she has grown into a beautiful young woman who now goes by the name of Hannah Theisen, as she too is now married. Her passion is to assist with the prevention of child slavery. We just spoke a few days ago, and she told me that although she is no longer works with the original organization that helped her to define her purpose and her passion she is still hard at work bringing light to the darkness that is the child slave trade. She explained that she had discovered that there was more power in working towards something than in fighting against it and so with that understanding she has initiated the birth of her own project which focusses on sustainable solutions. You can find out more about and support her work by visiting www.lifestylejustice.com.

Well, that pretty much sums it up, and after all these years, as I sit here writing the last few lines of this incredible story I am still in awe of the people who I have been blessed to have shared this journey with.

And so I leave you with a few more powerful words, written in 2010 on a day when I was feeling rather reflective about all that I had learned during my trip to the Philippines.

They call it simply Spiritual…

And it is...

Simple I mean; but we'll get back to that.

Lets' explore that other word for a first. Dissect it a bit; discuss for a moment its meaning.

Spiritual: defined by the experts at Merriam Webster as being;

1) Of relating to, consisting of or affecting the Spirit

2) a) of or relating to scared matters

b) Ecclesiastical rather than lay or temporal

3) Concerned with religious values

4) Related or joined in Spirit

5) a) of or relating to supernatural beings or phenomenon

b) Of, relating to or involving spiritualism

Which leaves us where? In my view nowhere close to simple.

The word itself has so many different meanings that are perceived by the masses in such a vast variety of ways that it would seem impossible for some to accept the word as being simple. Yet when we get back to the basics, take it down a notch, do away with all the hype and fancy explanations we can find ourselves in a place of simplicity.

There seem to me to be a lot of rules and rituals tied up with this one simple word. There are a whole collection of do's and don'ts, instructions and expectations that cause confusion and division. The trick, I think, to keeping it simple, is to get past all the outside influences and get back to inside where the spirit actually resides.

They call it connected, a state of oneness, being enlightened; I could go on since they call a lot of different things, but I feel at the moment as if I would be wasting your time. You see it is in my heart to tell you today that it doesn't matter what they call it, all that matters is what it is in ***your*** *heart that* ***you*** *feel it is. After much contemplation and consideration I have come to the conclusion that I myself have grown weary of the teachings and guidance of self appointed spiritual leaders. My reasons for this are my own yet I imagine that if I, a curious soul who is always asking questions, has grown tired of those who would force on me their answers, then perhaps there are others out there who have also become disillusioned by the whole scenario.*

Now don't get me wrong, the spirit within me is very much alive and well and still at one with the flesh, but then too, so is yours. Perhaps that's where in lies the confusion, that in this quest for knowledge and inner peace we forget that it is already ours. There within you, at your core, is the part of you that is, always has been, and always will be connected to all that is. When we tap into the creative side of who we, are we discover that our connection to the spirit ties in with our ability to create. Now in an age when we are being told if we want a better world we have to create it, we struggle to figure out with the help of others how exactly to go about it.

We seek answers outside ourselves; we go out into the world and look for that connection. We rely on the wisdoms and guidance of others to lead us to it yet it has never been something that we need to find. It's yours, right here, right now and it's not going anywhere. You see as much as we are human, prone to mistakes and full, at times, of doubt and fear, we are also all born of the spirit. Being born of it, we are a part of it, it is a part of us and therefore our connection to it can never be severed. Immortal, never ending, not needing to be redeemed or saved, we are as we are, perfect and complete, and simply cannot be anything else but that perfection.

Niki Norlock

I guess that's what makes it simple.

Simply put whatever it is in within you that dreams of a better tomorrow, that yearns to create a better world, whatever is in you that envisions something greater, more beautiful and more profound ; that is your you. Make it your reality...

Pick up a pen, write a tale that tells a story of love, a story of hope, a story that inspires. Pick up a brush and paint a picture that causes the viewer to stop and ponder it's meaning. Write a poem that whispers to the reader the secrets of the ancients, the secrets of your soul. Sing, full of joy and gratitude for all that we have been gifted, or just hum a tune that catches the ear of those walking by.

That is your connection, your creation done by you for you and benefitting all of us.

I will never understand why we choose to complicate matters, why we choose to add things to the mix that seem to confuse the issue. It's really not that hard. Basic and simple, a thing we all feel in our hearts to be a truth; when you walk out the door you are connected to ***all*** *that you see and when you lay your head down at night to rest you are connected to all that is, it will never be any other way.*

Spirituality and religion are often used to teach us things like compassion, understanding, empathy and love but honestly, your heart already knows these things; perhaps it is only that today your ***you*** *has chosen not to listen to your heart; or perhaps you were listening but have been afraid to allow others to share in what you have heard.*

We are all here together, and we all hold within us a magical ability to be and do whatever it is we wish, through our art, our vision, our creative energy there flows forth the change that our world needs, longs for and will have if we learn to let go and flow with it.

They say peace comes from within which means that it's already there within you. So maybe, just maybe, the time has come to stop searching for it and just start living it.

That would be keeping it simple.

And a few last final truths…

You never know how far the ripples of your compassion will take you; for none of these people had it in their hearts to be wealthy or famous or to inspire a great literary work or art. They were simply being who they were, and doing what they do and in the doing they motivated me to become a better person, a whole person, a person of whom they could be proud to call friend.

You cannot find unless you first choose to seek; and it is a choice and that choice made right *now*, today, could be the choice that redefines your existence and brings you one step closer to having intimate knowledge of the power of the Divine.

And power it is... for once you tap into your own ability to connect with the Divine and to, through that connection, create life exactly as **you** wish it to be, your life as you no know it will never be the same. Everything you ever dreamed will become your reality, everything you want and need will fall into your lap, every single person you meet will be there to help and to guide you to your next step... You will never again feel alone, or afraid or unsure of who you are... you will know your *you* and *you* will cherish and honor your *you* in every step you take for the rest of your life...

Such is a life lived in full faith that all is exactly as it needs to be for your highest good...

Such is the life of a SYNCHROMYSTIC.

Made in the USA
Las Vegas, NV
10 January 2026

39049899R00210